# THE MODEL MAJOR-GENERAL
A Biography of Field-Marshal Lord Wolseley

Wolseley F.M.

W. STRANG
1908

# THE MODEL
# MAJOR-GENERAL

A Biography of
Field-Marshal Lord Wolseley

*by*

JOSEPH H. LEHMANN

The Riverside Press Cambridge
HOUGHTON MIFFLIN COMPANY BOSTON
1964

PRINTED IN GREAT BRITAIN

# CONTENTS

The frontispiece portrait of Field-Marshal Viscount Wolseley by William Strang, signed and dated 1908, is reproduced by permission of the National Portrait Gallery, London

# LIST OF MAPS

# PREFACE

WOLSELEY. It is strange how quickly that name has passed into oblivion – or merged in confusion with that of a sixteenth-century cardinal. In late Victorian times the name was known throughout the kingdom: Wolseley, the supreme master of irregular warfare in an expanding Empire; Wolseley, the military reformer who strove no less valiantly to keep the British army abreast of the scientific changes that were revolutionizing the world he lived in. To restore that great soldier to his rightful place in history, this biography was undertaken.

The foundation of this volume has been pieced together largely from the correspondence and papers of the Wolseley family which have, until now, remained almost wholly undisturbed. The most valuable collection, containing family letters and unpublished manuscripts, is to be found at the public library in Hove. A second important source, consisting of some 4,000 letters exchanged by Lord and Lady Wolseley, is located in the library of the Royal United Service Institution (R.U.S.I.). (A fraction of this material was published, but its worth is marred by liberal alterations and deletions.) Wolseley's official papers are bound in some fifty volumes at the War Office Library, with a few additional pieces at the National Library of Ireland in Dublin.

Papers of persons who played a significant role in Wolseley's life were examined at the Public Record Office (P.R.O.), the British Museum (B.M.), the Historical Manuscripts Commission (H.M.C.), the Royal Commonwealth Society Library (R.C.S.L.), and the Queen's Library at Windsor Castle (Windsor). Additional material came from papers in the collections of private individuals, including those of General Ardagh (P.R.O.), Field-Marshal Buller (P.R.O.), General Butler (private), the Duke of Cambridge (Windsor), Mr Campbell-Bannerman (B.M.), Lord Cardwell (P.R.O.), Lord Cromer (B.M.), Mr Dilke (B.M.), Mr Gladstone (B.M.), Captain Glover (R.C.S.L.), General Gordon (B.M.), Lord Granville (P.R.O.), Lord Hambleden (H.M.C.), Lord Iddesleigh (H.M.C.), General Maurice (private), Lord Morley (B.M.), Field-Marshal White (private).

The significant published materials consulted are indicated in the notes at the end of the book.

I am deeply indebted to the many persons who helped in various ways to make this book possible. For private information and permission to use family letters, I owe special thanks to the Hon. Sir Albert Napier (son of Lord Napier of Magdala), Lady Napier (daughter of Field-Marshal Sir George Stuart White), Mr F. M. P. Maurice (grandson of General Sir Frederick Maurice), and Colonel Patrick Butler (son of General Sir William Butler). To Her Majesty the Queen, I am grateful for permission to use the archives at Windsor Castle. Though I alone am responsible for any errors of fact or judgment in this volume, I have profited greatly from the suggestions and criticisms of Brigadier Peter Young, Reader in Military History, Royal Military Academy, Sandhurst; Brigadier J. Stephenson, Director of the R.U.S.I.; Mr King, Director of the War Office Library; Major G. Tylden; and my colleagues at De Paul University, the Reverend Jeremiah C. Lehane, C.M., and Mr Henry Collins. I also wish to express my thanks to Mr Graham C. Greene of Jonathan Cape Ltd and Mr Craig Wylie of Houghton Mifflin Co. for their good counsel throughout our relationship.

JOSEPH H. LEHMANN

# THE MODEL MAJOR-GENERAL
A Biography of Field-Marshal Lord Wolseley

# THE SUBALTERNS' WAR

ENSIGN GARNET WOLSELEY believed that the best possible way to get ahead in the army was to try to get killed every time he had the chance. Daring and indifference to danger would attract his superior officers and lead to promotion and honours. The ambitious ensign had faith in a special providence that would preserve him through the perils of battle until he fulfilled a great destiny, one that would bring glory to the Wolseley name and advantage to England. The opportunity to test these beliefs in war would rarely be absent in the Victorian era, an age when the blood never dried on the British Empire.

Soldiering came naturally to a Wolseley. He was of a fighting stock that seemed to breed an hereditary aptitude for war. Garnet's ancestors claimed an unbroken line of warrior descent from the savage Danish marauders who settled in Staffordshire and cleared the land of wolves centuries before the arrival of the Norman. Their arms portrayed a wolf-hound; their proud crest was a wolf's head; and their motto was *Homo Homini Lupus* – man is to his fellow man as a wolf.

Like wolves the first Wolseleys came to Ireland to seize land for themselves and to exterminate the papist enemies of William III. General William Wolseley led a reckless, uncouth band of Orangemen to plunder and victory over the Jacobites in 1689. The following year this brilliant leader of 'Wolseley's Horse' rode beside 'Dutch' William at the crucial Battle of the Boyne, which put the Irish Catholics at the mercy of the Protestant king and his supporters. Richard Wolseley, a nephew of General Wolseley, failing to inherit legal title to the estates promised his uncle by an ungrateful sovereign (legend has it that William III never even returned the horse the general lent him at the Boyne), established himself peremptorily on confiscated lands in County Carlow. Thus, the Irish or cadet branch of the Wolseleys issued from the sword. Though Irish rebels burned their home in 1779 and revenged themselves on these English conquerors by entering the family burial-grounds, scattering their bones and rendering the lead coffins into bullets, the Wolseleys stayed on to breed soldiers. Garnet's grandfather served in the Seven

Years War as a captain, and his son, after whom Garnet was named, served in the West Indies until he retired as a major.

These Saxon settlers rarely mingled their blood with the native Celts. Garnet's mother, Frances Ann, daughter of William Smith, was largely of English ancestry and a pious Protestant. The future military hero was, therefore, born a true Anglo-Irishman, never wholly Irish but still no longer English. Living in close proximity with Hibernians, they often acquired some of their outstanding traits. Wolseley was a perfect example – fluent, boastful, imaginative, impulsive, audacious. Hybrids in a sense, but never sterile for they contributed more than their share of great soldiers, statesmen, and men of letters. Yet they were seldom claimed by either nation; they remained English to the Irish and Irish to the English. Wolseley made the best of both worlds, describing himself as English or Irish whichever suited his purpose for the moment.

The inheritance of a military tradition was only one source of Wolseley's devotion to a military career; the other was poverty, which Napoleon declared is the best school for a soldier. Garnet's father, a soldier with long service and little money, married late in life and was his wife's senior by twenty-five years. Lacking the cash for promotion to lieutenant-colonel, he sold out of the army, settling in Golden Bridge House, near Dublin, which he rented from his father-in-law.

Garnet was born on June 4th, 1833, the eldest of seven children. When Garnet was seven, his father, who had lived extravagantly like so many Anglo-Irishmen of his class, died leaving only a very small pension to his family. An aristocratic public school education would tax the family's slender financial resources too severely, so his mother taught him reading and writing and a strong belief in a personal God who watched over his welfare. She was a gentle, guiding influence to which he responded with profound affection. Later he gained his first formal tuition at a local day school where, with a driving determination to achieve perfection, he earned the praise of his masters. He excelled in history, mathematics and those arts which would prepare the future soldier. Barely fourteen, on the strength of his father's record of twenty-nine years of service, he submitted his application to the commander-in-chief for a commission without purchase. The Duke of Wellington promised to put the boy's name down as a future officer in Her Majesty's forces.

Commission without purchase was rarely granted in those pre-Cardwell days. The disposal of this honour rested entirely with the commander-in-chief and was restricted to successful students of the Royal Military College, non-commissioned officers who achieved distinction, and to the sons of men who had given great service to the nation. Wolseley, having qualified under the last-named provision, felt sure that by the time he was sixteen, the minimum age of appointment, he would successfully pass the educational requirements, which included an elementary knowledge in such subjects as algebra, history, geography, fortification, and a foreign language.

While Ireland in the late 'forties experienced dark days of potato famine, evictions, and ever-increasing lawlessness, Wolseley absorbed himself in an earnest, self-denying fashion in studies that would shape him for his future profession. To improve his knowledge of surveying, he took a job in a land-surveyor's office in Dublin while continuing his studies at night.

Garnet entered his seventeenth year but no commission was forthcoming. Purchase of an ensigncy in a Line regiment at £400 was still precluded by want of means. (Actually nearly double this amount was required for over-regulation commissions at the current 'black-market' price.) Wolseley wrote to the Duke of Wellington in the summer of 1850 urging him to consider his appointment and relating how his 'present inactive life was extremely irksome'.[1] The 'Iron Duke' ignored his petition.

Failing to rouse the hero of Waterloo, the impatient Wolseley tried to enlist the aid of Lord Raglan, the Duke's military secretary. He reminded him of the recent loss of officers in the Kaffir Wars at the Cape, for he assumed that his name had not been forwarded for a commission owing to the small number of vacancies in the officers' ranks. With undisguised anxiety, he concluded his petition by adding: 'I shall be prepared to start on the shortest notice, should your Lordship be pleased to appoint me to a regiment now at the seat of war.'[2] The Duke refused to act.

In September 1851, the boy's mother wrote a tearful letter earnestly entreating the commander-in-chief not to forget the 'cause of a poor widow of an old officer ... Having brought him up for the military profession it is out of my very limited means to educate him for any other station in life.' She prayed her son would not be reduced to entering the army as a private and working his way up to a commission. She assured His Grace that if he performed this act of kindness to a fatherless boy and widow, he would 'be rewarded in the world to come'.[3] On July 21st of the following year, after Wolseley's faith in the future was already seriously shaken, the Duke rather unexpectedly bestowed his favour on Garnet Joseph Wolseley by creating him an ensign in the 12th Foot.

Once commissioned, Ensign Wolseley sought immediate transfer to a regiment engaged in active service. The 80th Foot, later designated the

South Staffordshire Regiment, was the ideal unit for him to join because of its participation in the Second Burma War which was still in progress. Transfer was approved and he was ordered to Chatham where each summer beardless ensigns were sent to fill the inevitable vacancies of the Queen's regiments in India.

The callow officers received little training for what lay ahead. If these future warriors gained anything at Chatham, it was a romantic notion of war from those who had already served. The replacements were awed by veterans who wore medals, exhibited scars, and spoke of their recent adventures. After nearly a fortnight of exposure to these tales, glorious and grisly, Wolseley and his fledgling comrades embarked at Sheerness for India with deeds of valour crowding their young brains.

In the days before either steam or Suez annihilated the great distance the passage to India in a full-rigged East Indiaman occupied fully five months. During those apprentice days on board ship, Wolseley learned to despise the sea. The great expanse of water made him feel insignificant and humble. The ship was as confining as a prison. Worst of all was the wearisome monotony, where even the alarm 'Man overboard!' could be a welcome diversion. Macaulay said the boredom of long voyages to India was usually spent in quarrelling and love-making. But the quiet ensign, self-contained since childhood, remained aloof from his fellow voyagers, especially the young ladies. 'Marriage is ruinous to the prospects of young officers,' Wolseley soberly observed in his letters to home. 'Propinquity makes more matches than Cupid!'[4] He left the girls, cards, quoits, and tattooing to others and turned to his books. On board the *Maidstone* he spent hours reading and re-reading Voltaire's *Charles XII* and *The Meditations of Marcus Aurelius*, and he diligently sought to master the grammatical complexities of Hindustani before arrival at Calcutta.

Strange indeed was the officer of the Victorian era who approached war as a science and cultivated a taste for Clausewitz, or even Napoleon's comments on war. Professional knowledge was not encouraged. When a young officer discussed his profession at the mess-table, he was sternly suppressed. Reading and writing were largely ignored. Wolseley was appalled to discover colleagues who regarded the mere writing of a letter home as a somewhat risky venture.

Ensign Wolseley looked anything but the bookish type. He had the sturdy, well-proportioned appearance of an athlete. At a glance, it was obvious he indulged in the healthy tastes of youth, especially sport. Between readings, one might see Wolseley scrambling precariously in the ship's rigging, doing press-ups on the deck, or walking up and down furiously with his elbows flopping at his sides like some earthbound, featherless bird.

The manner of Wolseley was that of a soldier, quick and alert. He stood very erect, hoping to appear taller than a mere five feet seven inches. The tightness of his posture suggested a compressed spring easily released. His was a handsome face of clean-cut features; a fresh complexion; bright and penetrating blue eyes; a broad and lofty forehead that disappeared unevenly into chestnut-brown hair closely curled. There was but one rather poor feature, a weak chin and jaw that completely belied his resoluteness and strength of character.

Never was the sight of land more welcome. But the three days it took to tow the *Maidstone* to Calcutta against the strong currents of the Hooghly, westernmost channel of the Ganges, were sufficient to disenchant the future protectors of India. Under a cloudless and fiery sky, the muddy river oozed slime and corpses. 'Good God! Look at that awful thing!' shouted a soldier as he watched a motionless body float by on the sacred stream, serving at once as a perch and banquet to villainous-looking buzzards who tore at the decomposing flesh. After dark, thousands of mosquitoes descended out of the black and oppressively damp night to gorge themselves on blood enriched by sea air and good English porter. Being stout young Britons, many at first refused to conform to the effeminate practice of seeking safety behind a gauze curtain. Someone suggested that the youngest, tenderest recruit be staked out naked to appease the blood-sucking savages. The suggestion was enthusiastically seconded.

When the drafts for the various regiments serving in the Bengal Presidency disembarked, they were stationed at Chinsura where they awaited assignment. It was a dull existence. Idling through much of the long day, Wolseley occasionally put down his books to join his comrades in snipe-shooting and target practice.

As the war in Burma seemed to draw rapidly to a close, Wolseley regarded every hour away from his regiment as misspent. One of the last to leave Chinsura, he boarded one of 'John Company's' ships for Rangoon. But on arrival he discovered that military operations had been suspended. Instead of fighting in Burma, there was endless drill and picketing.

Drill consisted largely of goose-stepping across a parade-ground like wooden puppets. There was no attempt made to solve the problems of war, or to instil the lessons learned from combat. In no profession could one find greater disparity between training and actual practice. If an officer handled his men well in the formal evolutions of close-order drill, it was assumed he would be an excellent leader on the battlefield. Wolseley, who regarded the army as a serious profession, was discouraged by this ceremonial, spit-and-polish approach to war.

The want of adaptability to the actual demands of war was demonstrated by the soldier's dress and accoutrements. To Frederick the Great is credited the marvellous theory that colourful, close-fitting uniforms make the soldier a better fighting man. The Prussian practice was taken up by other princes, among them the Hanoverian kings of England. Thus, Tommy Atkins was a gaudily attired automaton, burdened with a pedlar's pack of inessentials so as to conform to every passing fad and fashion. He looked as if he were commanded by extravagant tailors. Great headdresses and helmets, enveloped in ribbons, feathers, or furs, became a miniature oven under a broiling sun and limited vision so severely that shooting with any degree of accuracy was often an impossibility. Tightly laced in his tunic with straps criss-crossing his chest, with knapsack, folded coat, and canteen on his back, with various brass and pipe-clayed trimmings – which required countless housemaid hours of rubbing and polishing – the soldier not only lacked comfort, his serviceability was sacrificed as well. One British colonel commanding a regiment of scarlet-coated lancers matched the uniforms with chestnut horses and tried to recruit red-haired men exclusively.*

Early in 1853, not long after Wolseley's arrival in Rangoon, the Second Burma War, which many observers had regarded as history, came noisily back to life, for in wars of conquest and annexation two separate stages often developed. First the regular forces of defence were overwhelmed and much of the land was occupied. In the second stage guerrilla fighting became common. The war in Burma followed such a pattern. After the defeat of the Burmese armies and the annexation of much of Lower Burma, an uneasy peace followed that was soon shattered by bands of irregular warriors composed of broken remnants of the army and dacoits. The most successful of these bands was led by a bold and resourceful dacoit chieftain, Myat Toon. Operating out of a treacherous wilderness in the district of Donabew, he successfully raided the supply ships plying between Rangoon and the advanced base at Prome. The expeditions sent to subdue him met with humiliating defeats that served to enhance the

---

* Wolseley and his comrades were amused by stories about the Pavlovsky Regiment in Russia where every soldier, from officers to drummer-boys, was required to have a turned-up nose like that of its founder, the mad Tsar Paul. Parents who hoped to make their son eligible for this crack unit would break his nose in infancy so as to give it the required upturned shape. A review of the regiment, with rows of snub noses pointed heavenward, was said to have been a truly astonishing sight.

prestige of this wily guerrilla, regarded as a bandit by the British and as a patriot by the Burmese.

The war soon became known as the 'Subalterns' War', for most of these minor expeditions gave eager young junior officers a chance to demonstrate their ability. As keen as any of the subalterns was Wolseley, who was assigned with 180 other men of the 80th to take part in a third expedition against Myat Toon commanded by Sir John Cheape. Wearing a tight shell-jacket buttoned up to his chin, buckskin gloves, and a pugaree wound around his pillbox forage-cap as the only concession to the heat, the teen-age officer boarded ship for the four-day trip on the Irrawaddy to Donabew.

The voyage up-river was made memorable by the crowding of General Cheape's entire draft on to one small steamer and an open tow. Drenching rains and oppressive heat added to their misery. The heat and dampness of the country, complained Wolseley, combined to create 'a steam as of twenty billion Turkish baths in full blast'. Reminding him that there might be a greater torment ahead if he fell into Myat Toon's hands were rafts floating down-river carrying the crucified bodies of comrades from previous expeditions. The mutilated soldiers were stretched out on a vertical bamboo frame so as to form an X or St Andrew's Cross.

On March 6th, Sir John Cheape's party of some 800 men left the broad Irrawaddy and plunged inland towards the dacoit chieftain's stronghold over twenty-five miles beyond. They followed a winding path, no more than three or four feet wide, through a dense jungle.

Silently, without warning, the invisible ally of the Burmese, cholera, struck first. To Wolseley, cholera seemed to fight in the van of the Burmese forces. Its blows were unseen and devastating. The fearful screams of the victim writhing from a sharp cramp were a shock to the nerves of his comrades. To relieve the pain, the sufferer was plied with strong drink or opium; the cramped area was rubbed with vigour. In a few hours Wolseley saw a robust young soldier begin to take on the appearance of approaching death. His skin greyed and tightened around the bony surfaces of the face, giving it a skull-like appearance. The eyes became glazed and the voice grew husky and weak. As the painful cramps continued, the face and body were as grotesquely twisted as that of a gargoyle. After the sufferer was completely dehydrated and the blood clogged in its vessels, death came mercifully to the stricken. The fresh corpse looked as if it had lain for a week. Most terrifying to the survivors was the appalling suddenness of the disease. Seizure and death – for few survived – were separated by only a few hours. In the presence of cholera, noticed Wolseley, all else seemed trivial – even battle. In the morning the soldier asked himself, which one will be next. During the day he wondered about the food he touched, the water he drank, the very air he breathed. At night he turned in thankful he had survived another day.

The dacoits soon kept up a provoking and desultory fire but showed no inclination to come to close quarters, though it was estimated that Myat Toon had at least 4,000 followers. These agile enemies, unencumbered by heavy equipment, their dark tawny skins barely distinguishable from the jungle, hovered about the struggling column very much like the vultures overhead. When they saw a chance to destroy one of Cheape's men, whose conspicuous red uniform made an excellent target, they moved in to snipe.

The march became a terrible ordeal. Over a narrow tortuous path admirably suited for ambush, the redcoats fought the sun, the rain, the mud, and starvation as rations began to run short. Cholera took a heavier toll each day. Over 100 men were lost in a few days. Wolseley was exhausted by long spells of picket duty each night. He often fell asleep on the march and awoke in the act of falling, saving himself only with difficulty from a bone-dislocating injury.

After pushing through the wilderness for twelve days, the enfeebled redcoats came into the vicinity of Kyault Azein, Myat Toon's stronghold. A flanking movement was precluded by a dense thicket on the right, and the left rested on an impassable swamp. The enemy's front, barely discernible through the jungle, was served by a moat-like creek. A short distance behind it, extending for nearly a quarter of a mile, were cleverly constructed stockades, abattis, stakes, or fences, according to what the ground required. There was neither a weak spot nor an undefended point along the entire line.

On the morning of the great assault it was the turn of the 80th to lead the way. Ensign Wolseley and four privates, all of whom were to be hit that day, were to form the point of the advance-guard. After probing the defences in the morning mist, Wolseley and his men joined the general assault. As the units became confused on the tangled battlefield, Garnet was offered a glimpse of some of 'John Company's' sepoys in action. The Sikhs, under British officers for the first time, 'were an example of splendid daring'. But most of the Bengal Infantry proved a cowardly lot who hugged the ground and had to be stepped over. Filled with disgust, Wolseley gave one of the cowards a mighty kick as he passed by him.

The assault failed. The general himself, the Scot named Cheape, now asked for volunteers to lead a storming party in an attempt to effect a breach in the breastwork. Wolseley and another young subaltern cheerfully obliged their chief and collected as many men as they could find. Shouting lustily in answer to the Burmese cries of 'Come on! Come on!', the party rushed down the narrow path that led to the fortifications. For a moment Garnet was 'in a heaven of ecstatic excitement'. Then the path opened up under his feet and he plummeted into a pit, barely missing being impaled on one of the sharp spikes that studded the bottom. Recovering his senses, the breathless subaltern scrambled out of the trap-hole to join his men. He made a mistake. The party of raw recruits had fled to the rear and, alone, Garnet faced the howling enemy less than thirty yards ahead. He turned and jumped back into the hole. Realizing he would be destroyed like a trapped animal if he remained, he waited until he believed the Burmese on the parapets had delivered a volley, and dashed back to his line. It was a dreadful, humiliating moment with the enemy trying to shoot him in the back as his comrades watched his ignominious flight.

Feverish with a desire to succeed where he had initially failed, Wolseley volunteered to lead another storming party. His little band from the 80th was conjoined in the attack with a small group of Madras Infantry under Lieutenant Taylor. As Garnet moved forward to conduct what was regarded as a suicidal charge, a fellow officer, whose spare shirt he had borrowed that morning, exclaimed in disgust, 'There goes my change in linen.'

There was a wild cry and a rapid tread of rushing feet. From behind the wall ahead came the explosion of muskets, kicking up little puffs of dust on the path about them. To Wolseley the pleasure was intense. His blood boiled. His brain was afire. Body and soul were purged of all petty thoughts of self, he declared. There was nothing in the world like it. He would never again experience 'the same unalloyed and elevating satisfaction'.

Almost simultaneously both officers were struck in the left thigh by gingal bullets and somersaulted forward. Wolseley sat up and hugged his leg. Seeing his men hesitate, he waved his sword and shouted for them to 'Go in! Go in! before they reload!' His plucky sergeant assumed command and led the stormers over the stockade. Only after the dacoits had bolted and the flag was waving over their works would Wolseley permit himself to be carried to the rear.

The wound was potentially lethal. A gingal ball the size of a small orange had furrowed his thigh, tearing through muscle and severing a vein. Wolseley staunched the bleeding as best he could with his fingers.

Near by, Lieutenant Taylor, whose femoral artery was cut, bled to death in a few minutes. A surgeon arrived in time to stop Wolseley's bleeding with a tourniquet, and he was removed to the rear.

The grievously wounded ensign was carried back to a steamer and taken on to Prome. For weeks he lay on his back with a soldier in constant attendance to screw on a tourniquet if the great sloughing of the wound ruptured the artery. The temperature rose to 100 degrees and the heat conspired with the stench of his own festering wound to rob him of sleep. To keep down the inflammation, the doctors began to starve him. The miserable patient, already severely weakened by wound and treatment, was further stricken with cholera, which came very close to being fatal. In May, still an invalid, he was ordered back to England by his physicians.

Before leaving Prome, Wolseley heard that Myat Toon had been decisively defeated, and though he escaped with 200 followers, his power was broken. It was the last and most furiously fought battle of the war. He also heard that his fiery courage and resource were acknowledged when the official report of the Donabew expedition was drawn up. Rare indeed is the ensign who earns mention in dispatches in his very first encounter with the enemy. On May 16th, 1853, he was promoted to lieutenant as a reward for his daring.

Exposing himself to death, concluded Wolseley, had paid off handsomely.

# CHAPTER TWO

# BLUNDERS AND HEROICS

O N returning to 'dear, dirty Dublin', the gallant young soldier from Burma received official confirmation of his well-earned promotion to lieutenant. He immediately exchanged into the 90th Light Infantry, then stationed in the Irish capital. By this transfer, the prospect of convalescing near his family for an extended period was considerably improved, for it was widely believed that light infantry regiments were not liable to service in India. And for the moment, Wolseley had had his fill of the East.

The newly-joined lieutenant was proud of the 90th. Throughout his years in the army, he always called it 'my regiment'. The unit, originally raised in Scotland, was regarded as one of the most splendidly drilled in the army. Many of the officers were high-born, and some were exceedingly wealthy. Wolseley described it as a 'home for gentlemen, and in that respect much above the great bulk of line regiments'.[1]

Dublin was always regarded as a first-rate quarter. The peacetime officers had little work and less responsibility. The drill and discipline, the feeding and well-being of the men were all left to the commanding officer, his adjutant, and various non-commissioned officers. What with cricket, hunting, balls, and dinners, every officer had more than enough to do. Lieutenant Wolseley was unfortunately somewhat handicapped by lack of funds and a leg that was useless for dancing and riding.

As soon as Wolseley had completely recovered from his wound, he began to crave action. In March 1854, England joined France and Turkey in a war against Russia. The 90th was alerted that summer to prepare for embarkation – to India! Since Waterloo, England had not been engaged in a war with a European power. It was a rare opportunity for an ambitious young officer; yet, Wolseley was destined to do service once more in 'the land of mosquitoes'. Discouraged, he contemplated seeking a transfer to a regiment in the field. Luckily the departure of the 90th was delayed until November, for by then, because of the heavy losses suffered at the Battle of Inkerman, its destination was changed to the Crimea. Had he not been attending church service at the time he received the welcome news, Garnet would have shouted for joy. He paid little attention to the service from that moment on.

At the time of embarkation, Wolseley was subaltern of the day and his duties included command of the regimental guard which marched to the rear of the battalion. Because eight or nine soldier prisoners were to be escorted on board, his small party proceeded with fixed bayonets. Marching through Kingston that Sunday morning, they drew the attention of hundreds returning from Mass. The crowd assumed these 'poor oppressed creatures' were enemies of England. Though there was not an Irishman among them, they were instantly adopted as heroes. The prisoners were cheered and many had purses pressed into their hands. The crowd became a mob. But Wolseley was not easily intimidated. The unperturbed English lieutenant gave every indication of instantly repelling an onrush with steel. The commander of the guard and his charges arrived at the docks without incident.

Wolseley had a theory about how to deal with the Irish, be they civilians or soldiers. Regarding himself as a member of the superior, conquering Saxon race, he believed 'Paddy' must be made to feel the presence of his superior in power and to recognize his 'determination to use that power'. He once wrote that the Irishman 'soon takes his hat off when he finds a master who is not afraid of him and who is always ready to tackle him'.[2]

Though he never denied his own Irish birth and background, Wolseley was convinced that he had escaped its baneful influence. To him, the Irish always remained an ugly people 'with noses so cut away that you can see the place where their brains should be ... They are a strange, illogical, inaccurate race, with the most amiable qualities, garnished with the dirt and squalor which they seem to love as dearly as their religion.'[3]

On the voyage out, Lieutenant Wolseley was tortured by anxiety lest Sebastopol should fall before he reached the Crimea. Arriving at Balaclava Harbour, he was assured by officer acquaintances of the Light Brigade who came on board that the war was still in progress, but it was no longer their kind of war. Siege operations, plus the discomforts and hardships which attended a Russian winter, took all the sport out of it. There was now little likelihood of a cavalry action and, after all, a campaign without a cavalry charge or two quickly degenerated into a vulgar brawl. Moreover, they were all lousy and advised the newcomers not to come too close. It was their intention, they told Wolseley, to go home as quickly as possible, even if this meant resigning their commissions. And scores of officers throughout the army did resign and leave the Crimea. Wolseley, who admired their courage in charging into the 'Valley of Death', nevertheless, believed them lacking in manliness for their craven desertion of the army in this time of trial.

Nor did the majority of officers he met after landing improve his general opinion of them. He soon found most of the staff officers to be totally incompetent. If any of them had been privates, he was sure their colonels would never have entertained the notion of promoting them to corporal. Such an individual was the brigade-major who sent Lieutenant Wolseley and his men out in the small hours of the morning to perform their first picket assignment with only the vaguest description of where to go. The company captain was of no help, because he was devoid of any interest in outpost duties or the war itself, for that matter, except for drill and dressing smartly. The captain let his uninitiated lieutenant lead the way. Stumbling through terrifying darkness in heavy rain, Wolseley, trusting largely to luck, found the company of Connaught Rangers they were to relieve, not a Russian prison camp.

Lieutenant Wolseley, already virtually the acting captain of his company, received official notice in the middle of December that his zeal and ability were to be rewarded; he was gazetted captain. A fortnight later his promotion was withdrawn; the authorities offered the excuse that a lad of twenty-one was too young to serve as a captain. Wolseley, incensed by the withdrawal of a promotion he had obviously earned, threatened to resign his commission if he were not reinstated. The order was rescinded.

To escape boredom and possibly see a little more action, Wolseley applied for duty with the Royal Engineers who were known to be shorthanded. Serving as a sapper, he would be in the most advanced position where defensive works and repairs were constructed in the hours of darkness, particularly after a day-time bombardment. The term of duty varied between twelve and twenty-four hours every fourth day. When not up front in the trenches, the sapper captain was writing reports and drawing plans; and as the ancient military rhyme put it, 'he was busy a-digging up of holes, and a-sticking in of poles, and a-building of barracks for the soldieree'.

At Christmas-time, Wolseley observed the festive season as best he could. Christmas in the Wolseley household was celebrated ever since he could remember with a tasty plum pudding. Though he abhorred the task of cooking, he was not to be denied; he and a friend prepared a pudding. They searched the port of Balaclava for the necessary ingredients and finally obtained a box of figs as a substitute for the plums; pounded-up

25

biscuit would suitably represent the flour, and a few pounds of very rancid grease would do for suet. The unsavoury mess was rolled up into a haversack and lowered into a pot of boiling water. While they impatiently sat around the bubbling kettle, they were unexpectedly required to go up into the trenches. The two famished soldiers decided to eat their half-cooked Christmas treat before departing. The squashy, greasy mixture called 'pudding', though heavy, stayed down with difficulty. No one cared for a second helping.

It was a still night in the trenches, except for the rumbling in Wolseley's stomach; it was as if he had swallowed a round of canister and the shot was rattling about inside. When his men discovered their poisoned captain doubled over with pain, a surgeon was called up. After fifteen minutes of brisk walking in the direction of his quarters, the pain began to leave him, and he insisted on returning to duty, despite the advice of his physician. For years after, the faintest reminder of this indigestible Christmas repast nauseated him.

It was a severe winter. It is always a severe winter for the invaders of Russia. Tsar Nicholas I boasted that his generals, January and February, would destroy the enemy as they did Napoleon's Grand Army in 1812. On the first day of the new year, snow and cold began a furious assault, and all major military operations were suspended. Soon not even an axe could make an impression on the frozen ground. Wolseley, however, was busier than ever in keeping the trenches clear of slush and snow, and repelling the frequent sorties made by the Russians at night.

The army, dressed in the same uniforms as those worn on ceremonial parades, suffered cruelly from the rigours of the arctic-like winter. After hard months of campaigning, the men went through their meagre clothing allowance and soon possessed only those garments that they stood up in and slept in. Without a change in underwear and little opportunity to wash what they wore, Wolseley noticed they became infested by vermin of a type described as the most exasperating of the Plagues of Egypt.

It was an army in rags, with greatcoats tattered and boots worn thin. Sorrowfully Wolseley meditated on the grim irony that England was the greatest manufacturing country in the world, and yet the dress of her soldiers was inferior to all in the Crimea, except that of the Turk. Even the cavalry when in full dress were all helmet and boots. The standing order against the stripping of the dead – Russian or British – had to be broken.

When the blue-nosed, red-faced, and often barefooted soldier returned to camp, he found little shelter from the icy wind that blew across the barren plateau. Wolseley winced as he watched them crowd as close as sheep behind boulders and bushes to escape the biting wind and cold. The camp equipment, much of it left over from the Peninsular War a half-century before, was either rotten or rusty. The canvas was torn by strong gales. The entrenching tools, carried largely for display, were so worthless that men used the wooden parts for fuel. And fuel was desperately scarce in this treeless country. What few shrubs there were disappeared into the camp fire in November; in December the men came back and dug up the roots. Because of the shortage of blankets, some wrapped straw round their legs and arms to shelter themselves from frost-bite. Many a shivering soldier who huddled around a small fire at night had his life flicker out as the flame failed before the dawn. The arrival of the first large consignment of blankets coincided with the arrival of the first heat-wave of the summer season.

Wolseley, serving as he did with the engineers, was closer to the common soldier than the ordinary officer. Keenly aware of their disposition and privations, he tried to set a cheery and gallant example. But as much as they, he was involved in the common struggle against the elements. He and another sapper officer managed to hold a makeshift tent together. They even enjoyed sleeping on a wooden floor rather than the muddy ground until they were forced to sacrifice their nocturnal comfort, plank by plank, to warm their food.

Their captain did not pity himself or any other officer in the army, for they had the money and means to go down to Balaclava and buy food, clothes, and other necessities. A few days after arrival, Wolseley bought a pony for sport and transport to the harbour-base eight miles from camp. At Balaclava, Greeks from Stamboul, Jews from Alexandria, Maltese, and other camp-followers had erected a row of shanties where they sold groceries and other goods at fabulous prices. Many of these merchants became wealthy from the gold they gathered in from needy British officers. On each trip to the crowded base, and there were many, Captain Wolseley permitted himself to be fleeced by the same publican who charged him a half-sovereign for a half-pint of what was labelled 'champagne'.

Sometimes he bargained with merchant seamen. Though Wolseley paid double the usual price, he was happy to purchase a comfortable pea-jacket and long boots from a sailor. 'I think,' said Wolseley long afterwards, 'I owe my life to that coat, and those boots; I lived the whole winter in them, and when spring came they were still intact.'[4]

Usually, he and his fellow officers sought food to supplement their tasteless rations. To get hold of an extra tin of sardines or cocoa and milk was a treat. The officers, of course, always had the additional luxury of a servant who would spend much of the day foraging for food and fuel. Rarely did a day pass on which Captain Wolseley and his tent-mate were not served a hot meal.

The rank and file began to starve and suffer from the debilitating effects of malnutrition, owing to the lack of proper organization. The diet of salt meat and hard biscuits without vegetables never varied. Tea, sugar, or the other minor comforts that would help sustain and warm them were totally absent. The men did receive a few green coffee beans, but with insufficient means to brew a palatable drink. A large quantity of rum was distributed with some regularity, though it had to be drunk on the spot. Frequently containers arrived already drained of their fiery contents. One enterprising private put the empty bottles to good use by constructing a glass side to his hut.*

Fresh vegetables were available at 'Ballyclava', as the men called it. Shiploads of potatoes, onions, cabbages, and other green foods arrived sporadically, only to be dumped on the shore and allowed to rot because there was not transport to convey these precious foods to the front several miles beyond. Wolseley, who saw what was one of the finest armies England ever sent abroad dwindle 'to a gaunt and stricken skeleton', joined other officers who took time off to carry what food they could on the backs of their mules and horses. But their puny efforts could hardly contain the spread of starvation.

What the army needed, in Wolseley's opinion, was an adequate transportation system. It was not the fault of the navy, for the Crimea was usually well served by ships from England, 3,000 miles away. Even after thirty vessels loaded with vital supplies were lost or disabled in a hurricane on November 14th, Balaclava harbour was soon crammed with cargo-laden transports. It was the land transport that had failed so disastrously. The final eight-mile link between the harbour and the army, between abundance and famine, became a clogged bottle-neck: a single narrow, clay road that was a sea of mud when it rained and wrinkled into deep ruts when the temperature dropped.

Initially, there wasn't even a land transport corps. Transport animals and vehicles were picked up wherever they could be found. The officers in charge, selected at random by the home authorities, had not the slightest knowledge of how to tackle the problems involved in conveying

---

* Glass, being almost indestructible, remained in huge piles around Sebastopol for years after the war, and the Russians delighted in showing the visitors these 'monuments to depravity' left behind by their former enemies.

supplies. The horses and mules turned to skin and bones because of the scarcity of forage. These starving creatures bit into the spokes of the gun-wheels and savagely ate each other's tails and manes. When a supply of compressed hay arrived, it was found to be weighted by swindling con-tractors with heavy stones and the stinking carcasses of animals.

The track from post to camp became littered with the corpses of horses and mules in every stage of decomposition. They became useful as guide-posts on the snow-covered ground to those civilians and officers who came up from Balaclava anxious to get a look at the front line. Wolseley over-heard one bluejacket give directions to a young officer: 'Well, sir, you must go straight on in that direction until you come to a dead horse on your right and an infernal stink on your left, and then you must turn half right and make for three newly-made graves. From there you will have no difficulty in fixing the position of Gordon's Battery ... '5 Wolseley hoped the young visitor would not lose his way with so many dead animals about and with so many bad smells prevailing.

It was painful to Wolseley to watch the troops struggling like beasts of burden with supplies from Balaclava. Their gaunt faces and weary bodies would haunt him the rest of his life. Yet never was he more proud of the British soldier. He worked and fought until he fell, accepting his fate with resignation, 'as if it were expected, as if he had been specially enlisted and trained to bear it ... he laid down and died uncomplaining like a gentle-man.'6

Rumours of peace, especially after the death of the Tsar (also a victim of the winter) at the beginning of March 1855, were welcomed by war-weary soldiers before Sebastopol, but they annoyed Captain Wolseley. Despite the hardships of a killing winter, war remained an exciting game. He prayed that the war would come furiously alive and give him the chance to earn further promotion – if he survived.

During dull intervals of quiet, Wolseley delighted in livening things up by having one of his men raise a forage-cap on a ramrod over the parapet to attract fire from the enemy rifle-pits while he stood at a near-by loop-hole with a cocked musket. The moment he saw the puff of smoke that revealed the position of the Russian marksman, he let go. If the enemy opened up with many guns and dropped a shell or two, he was flattered by the conviction that he had killed, or at least wounded one of the Mus-covites. On one occasion, the terrible row he provoked aroused the curiosity of the field officer of the day who came up from the rear to in-vestigate. When informed of the facts, he ordered Wolseley 'to shut up' and not draw fire upon them again.

But Wolseley could not resist this rare form of entertainment. He felt it served the purpose of demonstrating to the enemy that the English were keen, light-hearted, and always ready for a duel; in addition, it buoyed up the spirits of the men. On clear days, when he was free from duty, he went up into the advanced works and picked off enemy gunners, trench sentries, or anyone rash enough to expose his head. He envied a fellow officer who frequently joined him with a fancy, high-powered rifle with which he ran up a fabulous score. Once they nearly touched off a general engagement. In a letter to his dowager aunt, Lady Wolseley, he confessed that 'man shooting is the finest sport of all; there is a certain amount of infatuation about it, that the more you kill the more you wish to kill.'[7]

Wolseley had many visitors, 'T.G.s' or 'travelling gentlemen' as the army called them, who came up into the siege-works to see what war looked like just for the fun of the thing. Journalists, ministers, relatives, and ordinary sightseeing tourists came up by the hundreds and roamed about camp, batteries, and entrenchments at will. Neither passport nor permit was necessary. To Wolseley they provided a source of amusement whenever things got dull. He and his comrades would warn them to fall flat to escape harm when they heard gun-fire. Being callously indifferent to booming cannon and exploding shell because their own keen hearing easily discerned the shot that would fall close by, the soldiers enjoyed watching the 'T.G.s' hug the earth whenever they heard the whistle of a projectile and shudder in terror as they waited for the infernal thing to explode.

The conduct of one 'travelling gentleman' proved to be no laughing matter. Dressed in a shooting-jacket with his hands in his pockets, he carefully inspected the batteries for an entire afternoon. Suddenly he darted towards the Russian lines and made it before a bullet could catch him. One officer who witnessed his astonishing conduct exclaimed, 'One can hardly imagine so miserable a being – an Englishman, a spy on his country – to exist.'[8]

The 'T.G.s' cleared out on April 9th when the allied artillery began a general bombardment. The second great bombardment of Sebastopol – the first was in October – brought into play every gun and mortar the English and French could assemble. Over 130,000 projectiles were hurled into the modern Troy, everything from red-hot shot heated in special furnaces to 13-inch shells weighing 200 pounds and crammed with a composition not unlike Greek fire. The Russian artillery answered with three to the allies' every four shots. With this heavy retaliatory fire, Wolseley was kept busy repairing embrasures, laying platforms, and encouraging the men, largely by his own example, to face the danger bravely. The Russian marksmen were alert to their slightest exposure, and the artillery threw at the toiling sappers grape and canister, round shot, and exploding shell.

The second day of the cannonading, the enemy began to find the range. Wolseley was engaged in lifting sand-bags to repair one cheek of an embrasure when a round shot struck the wall behind him and spun away among the men, killing one of them outright and injuring several others. Their captain, who narrowly missed being killed, was only slightly wounded in the leg by debris the shot had scattered. Being an engineer with great responsibility, he regarded it as a point of honour not to report himself as wounded unless disabled.

After this 'near thing', Wolseley resolved always to turn and face towards the oncoming missile. The young officer had a dread of being hit in the back and dying like a coward. Moreover, he believed that with a practised eye and nimble feet, he could dodge any flying fragment, for he never found a small splinter.

The shrieking 13-inch shells, or 'Whistling Dicks' as they were named, terrorized the boldest because of their appalling size; but not Wolseley. He reasoned that the size of the shot was of little consequence, for a piece of metal not much larger than a pea could kill just as easily. The effect of artillery fire, he decided, was more moral than actual. The number of killed was always relatively small. It was the deafening noise, the way it shattered houses, shredded trees, and mangled a man's frame that caused the stoutest soldier to quake in mortal fear. Standing up to and facing a bombardment was also a way, thought Wolseley, of demonstrating his fearlessness for all to see. The captain's imperturbable coolness under fire was noticed by a general of engineers, who declared him to be the bravest man he ever saw under fire.

Wolseley held to the popular belief that most English gentlemen were born with courage. If an Englishman had the misfortune not to inherit this noble trait, he cultivated it; he stood his ground and steeled himself to appear brave. What surprised Wolseley most was that he was not only totally indifferent to death, but to the grisly scenes of war as well. On the third day of the bombardment, a sapper standing before him suddenly had his head taken off by a round shot. A second sapper, standing near by, had the first man's jaw-bone driven into his cheek so that at first glance it gave the shocking appearance of being part of his own torn face. Wolseley, bespattered with blood, remained calm and was not sickened in the slightest by the ghastly sight.

Yet ordinarily, Wolseley was a man with a finely sensitive temperament. The sight of raw meat always left him nauseated, and to pass a butcher's shop was an ordeal. Now these fine feelings became blunted even where his friends were concerned. He could look upon the dead body of a comrade with whom he had dined the night before 'with as much indifference as if it was a dog I had killed at home'.[9]

As the siege became more dormant, Garnet spent much of his time with his brother Dick, who had come out earlier in the year to serve as a surgeon. Dick found Garnet's appearance greatly changed. He had always remembered him as impeccably well-dressed. Now, after constant duty in the trenches, he looked like a badly-rumpled pillow. His face had lost much of its youthfulness owing to the growth of a large moustache.

The social life in this informal, almost casual war was well developed.* Wolseley made more military acquaintances than at any other time in his career. It was here that he met Charles 'Chinese' Gordon. He felt immediately drawn to this man in a way that he could not describe with words. This good-looking, curly-headed young engineer who was the same age as himself, impressed Wolseley with 'his full, clear, and bright eyes' that bespoke sincerity, and with his complete 'indifference to danger of all sorts'. This Christian warrior and hero startled him with a single-mindedness of purpose that made him feel inferior 'in all the higher qualities of character ... How inferior were all my aims in life to his,' he later concluded.[10] It was a strange friendship, for they rarely met or corresponded after the Crimean War. But they remained in each other's thoughts and closely followed each other's careers. Before Gordon went to be martyred at Khartoum, he told Wolseley that he was one of the two men for whom he prayed daily.

On June 6th the third great bombardment of Sebastopol began; this was regarded as the prelude to a series of assaults that would lead to the capture of the Russian stronghold. The combined action of the allied armies was directed against two great fortresses: the Malakoff, which stood opposite the French left; and the Great Redan, which was the main position before the British. The enemy had seized the ground before these strong points under cover of darkness and constructed works to improve the Russian defences and harass the French and English in the trenches opposite them. Therefore, as a preliminary to the great attack, the French had to clear the outworks known as the Mamelon and the British had to

---

* The casual approach was demonstrated by an officer in command of a force at Inkerman in danger of being overwhelmed. Rushing up to an officer commanding a detachment near by, he said politely, 'Excuse me, but we are in a dickens of a mess. Would you be good enough to come over and help us? I was introduced to you last summer at Lady Palmerston's.'

take the Quarries. On that brilliant summer afternoon nearly 600 guns opened a furious bombardment on the Russian position. Within a quarter of an hour, all the enemy ordnance replied. Not in the history of mankind, to that date, had so few men made such a violent noise over so long a period of time. At dusk the night mortars continued to batter the defences with monster projectiles. Their burning fuses traced a fiery, parabolic course across the night sky that ended in an earth-shaking concussion which spread death and ruin among the defenders who worked to repair the damage. At dawn the general cannonading was resumed as soon as the gunners could see to aim.

The enemy was almost completely silenced and their works were severely damaged by the slow, steady and accurate fire of the British batteries. The hour before the attack, the fire was intensified so as to kill as many Russian defenders as possible. The shells slashed and plunged into the troops massed in the Redan, blowing their victims into the air and leaving great ragged gaps.

At six o'clock in the evening the assaulting columns assembled in the trenches, nearly a thousand men, to be led by Colonel Campbell of the 90th. To the engineer officers was reserved the honour of showing the way to the storming parties; and then several engineers, including Wolseley, were assigned the job of connecting the Quarries before the Great Redan with their own trenches as soon as they were taken.

From an advanced position in the foremost trench Wolseley watched the men about him 'nerving their hearts', trying in good British fashion to disguise the powerful feelings within them and appear as unconcerned as possible. Reacting immediately to the given signal, the redcoats scrambled over the parapet and like an impetuous torrent they bore down on the trenches of the Quarries, indifferent to all danger and cheering lustily as they ran. Grape and canister from the Redan and musket fire from the Quarries thinned their ranks, but failed to slow their pace. They swarmed over the Russian trenches and rifle-pits, taking them at bayonet point. Some of the over-eager troops continued on beyond their objective and attacked the Redan itself until they were driven back by heavy Russian fire. The French enjoyed similar success in taking the Mamelon. This was the first great advantage gained by the allies since the beginning of the siege.

The supreme task was to hold what had been seized, for the Russians had abundant reserves to attempt to retake the lost position. Wolseley and the work party began the perilous labour of digging to the newly-won position and their own trenches on the right. As the losses mounted under

B

heavy fire, the captain and his men were forced to retire to the rear. Here Wolseley was informed of the sudden death of his friend, Captain Lowry, which left him in full command of the engineers at the front, and gave him the responsibility of constructing a vital passage connecting the British trench known as 'Egerton's pit' with the Quarries. As he nimbly made his way back to the Quarries trying to avoid the small Russian mines, he was struck by a canister-shot which whipped across his right thigh, inflicting a slight wound which bled profusely. He was too busy to have it attended to, but like all wounds he acquired serving Queen and country, he bore it with pride. This attitude was evinced by Lord Raglan, who, on hearing that one of his officers was wounded, said of the young man's mother: 'How proud she will be to hear that he has a bullet in his shoulder.'

It was hot work reversing the parapets of the Quarries and digging new connecting works. The Russian guns looked directly into the entrenchments and were fired incessantly. Most annoying was the Russian trick of filling a mortar with grape-shot. This iron shower pattered about the men, capable of cracking their heads like egg-shells.

When the artillery let up, the Russians attacked. Sergeant Gowing of the 88th counted fourteen separate counter-thrusts to retake the Quarries, or rather what was now dubbed the 'Shambles'. Many of the defenders ran out of ammunition* and used stones as they did at Inkerman, and it was not altogether certain that some of the men did not use their teeth. No more vicious hand-to-hand fighting occurred in the war. Wolseley fought and shouted and bullied his outnumbered men, succeeding each time in driving the enemy back with great slaughter.

Somehow, despite showers of shot and persistent assaults, through dust and smoke, Wolseley and his work party – of whom one-third were lost – succeeded in their task. It was most difficult digging where the rock was so close to the surface. The energetic and resourceful captain, in his haste to create a protecting parapet, used the bodies of the dead, friend and foe alike, along with gabions and piles of stone. Many a soldier continued to be of service to his comrades long after life had departed from his body.

Shortly before dawn, Wolseley made a final inspection of the Quarries and found the work successfully completed. To him it always remained the hardest day's work of his life. The men, overpowered by their labours,

* Two men received the Victoria Cross for bravely exposing themselves by bringing ammunition across the open from the rear. Later the story was told of one officer, who on being severely pressed by the Russians, urgently sent a request for ammunition and received instead a message which read, 'All communications to this Department must be written on foolscap paper with a two-inch margin.'

had fallen to the ground from sheer exhaustion. Many snored loudly amidst the sporadic firing of musket and mortar. The captain began to wish for the promised reinforcements; he doubted that the men had any fight left in them.

As Wolseley peered into the darkness trying to distinguish fresh troops arriving, he heard that peculiar, rasping, jackal-like cry, 'so unlike the manly British cheer', which heralded another Russian sortie. This would undoubtedly be the last and perhaps the most violent attack, for daylight was close at hand. Barely sixty men responded to the call to repel the enemy, and they were so drained of bodily strength they could barely stand.

Realizing that a few hundred Russians could clear them out in a few minutes, the engineer officers hoped to mislead the Russians regarding their true strength by making as much noise as possible. Captain Wolseley and Colonel R. Campbell, who had just come up from the rear, stood atop a small parapet and cheered themselves hoarse. A bugler, near by, was ordered to blow ear-shattering calls in rapid succession.

The dense Russian column came forward reluctantly; their officers seemed to be driving them. They halted a dozen paces or so before Wolseley and his comrades. The intrepid captain believed his time had come. But he stood his ground and emptied his revolver 'into the brown of them'. The Muscovites suddenly lost their nerve completely and fell back. Their officers could be seen pleading and threatening, even kicking and pushing, but nothing could bring them about to face the British and the terrors of another fight in the dark.

By the time Wolseley was relieved, he was giddy from physical exhaustion. He had been on duty for over twenty-four hours without a morsel of food, fighting and shouting until voiceless, even working with a pick, his wound all the while drenching him with blood. Stumbling forward, the weary captain barely got out of the Quarries when he collapsed among a row of recently laid-out corpses and fell fast alseep. He was awakened by the voice of his friend, Prince Victor Hohenlohe, who expressed his regret that poor Wolseley was dead. The corpse-like engineer, annoyed by the casual way he was dismissed from this world, managed to croak in a low whisper, 'I beg your pardon, I am worth many dead men yet!' Wolseley was assisted to his feet, given a strong drink, and pointed in the direction of his camp. He staggered and swayed, falling several times, until he met a mounted friend who lent him his horse. It took ten days of rest for him to recover completely.

Sherman tersely summarized the views of many a soldier when he declared, 'War is hell.' After that night in the Quarries, one might expect Wolseley to endorse this view heartily. Never! To Wolseley such statements should be relegated to a schoolgirl's copy-book. A night of fighting such as that in the Quarries was 'an evening's entertainment', the memory of which always made his blood tingle, his eyes narrow, and his lips expand like the recollection of an evening spent in the company of some exciting woman. After all, declared Wolseley, war is ennobling. Here was an opportunity to put aside selfish and material considerations, to place one's life in jeopardy for the advantage of one's country. True, widows and orphans were exposed to suffering and hardship, 'but what nobler heritage can a poor sinful man leave his children than the fact that he willingly died that England might be renowned and great, and her people safe and prosperous.'[11]

The taking of the Quarries and the Mamelon encouraged the allied commanders to press the siege operations to a successful conclusion with the capture of the two great fortresses, the Redan and the Malakoff. The day selected for the final assault on Sebastopol was June 18th, the anniversary of Waterloo. How appropriate! Englishmen and Frenchmen, friends and allies, marching and fighting side by side to commemorate that great battle and remove whatever bitterness remained in their hearts as a result of that bloody encounter. Lord Raglan, who had left an arm at Waterloo and still inadvertently referred to the enemy as the French, drew up the general plans for battle.

On June 17th, a fourth great bombardment opened with the guns of the fleet joining their fire with that of the many artillery pieces planted before the beleaguered city. They gained a quick mastery over the Russian guns, and with devastating explosions scorched and flayed their works, leaving acres of rubble strewn with dead, which resembled an overturned antheap on a monstrous scale.

To destroy whatever repairs the enemy would make during the night and prevent the hard-worked defenders from being reinforced, it had been agreed by Raglan and Pélissier, who recently succeeded to the command over the French, that the bombardment would be resumed at dawn for two hours before the storming parties moved to attack.

Only a few hours before the scheduled attack, the stout little Norman, Pélissier, arbitrarily decided to change the plan of attack by having the stormers advance without any preliminary bombardment. Though Raglan was convinced of the terrible consequences that would inevitably follow this sudden alteration of plan, he decided it would be futile to argue the point with the masterful, coarse-mannered Frenchman. Again, as seems to have been his habit, he acceded to the wishes of a French leader. The English commander was so sensitive to French feelings that when he heard of Marshal Canrobert, Pélissier's predecessor, tearing out his hair with rage over a suggested change in plans, he sent him some pomatum to make it grow again.

The Russians, alerted by the bombardment of the previous day, were well prepared to receive an attack. As the French advanced on the Malakoff, volleys of ball and shot tore them to pieces, littering the battlefield with human debris. While Raglan stood watching the French attack founder, he had to choose between ordering an attack that was sure to fail, costing hundreds of precious lives, or have his and England's honour impugned by the French. Of course, an English general who led 20,000 men was hardly in a position to dictate to a French general who commanded 120,000, but he could have offered some excuses to avoid participating in mass suicide. Above all, however, Raglan was a gentleman, a man of honour who, as Wellington used to say, was incapable of telling even the smallest lie. The attack was ordered.

On the night of June 17th and on into the morning that followed, Wolseley was on duty in the trenches close to No. 9 Battery where Lord Raglan and his staff occupied a fairly secure and commanding position to watch the attack. Wolseley was elated by the prospect of a brilliant victory and envied those who gathered for the assault, wishing he could share their glory. When daylight came and no preliminary bombardment followed it, he was less sanguine. The captain of engineers and the officers about him felt a sense of foreboding when they learned the stormers would be sent out without first silencing the Russian guns. And when the French effort against the Malakoff failed, the futility of any attempt to take the Redan became immediately apparent. Wolseley was not unique in believing that the Malakoff was the key to the entire defence, for the guns of this fort commanded the Redan and made it impossible for any hostile force to hold the position for long.

As the three columns of redcoats advanced, it looked to Wolseley as if the earth were covered by bright red poppies. In a few moments the Russian fire swept over the field and mowed them down like some great invisible scythe. Not a single allied soldier succeeded in reaching the Russian lines that day.

June 18th was a terrible mistake. The failure of the grand assault was the severest blow the allies suffered throughout the war. The bonds of the alliance were strained as the English blamed the French and the French blamed the English. Ten days later, a dreadful gloom hung over the

British camp when it was known that Raglan was dead: of a broken heart, it was said.

General Simpson – aged, uninspired and colourless – was appointed to succeed Lord Raglan. The news was greeted with little enthusiasm. This change in command, coupled with the bloody repulse before the Redan, ushered in a period of slackness; even the additional pay of sixpence a day to every man engaged in active operations against the Russians did little to stir the fighting ardour of the men. Wolseley and the other energetic engineers, anxious to resume their sapping up to the Redan and to lay out new batteries, shouted themselves hoarse with words of encouragement as they drove the listless men.

British work parties were naturally averse to swinging a shovel, and night duty with the engineers was exceptionally fatiguing. Moreover, on those short summer nights, between the customary issue of a tot of grog and the dawn serving of Bologna sausage, the Russians had a way of being most disturbing. It might be a quick sortie or a sudden bombardment. And the enemy developed the playful technique of sending up two mortar shells followed immediately by two more. With four of these lethal missiles in the air at one time, it was difficult – if not impossible – for Wolseley and the others to dodge them. They seemed to follow the soldiers wherever they ran, and sometimes the missile arrived at the place of 'safety' before them!

Towards the end of July, Wolseley had a serious bout of dysentery and was officially requested, very much against his will, to spend a couple of health-restoring weeks on board ship. It was hardly a luxury cruise as men stricken with cholera, dysentery, and fever lay on the crowded decks. There was little medicine to give them and only four or five drunken pensioners to attend to their wants and apply leeches. At dawn the physician and pensioners would make the rounds, separating the dead from the living and throwing them overboard. After a week on board this pest ship, Wolseley insisted he was much improved; and despite the protests of his surgeon, he demanded he be allowed to go back on duty to serve what was to be his last night in the trenches (August 30th).

The work that night was made difficult by the very rocky nature of the ground, the propinquity of the guns of the Redan, and the presence of a Russian rifle-pit less than a hundred yards from their most advanced position. Captain Wolseley's orders were to take a work party of 150 men, half with picks, the other half with shovels, and project the sap (an extension dug from a trench) as far forward as possible. Some fifty gabions of iron wicker-work, with their cylindrical shape filled out with stone for lack of a better material, were to be placed so as to create a parapet. Stones were always thought dangerous as a principal ingredient, for when struck by shot they scattered and hit with the force of a bullet.

Concerned with the safety of his detachment, Wolseley pleaded with the field officer in command to drive the enemy out of the near-by riflepit before the work was undertaken, or at least provide a strong covering party sent well forward to protect the work party from a surprise attack. The request was refused. The colonel, like so many officers in charge of the forward trenches, hoped either to avoid any unnecessary trouble during his tour of duty, or to pass on whatever disagreeable work was required to the field officer who relieved him.

Throughout much of the dismal night the men worked close to the ground like moles pointed towards the Russian batteries. They worked without talking or smoking, but the metallic ring of their picks and shovels on the stony ground drew enemy fire which took a steady toll of lives. The fire provided the sappers with an incentive to work harder, for their safety increased with each gabion they put in place and each shovelful of earth they removed. Wolseley was pleased, even a little proud of their progress, but he passed the night worried by the expectation of a quick sally by the Russians, who were capable of destroying their night's labour in a few minutes. And the sortie would be sudden, because the colonel had posted only a handful of sentries. Furthermore, they were drawn in far too close to provide much of an advance warning to the work party. The nervous captain was fully aware of the unpleasant fact that a soldier's courage was at its lowest ebb after several hours of darkness. Rare was the individual who possessed what Napoleon once described as 'two o'clock in the morning courage'.

Shortly after midnight, Wolseley relaxed and began to survey the work that had been done – then the Russians attacked. Except for the shrill, jackal-like cries and the sentries rushing by, there was little advance warning. The pick-and-shovel men were seized with unreasoning fear and rushed madly to the rearmost trench. Wolseley tried to stop them. In desperation he grabbed one of the men by the belt, but the bolting soldiers bowled him over, trod on him, and nearly kicked him into unconsciousness. As he struggled to regain his feet, he discovered he was alone in the trench, until a bearded and somewhat surprised-looking Muscovite poked his head over a gabion. To avoid capture, the proud engineer raced with unbecoming haste to the rear and rejoined his men.

Chagrined by the discreditable role he was forced to play, Wolseley aimed a verbal barrage of unparliamentary invective at the men who

39

had so shamelessly deserted their captain. Stung by these sharp words of reproach, the men rallied without command, swarmed out of their trench, and with a cheer charged the Russians, retaking the advanced sap with irresistible fury.

The unenterprising colonel who was responsible for the mishap now came forward somewhat abashed and asked, 'What is to be done?'

'I will do nothing,' answered the captain, 'until you have cleared out the rifle-pit I asked you to take before.' A small force carried the rifle-pit with a rush and Wolseley's work party spent the rest of the night repairing the mischief the enemy had wrought in the short time they held the sap.

As the morning turned grey, Wolseley began to reconnoitre and sketch the ground immediately before the sap so as to facilitate the work of the officer who succeeded him. He was impressed by what had been achieved in violation of the textbooks on siege warfare which ruled against any attempt to construct works under the muzzles of unsubdued artillery.

The guns were blind at night. But as the daylight increased, Wolseley began to cast a concerned eye towards one battery some 500 yards distant that bore directly upon his flying sap. While discussing the salient features of the ground before him with one of the sapper sergeants, his eyes were drawn once more to the menacing cannon. In that moment there was a brilliant flash from the mouth of the gun. He barely had time to shout 'Look out!' to the sergeant and two sappers working directly behind him, when the shot crashed into a gabion packed with gravel and scattered its contents with fearful violence among them. Wolseley was thrown to the ground with the two sappers on top of him. One was decapitated and the other lost a shoulder and a lung. The sergeant, who was unhurt, disentangled the captain from the mass of mangled humanity and led him at a funereal pace towards the doctor's hut behind the Quarries half a mile away. Wolseley in his half-conscious state, because of a numb feeling in his head, believed he had lost the uppermost part of his skull. As his fingers explored his head, he fully expected them to dabble with his brains which he was sure were oozing out.

At the surgeon's forward station, the captain presented an appalling sight. His face was torn and lacerated so that his features no longer resembled that of a human being. He bled freely from dozens of little wounds inflicted by jagged bits of pebbles, many of which were embedded in his face. His eyes, one of which protruded grotesquely, suggested complete blindness. The left cheek flapped down to his collar before it was sewn back in place. And when the patient pointed to what he believed was something foreign in his mouth, he was told by the surgeons that it was only the protruding portion of his broken jaw-bone. But Wolseley insisted on a more complete investigation, which resulted in one surgeon holding his head between his knees while a second with forceps extracted a large, sharp stone from the captain's jaw. (His sergeant companion saved the rock so that he might have a souvenir to recall his night in the trenches.) His right leg, pierced by many stony fragments, sustained a crippling wound that deprived him of part of his shin. His left leg had not yet recovered from the lameness acquired as a result of the fighting in Burma three years before.

After so many injuries, it was expected that he would be afflicted with tetanus or erysipelas; but he remained untroubled by further complications, and was sent to St George's monastery on the rocky coast near Balaclava, which had been converted by the English into a hospital. Here he was greeted by an old friend, Captain Sheehy, with whom he had shared a tent for several months. The genial Irishman, who was in charge there, made arrangements to have his comrade moved from a cell to a cave by the sea which he had converted into a comfortable residence. It was hoped that the semi-darkness of his dwelling would have a salutary effect upon his damaged eyes, for Wolseley would be threatened with total blindness for some time.

The invalid captain endured a period of great suffering, which increased when he heard that the final assault on Sebastopol would be made without him. While he lay brooding in his gloomy cavern, Private Andrews, his faithful servant, approached him with diffidence and stammered something about how he would appreciate the captain's permission to rejoin the 90th, which was to take part in the assault. Wolseley feigned anger and told him he was a fool; it was sheer stupidity to leave his duties and complete safety to participate in an attack where he might more than likely be killed. But as he peered with dimmed vision through his bandages, he saw Andrews as he had never seen him before. Such pluck, such daring – once more it was demonstrated to Wolseley's great satisfaction that courage was not the exclusive property of the well-born, the gentleman, the officer. Andrews was granted his request, on the condition that he was to return at once – if he survived – with news of the great event.

As Wolseley lay on his cot with his eyes closed, his mind's eye reeled off visions of the British army going into action. He knew every inch of scarred ground before the Redan; he could see the survivors of his old regiment crowded into the narrow trenches, waiting tensely for the signal to storm; he imagined how the officers, whose personalities he knew so intimately, would act and react. Then he seemed to hear the faint, low rumble of gun-fire. This, he was sure, was real and not fantasy for a strong wind was blowing from the direction of the battlefield. He could stand it no longer. He had to be there. Waiting with impatience until he was alone, Wolseley groped and limped his way to a pony and saddled it loosely with great difficulty. Trembling from exertion, weeping from frustration, he tried repeatedly to drag himself up on to the back of the little grey beast. His strength failed him. Ashamed and heartsick, the defeated captain returned to his stony home.

The attack began at noon, September 8th, after three days of relentless bombardment. The Russians contested their advance with destructive fire, but many Britons in the storming party succeeded in entering the Redan, including Private Andrews. Fulfilling his promise to Wolseley, he left the captured fort and galloped back to his captain to relate the good news. When Wolseley saw Andrews enter his cave smiling, he jumped to his feet with joy. His aches left him as his orderly related breathlessly the details of victory. Wolseley repeated them in the letters he prepared to send home. How proud they would be to hear of the great success won by England's heroes.

Three hours passed and Captain Sheehy returned to his domicile with a long face and bitter tidings: the attack on the Redan had ended in shameful disaster. Wolseley was astonished ... but Andrew's report ... surely Sheehy, that Irish rogue, was jesting! But Sheehy insisted his words were unfortunately true, as he disclosed the shocking truth of how the enemy counter-attacked, and forced the English to show their backs in disgraceful flight.

Though this mortifying tragedy left Wolseley heartsick, he insisted on learning the views of his brother officers who had participated in the battle. Each visitor was pumped for information until Wolseley knew as much about the event as he would have had he been there himself – if not more. It was as he had feared long before the attack took place: green troops* would be employed to carry out fatuous tactical plans. The fine regulars who had gone out to the Crimea had been whittled down to a pitiful few by privation and battle. Their shrunken ranks had been recently fleshed out with the weediest physical specimens he had ever seen in any army. And the schooling they gained in the trenches was all wrong for assault purposes. They had been taught to dodge, crawl, and take cover;

---

* W. H. Russell of *The Times* later asked one of the wounded boys, 'How many rounds did you fire?' Somewhat naïvely he confessed, 'None, sir, for I did not know how to load my rifle.'

they had no experience in advancing boldly, braving all the metal that could be hurled at them. All the dash was taken out of them.

While the British failed to hold the Redan on September 8th, the French took the Malakoff and all the honours in that final assault on the 'strong city'. The fall of the Malakoff precipitated the abandonment of Sebastopol by the Russians. The allies found a blackened ruin, and what remained of the fleet was scuttled in the harbour.

Now that Sebastopol had fallen, Wolseley resigned his post with the engineers. During the siege it was work that offered glory and danger; he had no desire to remain and participate in the building of roads and the construction of sanitary arrangements for camp. In recognition of his work in the trenches, he had received special mention in the dispatches of Lord Raglan. Napoleon III nominated him a Chevalier of the Legion of Honour, and the Sultan awarded him the Fifth Class of the Medjidie. In October, General Sir Harry Jones, chief of the engineers, recommended Wolseley for promotion to major. The advancement was denied by General Simpson because of insufficient years of service (six years were the minimum), but the meritorious manner in which he performed his duty in the trenches was to be placed on record.

Wolseley began to recover quickly, except for his eyes, and he intended to take the advice of his physicians and return to England where the best treatment possible could be given to them. But when Sir Richard Airey, the quartermaster-general, offered him an appointment on his staff, he felt it was too rare an opportunity for distinction to pass by.

He was soon ready to take on his new duties for he recovered the use of one eye, though he remained blind in the other. There was no trace of the defect in its appearance; it looked as bright and piercing in its glance as the other. Few people who met Wolseley were aware of this deficiency.

The fall of Sebastopol decided the outcome of the war. The allies had finally succeeded in their self-imposed task of destroying Russian power in the Black Sea. The conflict settled into an atmosphere of comfortable anti-climax. There was an occasional clash between patrols, and now and then a shot was fired across the harbour as a reminder that an armistice had not yet been concluded, but no effort was made to indulge in quixotic duels. All the life and drama had been drained out of this last of the romantic wars.

Nevertheless, Deputy-Assistant Quartermaster-General Wolseley was kept active reconnoitring, sketching, and preparing for the winter. In great contrast to the first winter, the authorities spared no expense in preparing for the comfort of the men. There were sturdy wooden huts now to shield them from arctic winds from the north, and food, firewood and warm clothing were provided in abundance on a plateau inhabited by so many ghosts from the previous winter who were victims of the Government's short-sighted policy. Wolseley and others of his party helped to organize drill, games and amusements for the men whenever there was a break in the weather. What sickness there was, was found almost exclusively among the French, who played host to typhoid, cholera, dysentery, and diseases induced by malnutrition.

By spring all parties were anxious for peace, save the British, who had assembled a powerful force of 90,000 to win greater glory and salve national pride. But Britain could not fight on without France. So on March 30th, 1856, the war was concluded by the Treaty of Paris, whose most important article provided for the permanent neutralization of the Black Sea, thereby eliminating the Russian threat in the Near East.

Wolseley was dissatisfied, but he took consolation from the fact that he could not be promoted to major until he had put in two more years of service, come peace or war. He wished the time spent in the field could be counted as double, but the regulation was not likely to be changed.

Through the spring and early summer, Wolseley assisted in embarking the troops. He was one of the last men to leave the Crimea. In July, as his lone ship pulled out of the strangely serene harbour of Balaclava – once bustling and alive with men, animals and ships – he asked himself, 'Have I done well?' After a few moments of recollection, he responded to his own cross-examination, 'I could have ... I ought to have done better.' But he was thankful that the good Lord had spared his life, reserved it for something better, perhaps. There was still 'an opportunity of becoming at least known if not famous'.[12]

# CHAPTER THREE

# THE DEVIL'S WIND

T HE chance to participate in another campaign came to Wolseley sooner than expected. In February 1857, after a few months' garrison duty at Aldershot and a long winter leave, he was ordered to rejoin the 90th in Portsmouth, where it was to embark on an expedition against China and afterwards go on Indian service. Wolseley spent his last few days in England buying enthusiastically whatever could possibly be useful to an officer stationed for years in the East.

He found the old regiment back to its full war strength of ten companies with over 1,000 bayonets. It was a fine-looking body of men led by some of the most experienced and capable officers in the army. They were mostly young men, lively and eager, who viewed the world as a place 'specially created for their own wild pleasures, of which ... war with all its sudden changes, and at times its maddening excitement, was the greatest.'[1]

Under the command of Colonel Campbell, seven companies and headquarters boarded the *Himalaya*. Wolseley's and two other companies shared accommodation aboard the *Transit* with the recently organized medical staff corps and drafts for the 59th in Hong Kong.

The *Transit* raised anchor on April 8th, 1857. By the time she reached the Cape she had sprung a leak. This was not an altogether unwelcome mishap, since it provided a substantial shore leave in Cape Town for Wolseley and his fellow officers. The men in the ranks could not be trusted to come back voluntarily. Ashore, the officers heard with dismay the disturbing and incredible rumour that the sepoys had mutinied. How this rumour was transmitted long before the swiftest ship carried the message from India remains a mystery. (The Mutiny began on May 10th; the *Transit* arrived at Cape Town on May 28th.) Though Wolseley's service in India was brief, he had the distinction of being the only man on the *Transit* who had been there. His companions sought his 'authoritative' opinion: 'Was it possible that the native army in India had revolted?' Wolseley believed it was.

Leaving the Cape, the *Transit* sailed eastwards into the low latitudes of

45

the Indian Ocean, a cyclonic belt where so many East Indiamen had been lost. Here in the great blue waste of water, where wind is king, the troop-ship was caught in a series of storms. Not until the *Transit* passed through the Sunda Strait, between Sumatra and Java, and made a sharp turn to the north towards Singapore was there a respite. The ship glided effortlessly along the glassy surface of the tropical waters, and after many weeks at

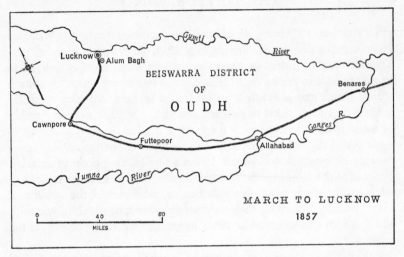

sea, the men enjoyed an occasional glimpse at the lush and varied foliage of the shore as they passed through the Strait of Banca, named after the island lying east of Sumatra. It was a treacherous, poorly-charted water-way, studded with rocks partially or fully submerged according to the tide. Many of these rocks bore names of ill-starred ships that had foundered upon them. On July 10th, 1857, another rock acquired a name – 'The Transit'.

Wolseley was preparing to enjoy his after-breakfast cigar on deck when he was thrown forward by the impact. On recovering his balance, he went to calm his men, who were suffering out their turn that week on the lowest deck, well below the water-line. Descending into the dark, stifling bowels of the transport, the captain lined up his men along the bulkhead and lied to them. He assured them there was no danger and asked them to remain silent and motionless until their turn came to leave in the boats.

A lone candle flickered and went out. Waiting in absolute darkness, they felt the deck slope slowly towards the stern. Obviously the ship was hanging on a rock, and if she slipped, would plunge to the bottom. The chance to swim for it in open sunlight, even in shark-infested waters, seemed preferable to being carried to the deep in a fast-flooding dungeon. Every man, however, was soon removed in disciplined excitement and deposited on a seaweed-covered reef about a mile from the wreck. Sufficient time was found to remove some provisions and arms before the ship slipped quietly out of sight.

The knots of stranded officers and men who stood huddled on the reef and watched their ship disappear were not completely rescued, merely reprieved, for the tide began to rise. Soon only the peaks of the reef, along with the fins of the sharks, remained above the water. The sailors worked their boats swiftly and by degrees transferred the shipwrecked party and their stores to a beach on the island of Banca, two miles distant, where it was hoped they would find relative safety and shelter from the equatorial sun. The cutter was sent on to the nearest settlement under the Dutch flag to relay a message to the authorities in Singapore.

For eight days the stranded men led a Robinson Crusoe existence. Shelters were constructed and the jungle yielded fuel and some fresh fruit. The food supply, however, was limited largely to salt meat, beans, and weevily biscuit. It was suggested that monkeys might provide fresh, nutritious meat. Many baboons were shot and mixed into a stew of salt pork and beans. But gastronomical prejudice is not easily overcome. Whenever a meal was served, Wolseley noted there was always a great deal of searching about in the pot to avoid fishing up any piece that was too unmistakably 'not pork'.

On July 18th a British gunboat arrived from Singapore with the disquieting news that India was in revolt and all the Europeans were being massacred. The orders were to steam to Calcutta, instead of China, where every soldier was urgently needed to restore British rule. Two days later the force was taken from Banca to Singapore, placed on board the H.M.S. *Pearl*, a handsome new corvette recently arrived from Hong Kong, and taken on to Calcutta. The officers on board shared their cabins and generously outfitted the officers from the *Transit* with clothes from their own wardrobes.

Anxious to unite all the companies of the 90th before the *Himalaya* group, diverted at Singapore, moved into the interior, the *Pearl* tried to proceed under full steam to Calcutta. But squalls, delays in finding a pilot up the Hoogley, and excited passengers falling overboard, caused the men on the *Pearl* to miss joining the main body of the 90th, which was attached to a relief column that hoped to fight its way into Lucknow.

The unusual sight of a sleek new twenty-one-gun corvette so far up the

Hoogley brought hundreds of curious natives out in small boats and to the banks of the river. When the *Pearl* fired a twenty-one-gun salute to the Union Jack flying over near-by Fort William, the onlookers fled in unreasoning terror and the small boats set off in every direction – many of their crews and passengers jumped into the river where they hoped to become less of a target. To the panicked natives, this sea monster was punishing them for the villainous deeds of the mutinous sepoys. To Wolseley and the other amused spectators on the *Pearl*, this demonstration confirmed the belief that the Indian was a cowardly rascal.

Fear was no less a stranger to the European community. Old Fort William, after so many years, once more resembled a citadel in a hostile land. The atmosphere was thick with rumours of disaster. The local newspapers reported the spread of rebellion to Central India and dwelt upon the heinous crimes and murders that had been committed. These stories were given a touch of realism by the bodies of English men and women that floated down the river. Wolseley heard that timid ladies came every night to sleep behind the stout walls of the fort. The less timid, many of whom had barely escaped with their lives from districts to the north, practised marksmanship during the day and slept with a revolver under their pillow. Some women carried poison in case of an emergency. Grisly tales of ineffable horrors involving women and children had a maddening effect upon the recently arrived soldier. Wolseley wrote to Dick, 'My sword is thirsty for the blood of these cursed women slayers.'[2]

The newly arrived were sent to Chinsura, forty miles to the north, where they were outfitted for the rigours of campaigning. Wolseley's company, numbering about a hundred men, was given new rifles and a 6-pounder gun. On August 29th Wolseley received orders to take his company to Cawnpore. The men boarded a train at Chinsura station that evening, but the 6-pounder was too large to take through the station door. It was too late to dismount the piece, or to take it some four miles down the line where means for boarding cannon were provided. Wolseley, however, was determined not to leave it behind. He called for an axe and a crow-bar to enlarge the doorway. The distraught, half-caste station-master at first forbade the undertaking in officious tones. Ignoring him, Wolseley directed his pioneer in chopping and prying. The station-master warned, threatened, and then begged. The 6-pounder was drawn through and on to the train while the helpless official looked on, open-mouthed, clutching a certificate written by the captain stating that the British army was responsible for the 'crime' of partially destroying the company's railway station at Chinsura.

The long journey up country really began at Raneegunge, 112 miles from Calcutta, which at that time represented the terminus of the railway line. At this point the Ganges became the chief highway inland, but in late August the sacred stream was very low. It was decided, therefore, that these three companies of the 90th should go to Cawnpore by way of the Grand Trunk Road, a truly superior military highway that connected Calcutta with Delhi and regions to the north and north-west. They would be the first troops to pass through the intervening country since the outbreak of the Mutiny, so Wolseley was warned to have his company ready to fight its way through if necessary.

The fate of the British in India, Wolseley told the people back home, now depended upon the 'bullock train', the mode of transport established along the Grand Trunk. He described how relays of soldiers, usually in company strength, travelled at night in bullock wagons, six to a wagon, or two officers with the luggage, while a third of the men and an officer moved along on foot and acted as a guard. The train travelled at a rate of two or three miles an hour, and at ten-mile intervals each wagon was furnished with fresh animals. At times there were unavoidable delays, related Wolseley. When it rained, for example, swollen rivers and streams became serious obstacles, especially at night. Time lost at night had to be made up with forced marches during the exhausting heat of the day.

Revenge was uppermost in the minds of all the men – not for the officers and men who had been victims of treachery, as soldiers they were expected to face death in every form and die when necessary, but for the innocent women and children who had been ruthlessly slaughtered. The British soldier was transformed by a passion foreign to his nature. Day after day, Wolseley's men spoke of their chances of joining General Havelock's relief column battling towards Lucknow. In the bungalows they chalked up messages to those who were to follow: 'TO HELL WITH THE SEPOYS!' and 'REVENGE YOUR SLAUGHTERED COUNTRYWOMEN!' The bullock wagons were given names such as 'The Avenger', 'The Rattler', 'Kill the Darkie'. Wolseley had difficulty in restraining his guard from doing harm to loyal native patrols after they pounced upon them. The men were rarely satisfied with their declarations of loyalty. Wolseley often overheard them complain, 'The captain has let off another lot of those d——d niggers'. It was not unusual for soldiers arriving in India to want to thrust their bayonet into the first suspicious-looking native they encountered.

Rebel marauders left a trail of destruction all about them and Wolseley expected his advance to be contested, perhaps in the form of an ambush.

If they entertained any such notion, the menacing-looking 6-pounder must have discouraged them. Less easily intimidated by this show of force was an enormous Bengal tiger. With no advance warning, the beast threw the entire column into confusion. The bullocks, ordinarily so phlegmatic, went wild with fear. The native drivers ran, and the wagons became tangled. Only the 6-pounder stood calm and dignified.

Wolseley ran up from the rear, expecting to find a sepoy barrier. Instead he saw the silhouette of a tiger etched in silvery moonlight against the dark forest background. The beast made a springing attack on the transport animals, failed, and retired a safe distance to debate attacking such a large group a second time. The master gunner requested permission to try a canister shot. The men, intrigued by the possible results of such a novel experiment, heartily supported the petition. Wolseley was tempted, but he reasoned that he could afford neither the time nor ammunition. He let the tiger remain master of the field. Anyway, it did not seem quite sporting, shooting tigers with a cannon.

Urged forward by the hope of overtaking General Havelock's column, Wolseley's company – the middle company on the march – caught up with the lead company at Futteepoor, forty miles from Cawnpore. These exhausting forced marches were in vain. At Futteepoor, Wolseley and his men were greeted by a disheartening message from Havelock to remain for the present at this civil station. The happy occasion of reuniting with the *Himalaya* companies and fighting on to Lucknow as a regiment was denied them. Each day they 'could hear the firing of Havelock's force which was most annoying', Wolseley wrote in a family letter. 'Indeed I know of nothing more annoying than being in the rear when fighting is to be had in the front.'[3]

In Futteepoor a search was undertaken to find the remains of the commissioner of the district, alleged to have been killed near by. The commissioner had been devoted to the welfare of the people and was known throughout the district as a kind and just man. When news of the Mutiny reached Futteepoor and the European community sought safety in Allahabad, he remained at his station. He refused to believe that the natives, in or out of uniform, would harm him. The good man's faith was rewarded with blows which left his body lying around in pieces. Wolseley and a detail of men found his skull and collected a few other bones. No coffin was available, so they buried him with full military honours in an empty brandy case. The sole inscription on the box in which his remains were laid to rest was 'OLD COGNAC'.

The next day a native trooper from the mutinous 2nd Cavalry was captured, tried, condemned, and handed over to Wolseley for hanging. When Wolseley called his company to attention and told them he needed a volunteer to execute a mutineer implicated in the Cawnpore massacres, every man stepped forward. Normally it was difficult to find a soldier who would accept the unpleasant role of hangman. A year before, in the Crimea, not one man in his company would accept the assignment, even when offered a discharge home and a £20 bonus.

The three companies of the 90th commanded by Major Barnston advanced on to Cawnpore on September 28th. Regarded as one of the finest military stations in the East, Cawnpore was now gutted and ruined. Wolseley inspected the crude entrenchment where General Wheeler and less than 300 men had struggled for three weeks, defending their wives and children against the local potentate, the Nana Sahib, and his sepoy allies. Faced with starvation and no hope of relief, Wheeler accepted the offer of the Nana Sahib to board forty boats moored in the river and paddle on to Allahabad. The Nana Sahib never had any intention of fulfilling his guarantee of safe conduct. Once the members of the garrison and their families stepped on to the boats, they discovered most of them had been damaged, and from concealed positions, the Nana's men fired upon them. Only one boat with four men escaped, all the other men were slain. The surviving women and children were herded into a dark little hut which a British officer had built to house his native mistress. Two weeks later, on hearing the sound of Havelock's avenging guns, the infamous Nana Sahib had the women and children hacked to pieces by local butchers, who then hurled the dead and dying into a well.

Wolseley's force, lacking tents, bivouacked in the open area around the little house and well where the butchery took place. Evidence of revolting barbarity was everywhere. Strewn about the area were bits of women's underwear and children's clothing and shoes. One officer found the head of a fair girl of about eighteen under some bushes. Wolseley picked up a handful of woman's hair before he fully realized what he had found. A tree in the yard was weirdly decorated with more human hair and fluttering fragments of garments instead of leaves. Inside the bungalow the floor was still covered with congealed blood, splashes of it clung to the walls. Gashes caused by the butchers' hatchets and knives scarred the walls and pillars. Here and there was the bloody handprint of a woman or child.

Trembling from 'un-christian passions', Wolseley ached for revenge against a race he regarded as inferior in every sense. 'The idea that a native should have dared to put his hands upon an Englishwoman', he wrote, 'was too much for our insular pride.'[4] The commanders saw to it that every man was given leave to visit the scene of atrocity so that he might see for himself how vile and debased was the enemy. Because Cawnpore was the base of operations for the entire region, one army after another was animated by a frenzy for revenge. Some scratched strong oaths on the walls; some divided locks of hair from the heads of countrywomen and swore vengeance; some just wept silently. Even an English bishop would have buckled on a sword, opined Wolseley, had he passed through Cawnpore.

The desire for revenge did not remain a vague sentiment among the British soldiers. Punishment for the Cawnpore massacres began with the arrival of the first British force. General Neil, whom Havelock left in charge of the station, was merciless in dealing with the rebels he caught. They were tried promptly, and unless their innocence was beyond doubt, hanged at once. A more fearful punishment was inflicted on ringleaders and principal culprits. Before being led to the gallows, they were taken to the slaughter-house and made to crouch and lick clean a portion of the blood clotted on the floor. If it was not done properly, the provost-marshal treated the culprit to the lash. The remains of the executed were buried in a public road. When Sir Colin Campbell, the commander-in-chief, arrived in November, he immediately put a stop to this practice which he believed unworthy of a Christian government.

Blowing condemned rebels from the mouths of guns, however, remained a common practice among the British in India. The victim was seized and tied with strong ropes to the uppermost part of the wheels of the cannon, usually a 9-pounder loaded with three pounds of powder. The muzzle was depressed so that either the small of the back or the pit of the stomach covered the mouth of the gun. The procedure varied slightly from one artillery officer to another. As one of Havelock's artillerymen explained it: 'Naturally this had not formed part of our curriculum at Woolwich.' Wolseley observed that even the most vindictive spectator had to have exceptionally strong nerves to witness the savage proceeding without strain. Before the officer gave the gunner the order to fire, the chief actor shattered the silence with curses and screams as he strained to free himself. The charge was exploded with a sickeningly muffled sound and the gun was enveloped in smoke which cleared, gradually revealing two legs lying before the gun. In the meantime, the blackened head, which had been thrown several hundred feet into the air, dropped among the bystanders, many of whom had already been bespattered with blood and shreds of humanity. The pent-up feelings of the witnesses 'found vent in a sort of loud gasp'.

Blowing men from guns was no cruel novelty devised by the British on the spur of the moment. It was the standard form of execution for rebels established by the old Mogul emperors and continued, intermittently, by the British conquerors, even after the Mutiny. In recent times it has been practised on the wrongdoers in Afghanistan. At the very onset of the Mutiny, it was first employed by the mutineers on European captives, and it was reported that women as well as men were executed in this manner.

To men like Wolseley, these executions were a simple matter of military expediency. At a safe distance, it was easy to be calm and talk like a gentle preacher. They were fighting to survive, not merely to win. Already outnumbered nearly ten to one, they ran the risk of turning the still loyal elements against them by displaying a merciful attitude that might be interpreted as a sign of weakness. Wolseley asked how one could consider these 'cowardly monsters' who murdered women and children 'in the same light as ... a white man or inhabitant of any other country whose son had pluck'.[5]

After Delhi fell to the British in mid September, all eyes turned on Lucknow and the attempts made to relieve the garrison trapped in the Residency. Throughout the summer, under the leadership of the vinegary and devout old Baptist general, Havelock, a small force of 1,500 men battled to reach Lucknow. Pushing forward against impossible odds, Havelock, with sword in hand and a prayer for success on his lips, resembled a warrior out of the Old Testament come to life. He won four victories, all of which he ascribed to the intercession of the Almighty, but then ran short of ammunition and men. Besides, the little band of survivors was so weakened by cholera and sunstroke that Havelock, even with the assistance of divine providence, decided he could not break through and turned back to Cawnpore to await reinforcements. Several weeks later, on September 13th, Sir James Outram arrived with additional men and a commission to supersede Havelock; however, he gallantly refused to claim command and allowed the heroic Havelock to lead the combined force of 3,000 men to Lucknow, serving himself as a mere volunteer. Outram resolved, moreover, not to use his sword on the mutineers but to strike them on the head with a stick, perhaps to show the troopers how easy a matter it would be to vanquish the enemy. But it was not quite that simple. As events proved, the column lost over 500 men in struggling to reach the Residency. Most casualties were the result of running the gauntlet through the narrow and heavily-guarded streets of Lucknow.

## 1857-9

The breakthrough of Havelock's forces into the Residency on September 27th was a bitter anticlimax to those who awaited their deliverance through eighty-five days of agony, for it was obvious that the Europeans and their native allies lacked the strength to carry off in safety the 600 women and children. What began as a relief expedition became a mere reinforcement. The original defenders, of which only one-third still survived, were greatly augmented, but there was no corresponding increase in badly-needed supplies of food and drugs. And still more rebels were pouring into the city every day from as far away as Delhi. Sir Colin Campbell, hurrying up from Calcutta, was forced to alter his plans and sacrifice his communications by concentrating all available men and resources for the relief of Lucknow.

While gathering his army of rescue, Sir Colin ordered a force of 500 men, including the detachment of the 90th under Major Barnston, to take a convoy of provisions from Cawnpore to the Alum Bagh (Garden of Delight), three miles outside Lucknow. The Alum Bagh was built by the last king of Oudh as an occasional residence for his favourite wife. The luxuriant garden, containing some 500 square yards of ground, was enclosed by a solid eight-foot masonry wall, and in the centre stood a large, three-storey brick mansion. After Havelock's force drove the mutineers out, it was retained and converted into a fortress and hospital. All attempts to recapture it were successfully resisted. Sir Colin intended using this garden-fortress, which commanded the road to Cawnpore, as his forward base.

Leaving Cawnpore on October 10th, 1857, the convoy (including some 300 wagons), with Wolseley's company forming the rear-guard, soon crossed over into the flat and fertile province of Oydh, of which Lucknow was the capital. British rule in the recently annexed kingdom was represented only by the imprisoned garrisons in the Alum Bagh and the Lucknow Residency. The British held only the ground covered by the range of their guns, for in this land chiefs and peasants, Muslims and Hindus were united in their hostility.

Because of the savage character of Oudh, Barnston's column anticipated a strong effort by the enemy to contest their advance. But not until the last day's march, eight miles from their destination, did sepoy horsemen venture forth and oblige an anxious Captain Wolseley by attacking the rearmost company which he commanded. As they thundered down on Wolseley's men, they received a staggering volley that stopped them dead. They continued to follow the rear of the column, but the great range of the new Enfield rifle kept them at a respectful distance. Whenever

54

Wolseley felt they were too close, he would halt his company and have them fire a volley or two, always in sections so that half of the men would be ready to repel a charge.

More serious was the possibility of a large force moving out from Lucknow and crushing the convoy by flank attack. Since the column was reduced to the pace of the slow wagons, the phlegmatic animals and drivers were liberally thrashed until all, finally, came under the guns of the Alum Bagh. Within the hour, great numbers of the enemy, more daring than usual, appeared before the improvised fortress. So strong, in fact, were the rebels that Barnston's detachment, which had been originally ordered to return to Cawnpore, dared not leave the Alum Bagh.

There was little to do but wait for Sir Colin to come up with the main body. It was a dull existence for the men confined in the Alum Bagh; even reading material was lacking. Wolseley, expecting to return to Cawnpore, had left his Bible and two volumes of Shakespeare's plays at Cawnpore with the rest of his kit. More annoying was an insolent enemy battery that dropped 32-pounder shots into the region of their tents every day. Major Barnston and the other officers who came up from Cawnpore pleaded with the old commandant to be allowed to make an early-morning foray and silence the battery, but he refused to sanction what he regarded as a foolish risk. To bumptious young officers like Wolseley, who had fought in the Crimea, a first-class war against a major power, the commandant was another example of the inefficiency and general inferiority of the Indianized officers who served in 'John Company's' army. Compared to the officers of the 'Queen's' army, they seemed to have had all 'the go' taken out of them – maybe it was too much sun, thought Wolseley.

Sir Colin Campbell arrived in November to begin the second relief of the hapless garrison in Lucknow and the last great campaign of his career. Standing on the roof of the palace, Wolseley witnessed the approach of Sir Colin at the Alum Bagh. He recognized from his Crimean days the soldierly frame, lean but wiry, and the pale, wrinkled but nevertheless handsome face. As the general came closer, Wolseley could see his face was contorted with anger. Sir Colin's bad temper was legendary. When his Highland blood became heated, it was as if a demon possessed him. And he was easily moved to wrath. One officer who rode alongside him complained, 'I felt like a mouse in the company of a large cat, for I did not know when I would be pounced upon.'

The object of his anger was the commandant of the Alum Bagh. It seems that while the commander-in-chief was marching up from

Cawnpore, he learned of the daring escape of a civilian named Kavanagh from the Residency and sent a brigadier ahead with a column of cavalry to obtain the important message he carried. But the commandant insisted to the brigadier that his orders from Outram were to turn the dispatch over to Sir Colin, personally, and no one else. The brigadier and the cavalry had raced forward to no purpose. Wolseley had no love for the unenterprising commandant who had once briefly placed him under arrest for drawing fire on one of the forward posts by attempting to get forage for the horses, yet he felt sincerely sorry for the soldier as he watched him being reprimanded by Sir Colin. The commandant stood like a delinquent schoolboy with his head bowed and his hands clasped behind his back while Sir Colin, his face blazing and his frame quivering, began a sort of war-dance. Round and round he went, shaking his fist and screaming at the top of his voice. Wolseley, the onlooker, was destined to provoke his commander-in-chief into an even more furious rage.

Looking ahead from the heights of the Alum Bagh, Lucknow, with its glistening white palaces, golden-domed mosques, and slender minarets, was a city straight out of the *Arabian Nights'*. But the picturesque silhouette framed against the bright blue sky concealed a tangle of dirty, crooked streets covering an area nearly as large as Paris, inhabited by 300,000 persons and guarded now by 60,000 rebels. For Sir Colin's little army of 4,500 this warren of brick and mortar could easily become a death-trap. Advised by Kavanagh, the general planned to skirt round the southern and eastern portions of the city by a flanking march from the Alum Bagh, keeping open ground – where the Europeans always had the advantage – between themselves and Lucknow. Upon reaching the Gumti River, which gently curved round the northern side of the city, the army would swing to the left and hug the bank, thereby protecting the right flank from attack until they reached the Residency some three miles up-river. This was the most vulnerable part of the city because the route close to the river was studded with palatial residences, mosques and other large buildings surrounded by many parks and gardens. Had Sir Colin been conducting a tour of Lucknow instead of a rescue operation, he could not have selected a more scenic route.

Before undertaking the relief, Sir Colin had his strangely variegated army drawn up for review in the middle of a great plain, encircled by woods. There were guns of the Bengal Artillery, which he had commanded when last in India; there were field-guns from Delhi, all blackened and service-worn, manned by gunners who looked trim and

56

swarthy; and there was the illustrious Naval Brigade, commanded by Captain William Peel (son of the former prime minister, Sir Robert Peel), consisting of 250 sailors and marines from H.M.S. *Shannon*. They landed some of their own 8-inch guns and made carriages for them. The readiness of the sailor to take part in the small wars of the nineteenth century became proverbial, and the way they worked their heavy guns evoked the admiration of everyone from the commanding general down. On the march, the men of the *Shannon* made quite a picture with their miscellaneous weapons – heavy guns, howitzers, and rocket tubes – drawn by elephants and oxen, and each sailor usually had a pet or two, including parrots, pigs, guinea-pigs, cats, dogs, monkeys, and mongooses, which together with the curses and cries of the men and drivers, created 'a Babel-like noise and confusion seldom to be enjoyed out of India'.

The cavalry, some 700 sabres, was composed of the 9th Lancers, who, though having just completed an arduous campaign, looked as if they were on their way to inspection at Wormwood Scrubs. Their colonel, Sir Hope Grant, maintained a high order of efficiency. They were all clad in smart blue uniforms and white turbans wound round their forage-caps, carried pennonless lances and sat with gallant bearing on lean but sturdy mounts; every man from the colonel to the bugler 'looked like a gentleman'. Next to them were squadrons of men from the Punjab, led by British officers and dressed in fawn-coloured robes, with gaily-coloured waistcoats, long boots, and voluminously folded turbans of blue or red. They were heavily armed with lightly poised lances, curved scimitars, and fire-arms decorated with silver. They bore the haughty air of aristocrats, and many of them were. Their steeds, which they owned, for they were all men of some property, were of every variety of horse imaginable, but they appeared as mettlesome as the riders who sat them so well.

The serried ranks of infantry began with bits and ends of regiments, many worn and bled like the men of the 8th and 75th. All were poorly outfitted from neck to knee in slate-coloured cloth. Amidst all this splendour, they stood grouped around their colours with the air of bored veterans. In the middle were the Punjab infantrymen dressed as brightly as their brethren on horseback – a superb-looking race that seemed bred to war. Tall, muscular, and straight of limb, they looked sternly proud with broad brows overhanging their piercing black eyes. The aquiline nose and neatly-combed moustache and silky beard gave them a finely chiselled countenance. They were mostly Sikhs, a military brotherhood as well as a religion, in whom warlike virtues were inculcated from childhood. Steel was to them a sacred metal, the metal of war, and under no conditions should a Sikh warrior die in bed; if necessary his friends would throw him from his sick-bed to the floor. They bore no grudge against the British, who had conquered them only a few years before, but they did nourish a feeling of revenge against the taunting Bengal sepoys who had assisted in the conquest. Many joined in the suppression of the Mutiny to pay off old scores.

Last in line were the 93rd Highlanders in full costume, a sea of tartans, feather bonnets, dark waving plumes, and spats. These 'petticoated devils', as the mutineers called them,* were the only complete regiment on the field, numbering nearly 1,000 tall, brawny-limbed warriors. They were in the prime of manhood, and over 700 displayed medals on their breasts for the Crimean War, where they formed Sir Colin's 'thin red line'. Swollen with *esprit de corps*, they told the girls in Portsmouth before departing for China, their original destination, that Lord Elgin wanted them to be his guard of honour at the Chinese court because they were 'a cut above other corps in Her Majesty's army'. No less impressed by the 'petticoated men' were the women of India, who crowded the streets and house-tops on their line of march. In time, many of the curious young females overcame their awe and bashfulness to ask personal questions about their 'petticoats' and if they were part of 'the Queen of England's regiment of eunuchs'. How the Highlanders responded to these questions is not recorded.

As the commander came down the line, he spoke a few words to each unit, which were received in absolute silence, but when he reached the 93rd, they cheered wildly and shouted their welcome. The old campaigner's face suddenly appeared youthful as his features smoothed into a smile. He acknowledged their greeting and launched into a stirring little Napoleonic speech. Pointing in the direction of Lucknow, he told of the desperate plight of the garrison and the dangers they faced in relieving it. 'Ninety-third!' said he. 'You are my own lads, I rely on you to do the work!'

'Aye, aye, Sir Colin!' answered a voice from the ranks. 'Ye ken us and we ken you; we'll bring the women and bairns out o' Lucknow or we'll leave our ain banes there!'

It was just as well that Wolseley and the 90th joined Sir Colin's army shortly after the review, for they were a disreputable-looking lot. Having lost their original kit in the *Transit* and left their second, makeshift kit in Cawnpore, the men were dressed in all sorts of motley costumes. Except

---

* When kilted Highlanders first appeared, some of the rebels wept with joy, believing that England had run short of men and was now reduced to enlisting women.

for some kind of helmet and dirty, yellow leather boots, which they pulled over their trousers, no two men or officers were clothed alike. Nor could the gaunt and sun-scorched men of the 90th, many no larger than Wolseley, compare favourably with the fine physical specimens found among the Sikhs and Highlanders. But for daring and energy, Wolseley would not trade his men for any company in the army. Most of the regiment had been recruited in London, and Wolseley contended that the average Londoner, because of his superior intelligence and general smartness, was ideally suited for light infantry work. And they had pluck. One evening, for example, Wolseley and his men stood around and admired the ease with which a group of exercising Sikhs handled heavy Indian clubs. The captain turned to one of his cockneys and asked him if he could do as well with the clubs. 'No, sir,' he replied smartly, 'but I'll fight any three of those fellows!'

The march towards the Residency commenced on November 14th across the grain-rich fields. Little was seen of the enemy until Sir Colin's force reached the Dilkoosha (Heart's Delight), the royal hunting palace, located on a plateau overlooking the city and surrounded by a luxurious park filled with deer. After an exchange of shots, the sepoys raced the deer in their flight before the advancing army. Many of both were not fleet enough; that night Wolseley and many of his men dined on venison in a field dotted with dead sepoys.

Less than a mile beyond was the un-Indian-looking Martinière College, built for soldiers' children by a French adventurer. It was now heavily fortified, but the fortifications faced in the opposite direction, for the mutineers had expected the second relief force to take the same route cut by Havelock and Outram. After an hour of pounding by Sir Colin's heavy guns, the position was easily carried and occupied. The army halted for the night, throwing out pickets – including Wolseley's company – to the near-by canal which represented the southern boundary of Lucknow. Wolseley remained on picket duty throughout the next day while Sir Colin fortified the Dilkoosha, which would serve as a hospital and general depot. The army was kept busy preparing for the grand advance, and the artillery was active all day and well into the night firing in the wrong direction so as to deceive the enemy as to the route the general had decided to follow. Relieved after thirty-six hours of duty, Wolseley slept soundly throughout the noisy night.

A semaphore had been erected on top of the Martinière and before dark a message was sent to Outram in the Residency – 'Advance tomorrow.' For four months the Residency had been subjected to a deadly and unceasing rain of shot, grape, and canister, supplemented by assorted lumps of rock and iron – even carcasses. Though their defences were by now reduced to a shambles, the defenders continued to fight desperately for their lives above and below ground. Enemy sappers constructing underground galleries for mining purposes were met by burrowing ex-miners of the 32nd Foot, a Cornish regiment, who engaged them in bloody subterranean combat.

November 16th began raw and chilly with an ominous blood-red sunrise. That morning the officers of Barnston's 'scratch battalion' were called together by the commander-in-chief, who delivered a brief address in which he emphasized the value of the bayonet in street-fighting, and suggested that when fired upon they should rush on with bayonets fixed, rather than halt and return fire. Shortly before noon the 'scratch battalion' moved out behind the 93rd and 53rd. They crossed the dry canal with little difficulty, Sir Colin having successfully misled the enemy as to his route of march. Moving first to the right as far as possible and then continuing close to the river, they moved forward unopposed. Alongside Wolseley was his fearless Madras servant, whom he had picked up on his way to Cawnpore. He proved invaluable as a servant, but he had a strong urge for loot. When they passed a home, he kicked in the door, charged in, and emerged a few minutes later with a smile of triumph as he jingled some coins. He always seemed to know where to look.

It was not until they arrived in the vicinity of the Sikandar Bagh (Garden of Alexander) that they encountered heavy firing. Ducking behind stone fences and into doorways, they kept up a musketry duel until the enemy gave ground. Wolseley and his men pursued them closely, darting over open ground and across bullet-swept lanes. As they neared the Sikandar Bagh, guns were brought up to batter the improvised fortress into submission. Wolseley's men lent a hand by dragging a heavy gun forward through ankle-deep sand. They were soon exposed to a hail of iron and 'the bullets dropped off the tires of the guns like peas off a drum'. Among the score of men who had assisted in pulling the gun, Wolseley was astonished to see so many unhurt. One sergeant had his upper lip shot away, but he refused to retire until the close of the fighting.

The Sikandar Bagh was 120 yards square, enclosed by a thick brick wall, carefully loopholed, and flanked at the corners by pentagonal bastions. The only entrance was protected by a traverse of earth and masonry with a two-storeyed guardhouse above. Stationed inside what they believed was an impregnable fortress were 2,000 sepoys, still wearing red coats, prepared to pounce on the flank of the army as it passed on its way to the Residency. Instead, they found themselves in the direct line of attack.

The violence of their fire soon became so great that Sir Colin's force was thrown into confusion. Men and horses were knocked down on all sides; the commander-in-chief himself was bruised by a spent musket-shot that had passed through and killed an artilleryman. Retreat would lead to disaster. Yet, no advance was possible until this stronghold was taken.

The large gun which Wolseley had helped to pull into position began to pound the wall of the Sikandar Bagh with heavy shot, as dark-plumed Highlanders and turbaned Sikhs waited on their stomachs until there was a breach large enough to admit stormers. When Sir Colin, sitting on his great white horse, waved his hat, they jumped to their feet and raced for the honour to be the first through the ragged hole. A Highlander won the coveted honour. Tumbling through the opening like a harlequin, he was immediately shot through the breast. A crowd gathered behind him to squeeze one by one through the small aperture. Some impatient Sikhs rushed over to the main doorway and beat their way in. A slaughter followed. The sepoys, having confidently sealed the rear exit, were caught in a death-trap, like rats in a barn. With no hope of escape or mercy, they fought with blind fury. Grimly imperturbable, with an occasional shout of 'Remember Cawnpore, boys!', Highlander, Saxon and Sikh executed the rebels with bayonet and shot as they followed them across the garden, up narrow staircases, and into every room. When it was over, in various corners of the Sikandar Bagh one was confronted with piles of dead and dying inextricably entangled, for the wounded could not pull themselves free. Imprisoned by the trunks and limbs of dead comrades, they gave vent to their pain and rage by cursing every British officer who passed by. Roses and other flowers were strewn about the dying mutineers by the victors, 'as if in derision'. Several hours after, Wolseley was given the distasteful chore of burying them. Two very long and deep trenches were dug alongside the main road into Lucknow. The bodies were hauled forth in great batches by elephants and flung into the holes. One observer kept a tally of the number buried and reported exactly 1,857!

A few yards beyond the Sikandar Bagh was the massive Shah Najif, mosque and tomb of the first king of Oudh. Around the great white-domed structure and its jungle-like garden was a high wall, exceptionally stout and loopholed with great care. The deadly fire from this rebel strong-point completely covered the road to the Residency. The Sikandar

Bagh was becoming a charnel-house when the Bengal Artillery galloped forward, unlimbered, and went smoothly into action against the hostile mosque. To protect the gunners' flank, Captain Wolseley was ordered by his brigade commander, Sir Adrian Hope, to clear a line of mud huts, adjacent to the mosque, of annoying snipers. Wolseley, still slightly lame from his wounds, had difficulty keeping up with his charging men until the brigadier offered him his stirrup-leather to hold on to. The rebels were easily dispersed.

Meanwhile, Sir Colin rode up and ordered the rest of the battalion of detachments to attack the mosque. Barnston and his men advanced at the double in skirmishing order to the wall. Ducking about under sepoy fire, they tried to find ingress, but all entrances were sealed. Barnston galloped back to the commander-in-chief to describe the situation. With a promise of reinforcements, he was returning to his men when he was struck in the thigh by a steel fragment that had exploded at the muzzle of a British gun. Leaderless and exposed to withering fire, the 'scratch' battalion began to waver, a few men started to run. Wolseley's company, along with other reinforcements, rushed forward in support but to no advantage. The assailants were raked with a storm of missiles – grenades, brick-bats, burning torches, boiling water, and steel-barbed arrows.

The infantry, having failed, was recalled and the artillery was massed for concentrated fire. After three hours of battering no impression was made on the wall. Evening shades were already falling. The crisis of the battle was at hand. Not only had the guns failed to subdue the Shah Najif, but the biting fire from its defenders into the jumbled mass of men, horses, and guns jeopardized the army's advanced position. Sir Colin collected his beloved Highlanders about him to tell them he had had no intention of using them again that day, especially after what they had already accomplished, but *that building* must be taken; since artillery could not drive the enemy out, it had to be done with the bayonet.

The grey-haired old warrior, sword in hand, led the charge himself. The 93rd followed, glowing with Highland fervour, advancing with great springing strides learned only on the heather. Joining them in one enormous wave was the Naval Brigade, who rolled their heavy guns within twenty yards of the wall. Captain Peel, calm and deliberate, acted as though he were laying the *Shannon* alongside an enemy warship. Broadside after broadside was delivered with quick, calculated energy. But the wall refused to yield. Bluejackets and Highlanders caught in the open before a wall twenty feet high without scaling-ladders began to fall all about. Members of Sir Colin's staff dropped and rolled on the ground.

As the unequal duel with the stubborn defenders, whose presence was indicated by little white puffs and flying missiles, continued, rocket frames were drawn forward, cocked up and adjusted to the proper angle. The war-rockets were then inserted and ignited. It was a fiery, fearsome projectile that went skimming close over the wall before the Shah Najif. Slowness of flight and the shifting of the centre of gravity as the propelling charge burned away, made it highly susceptible to wind, gravity and other accidental deflections. Like some wild, hissing fiend it seemed to be guided by diabolical cleverness as it veered to the left and the right, alternately rising and falling, but always screaming and pursuing. When it struck, the rocket exploded with great force, scattering carbine balls in every direction. It continued to burn for many minutes, exhaling a poisonous vapour all the while.

The rockets were employed to cover the withdrawal of the artillery, and represented an admission of failure by the attackers. The struggle would have to be postponed until the morning. The stormers were on the verge of withdrawing when word came that a narrow gap had been found near a far corner of the surrounding wall. The Highlanders, who slipped through the hole to open the main gate, arrived in time to see the last of the white-robed defenders, apparently terror-stricken by the engines of destruction that zoomed and plunged into the enclosure, disappearing into clouds of smoke and dark shadows. The rocket had inadvertently won the day when all else had failed. Sir Colin Campbell set up his headquarters in the mosque and ordered the pipers to march about the Shah Najif and play 'The Campbells Are Coming'. In this way the people in the Residency were informed of the progress that had been made.

Released from his duties after having bivouacked his men under the walls of the Sikandar Bagh, Wolseley looked for his wounded leader, Major Barnston. After a diligent search, he found him cheerful but cold. Wolseley gave him his overcoat and made a pretence at being optimistic, but he knew from the size of the major's wound that there was little chance for survival because of the fatal effects of the Indian climate. (Only two survived out of all who had a limb amputated at the relief of Lucknow.) When they parted, Wolseley already mourned the loss of a close friend and one of the ablest officers with whom he had ever been associated. Major Barnston was removed to Cawnpore, where he died a few weeks later. On learning of his death, Sir Colin caused his heavy guns to observe a two-hour silence.

It was a chilly night, doubly so for Wolseley who slept in the open with only a thin silk jacket. In the morning he was snapped into wakefulness by the smell of sizzling meat. The aroma was unlike that of pork or beef. Looking up the high wall of the Sikandar Bagh, he saw a dead sepoy directly above him whose clothes had somehow caught fire. A pale blue smoke curled from the body as the flames crackled the flesh and literally roasted him in his own fat. As Wolseley moved away, he saw a band of Sikhs farther along the wall behead three or four sepoy snipers they had persuaded to surrender. It was a grim beginning for what was to become an eventful day in his life.

The fall of the Shah Najif assured the success of the relief. The ground that remained to be won could be measured in yards. Sir Colin's plan was to take the direct road to the Residency, carrying the Mess House and then the Motee Mahul, thereby making it possible to effect a junction with Outram's men battling towards him. The action that morning, November 17th, was delayed until food was brought up for the men and ammunition for the guns. When the general moved forward, he did so cautiously, sending parties out to secure the flanks and the line of communication. It was nearly noon before Captain Peel was directed to commence fire with the heavy guns on the Mess House. The bombardment was steady and prolonged, for the commander was determined to spare his men as much as possible.

The Mess House of the 32nd (1st Cornwall Light Infantry), formerly the Khoorsheyd Munzil (Happy Palace), with its turrets and battlements, its moat and drawbridges, stood like a miniature castle out of the medieval past frowning forbiddingly at those who dared to approach. Three hours of slogging by Peel's guns seemed to have softened the defences sufficiently for a successful assault. A storming party made up of the companies of the 90th, a picket of the 53rd, and some of the Sikhs of the 4th Punjab Rifles was assembled. To lead them, Sir Colin selected Captain Wolseley. The young captain's eyes flashed with excitement as he stood before the general. The old Scot prefaced his orders with a few flattering remarks about his outstanding conduct in the Crimea. Then he related what he knew of the defences and instructed Wolseley to fight his way up to the ditch. If a crossing could be made, he was to place his men under cover and return with detailed information about the defences. Of course, if he saw a chance to take the Mess House, he should do so by all means. Before he dismissed him, Sir Colin promised to recommend Wolseley for the coveted Victoria Cross.

With fifty of his own cockneys leading the advance, Wolseley rushed across the intervening space to the Mess House. Under heavy fire, the slight figure of the captain who led them seemed to be indestructible.

He was the first to scramble over the crumbling mud wall battered by Peel's guns. As he stood before the masonry-riveted ditch, he was greeted by the happy sight of 'niggers ... bolting from the house; so [he] dashed at it, found the drawbridges down and was to it like a shot.'[6]

His bugler sounded the call and the supporting companies came up across the ditch and followed him into the area surrounding the Mess House. His own sober Saxons, accompanied by murderous-looking Sikhs and reckless, daredevil Irishmen of the 53rd, dashed about flushing luckless sepoys who had failed to escape by way of the drawbridge to the rear. Sir Colin, his eager eyes straining to catch every detail of the advance, ordered Lieutenant Roberts (later Field-Marshal Lord Roberts) to go and place a regimental colour at the top of the newly-won Mess House so that Outram would be informed of his latest success.

Sir Colin was enormously pleased by the success of Wolseley's mission. There was no longer any doubt that contact would be made with the besieged that evening, with his favourite Highlanders leading the way. But once the impetuous young captain had taken the Mess House, he had no intention of stopping short of the Residency as the general had planned. From the moment Sir Colin had given him his instructions, the nagging suspicion kept crossing Wolseley's mind that his men were being employed to clear the way for the general's pet 'Hielandmen'. There was no mistaking Sir Colin's partiality. The old warrior would like nothing better than to have his dispatches relate, and history record, how his 'own lads' were first to grasp the hands of the feeble defenders. How the public would conjure up visions of pipes playing and tartans waving as the distinguished regiment fought its way into Lucknow. Bonfires would be blazing 'on every hill north of the Tweed in honour of such a national achievement'. Wolseley resolved it should be otherwise, and all ranks of his company expressed themselves 'in very explicit Saxon English ... that no breeches-less Highlanders should get in front of them that day.'[7]

Three hundred yards beyond the Mess House stood the Motee Mahul (Pearl of Palaces), the last obstacle before the relieving army. Though Wolseley was unaware of the move, the besieged had on the 16th begun seizing such buildings as lay in the direction of Sir Colin's advance until they were just beyond the Motee Mahul. The Pearl of Palaces was not unlike the other palace fortresses: a garden of orange and lemon trees, with bubbling fountains, girdled by a twenty-foot wall. Standing before the principal entrance was an extra wall built out and loopholed so as to command the approach. All other entrances were bricked up.

Exercising what he called 'initiative', Wolseley sent one company to force the rebels out of a large bungalow to his left, the residence of the king of Oudh's astronomer, while his own company pressed on to the Motee Mahul to his right, along the banks of the Gumti. Quitting the garden of the Mess House, Wolseley's men tumbled over the garden wall and rushed down a broad street in the direction of the Residency, speeded on their way by bullets whizzing out of the Kaiser Bagh (king's palace) and other near-by buildings. Before the wall of the Motee Mahul, they found shelter in an arcade-like structure. Pausing for a moment, Wolseley sized up the loopholed entrance to the palace. Happily the sepoys had failed to dig a ditch before their position. So, after the enemy fired a volley, he rushed his men up to the wall to gain control of the loopholes. There they stood, the enemy on one side and they on the other, striving to gain mastery over the opposite side of the wall by poking their weapons through the same loopholes. The mutineers were first to abandon the struggle, though frequently one of them would crawl along the wall, pop up and fire a quick shot.

Confronted by a wall too high to climb, Wolseley sent an officer and several men to the rear to fetch crow-bars and pickaxes to dig out the newly-laid bricks in front of the entrance. When the party returned with the tools, they were seen to be going astray. Private Andrews, Wolseley's former servant, sprang forward to direct them. He had no sooner crossed into the open than a shot from one of the loopholes along the wall struck him down. Wolseley rushed forward to scoop him up in his arms. While carrying him to safety, another bullet, meant for Wolseley, passed through Andrews's body. Private Andrews lived to collect a pension of eightpence a day for his services and wounds.

While the soldiers were prying and hacking at the bricks, 'Lucknow' Kavanagh, the civilian messenger who had escaped earlier from the Residency, came up on his own and volunteered to lead the assailants to another entrance. Captain Wolseley accepted his offer gladly and the pair, dodging occasional musket fire, made their way round the palace, only to find a second gateway sealed. Returning to his company, Wolseley arrived as Ensign Haig was wriggling on his belly through a small opening. It was a daring deed that could easily have earned him a bashed-in head. The rest of the attacking party followed the ensign into the courtyard and pursued the sepoys from one lavishly-decorated room to another where only a short time before the king of Oudh had entertained his European visitors. Some of the rebels dived into the Gumti and tried to swim to a safe shore; Wolseley and his men 'had capital practice at them in the water'.[8] They were interrupted by a loud explosion at the west wall of the courtyard. Out of the dust and smoke emerged another company of the 90th under Captain Tingling, part of the Lucknow garrison which had placed a mine under a wall to open a way for the relieving force. The 90th was dramatically reunited as Captain Wolseley and Captain Tingling clasped hands. Lucknow was relieved and Wolseley had won the distinction of being the first of Sir Colin's army to reach the beleaguered garrison.

With communications between the two forces established, Havelock and Outram rushed past the Motee Mahul and down to the ground before the Mess House, where Sir Colin waited to greet them. As the leaders shook hands in that historic meeting, there was a deafening cheer which was taken up in succession by the men all the way back to the rearguard, sounding like a gradually diminishing echo. Wolseley visited his old comrades of the 90th, some of whom he barely recognized because of the marks of toil and privation written into their faces. He had planned ahead to this reunion by carrying with him a large supply of tobacco and a keg of rum before he attacked the Mess House. The liquor being bulky had to be left in front of the Mess House until Wolseley could spare the time and men to go back and fetch it. To men who had smoked nothing but evil-tasting vines and tea-leaves, and thirsted for strong drink, Captain Wolseley was the most thoughtful hero of that glorious day.

Wolseley anxiously anticipated recognition from the commander-in-chief for daring and enterprise in taking the Mess House and Motee Mahul, and effecting the relief. On meeting Brigadier Hope on his way back for the rum, his dazzling visions of rewards and honours vanished. The brigadier praised him for his splendid work, but told him that Sir Colin was furious because he had gone far beyond the letter of his instructions. Hope declared he had never seen the 'Lord Sahib' so angry and advised the captain to stay out of his way.

Wolseley knew the true reason for his anger: he had upset the general's little scheme to put the 93rd Highlanders in the limelight. He was hurt. The old veteran, he thought, should have been enough of a soldier to appreciate his accomplishments. After all, ardent Scots like Sir Adrian Hope and Sir Hope Grant were never slow to honour and reward men who were not fortunate enough to have been born in the land of the heather.

That night a disappointed captain slept on the side of the road near the Shah Najif. His sleep was disturbed by a stumbling late-comer whom his neighbour denounced as a 'beastly nigger' for stepping on his stomach. With the first ray of dawn, Wolseley sat upright and discovered that the

'beastly nigger' who slept opposite him was His Excellency – the commander-in-chief. There was no chance for escape, for the irascible general
had recognized him. Shaking his fist, he shouted, 'How dared you attack
the Motee Mahul without instructions?' But he said it with a smile. His
anger had left him. He told the young captain how fortunate he was that
he had not found him the night before. Never was he so enraged by any
man in his life. With a quick motion of his hand, he invited the delinquent
subordinate to pace up and down with him while he delivered a very
outspoken lecture on the heinous error of being too zealous. He concluded by congratulating Wolseley for his courage and signal ability,
and told him he would be promoted. He was not aware that Captain
Wolseley had been promised a promotion in the Crimea but had to
complete the six years of service required. There was no mention of the
promised Victoria Cross, nor was Wolseley's exploit, which reunited
the companies of the 90th in the big square of the Motee Mahul, mentioned in any official dispatch.

The shrewd old general had recognized that this young officer was
extremely ambitious and he exploited his aspiring nature. But in Wolseley's case, where ambition was boundless, he got far more than he bargained for.

The garrison was relieved but Sir Colin Campbell had not wrested
control of Lucknow from the rebels who still held most of the city and its
chief stronghold, the Kaiser Bagh. Having already lost well over ten per
cent of his army and encumbered it with 500 women and children and
1,000 sick and wounded, he resolved upon 'a strategic movement to the
rear'. Besides, there was no news for several days from the slender force
under General Windham at Cawnpore. Sir Colin's military intuition
told him that no news was bad news and that the Cawnpore garrison was
in danger. It was.

The decision to pull out of Lucknow was received with grumbling
and regrets by the survivors of the long siege. Their pride rebelled at the
thought of meekly abandoning to the enemy what they had fought five
gruelling months to hold. Their leaders asked for just one regiment to
remain in the Residency and keep the Union Jack flying from the top-
most roof. But the general remained firm in his decision. The next day
arrangements were made for the withdrawal that night without detection,
if possible. To achieve this difficult end, the line of retreat was to be closed
off to enemy view. Wolseley and his company laboured all day putting up
canvas, dragging doors, shutters and whatever other debris could be
found to screen the open spaces. Walls and bungalows behind which

sepoys might lurk were torn down. Throughout the day Peel's guns bombarded the Kaiser Bagh and other enemy strong-points with increasing intensity, as if the Europeans were planning to launch a grand assault.

The evacuation that night of November 19th began with the women and the sick, who were quietly brought out in twos and threes under the noses of thousands of rebels. Every person that came out of the Residency had to pass Wolseley's picket along the Motee Mahul. Down the lane with muffled steps came unsmiling women with careworn features, leading the children and carrying bundles of personal belongings. They seemed reluctant to leave the crumbling prison which for so long had been their home and where loved ones were buried. 'They appeared almost wedded to the Residency,' declared one witness. There was not a happy face among them, nor a kind word for the soldiers who had rescued them. The only smiles to be seen were those of the little children when they reached the Dilkoosha Palace where a feast had been prepared for them. One little girl ran up to her mother and exclaimed ecstatically, 'Oh, mamma! There is a loaf of bread upon the table. I am certain of it; I saw it with my own eyes.'[9] The men who followed were a toil-worn, ragged remnant, sinking fast under the effects of combat, malnutrition and disease. Among them were hundreds of faithful sepoys who had refused to join their comrades in mutiny. Without them the Residency would never have been defended. The measured tread of the retreating soldiers was mingled with the pattering sound of camels' and horses' hoofs, soft jingling harnesses, and the rumble of gun wheels. Everything that could be moved under such conditions – food, ammunition, and treasure – was taken from the Residency with exactness and efficiency down the winding roads of Lucknow.

At midnight on November 22nd, with all the lights burning and the sepoys still dropping an occasional shell into the deserted building, the last of Outram's men passed silently into the thick darkness. Not a single life was lost in this delicate operation that took place over several days in the presence of thousands of the enemy.

A column nearly three miles long wound its way out of Lucknow and halted at the Alum Bagh. Sir Colin Campbell decided to leave a force of 4,000 here, among them the 90th, under Sir James Outram. It was a dagger pointed at the heart of Oudh, designed to keep the rebel army of Lucknow intimidated until he could return with sufficient strength to crush them. The rest of Sir Colin's army departed for Cawnpore on the morning of November 27th. As they marched out, the drums and fifes of each regiment burst forth with a gay tune. To those unfortunates who had to stay in the Alum Bagh, it seemed as if the music was intended to 'cheer up sorrowing hearts in the division', a weak division that had to face the music of tens of thousands of enemy muskets.

Outram's force held an area over eleven miles in circumference with strong-points on the periphery such as the Alum Bagh, the tumbled fort of Jellalabad, a deserted village, etc. In the flat open spaces between these positions of natural strength, the men constructed batteries, abattis, and trenches. Inside this perimeter the officers got up some races and organized sports for the men. Wolseley, confined to these same grounds once more, grumbled about his monotonous existence while so much fighting was going on elsewhere in India.

But the enemy soon kept things from being altogether dull. For the first few days, the mutineers ignored the presence of Outram's division; they concentrated on looting the silver plate and whatever other articles of value had been left behind in the Residency. They took their revenge on the dead defenders by desecrating their graves and throwing their exhumed bodies into the river. Early in December they began mischievous feints on the various outposts of Outram's extended lines, rarely attacking in strength though they numbered nearly 100,000 by the end of the year as more and more sepoys and their sympathizers poured into the city from all over Bengal. They preferred to keep up a steady, perfunctory cannonading. They knew if they massed in sufficient numbers, Outram's heavy ordnance, always alert and searching, was prepared to disperse and slaughter them.

Now and then a religious leader would encourage fanatics to act boldly. On January 16th an influential Brahman, who claimed to represent Mahavira, the monkey-god, appeared before Wolseley's picket guarding a partially-built battery near the Jellalabad. Painted and dressed like a monkey, tail and all, he screwed up the courage of several hundred followers to the point where they made a sudden, reckless rush on the outpost. They came on in grand style until a tearing fire cut down their leader and dozens of co-religionists. Monkey or no monkey, they came to the conclusion their sacred cause was lost that day. The fanatics promptly fled, pursued by a band of Sikhs who had come running when they heard the alarm. The pitiful 'monkey-god', with both eyes shot out, was taken by the Sikhs who, Wolseley learned, kept him as a pet.

During periods of quiet, the entire force in the Alum Bagh camp was busily employed in preparations for the final operations against Lucknow. To Wolseley it was like being back before Sebastopol, constructing gabions, fascines, scaling-ladders, sap rollers, and other siege materials.

One party built a cask bridge to be thrown across the Gumti, another experimented with bag powder to discover the quickest and surest way of blowing down doors and walls.

On March 2nd the men at the Alum Bagh saw the commander-in-chief arrive in a pelting rainstorm with a large part of his force behind him. They did not pause but went on in the direction of the Dilkoosha Palace, which they took after a brief skirmish. The so-called 'siege of Lucknow' had begun.

The various component units of the army of reconquest began to assemble before the doomed city. Brigadier Frank's column, after doing excellent service in the south of Oudh, came up on March 5th. Included in his force were 3,000 Gurkhas, participating for the first time as highly-valued allies of the British in India. Another 8,000 of these flat-faced, high-shouldered, bow-legged little men from the mountain kingdom of Nepal were expected to arrive under the Prime Minister and de facto ruler, Jung Bahadur, regarded as India's greatest fighting prince. Sir Colin's army would then number 31,000 men with 164 pieces of artillery, the largest army Britain had ever assembled in India. Opposed to them, behind walls and entrenchments, were 120,000 armed men, half of whom had lately served as sepoys. Though 90,000 men stronger, the difference was not one of arithmetic but one of organization, leadership, and resolution. There was not the slightest doubt among the men of the British army as to how the struggle would end.Wolseley predicted an unqualified success.

During the three months' interval while Sir Colin's army was engaging rebels elsewhere, the sepoys and people of Lucknow repaired the old positions and constructed new ones. Besides these principal strongholds, hundreds of houses were loopholed and the streets were blocked by numerous barricades with batteries carefully placed to sweep the approaches. It was the ideal defence, assuming, as did the unimaginative mutineers, that the British would follow the same general plan of attack they did the last two times. Sir Colin, however, acting on the advice of his brilliant chief engineer, Colonel Robert Napier, decided to send a division under Outram across the Gumti to seize the weakly-defended posts there and deliver an enfilading fire across the river which would make the carefully prepared lines before Sir Colin's main force untenable.

Two pontoon bridges were constructed over the Gumti on March 5th, and the following day Outram's trans-Gumti division of 6,000 formed up on the bank to cross. It was a moment of disappointment to Wolseley, for the 90th was not part of the force commanded by a man he believed was the best general in India. As he watched the troops – most of them newly arrived from England – waiting for the signal to move out under a bright morning sun, he was dazzled by the spectacle of gaily-coloured uniforms: the deep green of the Rifles, the dark blue of the Bengal Fusiliers, and the Queen's Bays in scarlet coats and shiny helmets – all trim and tailored. Such a sight was not to be seen in India for long. The more sombre and serviceable khaki, already to be found among a few of the troops from Delhi and up-country, was destined to bring uniform drabness to armies in the field.

To prevent a 'big butcher's bill', the frugal Scot relied chiefly upon his artillery. No unnecessary risks were to be taken, and young officers – like Wolseley in particular – were not to move 'without precise orders'. On March 9th, after being subjected to heavy artillery fire, the Martinière College was taken with the loss of only one man. Wolseley's company, relieved of the duty of guarding Outram's bridges, took possession of the Martinière that night. The next morning the company was ordered to give protection to the gunners. The latter took a very casual attitude towards their work. In the intervals between loading and firing, they 'squatted in parties of four ... and proceeded with games of cards, in which they seemed to take as much interest as in the effect produced by their fire'.[10] It was a pretty dull affair for Wolseley and his men, as well as the gunners, until treated to the amusing sight of tiny Gurkhas carrying umbrellas and parrots, and drawing their own guns like beasts of burden. Clad in dirty scarlet, crouching and hopping around their cannon, they looked 'like a lot of monkeys on a barrel-organ'.[11]

It was the gunners' and sappers' war, with the infantry playing a subordinate role of cleaning out pockets of resistance as the main enemy force retired. On March 11th the advance was halted at the Begum's palace, a block of strongly-built structures situated in front of the Kaiser Bagh. A breach was made by the monster guns of the Naval Brigade, and the 93rd and 4th Sikhs stormed the building. Since that first day when they fought side by side at the Sikandar Bagh, mutual admiration led to fraternization and a gallant desire of emulation which made them an exceptionally dangerous team to any who opposed them. Side by side, in grim silence, they stalked into the rooms and courtyards of the Begum Kothi. While bloody scenes were being enacted within, the Scottish pipers were playing wildly outside, their shrill notes vibrating through the nerves of Highlander and Sikh, giving them a lust for battle.

A few hours later Wolseley, relieved from his duty with the guns, came up through gardens and streets littered with fallen masonry. Walls were blackened and broken. Dwellings were deprived of roofs and tenants, except for the lifeless sepoys who lay riddled and ripped. Where sepoys were found still alive, they were 'mercifully' put out of their misery as calmly as if they were wounded animals. No prisoners were taken; a man caught with arms was a traitor. Moreover, it was regarded as not practicable further to reduce Sir Colin's army by detaching Europeans for guard duty. The rebels, too, put to death any white man who fell into their hands. When the British troops broke into the residence of a rebel leader they found the gory heads of recently captured British soldiers. William Howard Russell, special war correspondent for *The Times*, who came out to India to report the war and verify atrocities,* was shocked far more by the conduct of Sir Colin's men than by the sepoys. As he accompanied the army advancing into Lucknow, he witnessed a detachment of Sikhs roast a sepoy alive over a small pyre while English officers looked on without protest.

Wolseley spent the entire night on picket in the open ground before the Sikandar Bagh, where 1,857 sepoys were lost when Sir Colin relieved the Residency. To the sepoys, who had learned a terrible lesson, it was a place of evil omen not to be defended a second time. It was an unpleasant assignment for Wolseley because of the intolerable odour that clung to the place. Even now, he found large quantities of human hair and a few bones inside.

The next morning fire was concentrated on the great citadel, the Kaiser Bagh and its defences. After the commander decided there were practicable breaches, a regiment of Sikhs, the 10th Foot and the 90th forced their way in by various entrances.

When Wolseley's company, one of the last of the 90th to enter, came up, most of the enemy had fled. Like all who entered the Kaiser Bagh that day, Wolseley was overwhelmed by its lavish magnificence. The gardens rivalled Kew. As for the main palace, Wolseley believed 'the Tuileries and Buckingham Palace might have been stolen from it'.[13] All the treasure of India seemed to be housed here. The dazzling sight of gold, silver, and crystal drove the soldiers mad for plunder. Rude hands scooped up brocades, rich scabbards, golden shawls, bejewelled clocks, and often, hard cash. Closed doors, behind which sepoys cowered, were blown in with bags of gunpowder to facilitate the search. Hundreds of bodies were strewn about, some half-burnt, some with life still quivering and palpitating within them. The stench was sickening. Here in the palace of

---

* To the people in England, however, affairs in India had by now become anticlimactic. Events that had evoked horror became a subject for levity. 'Mrs Dudley Carleton', wrote Lord Houghton, 'is so idle and apathetic that one feels a short residence at Lucknow under the late circumstances would have been a very good thing for her.'[12]

pleasure where voluptuaries once frolicked, Wolseley saw Welch Fusiliers and Sikhs revelling. The latter, with a superior instinct for valuables, gave Tommy Atkins a lesson. The feverish desire for loot was soon merged with a craving for destruction. Using their guns as clubs, mirrors, chandeliers, costly vases, priceless collections of porcelain were wantonly smashed; bayonets tore into oil-paintings; pages from illuminated manuscripts lit the pipes of looters. That which could not be carried was destroyed.

Wolseley objected to looting. It was not that he had any scruples about taking an enemy's possessions. Plundering was a natural by-product of war. It was not so long ago that the military made its living by seizing the property of the enemy; and it was still thought of as a military privilege. He simply believed it not in the best interests of discipline and military efficiency. He saw officers, for example, bicker with privates about the ownership of valuable articles. Invariably, the army was demoralized and did not recover from the effects of pillaging for weeks.

There were many prizes that Wolseley admired. On first entering the garden he was struck by the beauty of a handsome marble throne. The next time he saw it, it was in the King's Garden at Windsor Castle. Wolseley did buy a few small objects for presents from prize-agents a few days later, and a fellow officer offered him the choice of any one of dozens of cashmere shawls to sleep on. The shawl he took was 'looted' from him before he had a chance to use it that night. Later the men of his company presented their captain with two silver bowls, and though he slept with them at the head of his bed, they too were stolen.

With the fall of the Kaiser Bagh, the other major buildings were quickly stormed and taken. The Union Jack was once more raised over the Residency, and there it was to remain as a reminder of the gallant defence by Englishmen and Indians, the only flag throughout the empire to fly night and day, through calm and storm, hauled down only for replacement. An aide-de-camp of Sir Colin Campbell sent out a proclamation of victory, as if dictated by the general himself – '*Nunc fortunatus sum*' ('I am in luck now').* It came at a time when a joke, no matter how small, was gratefully received, wrote Wolseley.

With the fall of Lucknow the last hope of the rebels for success was shattered. There was no longer a centre where they could rally, so they scattered to distant parts. The grand army Sir Colin had collected for the siege was broken up and divided into columns, or field forces, which went

* This was in imitation of the more than innocent pun '*Peccavi*' ('I have sinned') used in announcing Sir Charles Napier's rascally annexation of the province of Sind in 1843.

out in different directions to hunt down the sepoys and purge the various districts of rebellions. Sir Hope Grant was put in command of one such powerful column called the Lucknow Field Force with its headquarters in the Tara Kothi, the king's observatory in Lucknow. Much to the astonishment of Captain Wolseley, he was made deputy-assistant quarter-master-general of Grant's force. The pay was small (150 rupees a month in addition to regimental pay), but Wolseley was elated by his appointment and declared to Dick, 'I am now a great swell.'[14] He had been angling for a staff appointment for months, having applied first to the commander-in-chief and then to Colonel Pakenham, who as the adjutant-general in the Crimea had appreciated his talents to the extent where he could be expected to drop a good word in the right place. Wolseley had given up hope when a vacancy suddenly occurred on Grant's staff; Lieutenant Frederick Roberts, destined to become Wolseley's great rival, was given sick-leave to return to England. A few days later Wolseley received his brevet majority.

Sir Hope Grant's column, with its base at Lucknow, struck out in every direction, wherever the enemy had the courage to show himself. The young quartermaster-general worked under incessant strain assigning quarters, superintending the transport, compiling a mass of useful information about every section the little army passed through, reconnoitring and drawing a series of maps (none existed of Oudh) which were to be of immense value for subsequent campaigns.

They marched and countermarched across the length and breadth of Oudh, pursuing the ever-vanishing rebels. Nevertheless, there was often ample excitement for Wolseley to outweigh the discomforts when the enemy made a stand at such long-forgotten battlefields as Baree and Sirsee.

If the insurgents expected the British to remain in the shade during the hot weather, they were sadly mistaken. During the furnace season, the burning days grew increasingly hotter, with the thermometer rising to 120°, at times 130° in the shade, and there was usually no shade. Kipling described the Indian summer as a time when there is 'neither sky, sun, nor horizon. Nothing but a brown-purple haze of heat. It is as though the earth were dying of apoplexy'. The gasping army continued to march, often in full regimentals, until there seemed to be 'only a sheet of brown paper between them and the infernal regions, and that had been nearly scorched through'.[15] General Grant, a cavalryman by training, failed to appreciate the difficult circumstances attending the march. The infantry-men – burdened with rifle, bayonet, sixty rounds of ammunition, and other accoutrements – were foolishly ordered to advance in a close formation common to temperate zones. The effect was disastrous. Those in the centre of the line of march were smothered by the heat and want of air as choking clouds of dust were stirred by stamping feet. Men and beasts staggered about and then would lie panting by the side of the road. Wolseley reported that the medical officers knew of only one remedy: the victim was placed in the shade and his head was soused with water by the *bheesties* (water-carriers). Those who died were wrapped in blankets and buried. Most sufferers actually died in their tents at night. They would fall into a deep sleep and never wake again.

The heat struck like a drawn sword. In May, in Central India, Sir Hugh Rose's entire column collapsed under the terrible temperature and prolonged exertion. In that same month, in an atmosphere of sweltering mortality, over a thousand British soldiers were destroyed by sunstroke and disease while less than a hundred were killed in action. Wolseley later observed that many lives could have been saved if mounted infantry had been employed, but at the time such an innovation was quite undreamt of.

The subjugation of Oudh continued without respite into the rainy season. The air was cooled, but the heavy torrential rains of July and August muddied the roads so that they became almost impassable and swelled even the smallest rivers to the extent where they were unfordable. In September, Grant's column returned to Lucknow for a well-earned rest. Not for long, Sir Colin, now Lord Clyde, for he was made a peer of the realm for his successful siege of Lucknow, made preparations for the final pacification of the province. Enemy forts were quickly abandoned and garrisons surrendered and returned to their former peaceful vocations. Lord Clyde, ever cautious and moving according to a well-prepared time-table, cleansed the province of wrongdoers by the end of the year, having lost only eighteen killed and eighty-four wounded.

Wolseley became 'thoroughly tired of this vagrant life' which had degenerated into chasing small bands of rebels without cannon, and 'annihilating not fighting them'; this was 'police duty and quite derogatory to a soldier's profession' – worst of all there was no longer any 'chance for honour or glory to be acquired by it'.[16] He was relieved when the last action of the campaign – and the war – was fought on May 23rd, fully two years after the beginning of the Indian Mutiny, or the 'Devil's Wind', as the natives described it.

The Lucknow Field Force retired to Lucknow to enjoy a long period of repose on June 4th, 1859, the twenty-sixth anniversary of Wolseley's birthday. No gift could have pleased him more than the news that he had received the brevet of lieutenant-colonel. He was sure that he must now, at twenty-six, be the youngest colonel in the British army, and he had the added satisfaction of moving up through every rank without purchase. This latest triumph in the scramble for promotion was somewhat unexpected after his recent step up to major. Not that it was undeserved. Wolseley's name had been mentioned several times in dispatches and on one occasion Grant gave him charge of the advance, heartily commending him for the perfection of his preparations.

For the moment, the pressure for higher appointment was off – and Wolseley relaxed. He would now remain in India, where the climate seemed to agree with him, collect £800 annually, and after a couple of years he would return to England and live in style. As a quartermaster, he kept active applying his experience in quartering troops to the construction of new cantonments in the city.

At the beginning of October 1859, it was announced that a large force would be sent to North China to force the Imperial Government in Peking to terms, and Sir Hope Grant was nominated to command the expedition. Sir Hope wanted to put his bright young colonel in command of the quartermaster-general's department; Lord Clyde, however, insisted upon another, a worthy Scot named Colonel Kenneth Mackenzie. Wolseley, unaware of Lord Clyde's veto, was more than satisfied at the time to take the field as Mackenzie's deputy-assistant in charge of the topographical department. On the day of his appointment, he was reminded of his Irish nanny who always called him 'lucky boy'. Wolseley reasoned that she must have been clairvoyant.

# CHAPTER FOUR

# THE SHOPKEEPER'S VENGEANCE

SINCE the China expedition would not get under way until the
following year when the weather would be propitious in North
China, Sir Hope Grant and his staff indulged in a much-neglected
social life. Lucknow, scene of the heaviest fighting, suddenly became the
social centre of India. The season opened at the end of October with the
arrival of the governor-general, Lady Canning and Lord Clyde. The dig-
nitaries, with their enormous retinues and accompanied by five regiments,
paraded through the streets of the partially rebuilt city as salutes were
fired from the various forts. Wolseley rode about in a red coat and cocked
hat, endeavouring to keep 'the civilian and all that sort of ragtag and bob-
tail' from crowding in. One civilian's horse nudged into his spirited little
Arab, who backed into the carriage of Lady Canning and 'immediately
let fly with his hind legs, making the footboard behind resound with his
kicking'.[1] Fortunately, he gained control of the beast before it succeeded
in knocking a hole into the panels of her ladyship's carriage. For a brief
moment the face of Lady Canning lost its bored expression.

Reviews, levees, and durbars followed in rapid succession; noblemen
from all over India crowded into the city to receive presents; and soon the
families of British officers and officials came out from England with many
young ladies among them. The latter, almost without exception, were
searching for husbands in this land 'where they hang like flocks of the
golden fleece, which daring argonauts from the schools may pluck as
they will ... '[2] Wolseley suddenly discovered India to be a very pleasant
place. He had almost forgotten how charming English girls could be.
They were, of course, a fickle lot: after only two years in India, Lizzie
Elliott had 'proved false' and married another; Kate Hill now smiled upon
William Wolseley as she once did on his brother, Garnet; and his Marion
not only married but she wed a civilian instead of a good soldier – unfor-
givable!

Wolseley and two other officers established themselves in a little
country house surrounded by a handsome park. Built by the former king
of Oudh, it was called Beedeeapore, or 'the place of the women'. They

brought furnishings and table requisites up from Calcutta so as to entertain the ladies in style. The occupants, however, entered into a compact:
'any of the three who marry is to be turned out ignominiously'.³

With his high rank and 'fascinating manner', he wrote to his sister,
Caroline, he was 'considered a most desirable match for any young lady;
and designing mothers and intriguing sisters' tried to lure him with their

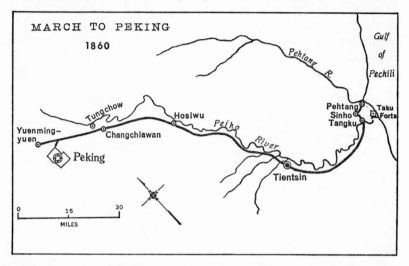

'nasty ways' into the coils of marriage. Wolseley accepted their invita-
tions and hospitality with pleasure, but privately he laughed at their silly
little efforts 'to catch a live colonel'.⁴

For a 'poor officer' such as himself, marriage was out of the question.
Think of the unfortunate girl, chained to a pauper – a pauper who possessed only his ambition. Advancement, not marriage, was his goal in life;
the latter would extinguish the former, and life would thenceforward
become 'a shoreless sea'. The possibility of marrying an heiress, of having
a wife whose affluence could be a stepping-stone for his ambition, occurred
to him; but then he would owe his triumphs to his wife, and he was too
proud for that.

He warned his brother, Dick, who had come out to India, to beware of
falling into the 'hymeneal pit'. All about him he saw young and foolish
subalterns without a shilling to their name marry young ladies, equally
poor, and by a peculiar quirk of nature they always bred like rabbits.
And those children! There are all kinds, of course, but imagine having a
nasty little red monster 'who is neither exactly biped or quadruped, who

cannot crawl or talk, who with large unmeaning eyes has no nose, but a weakly supported bald head, who bawls and screams by the hour and is only quiet when asleep, and who, pardon me, smells high. I know of no more unpleasant insect, and would prefer fondling a young crocodile to taking in my arms a newly-born embryo of humanity.'[5]

After Dick had spent a year and a half in India, Garnet wrote to congratulate his brother on having successfully avoided that 'great stumbling block, marriage'. All the while he had been 'in a funk that some bitch might have caught' him, but he had 'passed through the fiery ordeal most heroically'.[6] The following month Dick sheepishly announced to Garnet that he had married one of the young ladies who had come out from England.

When George, another brother, arrived in India a totally inexperienced subaltern, Garnet saw him briefly on a quick visit to Calcutta. Then, and in subsequent letters, he lectured him upon the immorality of marriage, 'unless he should be lucky enough to encounter an heiress'. Above all, he admonished him 'to beware of Indian ladies, for bad as the class of women are, Indian ones are the devil incarnate'.[7] But later Garnet confessed to Dick that he managed to console himself with an attractive 'Eastern Princess' who answered 'all the purposes of a wife without giving any of the bother'.[8] Moreover, it was an excellent way to improve one's Hindustani.

British officers were, for the most part, fairly virtuous, but the practice of taking a native mistress, or 'buying a native dictionary' as the expression went, was not uncommon in India where men might be exiled from home for many years. Superiors often recommended the custom quite openly. To say that an officer 'lowered' himself when he took an Indian girl for a mistress was regarded as a debatable subject. And as far as the girls were concerned, 'it broke no caste, offended no religious prejudice' and possibly improved 'their social position in most cases'.[9] One of Wolseley's contemporaries rationalized that India, in all probability, would never have been a great imperial addition 'if some of our greatest men had not gained the affection of their coloured mistresses and thereby a knowledge of native affairs'.[10]

Wolseley's interest in languages soon extended to Chinese, and he ransacked the bookshops in Calcutta on this and other subjects related to the Celestial Kingdom, where he hoped to win greater honours. Early in the evening, because his sight was growing worse and would not allow him to read by candlelight, he would close his eyes and consciously dream of the future. He was certain to add another medal or decoration to the six he had already won. Surely he would return home a full colonel with a well-deserved knighthood. His determination to succeed took a savage turn when he learned shortly before leaving for China that Sir Hope Grant had applied to have him made the 'second *swell*' instead of the 'third *swell*' on his staff. Old Clyde had no business interfering with the choice of staff officers by the supreme commander of the China expedition! But he was going to succeed in spite of the 'bigoted Scotchman' who had thrown him over to make room for one of his 'greedy friends'. In his family letters, he denounced all the 'job-hunting Scotchmen in Christendom or elsewhere and . they are to be found everywhere'.[11]

Though Sir Hope Grant was born a Scot, Wolseley never held it against him. He described his chief as a well-born, gracious and considerate officer, and the finest general in the army. His admiration of the general was such that he even wore his whiskers in a similar fashion, with a clear space of an inch or so between his bushy sideburns and his moustache, which was shorn off at the angle of the mouth, a style called 'Piccadilly weepers'.

Actually, Sir Hope was fortunate in having won command, for he had many detractors. Never was there a general in command of a British army who seemed more confused than he. During a campaign he was unable to read a map. He could not tell the points of the compass. Nor could he correctly describe the direction from which he had come, or the place he hoped to reach. When he resorted to verbal expression, he rarely found the words to convey his ideas. His sentences followed no logical sequence. Not only did he fail to say what had to be said, sometimes he said quite the wrong thing. That which he committed to writing was even less intelligible, for he wrote a very bad hand. This pitifully inarticulate general was fluent only in the realm of music, where he expressed himself with clarity and precision on the violoncello, or the 'big fiddle' as he irreverently called it. He was never without it. Throughout the Indian Mutiny, though room for baggage was often scarce, he had the enormous instrument carried by a well-behaved camel. Its appearance was so singular that the natives ran from it whenever it appeared, calling it 'shaitan', or 'the devil'.

It was the 'big fiddle' that provided Sir Hope Grant with the opportunity for a successful career in the army. As a cavalry captain with little chance of promotion, Sir Hope was on the verge of resigning from the service when he was recommended to a violinist and general, Lord Saltoun, who sought a musical brigade-major to accompany him in pleasant duets in what otherwise promised to be a tedious six-month voyage to China. In the First China War that followed, Sir Hope gained distinction as a soldier in the eyes of his commander and a fellow officer, Sir Colin Campbell, who was to rely upon him so heavily during the Mutiny and support his being given command of the North China expedition.

To his enemies, jealous perhaps of his popularity, Sir Hope remained a puzzle-headed incompetent. To those who knew him and served under him, he was a first-class general. They would admit that he had little professional training, but insisted he was an able strategist and clever tactician with an instinct for doing the right thing at the right time. Once the members of his staff acquired the habit of grasping the meaning behind his blundering words, they functioned as a smoothly efficient team. And his supporters admired his unusual courage. It was the kind of courage that on one occasion compelled him to put his commission at stake by arresting his commanding officer for drunkenness. It was the kind of courage that was reinforced by a deep religious conviction which influenced his every act. 'To die is nothing,' he once explained to a subordinate, 'it is only going from one room into another.' On a campaign he was always concerned with the spiritual welfare of his men. Lean and wiry, as though he were made of the same strings that stretched across his big fiddle, he seemed never to tire, though he had passed the half-century mark. After a day of hard marching or fighting, he would serenade his soldiers with the soft strains of the violoncello, as if to remind them that there was a gentler, more serene world.

The general was no Puritan. Always young in spirit and full of good humour, he sought the company of his young officers and joined in their games and daily fun. The fun-making continued unabated aboard the steamer *Fiery Cross* when the general and his staff embarked at Calcutta and voyaged to Hong Kong in February 1860. The presence of Lady Grant, the only woman on board, enhanced rather than inhibited sociability. There were musical sessions, chess games – in which Wolseley excelled – and rough play such as 'cock-fighting' and 'high cockalorum', in which Sir Hope demonstrated that he could carry more to the floor than any of them as he leapt successively astride a row of arched backs.

Sometimes they sat around and spoke of their mission, a journey into the unknown with elements of mystery more akin to the expeditions of the conquistadores centuries before. Like Cortez in Mexico, Sir Hope would be waging war on unfamiliar ground with an enemy whose military potential had never been fully assessed. Peking and its surroundings were little known to the British, except for exciting tales of exotic places housing untold riches. The ignorance of the Chinese regarding their Nemesis from the sea was even more profound. After the war, Prince Kung, brother to the Emperor, revealed to Lord Elgin that the Chinese Government was unaware of the fact that the British held India, and believed that the lonely island from which they came was so small and the population so large 'that the greater half of the people were compelled to live afloat'.[12]

The various parts of the expedition, which came from distant points of the empire, were assembled at Hong Kong and Kowloon, the rocky promontory which extended from the mainland towards the harbour of Victoria. The quartermaster-general's department worked overtime to accommodate the thousands that were disembarked each week. The barren ground of Kowloon mushroomed neat little rows of tents until there was a large settlement. Great crowds, spurred by curiosity, crossed from Hong Kong daily to see how the 'pretty soldiers' lived and to watch them drill.

India was about to invade China! There were sepoys from Bengal, Madras and Bombay, and cavalry recruited from among the wild tribes of Northern India. Two irregular regiments (Probyn's and Fane's Horse) which had been raised expressly for the war in China, excited the greatest interest. The tall, noble-looking Sikhs sat their mounts as if they were never intended to walk; in fact, their legs were rather puny and large boots were worn to disguise their true size. Their field dress consisted of blue serge tunics, red cummerbunds and white cotton trousers. The colour of their turbans was either blue or red, according to the regiment. Led by two of the most handsome Englishmen in the Indian army, they exercised their skill each day by piercing oranges with keen-edged lances, which were afterwards stuck in the ground before their tents. With their blue and red pennons fluttering at the top, they gave the camp the colourful appearance of a medieval tournament.

The soldiers, for their part, were just as interested in seeing China and its people. Many, Wolseley among them, made excursions to Canton. Most of the sights of Canton filled Wolseley with disgust. The walls throughout the city, for example, were filled in with the skulls of those who had been beheaded by the governor of the province. When captured by the British during the Second China War, this same governor boasted he had beheaded over 60,000 subjects in one year. Between the walls, Wolseley found narrow, ill-paved streets swarming with leprous-looking beggars who importuned him with requests for alms. Wolseley was told by a companion that, in China, unlike the West, begging was a popular

83

profession. At least one son in a large family among the poor was trained to be a mendicant. Frequently an eye or two was removed or a loathsome disease was contracted so as to excite the pity of the potential donor. He also learned that many of the girls born to impoverished families were neglected and allowed to die in infancy. So many were drowned in convenient pools that in some sections signs were posted reading 'GIRLS MAY NOT BE DROWNED HERE' to prevent this nuisance.

Though Wolseley called it one of the best organized expeditions in the history of the army, there was always the possibility that military operations would be called off. Lord Elgin, the mild-mannered ambassador with the face of a bewhiskered cherub, never abandoned hope of finding a diplomatic solution to the problem, and in April the new government under Lord Russell instructed him 'to employ every means calculated to establish peace with the Emperor of China'. To maintain good relations with Chinese authorities, the British actually paid rent for the land they occupied at Kowloon.

When Wolseley heard that negotiations had been resumed, he prayed they would fail. After the repulse of English forces at the Taku forts a year before, Britain's prestige was at stake. No Englishman's life would be safe in China, he argued, 'until we make it universally felt, that as a nation we are so much their superiors that we can always punish an injury inflicted upon the most lowly of our people.' If war should be averted by diplomacy, it would be a great national misfortune, 'for now we are ready and prepared to carry it on which we seldom are at such a distant part of the world as the neighbourhood of Peking.'[13]

The British Government finally lost patience and put its demands into the form of an ultimatum: immediate ratification of the Treaty of Tientsin, with its many commercial advantages, and an apology from the Emperor, as well as an indemnity, for the insult to the European representatives at Taku the year before. Peking countered with a swift and categorical rejection of these demands. On June 26th the British Government informed the Western powers that a state of war with China existed. The French Government, having associated itself with Britain's actions, followed suit.

Never was there a military alliance less wanted by English soldiers than that with the French in China in 1860. The alliance was a burden, not a boon, to the British forces, and reduced their chances of success. To placate French susceptibilities, for example, Sir Hope's force had to be reduced to 11,000. The French were to provide 7,000 under General Montauban, who was to exercise complete independence of command;

yet, in every way other than command, the French were wholly dependent upon the English. They had no convenient base in the East such as the British had at Hong Kong, and certainly no experience of fighting in this part of the world. The French arrived utterly unprepared. Regular cavalry they had none; they even lacked horses for their field batteries. Their transport consisted largely of coolies lent to them by the English, who first organized and trained them.* Time and again they fell back on the ample resources of the British. It was to be a cheap military undertaking for the glory-hunting Napoleon III, so long as the English paid most of the bills.

Francophobia was endemic, for a centuries-old antagonism between nations dies hard. Wolseley, like so many of his contemporaries, grew up hating the French. The comradeship fostered by the Crimean War improved relations only temporarily, and in some ways the war raked up ancient rivalries and promoted jealousy. Wolseley, along with the rest of the English soldiers in the Crimea, was chagrined to fight beside the French and see them succeed with superior strength where the English had failed. He would always regard them as potential enemies and was convinced that one day they would attempt to invade England as they did in the time of Napoleon I and the Bourbon kings before him.

Having associated with the French, there was scarcely a man in the British army who did not wish them away, most of all the general. Sir Hope was extremely wary of their leaders. They were 'a cunning sort' from whom he never knew quite what to expect. At the first meeting with French officialdom in Shanghai, he and Lady Grant sat in silence and made only mental comments as the crafty French representative, Bourboulon, oozed charm and his wife puffed heartily on the biggest, blackest cigars. He dreaded meeting the French commander, Montauban, a cavalry officer of distinguished service in Algeria, when the members of his staff who had served in the Crimea assured him that he could expect to be embraced and kissed on both cheeks.

Organizing the transport kept Sir Hope and his staff busy, but time was taken by the general to celebrate Wolseley's birthday properly. Except for the Bible, Sir Hope had little use for books; however, he carefully selected four handsome volumes as a gift for his intellectual young colonel. Another officer, Major Anson, gave him a tankard inscribed 'To Garnet

* With absolute candour, Wolseley estimated that one coolie was worth three baggage animals. Best of all, he testified 'they were easily fed, and when properly treated most manageable'.

Wolseley on his 37th birthday', instead of '27th' because his hair was so grey. Wolseley saw no humour in the jest.

Before embarking his troops from the advance base on the Liotung Peninsula, Sir Hope held a review. Never was an army in better condition, so healthy and full of fight. As Montauban walked down the line with their proud commander, he declared it was the sort of magnificent military display one might expect to see in Hyde Park or the Tuileries but not in China. A few days later, on July 26th, the men folded their little bell tents and re-embarked their guns, ammunition, horses, coolies, and supplies, leaving behind them an invigorating climate, excellent food, and lands and orchards not unlike Devonshire or Gloucestershire.

The trip across the bay proved an imposing spectacle, reminiscent of the crossing from Varna to the Crimea during the Russian War. Two lines of ships, nearly 200 in number, with full sail opened to a light favourable breeze, stretched from horizon to horizon across the smooth, sapphire waters of the Gulf of Pechili with steamers darting along the flanks signalling the merchant skippers to maintain a proper interval. The smaller French transport joined them towards evening to add a third line. To Wolseley it was an animated picture of maritime strength that filled him with awe and pride. Imagine, he wrote, old England sending her sons half-way across the world to punish a treacherous and arrogant government.

Nearing the shallow waters of the Peiho on July 28th, the vessels anchored in the same careful line. Against the evening sun, the little mounds representing the Taku forts became visible on the flat shoreline. Behind this point the Peiho curled through a vast plain, the province of Pechili, as level as the sea and as large as the whole of England, with approximately as many inhabitants. In a straight line nearly a hundred miles to the north-west stood their objective: Peking, the northern capital.

Avoiding the prepared front at the mouth of the Peiho, the fleet moved a few miles north to Pehtang. The two small but menacing forts guarding the entrance of the Pehtang River drew nervous glances from the troops nearing the shore in launches. They expected to be fired upon at any moment. The forts could have done fearful damage to the closely-packed masses. But the guns proved to be dummies. The only foe the invaders battled with that day was the sticky mud and the evil smell that enveloped Pehtang – an enemy as mean as any they ever hoped to encounter.

The last mile was too shallow for boats, so the troops in heavy marching order and with three days' provisions were deposited on knee-deep flats. A gallant brigadier, popularly called 'Blaspheming Billy' because of his propensity for strong language, was the first to step ashore after carefully removing his trousers, boots and socks. An army of onlookers was convulsed with laughter as this fierce-looking bandy-legged old campaigner waded through the mire attired in an enormous white helmet and a dirty red serge tunic, with trousers and boots draped over his shoulder on a sword, cursing at the top of his voice everyone and everything around him every step of the way. Not far behind his fluttering shirt-tails were many trouserless officers and men who decided to follow his sensible example. A few of the far-famed Tartar horsemen appeared on the causeway connecting Pehtang with the communities to the south. For a few moments they peered with unbelieving eyes at an army floundering towards them *sans culottes*, and rode off.

The commander and his staff were not far behind, scrambling in the slush. One clever officer got a sepoy to carry him on his back, but the Indian found it impossible to keep his footing and they fell headlong into a muddy pool. Before reaching the firm ground of the causeway, the landing party waded waist-deep through a noisome moat that drained the vile-smelling animal and vegetable decomposition from the town. Neither trees nor grass brightened this cheerless land. The doomed town of Pehtang was a sort of repulsive-looking Venice surrounded by water, mud, and marsh.

The sordid collection of houses, composed of mud and straw, had but one road to the mainland, the elevated causeway. It was on this causeway that the army bedded down for the night, for the general would not risk entering Pehtang so late in the day. The men, wet and dirty, consumed their salty provisions and began to thirst, for they had drained their allotted pint during the exhausting march ashore; none of the water about them was fit to drink. Wolseley remembered leaving a water keg in one of the launches. Together with another officer, he made the fatiguing journey back across the great expanse of mud in the dark. The two were cheered as they tramped into camp with the keg slung upon an oar between them. Subsequently the coolies came up with additional supplies.

During the night the indefatigable Mr Parkes, Lord Elgin's interpreter, accompanied by a staff officer, found his way into the town. Friendly inhabitants told him the forts were deserted, but that the soldiers had left mines, or ground torpedoes, buried inside to destroy the inquisitive and unsuspecting. The people of Pehtang were quick to relate how they detested the Tartar troops who patrolled the area. They described them as an uncouth people with alien manners and tongue who never washed, and ate raw mutton. To the Chinese the white man has an offensive odour, but they declared within Parkes's hearing that 'the Tartars stink more than the English do'. It was obviously meant as a compliment, but to a race that prided itself on being the cleanest of mankind with a 'national smell' above reproach, it came as a shock. Moreover, it was difficult to imagine the noses of these people having any sensitivity left after living in this vile-smelling hole called Pehtang.

In the morning the allied army cautiously moved in and took possession of Pehtang. The townsmen welcomed them, for news of the fair treatment accorded the people of the Talienwan Bay area in the Liotung Peninsula had preceded the British, and led them to expect profits rather than pillage. They repeatedly assured the invaders that this war was a Peking affair of no concern to them.

The occupation of Pehtang was a badly managed affair. The English leaders blamed the French. Mr Parkes decided it was useless to 'tell the people that we will protect them ... with the French in company'.[14] Wolseley noted how the English were kept busy working on the wharves or repairing roads and then confined to quarters, while the French looked on with their hands in their pockets and wandered about searching for anything of value. They dressed in silks and furs, sat at the door steps of the homes they looted and affected the manners of the gentle sex. Because of the defects of their commissariat, a good deal of their time was spent searching for food. They pursued and bayoneted pigs and dogs through the muddy streets. One Frenchman living off the country was observed dragging a dead dog behind him. 'Do you eat dogs?' he was asked by a surprised Englishman. 'I should think so,' was his reply, 'and I wish I could get as good food every day.'[15]

Having ascertained the strength of the enemy's position before Sinho (seven miles south-west of Pehtang), Sir Hope asked Wolseley to take a body of men, 200 cavalry and 100 infantry, to search the region west of the causeway for a road, so as to turn the flank of the Chinese position. Virtually nothing was known of the topography of the interior. So far the Europeans had seen no hard ground beyond the city; Pehtang seemed to be floating on one enormous pudding of earth and water. It looked like the beginning of the world – or the end of it. Wolseley was further instructed by his chief, who was well aware of his lust for combat, to avoid a fight unless it was forced upon him.

On the morning of August 9th, Wolseley moved down the causeway for a couple of miles, placed his infantry on the road to secure his flank, and then swung out in a broad arc with his cavalry. Having surveyed the region carefully to within sight of Sinho, he returned to construct a plan from his sketches. The road he indicated was a poor one, but it would support the weight of artillery and provide fresh-water pools for the horses, a matter of great concern to the general. He worked all that night making copies of the plan for the staff officers of both armies.

It was on the evening of August 11th that Sir Hope, despite Montauban's objections, gave the order to march the following morning. Wolseley was so enraptured by anticipation, he declared that all 'subsequent sensations are but the tinkling of a doorbell in comparison with the throbbing toll of a Big Ben'.[16] His dreams that night were of leading storming parties against a never-ending series of forts, and planting colours on the highest turrets.

Leaving the devastated pigsty called Pehtang, which only Balaclava rivalled in dirt and confusion, was thrill enough for most men as they marched out at dawn. The First Division (under Sir John Michel), accompanied by the French, moved along the causeway to attack the enemy's works in front. The Second Division (under Sir Robert Napier), with the cavalry, took the western track reconnoitred by Wolseley, their guide, so as to turn the flank of the Chinese position. It was heavy going for the Second Division. Sir Hope joined them to assure himself that they could get across the marsh. 'The horses got bogged, the guns sank up to their axle-trees and the wagons stuck fast,' wrote the general, 'and even the infantry found it hard work, and lost many a good pair of boots.'[17] Sir Hope thought they would have to give it up, but they eventually reached solid ground.

Among the heavy pieces of artillery dragged through the mud with rope and perseverance, was a battery of the new Armstrong guns. This was a breechloading, rifled gun which fired an elongated shell. It was not a solid casting, but had been built up scientifically by its inventor, Sir William Armstrong. The weapon was highly controversial. When Sir John Bloomfield, inspector-general of artillery, was asked what he thought of these rifled guns, he replied: 'I do not like them at all; we did not have them at Waterloo, and, besides, they are a change, and every change is an innovation, and every innovation is to be deprecated.'

The Chinese had an even more exaggerated fear of military innovations: their army would have been more at home in the age of the Tudors. Regulations required the Chinese infantryman to possess a shield and helmet, carved or painted to resemble some frightful monster. To frighten their enemies even more, they were taught to make hideous faces. Each soldier was to carry two swords, matchlock, spear, bow and arrows, and on occasions, a stink-pot, though he was usually content with a sword and matchlock – or merely a club.

China's army had become a great rotting mass veined with graft, peculation, idleness, and addiction to opium. At Peking, for example, a special force of 20,000 Tartar cavalry was established to meet any emergency. When it was learned that the barbarians had landed at Pehtang, this force was called out for review. Only then was it discovered that they had no horses, their commander having pocketed the money allotted for the purchase of mounts. Prince Sankolinsin,* the commander-in-chief, was obliged to send an improvised cavalry, with horses hired or borrowed, on forced marches to drive back the invaders.

Wolseley watched as some 3,000 of this force of Tartar cavalry swarmed out of the Sinho entrenchments to attack the Second Division. He had heard that these were the same men who had turned back an army of Taiping rebels seven years before. All wore cuirasses of gilded leather or chain mail, and long-furred black boots into which they tucked their blue trousers. The two squirrels' tails projecting from behind their ordinary Chinese hats of black silk with brim turned up all round were decorations worn only by the military. Mounted on sturdy ponies with high wooden saddles, they drove forward in a furious wave, pointing their strange spears with red horsehair collars straight at English hearts.

The untried Armstrongs now had a chance to prove their worth. Swiftly and precisely, at great range, their shells burst among the advancing skirmishers. The damage was not as great as it might have been, for the horsemen were scattered and on the move. The Tartars came on steadily, fearlessly, without hesitation, though at closer range every shot tore a lane in their lines, leaving riderless mounts and men without horses flying in all directions from the explosions. If the English had any notion that they were opposed by cowards, it left them at this moment. Once the Tartar lines came within range of the Enfields of the infantry, they began to waver. Only then were the two regiments of Sikh cavalry, supported by squads of the stout old King's Dragoon Guards, all nearly mad with impatience, released in a wild rush. The Tartars embraced them in close conflict with loud, savage yells. The superior weight and mettle of the Sikh and Dragoon chargers bowled over the light ponies, and the Tartar riders dropped under measured blows like so many puppets with their

* There was a rumour that 'Sam Collinson', as the English soldiers called him, was in reality an Irish deserter from the corps of Royal Marines.

strings cut. The fight was over in a minute. The Indians and British followed in pursuit, but the fleet, well-cared-for ponies* easily outdistanced horses that were hardly in galloping condition after so many days on board ship.

The Tartars had been cut up in style, and 'the performances of individuals were spoken of afterwards much as one would speak of the success on that same day on the moors.'[18] Major Fane, who commanded one regiment, was said to have bagged three, another officer cut down five, and so on. The Chinese later complained it was 'extremely unfair' of the barbarians to use cavalry, because in all previous encounters they employed only infantry.

As the Sikhs rode in shaking their lances, leaving the field behind them speckled with Tartar dead, the First Division went into action against the fortifications before Sinho. The Armstrongs punched holes in the mud walls and knocked the defenders over. Those Chinese who could flee (some less fortunate defenders had their legs tied to the guns) ran back through the town with rockets whizzing menacingly over their heads. They abandoned their gingals, matchlocks, and primitive bows and arrows, which were so outdated by Western standards of warfare that the victors kept them as souvenirs. The town of Sinho was entered without further interruption and looted. Hen- and pig-sticking Frenchmen were soon dashing all over the place. The men were to dine well that night; for, unlike Pehtang, Sinho was surrounded by a paradise of vegetable gardens and orchards of tasty apricots and peaches.

There were many suicides. Colonel Schmitz of the French army entered a Chinese home shortly after a mandarin and his family had cut their throats. Their members were still trembling in the last spasm of the death agony. The children, their faces 'smirched with blood like those of babies eating jam', were playing with the tresses of their young mothers. The mandarin sat immovable in ropes of silk, his right hand slowly working a fan to keep the greedy flies from settling where his throat had been opened, and, under the fanning, the blood had already congealed and was turning brown. Many Europeans began to ponder the question that was in the French officer's mind: 'If these people have such a horror of us that they do not hesitate to kill themselves, what would they do with us?'[19]

By making a ninety-degree turn to the south-east at Sinho, General Grant was in a position to take the Taku forts from the rear. The only

---

* The tartars pampered their ponies; one of their commandments was: 'Never strike a horse.'

obstacle remaining was the fortified town of Tangku half-way to the Taku forts and three miles beyond Sinho.

Wolseley reconnoitred the Tangku area the next day and found the enemy, except for those in the fort, had fallen back towards Taku. Close inspection revealed hard ground near canals and streams which could be bridged so as to deliver an attack on an extended front right up to the crenellated walls and ditches of the Tangku fort.

On the morning of August 14th, with the line of artillery massed before the fort, the assault began. The French were on the left with their flank resting upon the causeway; the First Division extended its right flank to the Peiho River. It was a hot day as Frenchman and Englishman filed across the hastily-constructed bridges behind a protective rain of iron. Soon Chinese guns opened fire from junks and elevated positions across the river, as well as the forts. They also used rockets, fired singly and in bouquets, with iron-barbed arrow-points. The Europeans' hot and accurate fire quickly silenced all opposition.

Allied losses were slight, and the Armstrongs had 'beautiful exercise practice' on the defenders, many of whom were torn in a horrible manner. The coolies would run up first to turn over their unfortunate countryman, point at his immobile features, laugh, and proceed to rifle his pockets. The reactions of Englishmen to the scene of mutilated dead were varied. Tommy Atkins would sigh, 'Poor heathens! They little know our strength.' The officers would gather round some fine specimen of a carcass and remark, 'Egad! What fine soldiers they would make, if properly drilled and led by plucky spirits.' The surgeons with a detached, professional air, would bend over the corpse, send a probing finger into the wound and observe, 'Wonderful instrument that Armstrong.'[20]

The army paused. The military position resembled a right-angle: at the top was Pehtang with the stores from which General Grant was drawing ten days' supplies to Sinho, the corner where the army was camped; at the other end, roughly the same distance as from Sinho to Pehtang, stood the Taku forts, sea gate to Peking. Here the Mongol General Sankolinsin received a letter from the frightened emperor exhorting him to obey tremblingly his request that he and his army do their utmost to resist.

Sir Hope, too, was beginning to feel pressure from civilians. The diplomats and correspondents made gibes at his circumspect and dilatory conduct of the war. Wolseley, who along with the rest of the staff regarded all civilians at the front as an intolerable nuisance, heard them grumble by the hour. 'What nonsense it is bringing up heavy guns!' – 'Why don't we push on?' – 'I would take the forts tonight if I had a couple of hundred men!' To the impetuous Parkes, the most outspoken among them, the campaign had no dash. 'One would think', he wrote, 'that the British soldier was a creature that should be wrapped in tissue paper and put away in a glass case!'[21] The prudent Scot remained unperturbed. He was as eager as any man to get on, but he knew his profession and was aware of his responsibilities; and he was buoyed by the knowledge that he commanded the confidence and unqualified respect of all of his troops.

Wolseley was kept busy surveying and drawing plans until his eyes were sore. Much of this work was done during a time of torrential rains, and he was forced to slosh through miles of water and slime. At night he returned to camp to eat a cold ration of biscuit and canned beef. On one occasion he found his belongings floating in a mud puddle that had engulfed his tent. Tired and dirty, he was by no means disheartened. He wrote to his mother, 'I am jolly and well and enjoy my profession as much now as I did the day I first donned Her Majesty's Scarlet.'[22]

Wolseley soon discovered that the Taku forts were a marvel of strength, a tribute to the engineering skill of Sankolinsin, considering the men and materials he had to work with. They had proved impregnable from the sea side when he turned back the English the year before, but they were not designed to withstand an attack from the land side. Here, the forts' principal strength was in the character of the surrounding country. Numerous watercourses ran in every direction across mud flats, necessitating the construction of many bridges. When it rained, the land was transformed into a perfect swamp, difficult for cavalry and impassable for artillery. The first northern fort, somewhat smaller than the other, had solid faces supported by great blocks of upright timbers. Some twenty guns had been reversed to receive an attack from the land side. Where the thick, looped walls did not rest along the river, they were surrounded by man-made ditches, one dry followed by two filled with water. The ground between each was thickly planted with sharp stakes.

During the night of August 20th, Sir Robert Napier brought up guns, mortars, and a rocket battery along the newly-created causeways and bridges until they were less than 1,000 yards from the closest fort. At dawn the long row of guns, with the infantry drawn up behind them, opened fire. The artillery of the Celestials, among them guns they had captured from the English a year before, responded with shots usually off the mark. After an hour of cannonading, a shell, apparently from one of the co-operating gunboats, exploded the principal magazine of the fort and 'a tall black pillar, as if by magic, shot up from the midst of the nearest fort,' wrote Wolseley, 'and then bursting like a rocket after it had attained a great height, was soon lost in the vast shower of wood and earth into which it resolved itself – a loud, bursting, booming sound, marking, as it were, the moment of its short existence.'[23] The fort was believed to have been destroyed, for it was completely enshrouded by smoke; but as the smoke cleared, the survivors came to life and recommenced firing.

As the enemy fire was beaten down, the men of the Second Division (the First remained in camp) lay in readiness behind a gentle slope. Napier was about to signal the advance, when he was ordered to wait for the French rushing out of their camp. Montauban had decided at last to send his promised, face-saving party of 400 infantry to join in what he regarded as a 'hopeless undertaking'. The French general, who had not bothered to put on his sword, appeared – or pretended – to be slightly bored as he remained well to the rear with the red-legged gentlemen of his staff and his escort of fifty Spahis (Algerian cavalry) dressed in native costume. The Arabs' eyes lit up with the excitement of battle as Englishmen and Frenchmen rushed towards the crackling matchlocks. The artillery followed more deliberately, fired a shot or two until the enemy got the range, limbered up, advanced, halted, and fired once again.

To negotiate the formidable ditches, parties of engineers brought up a copper pontoon bridge. Light bamboo ladders, used extensively in India, had been suggested, but the engineer in command rejected them because he could not find them mentioned in the book of regulations. The French, unfettered by regulations, used light ladders and soon led the advance on the right flank near the river. Their coolies formed a human bridge as they stood in water up to their necks holding ladders horizontally over their heads so the soldiers could scramble across. Meanwhile, a round shot had banged through one of the British pontoons, rendering it useless. The clumsy bridge fell across the causeway and slowed the advance. Milling stormers, exposed unnecessarily, began to drop. Wolseley, who had come up with the advance party, laboured to separate the damaged pontoon and lift it to one side so that the bridge might be launched.

Many of the stormers did not wait for the bridge to be laid. They jumped into the dry ditch and clambered up the side, and then waded or swam the wet ditches. Far ahead was Major Anson, aide-de-camp to Sir Hope and close friend to Wolseley. Riding a white charger, he had bolted from the general's side to lead the attack.

Among the first to cross the last ditch, Anson tackled the raised drawbridge to enable others to cross more easily. He struggled up a pole with a sword between his teeth and contrived to hack through the supporting ropes. The bridge came down with a great crash. Hardly serviceable after being riddled with shot, only one shaky beam seemed capable of supporting any weight. When the men crossed over, it rolled and pitched. With death all around them, it became a source of comic relief to watch an unlucky comrade lose his footing and fall into the ditch, 'from whence he climbed up the muddy bank opposite, there perchance to meet his death-blow, ere the very smile at his own mishap had passed from his countenance; such is life, death, and war,' philosophized Wolseley.[24]

Most amused, by far, were the coolies. They were thoroughly delighted by the bombardment and all the commotion of the assault. As they coolly carried out the dangerous mission of removing the wounded or bringing up ammunition, they would pause and cheer every good shot that knocked some poor unfortunate, whether friend or foe.

A few soldiers who had cleared all obstacles and braved the raking, rattling fire of slugs from gingals, bolts from cross-bows, and round shot from this or one of the other forts, prowled under the walls searching for a breach or scalable point. While some of the English stood on their comrades' shoulders, the French had coolies bring up scaling-ladders and hold them firmly against the fort, which they did with courage and steadiness while the stormers fought for every rung.

The Chinese manned the walls with uncommon determination, showering down every conceivable missile from buckets of lime to round shot dropped by hand. As the ladders – human and otherwise – touched the parapet, the defenders shoved them back, often causing the falling assailants to be impaled on the bamboo stakes below. A little French drummer was the first to bound to the top and wave the Tricolour, while everyone joined in his maddening cheer. 'Amidst the wild clamour, his spirit passed away from him to another, and let us hope a better world,' Wolseley wrote.[25] He had been shot through the heart.

In a matter of seconds an ensign of the 67th, wounded three times in the attempt, hoisted the colours of his regiment, normally a flag too dearly prized as a military emblem to risk being captured at such a forward position. The honour of being first into the fort was shared with men of the 44th and 67th who managed to force their way through the sally-port below.

The Chinese continued to fight with fury as the English and French poured over the wall and through different breaches. It was the re-enactment of the last terrible scene at Sikandar Bagh, for the only exit was the point by which the Europeans had entered. A few defenders escaped by hurling themselves through the embrasures on the sea front; even then many were drowned, transfixed by a sharpened stake, or shot in the act of swimming. Most stood their ground and died. Some shut themselves up in their barracks and resisted until they were bayoneted to a man.

Wolseley came up as the last of the garrison were overwhelmed, and surveyed the debris of battle. Around the broken gun-carriages and over-turned cannon were three to four hundred dead and dying. In contrast to soldiers who had died huddled in a trench, or were strewn about hap-hazardly on a field, there was something purposeful and noble about dead men lying beside a cannon.

As the wounded defenders were taken to the rear and given careful attention by the surgeons, fatigue-parties dragged the dead by their pig-tails and dropped them into smoking craters, which made perfect graves. Their work was interrupted by the eminent Italian photographer, Signor Beato, who kept entreating them not to move the 'deada mansa' until he had completed his picture. And while in one corner of the fort a French Catholic priest was consoling a couple of dying men, the soldiers laughed and joked over the macabre scene and tossed dead dogs and cats into the craters with the corpses. 'To such an extent the finer feelings of human nature become blunted by war and its attendant circumstances,' observed one Englishman, 'a very brief experience with which had rendered young soldiers indifferent to scenes that perhaps a few weeks before would have filled them with horror.'[26]

Preparations were quickly made to take the second and larger fort about 1,000 yards down the river. Colonel Wolseley took a small party to re-connoitre in advance of the main body. On seeing the barbarians approach, the Chinese suddenly ceased fire and white flags began to appear on the walls. After prolonged negotiations, the Europeans marched in and took possession of the place without incident. When Wolseley entered he found the soldiers of the garrison, who had made menacing gestures only a short time before, were now out of uniform assuming the guise of humble civilians. Much to the astonishment of the dissembling defenders, they were actually treated as peaceable citizens. They had expected to be slaughtered en masse as they cowered in the corners of the fort, or perhaps taken out individually and beheaded. Slowly, with a look of disbelief in their eyes, some 2,000 shuffled out of the fort to freedom.

Disheartened by the loss of the northern forts, which made their own position untenable, the Chinese on the south side of the Peiho gave up their formidable works before sunset with upwards of 600 guns and some ancient catapults which looked as if they had seen service at the walls of Troy. Under cover of night, while Sir Hope played vigorously on the violoncello, the renowned Sankolinsin took what remained of his army, mostly cavalry, and retreated towards Tientsin where he was degraded by the Emperor, who deprived him of his command of the Manchu banner force and his three-eyed peacock's feather.

'The Third Chinese War is *over*,' Wolseley told his mother, 'and thank God I am well and hearty, without a scratch of any sort.'[27] He declared that the honour of the British army, which had been tarnished the year before, was now gloriously vindicated and they had suffered only 200 casualties (the French around 300).

But peace still lay well beyond the Taku forts. And not a moment was lost in marching the army along the Peiho to Tientsin, sixty-eight miles beyond. From here, Lord Elgin would launch his diplomatic offensive. Sir Hope and staff boarded the *Grenada* and steamed on in advance with the gunboats while Wolseley remained ashore, busily sketching and mapping every step of the way. No resistance was anticipated, for the Taku generals had surrendered all the forts and troops under their jurisdiction, which extended as far as Tientsin. Only the miserable roads retarded the advance.

It was the same flat, monotonous country, but the army soon left the disgusting mud flats and entered an exceptionally fertile land – a land of plenty where beef, mutton, ducks and chickens were offered for only a few coppers by the friendly inhabitants. Fruits and vegetables of every description were found ripening in riverside gardens. As the long, thin red line wound its way through the green land, they wanted for nothing in the way of food. Only the heat was at times oppressive, but as the army approached Tientsin, tons of ice were offered for their convenience. Crushed ice was used by the Chinese not only for drinking purposes but also for scattering under a mat on sultry afternoons before they lay down for a refreshing siesta. The soldiers soon learned that for an empty bottle, the hawkers would part with large clear blocks of ice. For another bottle, they could purchase a load of delicious grapes weighing nearly 200 lb. At these prices, the troopers could afford to feed their horses sweet grapes and ice water.

'What a campaign!' exclaimed Wolseley. There were sights one would never expect to witness in a war: at Pehtang, thousands of soldiers could be seen devouring oysters (though many had regrets the following morning); at Sinho the army consumed peaches in orchards said to be the property of the Emperor himself; and now at Tientsin the men dined on

D

iced grapes. The sailors did not have it so bad either. According to the army, they never do. It was rumoured among the soldiers that 'Jack Tar' had become so particular, he could not possibly get through 'his grog without his lump of ice'.[28] Wolseley was sorry that brother George had not been transferred to Sir Hope's army.

Tientsin, a city of 150,000, was taken without a shot. There was absolute civility on the part of the Chinese. The army pitched tents in a grassy field two miles south of the city, and Lord Elgin and the diplomats began negotiations with two high-ranking commissioners who had been sent from Peking. In the battle of words that ensued, the Chinese envoys agreed to all demands. The sanguine diplomats assured the soldiers that the last gun had been fired and that peace was certain. Everyone began to speculate as to when he would reach home as the army began to break up. The 44th was sent to Shanghai on August 25th to deal with the Taiping rebels and arrangements were made for the staff to have leave in England. Wolseley estimated he could be home in time to eat Christmas dinner with his 'dear mother'.

A great meeting took place on September 6th, and everyone was in high spirits as the Emperor's ambassadors were invited to come forward to sign the convention. But when asked if they were ready to place their sovereign's seal on the document, the mandarins confessed they posessed neither seal nor plenary powers. They admitted quite frankly that they had been lying. Lord Elgin, more red-faced than usual, replied that if such were the case, he must go to Peking and deal with the Emperor himself.

The Chinese had a natural fear that it was the purpose of the Europeans to wrest the country from them. Too weak to resist, they resorted to treachery and specious negotiations with 'that fat barbarian Elgin'. If they could delay the enemy long enough, the cold weather would come to their aid, freeze the river, and drive the barbarians back to the sea. The sham robbed the allies of eight irretrievable days of fine weather and deprived Grant of the use of part of his army owing to a serious loss in transport facilities. For while the diplomats were at work, the Chinese contrived that most of the native drivers and their animals, which had been collected in Tientsin with great difficulty, should vanish during the night of September 9th, just as the army was getting under way towards Peking.

Wolseley, who was still leading a small surveying party, left his mule carts and drivers in the care of a sepoy, warning him that he and their party would never reach Peking unless he kept a close watch over them. While others deserted the European force, Wolseley never lost a man. On the morning following the great departure of drivers, Wolseley asked his duffadar of cavalry, 'Are your mules and drivers safe?' He answered with a broad grin, 'Yes, sahib.' The colonel became curious as to why his coolies did not desert. After some investigation, Wolseley found that at the end of a day's march, the drivers were tied by their pigtails to a tent pole. And no Chinese would think of exchanging his precious pigtail for freedom!

Because of the limited land transport, the French and English advanced from Tientsin by detachments. Napier and the Second Division were to remain in the city, ready to advance when called. The party under Wolseley, including two officers and an interpreter (Mr Swinhoe) and a small escort from Fane's Horse, was to survey the river and roads, and to a certain extent, provide intelligence. He had the authority to go where and when he liked. Sometimes he was in front of the army, sometimes behind it; usually, however, he followed in its wake. Should hostilities be resumed, Wolseley was to rejoin headquarters.

To be his 'own master of course' suited Wolseley's disposition. And there were those happy to see him go. The studious young colonel who expounded all those fancy theories on war was a bit too much for the more tradition-bound officers, many of whom could not help being offended by his rapid advance and the way Sir Hope sought him out for companionship and important missions. When protesting officers expressed their annoyance with Wolseley's radical ideas on war to Sir Hope, he would chuckle and reply, 'Nonsense, that is merely Wolseley's way of talking; he is a very able officer and a very good soldier.'

Peace still prevailed. The Chinese once more insisted they sincerely wished to negotiate. Only when they realized that Lord Elgin could not be persuaded to stop short of Tungchow did they agree to all conditions demanded, provided that the European army itself did not march beyond Hosiwu while the Western ambassadors came forward with a small unarmed escort to Tungchow. Here, they said, the final settlement would be made and they could then move on to Peking to exchange the ratifications. Lord Elgin, optimistic and ready to accommodate what appeared to be a sincere offer, sent Parkes, who had grown up in China and knew the people, to take diplomatic soundings and adjust details at Tungchow. These details included Elgin's demand that instead of a small unarmed party, a force of a thousand armed men accompany him and another thousand men escort the French ambassador. Moreover, the army would advance to Changchiawan, four miles south of Tungchow, instead of halting at Hosiwu.

The Celestials set a trap. The shrewd young Parkes was thoroughly deceived by the clever Prince of I, who was said to be one of the three men who actually governed China. The Prince, amiable to the point of being unctuous, agreed personally to all Parkes's demands while he secretly plotted to ambush the 'outer barbarians'. A Chinese official later explained his conduct with the comment: 'You foreigners always think in straight lines, but we think in curves.' Meanwhile, Sankolinsin, reinstated in the Emperor's favour, took an army of 20,000 into the area south of Tungchow and vowed that the surprised barbarians would never return to Tientsin alive.

When Parkes, on the morning of September 18th, went to inspect the camping site selected for the European armies two miles south of Changchiawan, he was astonished to find large bodies of Chinese troops with masked batteries all about. Obviously, the Celestials were preparing an ambush, so Parkes sent Mr Loch, Lord Elgin's private secretary, to gallop on to Sir Hope and report what he had seen. Colonel Walker was to remain on the ground to observe the enemy, while Parkes himself retraced his steps to Tungchow to warn the remainder of his escort and remonstrate against this apparent breach of faith to the Prince of I.

The Europeans had begun their march to the designated camping grounds early that same morning. Already fully aware of the presence of a large hostile force in the neighbourhood, Sir Hope was preparing his army for battle when Loch rode up. Concern for Parkes and his party and the opportunity to gain further knowledge about this puerile stratagem, persuaded the general to allow Loch, still under a flag of truce, to return.

As Loch prepared to go back and collect his people and lead them to safety, Sir Hope offered to send one of his trusted staff officers to assist him in his mission. 'Where is Wolseley?' called the commander. When he learned that he was still on a mapping assignment far to the rear, Sir Hope selected Captain Brabazon to go in his place.

Wolseley, at the very moment his chief sought him, was himself close to capture or death. With Sir Hope's permission, he had stayed behind the army that morning, anxious to complete his survey of the road. It was an arduous task, more difficult than he had expected, for the face of this level land was decked with fields of millet and maize, tall enough to conceal a horse. To ensure accuracy, Wolseley often felt it necessary to pace the road.

While the surveying party was at breakfast, an officer of the Dragoons rode back to say that the rear-guard had halted four miles ahead owing to suspicious activities at the front. Wolseley thanked him for the warning, but his voice betrayed his unconcern. He leisurely finished his tea, confident that the diplomats had the peace well in hand. His aplomb was shattered in a twinkling when a Sikh officer of his escort rushed to his side with his arm extended towards a great cloud of dust and reported in an excited, high-pitched voice that a large body of Tartar cavalry was close by. Tea cups rattled, tent poles were struck, and Wolseley hastily stuffed his pockets and holster-pipes with his sketches. All was made ready for an instant start. It was ascertained that the enemy force was moving on a path between them and the rear-guard. Though his party had excellent mounts, Wolseley refused to flee to safety. He remained sword in hand, next to his charger. His fellow officers were baffled by his conduct until he said very quietly, 'We can't leave the dismounted men.' Realizing his concern for those in the party who were on foot, the others dismounted and stood beside him. His officers observed a display of 'quiet, calculating courage' which they recognized as superior to 'the headlong and somewhat rash bravery which frequently wins more tangible recognition'.[29]

The Tartar cavalry, absorbed with its mission of slipping around behind the 'foreign devils', failed to discover the party fairly concealed by the tall Indian corn. When the immediate danger had passed, Wolseley's party rushed forward to rejoin Sir Hope's force as quickly as their clumsy carts would allow. Those were the longest four miles Wolseley ever travelled. Time and again the cart-wheels would stick in the ruts as the clouds of dust seemed to come closer and closer. Any moment, the colonel expected to be discovered and he resolved to take his men into the first hut along the road where they would die fighting rather than submit to capture. Having at last brought his carts up as far as the rear-guard, Wolseley cantered on to join the commander. Sir Hope was having an anxious moment. He had already held up the battle for nearly two hours, Montauban's protests notwithstanding, rather than jeopardize the safety of Parkes and the rest of the party.

Colonel Walker, standing with his men in the middle of the Chinese army, also waited for Parkes. Suddenly the Celestials became surly. One tried to take Walker's sword from him. Several others began to close in on a French officer near by. As a general mêlée developed, Walker called out to his men to ride for their lives. Wolseley stood near Sir Hope on a little mound watching the enemy through a telescope, when he espied on the clear ground before them the scarlet coats of Walker's Dragoons colourfully framed against the grey uniforms of the Chinese army. Galloping at top speed, they were cutting their way through the troops that surrounded them. All the enemy seemed to be firing in their direction, including the batteries. Somehow they managed to escape without losing a man, though many of them and their horses were wounded.

The firing, having once commenced, continued steadily. The battle was on. All hope for Parkes and the rest of his party had to be abandoned.

Despite the difference in numbers – 20,000 against 4,000 – the allied leaders did not hesitate in taking the offensive. The Chinese line extended for nearly four miles, from the Peiho to the lofty but crumbling and moss-grown walls of Changchiawan. Artillery gave the allies the initial advantage. Each shot crashed with telling effect as the Armstrongs were gradually drawn around the right flank of the enemy. Musbee Sikhs, on trial as irregular cavalry, gallantly cleared the way – passing their test with honours. Punjab infantry followed through reaped cornfields where only six inches of sharp, diagonally-cut stalks remained. They rolled up the Celestials' right flank in a ghastly second harvest. The French swung around the left flank to enfilade the Chinese position. However, they encountered strong resistance and were vigorously attacked by Tartar cavalry. A squadron of Fane's Horse, lent by Sir Hope to the French, vied with Arab Spahis in counter-attacking and pursuing the Tartars. At this point, the Oriental army, whose fire had never been very effective, retired. The French were too exhausted to pursue and remained behind as the English went on to capture Changchiawan. The pursuit continued as far as the enemy camps beyond the city. The cotton tents, containing considerable quantities of gunpowder, were put to the torch. The subsequent explosions and tall columns of smoke that shot high into the air gave Peking an early announcement of defeat. The town of Changchiawan was occupied by the English and given up to plunder as punishment for Sankolinsin's treachery.

Sankolinsin had not retreated very far. His army was only a short distance away, in the vicinity of the canal that linked Peking to its port of Tungchow. It was heard in camp that night that each of the forty-eight princes of Tartary had sent a thousand picked warriors to protect the Emperor and his throne. No doubt the Chinese command was determined to fight again to save the capital. Sir Hope, ready to oblige, moved his army out of Changchiawan at dawn on September 21st. The French on the right were to strike towards the marble bridge of Palikao spanning the canal three miles outside Tungchow. The English were to cross a wooden bridge a mile farther up towards Peking. The cavalry was to make a wide flanking movement to the left and drive the Chinese up against the advancing infantry.

The battle that ensued was largely a cavalry action, for the Tartar horsemen, among them the warriors of the Yellow Banner believed to be the pick of the force, were out that same morning to outflank the advancing barbarians. Their charges were halted by the Dragoons and Irregulars, who, in Wolseley's words, 'went through and through them bowling them over like ninepins'.[30] The Tartar cavalry never came close to the English infantry.

Sir Hope and his staff were well up in front during much of the fighting and, at one point, nearly surrounded by stalwart warriors on little Mongolian ponies. To be captured by Tartar horsemen was a grim prospect. One Sikh, who was carried into their midst by an unmanageable mount, had his eyes gouged out and then was cut to pieces limb by limb.

The enemy was chased to within six miles of Peking, shell and sabre overtaking many of the less fortunate. Their abandoned camps were looted by the villagers who rushed in as soon as the imperial soldiers streamed out. When the English arrived, they assigned the tents to flames and destruction. Wolseley, who left the general's side to join in the pursuit, saw sights that would have inspired even the most faint-hearted. 'Had the Chairman of the Peace Society been there,' he opined, 'I am sure he would have shouted in exultation as he saw those gallant horsemen charge at full speed amongst the enemy's hordes.'[31] Riding back to rejoin his chief, he witnessed the more sordid side of battle as parties of Sikhs lingered about the battle-area testing the fallen foe with spear's point, and if they screamed or writhed with pain, 'some of the party would dismount and deliberately saw his head off'.[32] Oddly enough, the Chinese called the gaudily-dressed Sikhs 'the dark-coloured princes' rather than 'barbarians'.

The way to Peking, the mysterious and forbidden city, was now open. The Chinese army retreated to the north-east of the city; the Emperor of China, Hienfung, fled north to Jehol with his thirteen wives and much of the court. Had Sir Hope not been misled by the over-confidence of his diplomat colleagues, he would have lost no time in besieging the Chinese capital. But without his siege-guns, for the walls were too high to be escaladed, he was forced to wait for the siege-train to be brought up-river to Tungchow, which had opened its gates to the barbarians without the slightest difficulty. Sir Robert Napier and the Second Division were already on their way. The French, meanwhile, left all these prosaic details – moving siege-trains, guarding lines of communication, garrisoning towns, etc. – to the English.

With their armies routed, the Chinese leaders once more fell back upon negotiations to save Peking from capture by the 'foreign devils'. While the last shots were being fired Prince Kung, younger brother of the Emperor, wrote to the allies stating he had been appointed High Commissioner with plenipotentiary powers, and indicated he was anxious for a truce. To gain the withdrawal of the approaching army, the Prince offered to exchange the European prisoners. But Lord Elgin insisted he would not consider any terms until the captives were released. The new High Commissioner, feeling this was the only trump card he held, refused to surrender Parkes and his fellow captives without some kind of diplomatic advantage. And since some of the prisoners were already dead and all showed signs of maltreatment, the Westerners might exact some fearful reprisal when they discovered the true nature of their condition.

While the daily exchange of letters failed to produce any concession on either side, General Grant sent out parties to reconnoitre the Peking area. Wolseley was out every day, from dawn to sunset, collecting data to fill the many blank spaces on his map. On September 26th, he led a strong reconnaissance force consisting of troopers from Fane's Horse and the Arab Spahis. He took his party up to the very walls of the Forbidden City, which he found to be over forty feet high, and broad enough at the tapering top to accommodate three carriages driving abreast, like the ancient walls of Babylon. They were said to surround many marvels which few Euopeans had ever seen. A few soldiers came out, fired several shots and ran back when the 'foreign devils' advanced towards them. Searching the walls with his telescope, Wolseley discovered that they were guarded by armed 'sentries' who were in reality dummies. Why bother to use live soldiers who had to be fed and paid, reasoned the Chinese, when men of straw would serve the purpose just as well?

Having drawn up their siege-train and reinforcements, the army was again in motion on October 3rd, marching alongside a neglected highway of granite blocks that bespoke a glorious past. Nearing the great city, the army moved cautiously through a land where the view was shortened by numerous groves of trees, for Sir Hope was concerned with the whereabouts of Sankolinsin and his hordes of Tartar cavalry. By October 6th, the British general lost contact with the French and his cavalry, which had been ordered to work round to the north of the city and block the most likely line of retreat. However, all the information that had been garnered at this time convinced the general that the Chinese army had fallen back towards the Summer Palace, Yuenmingyuen, which housed the heads of government. Rather than venture forth towards the Summer Palace without cavalry, the commander-in-chief rested his fatigued troops north-east of the capital and serenaded them with his violoncello until the horsemen could rejoin them.

Early on the morning of October 7th, Sir Hope sent Wolseley with a squadron of Dragoons to establish communications with the rest of the European force. After some beating about, Wolseley found the French and the cavalry at the Summer Palace, five miles north-west of Peking. He raced back to inform Sir Hope, who, along with Lord Elgin, returned with them to the gates of Yuenmingyuen (Garden of Perfect Brightness).

The Summer Palace, the cherished residence for two hundred years of Manchu majesties, was enclosed by a lofty granite wall five miles in circumference. It was in reality a series of palaces, a Versailles, with numerous decorated dwellings in which government officials and the Emperor and his relatives dwelt. The extravagantly decorated palaces, pavilions and pagodas, each a mine of treasures, were surrounded by many gardens, landscaped with stunted trees in the approved Chinese fashion.

The Emperor's younger brother remained at Yuenmingyuen until he learned the enemy were close by. He instructed some 300 eunuchs to defend the palaces to the last and then made a quick exit from the premises. That evening, while Sir Hope was lighting signal fires to draw the attention of his cavalry, the French banged through the doors of the main palace while the British cavalry remained outside, forbidden to enter a walled place. The emasculated defenders made a feeble show of resistance and shouted, 'Don't commit sacrilege!' as the 'white devils' entered the sacred precincts of the great Dragon Hall. While the heavily-armed barbarians profaned the forbidden magnificence with their sacrilegious gaze, only a few Pekingese dogs, the exclusive pets of the royal family, stayed to bark in protest.*

It was early the following morning when Wolseley guided the English leaders through the main gate, on either side of which were brass lions couchant similar to the entrance of some great country estate. Once inside the pleasure gardens, they found the French camped outside the Dragon Hall, or Great Audience Hall, which stood before the main residence of the Emperor, the Cousin of the Stars. Montauban came forward, greeted the English chiefs, and requested that the staff remain outside, away from

---

* It was a capital offence for any but royalty to own one of these sacred symbols of the throne. Most were thrown into a well rather than permit their capture by barbarians. One was eventually presented to Queen Victoria, who, having no delusions as to how this unique canine was acquired, promptly dubbed it 'Looty'. The pampered emigrant Pekingese was forced to adjust itself to something other than an exclusive diet of sharks' fins, curlews' livers, and the breast of quail.

the valuables. Sir Hope assented. Then with a solemn face, the French general assured Sir Hope that all looting had been forbidden so as to permit the English an equal opportunity. While he spoke, French soldiers were openly engaged in plundering.

Wolseley stood outside the palace and smiled with amusement as the French filed in one side empty-handed and came out the other richly attired in skirts embroidered with floss silk, struggling like ants under loads of jade, pearls, ivory, furs, clocks, and other art objects of every description. One generous soldier noticed the English colonel without spoils, stopped, reached into his bag and offered him an enamel figurine, the gift of another Frenchman, Louis XV, to the Emperor of China. Wolseley thanked him and pocketed the article, the only piece of loot he was to carry away from China. In defence, he might have said as did the great Lord Clive, 'When I recollect my opportunities, I wonder at my own moderation.'

Lord Elgin was not amused. His face registered stern disapproval as he accosted Montauban and said quite plainly, 'I would like a great many things that the palace contains, but I am not a thief!'[33]

Eventually Wolseley was permitted to enter the Dragon Hall. He crossed the great marble floor where countless thousands had grovelled before the Sun's Brother as he sat in the now vacant rosewood throne. Beyond the throne were the private apartments which the French command had, so far, prevented from being pillaged entirely. The quarters of Hienfung were almost exactly as he had left them, with his small cap, pipe and tobacco pouch next to his couch. There were the silver tablets on which all messages to his august person were inscribed, for no one was permitted to gaze upon his sacred person, and the silver trumpet which he used to swell his voice to thunderous god-like tones for the benefit of his awed subjects. So lavish were the decorations that even the curtain-rods and door-handles were of pure gold. The adjoining rooms contained a wardrobe of the costliest silks, satins, and furs, sufficient to adorn all the princes of the *Arabian Nights'*. The furniture was covered with yellow satin, the imperial colour, which only those of royal birth were permitted to wear.

When the French first arrived at the Summer Palace, they were like children let loose in a toyshop, impressed by the novelty but somewhat puzzled as to where to start. Frequently they pawed over trifles. By the next day, when Wolseley arrived, they were already intoxicated by so much splendour. It was as if the men 'had been seized with a temporary insanity', wrote Wolseley; 'in body and soul absorbed in one pursuit, which was plunder, plunder'.[34] Discipline was annihilated. In one regimental camp near the gate, the drums beat 'assembly' over and over again, but no more than ten men per company could be mustered as their comrades ran about in women's clothes, disregarding their forage-caps for the turned-up hat of a mandarin. Furniture, clothing of all kinds and rolls of silk were thrown out by the armful and strewn about the camp.

Soon the French soldiers approached the last stage of unrestrained looting: vandalism. No longer did they bother with the handle of a door, they kicked it in. Armed with heavy clubs, they destroyed what they could not carry, or what their limited education could not comprehend. A series of 4,000 illustrations depicting the entire history of the Celestial Empire was stamped to pieces and used for kindling. What little aesthetic appreciation they possessed was gratified by the adornment of fine statues with an absurd, painted moustache. They hurled chairs through windows, used golden vessels for footballs, and took pot-shots at chandeliers. Mirrors that once reflected serene and gentle scenes were mercifully shattered. Even the sack of Kaiser Bagh, which Wolseley had witnessed, faded in comparison with this hashish-taker's dream. Had Sankolinsin and his Tartars chosen this day to come back to Yuenming-yuen, the vivacious pilferers might well have joined the eunuchs lying on the ground dead, manacled, or writhing from their wounds. Montauban could no more have stopped them than Napoleon could have stopped his routed regiments at Waterloo.

Three days later when these soldiers marched into position before Peking, the French had completely recovered their discipline; their behaviour was so correct, one would never have suspected their recent debauchery. Wolseley believed plundering English soldiers would never have shaken off the demoralizing effects of such an experience in so short a time. He thoroughly approved of Sir Hope's order preventing the soldiers from leaving their camp. The commander, however, yielded to the extent of permitting half of the officers of each regiment and some from the cavalry stationed near by to go to the Summer Palace and join in the looting. They were to return at a given time so that the other half could have a turn.

The looting by the English began on Sunday, and one chaplain became so excited that it was only after the utmost persuasion by the men that he gave the customary morning service. It was the shortest service he ever delivered. The chaplain returned that night with a mule cart stacked with spoils. The next Sunday he was back in form 'to preach an admirable sermon against covetousness, to the surprise and edification of his hearers'.[35]

By October 7th most of the British army quietly established itself before the north wall of Peking near the Anting gate, and Lord Elgin sent an ultimatum demanding the immediate surrender of the prisoners, failing which the attack on the Forbidden City would begin. The next day, those prisoners held inside Peking, including Parkes and Loch, were restored. Gradually others were brought out – some dead. Of the twenty-six British taken, half survived; and of the French, but six of the original thirteen. The coolies who fell into the hands of the Chinese authorities were less fortunate. They were buried so that only their heads were exposed, and left to the mercy of the dogs. These scavengers would begin by licking their faces; licking turned to biting; and soon they gnawed their heads off.

Wolseley, though not a prize-agent, was busy until October 10th attending to matters relating to prize-money. On that day he joined the commander and his staff in a reconnaissance about the northern face of the great wall of Peking. They rode to the edge of the ditch before the wall, and the general selected a position for the breaching batteries close to the Anting gate. The Chinese were given until noon of October 13th to surrender the gate, for the guns could not be placed until that time. The interval was devoted to negotiations and threats. There were so many ultimatums sent to the Chinese that a Church of England chaplain remarked that it sounded 'like the end of a Presbyterian minister's sermon'.

As the hour of bombardment approached, the Celestials made no move to surrender. The guns of the siege-battery, now less than 200 yards from the last stronghold of the Chinese seclusion, were sponged out and loaded. Wolseley took his place next to the right gun and, with match in hand, waited. He was uneasy. The siege-guns had hardly enough rounds to batter a breach in those immense walls of brick and earth. What if the Celestials called the Englishmen's bluff? Scanning the rim of the wall, he looked anxiously for some sign of capitulation. The Chinese delayed until a few minutes before noon. Convinced that the menacing muzzles were aimed in earnest, they opened the Anting gate, through which the Manchus had entered as conquerors two hundred years before. Peking, the pride of the Flowery kingdom, capitulated to the barbarians after twenty years of conflict, and the representatives of the Queen entered within the walls of the inviolate capital.

Peking itself was a lie, thought Wolseley, as he looked the city over. 'Everyone has been disappointed,' he wrote his sister Matilda. 'In childhood we learnt it was the capital of China, and all had imagined it to be something very wonderful.' When the army came near the city for the first time, the men strained their eyes, climbed trees, and speculated as to the wondrous sights behind those great walls. Then they saw it as it really was, Wolseley related, an ordinary, dirty city with black filth covering the streets and a population far smaller than anyone had expected. 'Never have we had a war', he concluded, 'in a country of which we knew so little when entering it, and never were preconceived ideas of what it was like so utterly mistaken as they have been regarding the country from Ten-tsin to Pekin ... '36

The day after the entrance into Peking, Wolseley was reconnoitring the little-known territory west of the capital when he met a body of Tartar horsemen escorting five carts, each carrying a crude coffin containing what remained of some of the murdered European prisoners. One of them held the bones of Mr Bowlby of *The Times*, the first war correspondent to be killed in the line of duty. He had been thrown from a window and partially devoured by pigs. The bodies of the beheaded Brabazon, who had taken Wolseley's place, and two Frenchmen, one of them the interpreter Abbé de Luc, were never returned.

Lord Elgin decided upon a quick and drastic punishment: burn the magnificent Summer Palace. Sir Hope agreed. By putting the judicial torch to Yuenmingyuen, the Son of Heaven and the imperial party would be made to suffer directly. It would strike a blow at his royal pride and puncture his boast of universal supremacy, for his property, like his person, was said to be sacrosanct. In addition, the Summer Palace was the scene of recent atrocities where European prisoners had been taken, trussed up so tightly that maggots entered their wounds, and then flung to the ground before the Emperor.

Sir Hope remained in camp while Michel's First Division and the greater part of the cavalry were detailed to burn the Summer Palace. Wolseley went to Yuenmingyuen more as a spectator than a participant and watched 3,500 men rush about, burning and looting, discharging their duty zealously. With them were hundreds of peasants who fought over the spoils long after the Summer Palace became a monumental ruin. Several days later, Wolseley encountered one villager beating another on the head with a hammer. Though he prevented the assailant from pounding the victim's brains out, he could not guarantee the latter's survival after he rode off.·

Wolseley held the view that the charred, smoking ruins of the sinning monarch's rural palace gave the Europeans one advantage: it frightened

Prince Kung into a quick settlement. A gentle wind wafted a great black cloud from the Summer Palace to Peking and showered hot embers over the city. For days it hung over the city casting a dark shadow, demonstrating the avenging power of the Europeans and suggesting the doom of the Manchu Dynasty unless their terms were accepted.

All terms were accepted without further demur. On October 24th, Lord Elgin was to enter Peking in state; ratifications of the Treaty of 1858 were to be exchanged, and the Convention of Peking signed.

Shortly after noon on the day of the signing, Wolseley rode at the head of the procession with two bands as Lord Elgin entered the city in an ornate sedan-chair streaming with tassels of many colours and carried by eight coolies outfitted in elegant scarlet jackets. The ambassador was surrounded by a strong escort and attended by the diplomatic staff, and Sir Hope with three officers from every regiment. The throngs of curious spectators, who had never seen an 'outer barbarian', acted friendlily enough as the imposing procession passed by slowly and with great dignity. They had a look of wonderment on their faces as they listened to the band; and when it stopped playing, the people roared with laughter. Nevertheless, Wolseley believed this display of military strength in the city would have a 'far more important and beneficial influence in our future dealings with China than all the treaties now ratified or that may be hereafter concluded'.[37]

After two hours the ceremony was about to be concluded when Signor Beato, the energetic photographer, came forward with his terrifying apparatus and aimed the lens directly at Prince Kung. It looked to him like some diabolical mortar 'ready to disgorge its terrible contents into his devoted body'.[38] The royal brother, expecting at any moment to be blown to bits, quivered and blanched. Only after Lord Elgin and Sir Hope, who flanked him, explained the purpose of the camera, did he settle down to a hollow smile.

That evening Wolseley wrote: 'I sincerely hope that every war may be as ably planned and as well carried out as this war by Sir Hope Grant.'[39] And he gained invaluable lessons in the art of war from a master. Delivering an address at Aldershot several years later, he explained, 'If I have attained any measure of military prosperity, my gratitude is due to one man, Sir Hope Grant.' Sir Hope, in turn, had nothing but praise to bestow upon Wolseley and often mentioned his name in dispatches during his campaign. He admired his thoroughness, especially the way he completed his surveys around Peking after the war. The general also encouraged and appreciated his bright views, and enjoyed his strong opinions and independence of judgment. When Wolseley was too quick to find fault with others and displayed an intellectual contempt for the 'bow-and-arrow' school of officers, Sir Hope found it necessary to reprove him in a kindly, constructive way. Wolseley, being devoted to this thoughtful general, would accept a rebuke from him as he would from no other.

Having conveyed the troops to the fleet, Sir Hope and most of his staff took an extended pleasure cruise around Japan in a chartered steamer. Soon wearying of sightseeing in the East, Wolseley expressed a desire to visit the 'nice little islands of Great Britain and Ireland'. It was his intention to hurry home 'as fast as possible, stopping nowhere on the way'.[40]

The general, however, had just one more assignment for his bright young colonel: a semi-diplomatic mission up the Yangtze to the ancient capital of Nanking to gather information on the strength and prospects of the Taipings who now entered their eleventh year of rebellion against the Manchu Tartars.

The Taipings attracted considerable attention in the Western world at this time. Britain and the United States seriously considered recognition and support of a Chinese administration which had converted millions to a nominally Protestant Christianity. But their excesses soon made them appear more as a cult of plunderers than dedicated malcontents. And once the treaties, which offered such great commercial advantage, were signed in Peking in 1860, England and France were more or less committed to supporting the Manchus against the Taipings so as to preserve their material interests. Wolseley's recommendations, based upon personal observations, would carry considerable weight in deciding exactly how to deal with the rebels.

Travelling up the Yangtze, the observant colonel found a harvest of misery and suffering wherever the Taipings had touched the land. In Nanking itself, the people were wretched and starving. As in Russia after the Bolsheviks seized power, money and trade were abolished and the citizens were completely dependent upon rations the government doled out with a patriarchal hand. The smallest crimes against the order were punished with unusual severity. In the 'New Jerusalem' (Nanking) the heads of the decapitated were publicly displayed. Adulterers were bound in oil-soaked rags and set aflame like Nero's 'Christian torches'.

Since entering his new capital, the Heavenly Young Brother of Jesus Christ, as the leader styled himself, lived secluded from all society except that of his generals (who were elevated to the exalted position of 'kings'), his eighty-eight wives, and a host of female servants and concubines who catered to his slightest whims. Wolseley soon learned why there were at least two women for every man in the city, for with 'admirable discrimination' the best-looking females were spared from the general massacre that followed a Taiping victory. Nor were the kings of the movement handicapped by the tenth commandment; they had frequent revelations similar to those of their master which permitted them to transfer another man's wife to their own harem. By the time of his visit, Wolseley recognized that 'Christ's Brother' was fast becoming a harem sluggard. Not unlike some of the great conquerors of the past, the leadership was undermined by good living and bad women.

The English officer was well received. He was given rooms in one of the king's palaces where his wants were generously supplied. After dispensing his official duty of informing the Taipings of the terms of the Peking treaties, he was given the freedom of the city and surrounding country. For a week he sketched and made notes. To his amazement, he found not one church or place of worship. As far as he could see, the only virtue their religion held was freedom from idolatry. He was equally unimpressed with their military strength. The rebels were poorly armed and what zeal they possessed was for plunder. The fortifications reminded him of the castles of toy bricks and cards he built as a boy. Consequently, in his report, he described the Taipings as militarily weak and anticipated their eventual ruin. The strength of the rebels, he observed, was to be found in the weakness of the Imperial Government. Though this was controverted by British officials who lived in China for years, subsequent events vindicated his observations.

His old comrade from Crimean days, Major Charles Gordon, soon to be known as 'Chinese' Gordon, helped to prove him right. Gordon took command of a foreign-led Chinese legion in 1863. This force of 3,000, officially known as the 'Ever Victorious Army', had been created along Western lines and capably led – until he fell – by an American soldier of fortune, Frederick Townshend Ward. With this small army, consisting largely of enlisted prisoners led by white adventurers, Gordon won thirty pitched battles, took one walled town after another, and did not halt until he reached Nanking. Madness entered the beleaguered city before the imperial armies. The Heavenly Younger Brother, after instructing his starving followers to eat grass, took his own life by drinking a cocktail of gold-leaf stirred into wine.

Actually, for some time it had been debated by the British command in China whether Wolseley or Gordon should lead the Ever Victorious Army against the rebels. Wolseley felt that they made the right decision in selecting his friend. When Gordon returned from China, Wolseley said to him laughingly, 'How differently events might have turned out had I been sent on that mission instead of you. I should have gone there with the determination of wiping out the rebellion and becoming myself Emperor of China!'[41]

# CHAPTER FIVE

# THE BURNING EDGE OF WAR

AFTER four years of perilous service, braving shipwreck, pestilence and battle, Wolseley was given a substantial leave of eighteen months. As an idler he hunted and courted, and visited Paris to study painting. Returning to Ireland, Wolseley spent a week-end with the Fortescues where he met the beautiful Miss Louisa Erskine (the future Mrs Wolseley) and fell 'most dreadfully in love'. Not being one of the marrying kind, he tried to forget her; and the best way to forget was to buy a couple of horses and spend much of the winter fox-hunting in County Cork. The season had hardly begun when he realized the need for a third horse. He was on his way to buy the animal he already had in mind, when he stopped at the village post office to pick up his mail. The newspapers reported an international crisis that threatened to draw Britain into war with the Federal government of the not-so-united United States. An official telegram at the bottom of the mail ordered him to be ready to embark in four days. Wolseley never bought that third horse.

Britain's rights on the sea had been violated. A Federal warship under Captain Wilkes had stopped a British Royal Mail steamer, the *Trent*, on November 9th, 1861, and carried off two Confederate envoys on their way to Europe. The North, depressed by early defeats and annoyed by the British Government's unguarded expression of sympathy for the South, hailed Captain Wilkes's feat as a victory and treated him as a national hero. While the bold captain was receiving the thanks of Congress, a storm of protest arose in Britain which threatened to sweep the nation into war. British blood 'boiled', as the Queen herself expressed it. Palmerston, the Prime Minister, reacted in the customary high-handed, precipitate manner, demanding the release of the prisoners and an apology. His strong protest was backed by a show of force: reinforcements were to be poured into Canada immediately. At the time, there was only one regular battalion of the British army in all Canada, but, wrote the Secretary of State for War, 'we shall soon iron the smile out of their face.'

War seemed imminent when Wolseley reported to Colonel Mackenzie, the quartermaster-general in the China War, who asked him to serve as his assistant once more. Mackenzie requested that he and his special service officers should be sent by the next swift mail steamer so that they would arrive ahead of the troops and prepare their reception. But the War Office insisted on assigning them to passage on the notoriously slow and unseaworthy *Melbourne*, which possessed the single virtue of being ready to sail immediately. Mackenzie and his officers knew her well by reputation as an uncomfortable 'lame duck' that had been condemned as a transport in the Crimean War and had broken down repeatedly during the China War. Their argument against employing the *Melbourne* was well understood, but the Government was concerned with the political, not the military aspects of their departure. Because of the sobering effect that it would produce in Washington, they wanted to announce in Parliament as quickly as possible the embarkation of these officers; they wanted to show the Americans that Britain meant business.

The *Melbourne* was not out to sea more than a few days when her unseaworthiness became apparent. Encountering dirty weather, the ship began to tumble and roll frantically. Her convoy, the frigate H.M.S. *Orpheus*, which was to guard her from roving Federal cruisers commanded by impetuous captains like Wilkes, was soon lost sight of and never found again during the voyage. As the weather grew more tempestuous, the ship shuddered as each wave hit her and the sea spouted in at all the portholes. Constant repairs were necessary to keep her afloat.

After nearly a month at sea, 'cabin'd, cribb'd, confined', they neared the Nova Scotian shores. Arriving safely at Sydney Harbour, as if by a miracle, they were greeted by the news that the crisis had passed. Largely because of the wise counsel of Prince Albert, the Government decided to forgo an apology and expressed its satisfaction with the release of the envoys and the assurance that Wilkes had seized them without orders. Though the tension was eased, the recent arrivals were greatly saddened by the further news that Prince Albert had died. They all felt a deep sympathy for their widowed Queen.

From the inhospitable shore of Sydney Harbour, where the land was covered with snow and most of the inhabitants spoke only Gaelic, the *Melbourne* proceeded to Halifax where three transports had already disembarked their troops many days before, though they had departed from England long after the *Melbourne*. Of course, everyone was happy that the leaky old tub had made it at all. At one point, the ship was in such a bad way that the alternative of landing at New York was considered. If such had been the case and war had broken out, most of the staff of the Canadian army would have become the first prisoners of war.

It was originally intended that since winter was late in coming to Canada, the transports might sail up the St Lawrence as far as Rivière du Loup, the eastern terminus of the Grand Trunk railway, where they could be sped by rail to the interior. In the dramatic race with winter for Rivière du Loup, only one transport reached it in time. The others had to turn back to Halifax. The troops would have to be sent overland on a 'snow road' operating between New Brunswick and Canada.

To hasten the staff on their way to Montreal before the troops, permission was requested from Washington to allow them to travel from Boston to Canada by rail. It was a preposterous situation: asking consent for officers of the Canadian army to travel across the territory of a neighbouring nation so as to be in a better position to fight them, if necessary. To prevent an untoward incident in Boston, where the hysteria resulting from the *Trent* affair might still be present, the officers were cautioned to appear as inconspicuous as possible, even to the extent of removing military titles written before their names on the baggage.

Stepping off the Cunard mail steamer in Boston harbour, it soon became evident that there was no danger; Wolseley and his fellow officers were treated with kindness and consideration. Wolseley renewed the acquaintance of an American he had met in China, who took him on a tour of the city. When they visited the Stock Exchange, he was welcomed by a 'sort of ovation'.

The trip to Montreal was cold and dreary. In a few days the assistant quartermaster-general was ordered to Rivière du Loup to arrange the necessary accommodation for the daily detachments of 200 men who arrived by sled from St John, New Brunswick, and were transhipped by rail to Montreal. While in India and China, Wolseley frequently wrote of his desire to be quartered in Canada, 'that paradise of soldiers'. Next to Corfu, it was regarded as the best station in the British army. Now he was overwhelmed by a monotonous life in this cheerless, primitive village. There was a shortage of reading material and the snow offered little challenge to his sketching ability. Learning to skate and to walk in snow-shoes provided temporary amusement.

In March, Wolseley was happily transferred to Montreal, the head-quarters of the army in Canada, where he took on the duties of deputy quartermaster-general during the absence of Colonel Mackenzie in England. The demands of his office were light and the opportunities for social life seemed limitless. During the long winter there was skating, toboganning and sleighing, which were replaced by shooting, fishing and cricket during the summer months. The people were hospitable, and the young ladies most charming. Society being less restrained than in England, the young men and women associated together quite freely. The one great difficulty was remaining single, for these pleasant relationships often led to 'imprudent' marriages. The Canadian women, though attractive, were poor. Several impressionable young officers had to be sent home in a hurry to keep them from unfortunate marital entanglements.

When ordered to America, Wolseley regarded the move as another 'rung on the ladder', for war with the North seemed imminent and with its advent the opportunities for distinction would be multiplied. The chances for war after the *Trent* affair were still good. The sympathy of England as reflected in the press and society was wholly with the South. Not that the English favoured the institution of slavery. They emphatically did not. Rather, the conservative ruling class had a natural affinity for a people whose blood and traditions resembled their own. Stronger than their sympathy for the Confederacy was a basic antagonism towards the democratic North. Aristocratic Englishmen never reconciled themselves to the Great Republic of the West. They looked with favour upon its destruction through civil war. *The Times* wrote gleefully of the possibility of having 'the bubble of the Republic' pricked.

Wolseley's attitude was typical. He favoured recognition and support of Dixie only to the extent of ensuring the division of the Republic into weaker states. He even feared a complete Southern victory that might reunite most of the northern and western states (except for New England) with Jefferson Davis as President, 'thereby reconstituting a government which would be more powerful than it is in our interests to have established anywhere under one recognized head upon this continent.' He liked the people from the South, but he had no great love for the Confederacy; 'indeed most of my good wishes', he confided to Dick, 'arise from my dislike to the people of the United States, taking them generally, and my delight at seeing their swagger and *bunkum* rudely kicked out of them.'[1]

He differed with most European military observers who felt there were no lessons to be learned from a vulgar brawl between hastily recruited civilians. Always ready to consider the adoption by the British military system of new methods as revealed by these virile armies fighting under ever-changing circumstances, Wolseley studied the campaigns carefully. Dissatisfied with the meagre information that reached him in Canada, he decided to take what leave remained to him and visit the war zones.

Should he visit the Federals or the Confederates? Since a rupture with the North seemed likely, it might be wise to gain some experience in their country. On the other hand, he had developed a great admiration for General Lee and hoped to see him personally. Furthermore, there was less reliable information about Southern plans and operations, for no English officer had yet penetrated the Southern lines, though many had visited the Union army. His friend William Muir, the chief medical officer, who also planned to take his leave south of the border, suggested one should join the headquarters of the Federal army and the other that of the Confederate army; afterwards they could compare notes. So they tossed a coin to decide the direction each would take. Wolseley won and elected to go south. This 'soldier's holiday' would entail great risks. It would be difficult to cross over Northern territory to enter Southern lines, and if he were caught, he might be treated as a spy. Certainly his own government would not approve his conduct at a time when relations with the United States were strained. He placed his commission in jeopardy.

Wolseley began his two-months' leave to visit a war armed with letters of introduction to prominent men of the South written by Confederates and their sympathizers in Canada. A strange American custom, he thought; many of these 'open sesame' billets were written by persons with whom he was only barely acquainted and addressed to individuals they often knew only slightly. When he reached Baltimore, a city with pronounced Southern sympathies and occupied by Federal troops, his letters of introduction opened doors and made him new friends, and he was agreeably surprised to find that the 'better classes' of the South 'approach nearer in manners our people at home'.[2]

The very first day in Baltimore, Wolseley was invited to a ball and offered the companionship of an attractive Southern belle. Astonished at being allowed to drive her to and from the ball without a chaperon, he soon learned that the parents in this part of the world trusted their daughters in the company of a young English gentleman, which was sufficient guarantee to the well-born people of Maryland. These ladies of the South with their 'unspeakable charm' seemed to exercise a great fascination over him. When he met the beautiful nieces of General John B. Magruder, C.S.A., in Montreal several weeks before, he immediately fell in love with both of them. They were so modest and kind; only when they spoke of Yankees did they show another side to their sweet personalities. Dr William H. Russell, also visiting the South at this time, told how painful it was to hear a delicate little maid with a silvery voice say, 'I am so delighted to hear that the Yankees in Fortress Monroe have got typhus fever; I hope it may kill them all.' It was as if she had remarked, 'I hear all the snakes in Virginia are dying of poison.'[3]

The sound of cannon fire at Antietam, twenty-eight miles away, spurred Wolseley on in his efforts to reach the Confederate headquarters. While he was preparing to leave Baltimore, he met the Honourable Frank Lawley, a former Member of Parliament and an adventurous *Times* correspondent, who had the distinction of having been Gladstone's private secretary and resembling George Washington. Lawley was on his way south for a story, so they agreed to run the Federal blockade together. Their mutual host in Baltimore made arrangements to move them along the 'underground railway'.

Their journey began in style as they rode a two-horse buggy through well-cultivated lands and stayed at a succession of country houses owned by secessionist gentlemen, one of whom was a Calvert descended from Lord Baltimore. The way grew difficult as the interviews with Federal cavalry patrols became more disagreeable and when they had to take lodgings one night in an inn. As English gentlemen accustomed to the luxury of their own bed, they balked as the innkeeper offered them a bed to share. But since it was the established custom of this strange land for two or even three men to sleep together in one bed, they made the best of a bad situation – one of them slept on the floor. Actually neither of them got much sleep because the room was alive with vermin.

Only after many disappointments did they find a smuggler along the Potomac who was willing to risk taking two conspicuous Englishmen across the river. To cross the broad Potomac (in reality more an arm of the Atlantic than a river since it was nearly ten miles wide at this point) without being detected by gunboats or a patrol, proved more difficult than the travellers imagined. Hour after hour they were slipped along the northern shore of the river by the smugglers, who showed an obvious distaste for handling such English-looking contraband. Gunboats equipped with powerful telescopes that swept the shore steamed up and down; and then with little warning a patrol boat landed near the shack in which they tried to conceal themselves. A Federal officer and seven men made straight for their door. Since it was no longer possible to escape detection, the *Times* man put on a bold front and stepped forward to greet them. He told the officer that he and his companion were duck-hunting and asked if a boat could be hired to pursue their sport. The officer answered curtly that no hunting was now permitted on the river. While Lawley asked him how they could get back to Washington, Wolseley stepped up and offered the lieutenant a cigar. The cheroot tipped the balance against suspicion. The officer smiled, adopted a co-operative manner and told them how they could take a steamer to Washington in the morning. Though they posed as hunters, he never asked to see their guns, and thereby missed the opportunity of making a distinguished colonel of the British army his prisoner.

That evening coffee, sugar, and Englishmen were loaded into a little cutter by the smuggler and his two sons. It was a perfect night for a crossing, misty and smooth. Occasionally, when a gunboat could be heard approaching, they would stop rowing and lie down below the gunwale. Once on the Virginia side, they paddled up a small creek for a mile or so before making a landing. Each of the passengers handed the smuggler twenty dollars in gold. A few weeks later the smuggler was captured carrying others across the Potomac and was sent to prison.

Continuing their journey south, it was not long before they were picked up by a Confederate patrol. The officer in charge was an extremely polite young gentleman who apologized for placing them under arrest. He took them into custody to his headquarters at Fredericksburg, which in a few weeks would become the bloody focal point of the war. The English travellers were quickly released with more apologies and allowed to board a train for Richmond. The trip was rough, and they had to stand all the way because the train was crowded with the sick and wounded of Lee's army moving from the front. A great stench clung to this human wreckage and at every jolt the badly wounded and amputees would moan. It was a disagreeable experience even for a battle-hardened veteran. Lawley nearly fainted.

The Confederate capital was densely crowded. At the railway station an armed guard with fixed bayonets was employed to keep open a passage through the throngs of relatives who sought their loved ones from among the wounded. The streets were equally jammed with traffic. At the hotels they had to elbow their way to the reception desks, only to be told there were no rooms available, for the Congress was in session. With luck, the weary Englishmen found uncomfortable quarters in a second-rate hotel. They expected to have a refreshing cup of tea until they were told that it sold for sixteen dollars a pound.

Again all doors were open to the English colonel. General Randolph, the Secretary of War, was 'kindness itself'. When Wolseley expressed a desire to see the battle-grounds around Richmond, Captain Lee, formerly of the U.S. Navy, a brother to the commander of the Army of Northern Virginia, was assigned as one of his guides. To wander across the fields with so many freshly-marked graves 'where lately two English-speaking armies had met in deadly strife was a sad but an instructive opportunity for a British colonel'.[4]

Anxious to be on his way (for his leave time was running short), he asked for permission to visit Lee's army. General Randolph responded with alacrity by signing his passport to visit the front and by writing a personal note to General Lee which stated: 'I have not asked Colonel Wolseley to take the usual oath that he would disclose nothing of what he sees here to our enemies, because I know I can rely upon the honor of an English officer.'[5] Wolseley was deeply touched.

Another miserable journey over the same Virginia Central Railroad brought them to a railway terminus in the beautiful but battle-scarred Shenandoah valley. Four dreary days later, travelling with an ambulance train, the only means of transport available, they reached Winchester, six miles from Confederate headquarters. The war at this time was between campaigns. Lee's army was recovering from the indecisive Maryland venture, while McClellan's remained on the other side of the Potomac, slowly, deliberately renewing its strength, despite Lincoln's urgent requests to the Federal commander for action.

Having presented the adjutant-general with their letters, the two visitors were taken to see the commander-in-chief. Lee watched them approach, the one with a strong resemblance to George Washington and the other spare, erect and soldier-like, obviously a military man. Wolseley was somewhat diffident, remembering how he had always regarded 'travelling gentlemen' at the front as an absolute nuisance. But he was immediately put at ease by the general's kindly face and stately courtesy.

Lee discussed the war and the recent action in Maryland. As he spoke in a frank, open way, Wolseley was impressed with the dignity of his speech. Though no one would ever accuse Wolseley of being humble, he felt strangely insignificant in the general's presence, awed by his inherent greatness. He seemed taller and more massive than he was, and when he looked at Wolseley with his handsome, benevolent dark-brown eyes, they seemed to search his heart. It was inconceivable that this man had any ordinary human weakness. Wolseley believed if he had lived among the ancients, they would have worshipped him as a demigod. After a long and varied life in which he met virtually all the great men of his time, Wolseley wrote, 'I have met two men whom I prized as being above all the world I have ever known, and the greater of these two was General Lee.'[6] (The other was General Charles 'Chinese' Gordon.)

Lee asked one of his colonels to escort the English visitors about the camp. Wolseley had seen many European armies in the field, but never one so completely devoid of the 'pomp and circumstance of war in and around their encampments'. The small headquarters tents were pitched at various angles over rocky ground, with two or three officers crowded into each. A large farm-house stood close by, which in any other army would have become the general's residence; but since liberties with private property were forbidden, Lee was careful not to set a bad example himself. There were no guards or aides-de-camp, only wagons drawn up and left without any semblance of regularity. And when the men approached the commander it was with marked respect; yet, there was 'none of that bowing and flourishing of forage-cap which occurs in the presence of European generals'.[7]

The visiting party drove on a few miles to Bunker's Hill to meet the renowned 'Stonewall' Jackson. Fearing that he might be quiet, if not morose, they were happily surprised by his smiling countenance and affable manner. Though he appeared a bit shy as he received them and fumbled with their hats until he found a place to put them down, in conversation he was more sure of himself and he gave them an hour-long dissertation about Durham Cathedral, its architecture, history and setting, pausing now and then to cross-examine his listeners about their national monument. Obviously, he had no intention of allowing his guests, honourable Englishmen to be sure, to probe military subjects and ask questions that might prove embarrassing. Wolseley, recognizing his desire to preserve military secrecy, confined himself to asking such innocent and ordinary questions as, what recollection did he take with him from Britain upon which his memory dwelt most? Jackson reflected for a moment and answered enthusiastically, 'The seven lancet windows in York Minster.'

As Wolseley looked into his strange 'blue eyes, and studied the movements of his calm, frank, and charming face as the sentences came slowly out of the firmly set and determined mouth', he understood the influence the mighty Stonewall exercised over his soldiers. It was a complete self-assurance, based upon an absolute trust in God, that inspired men to utter devotion. This great hero, as Wolseley described him, reminded him strongly of Macaulay's description of the Roundheads. If Jackson had fought in the English civil war, he 'would have been more at home amongst Cromwell's Ironsides'; Lee, the 'proud cavalier', on the other hand, 'would certainly have fought for his king had he lived when Rupert charged at Naseby'.[8]

Later he visited General Longstreet, Lee's other corps commander. The esteemed and hard-hitting Longstreet invited him to inspect part of his force. It was a sight he would never forget. The men were wretchedly dressed and poorly shod. He was told that some who wore only rags and were barefooted stayed out of the ranks rather than face the humiliating ordeal of marching before an English officer.* Though many of them were men of large property, they served as privates, while officers who were sons of small farmers of inferior social position frequently led them. Wolseley tried to distinguish the gentleman of property from among the mass, but he found it impossible except, perhaps, for an occasional soldier who carried a tooth-brush stuck in the buttonhole of his jacket. His face could not conceal his astonishment at the unmilitary sight of tattered shirt-tails and ragged breeches as Hood's men filed past. 'Never mind the raggedness, Colonel,' Lee said softly, 'the enemy never sees the backs of my Texas Brigade.'

Wolseley knew that it took more than clothes to make a soldier. And these were *soldiers*, vigorous and healthy, with an elastic tread; more than a match, he believed, for the mobs of Irish and German mercenaries who fought for fifteen dollars a month in a cause they knew little or nothing about. In his lifetime he witnessed many parades of sartorially splendid warriors with well-polished accoutrements, but he never saw one composed of men who 'looked more like work'. The future head of the British army came away that afternoon with the conviction that young citizen-soldiers with spirit could be moulded into fighting men.

Wolseley returned to Montreal to write an article describing his visit to Lee's headquarters which was published in the January (1863) issue of *Blackwood's Magazine* and received with great interest in Britain and America. His article offered cogent arguments for the recognition of the Confederacy to safeguard the position of Britain's possessions in North America. Besides serving her selfish aims, England should interfere in the name of humanity to end this fratricidal struggle in which 'the military despotism of one portion of the States under the dictatorship of an insignificant lawyer [Abraham Lincoln] attempts to crush out the freedom of the rest'. He warned his countrymen that once the North had subjugated 'the descendants of our banished cavaliers', their insolence and arrogance would know no bounds, and might very well provoke a war with Britain.[9]

The first eight years in service Wolseley had been constantly in the field, always at the front, always fighting. Quick promotions had followed from ensign to lieutenant-colonel, every new rank was won at the point of the sword. Now in Canada, where the opportunity for active service

---

* They were less shy when meeting Yankees. One ragged private when taunted by the enemy replied, 'We 'uns don't put on our good clothes to butcher hogs.'

once seemed so good, each passing month became a torment to Wolseley, saddled as he was to a humdrum desk job that 'an intelligent lance-corporal could do with ease'. He could well complain as Napoleon once did to Talleyrand, 'What a beautiful fix we are in now – peace has been declared!'

At times he grew very irritable and depressed. He asked for employment in China reorganizing the imperial army. The request was denied. Wolseley ached for active soldiering, even if he had to 'go to Timbuctoo to get away'. As Sherman was marching through the deep South with 'an excess of ruthlessness' that was to hasten the end of the Civil War, Wolseley wrote of 'these wasted years' in America that 'have pushed away the ladder from under me and I am left hanging here without any prospects ... I am of no use to anyone and all my visions of being able to advance have all vanished.'[10] His thoughts turned to leaving the army and becoming a civil engineer, a profession for which he felt qualified by training and experience.

Part of Wolseley's dissatisfaction stemmed from his financial burdens, for he maintained an expensive establishment and refused to deny himself an extravagant social life. The money, of course, was spent with a purpose: to cultivate important friendships and influence the 'right' people. 'If I lived otherwise,' he explained to his sister Matilda, 'I might perhaps have a few pounds a year to send home, but I should not stand where I do in the world, and as I look upon myself as the only one of my family ever likely to make anything that those who came after me are likely to be proud of, I consider the money I squander as well spent.'[11] Nevertheless, if he had remained in the East, Wolseley pointed out, he could have saved much of his £800 a year.

The greatest drain on his resources was actually his family. He made no objection to supporting his mother or giving money to his unwed sister, but his brothers were another matter. Garnet, taking on the responsibilities of a father, tried to embark them on a successful career. Dick, once having earned his degree as a physician and entered the army, in time became a successful brigade surgeon. Whatever money was loaned to him was invariably paid back. Fred was an inventor who went to Australia to seek his fortune. Garnet backed him financially in all his enterprises, but they failed through lack of business acumen and brought about the loss of a considerable sum to his generous brother.

Finally, there was George who 'has been the drawback to my happiness'. George, with Garnet's aid, purchased appointments in the army, but the young officer was constantly in debt and when he could get no more money from Garnet, he borrowed from Dick and their mother. His colonel brother thought him 'the damndest young fool I have ever let loose on the army'.[12] After going deep into debt himself to pay his youngest brother's bills, Garnet began to fear he was 'worthless' and 'it would be better that Master George should leave the service and go to the devil quietly in Australia ... Looking after sheep or breaking stones is far more in his line than honest soldiering.'[13] George eventually rose in the army to become known as General Sir George Wolseley.

With the overthrow of the Southern Confederacy, the United States, now the strongest military power in the world, was free to use her full weight in foreign affairs. Napoleon III was forced to withdraw his troops from Mexico, and the British began to feel the pressure of American ill-will. England's un-neutral policy of recognizing the belligerency of the South and allowing privateers such as the *Alabama* to be built in her ship-yards, left a hard residue of animosity in the United States long after Lee's surrender. With relations strained by America's surly post-war posture, the Fenians hoped to provoke a war; after all, England's difficulty was Ireland's opportunity.

The Fenian Brotherhood was founded in New York in 1859 with the intention of liberating Ireland to establish a Republic (a kindred society in Ireland itself was called the Irish Revolutionary Brotherhood). Following the great famine of 1846–7, which many believed was a cold-blooded English plot, hundreds of thousands of Irishmen had migrated to the New World, carrying with them little more than their ancient grievances. Hate is a fertile field for agitators, and thousands of Irish-Americans were recruited by the Fenians, among them veterans of the war who were to be organized into effective militia units. Many blue-coated Irishmen marched home from Appomattox with the cry, 'On to Dublin.'

The bellicose Celts, claiming hundreds of thousands of adherents, met in Philadelphia after the war and set up a republic without a territory. They elected a senate, a president – who appointed a cabinet – and rented a huge mansion, over which the Irish flag was raised and before which guards in green uniforms were stationed, part of the republic's great army which was being organized from Maine to Texas. Letters of marque were issued and a navy of Irish privateers, *Alabama* style, was promised. All this was to be supported by bonds sold to Irish servant-girls and the like. Always, there was a lot of wild talk of knotting the tail of the British lion by invading Ireland and burning London with Greek fire. But an uprising in Ireland soon proved abortive and an invasion from America was pronounced impractical. Thus, the way to Dublin, it was decided – but not without a split in the movement – was through Canada.

The danger to Canada with its straggling, ill-defined, virtually undefended frontier became acute by 1866. Bands of Fenian filibusters began to gather along the border, encouraged by an irresponsible anti-English press and the calm countenance of the United States Government. The American politicians were not anxious to break up these armed bands of Irishmen: Radical Republicans enjoyed the embarrassment suffered by the Johnson administration; Democrats, with the first post-war election coming up in November, were more dependent upon the Irish vote than ever; and any politician, in or out of office, who supported a programme that could be construed as pro-English, committed political suicide. Yet, if the Fenians were not restrained, they might bring on the general war they worked towards.

The true defence of British colonies, according to the views of the home Government, was that they lived under the aegis of the name of Britain, and that a war with them meant war with Britain. Therefore, the regular army in Canada never numbered more than 18,000 to augment the local militia, despite the danger of war with Americans during the early 'sixties.

The Canadian people accepted the challenge of the Brotherhood. Volunteers swelled the ranks of the militia. To test the efficiency of the militia officers trained by the Canadian military school, a Camp of Instructions for Cadets was established at La Prairie, nine miles outside Montreal, on the other side of the St Lawrence. Appointed as commandant of the first cadet training-school in Dominion history, was Garnet Wolseley, recently made a brevet colonel. Under his able direction, the experiment proved a great success. Ignoring time-honoured traditions that were fast becoming obsolete, and placing little stress on childish parade-ground manœuvres, Wolseley taught them the practical side of war. This was the kind of employment that suited him; and he was very proud of the results, feeling the Canadian Government had taken a significant step in improving the military efficiency of its local forces.

Throughout the winter of 1865–6 there were Fenian 'scares'. No leaves were granted to officers, though Wolseley felt unaffected because he was 'too poor' to go anywhere. To prepare for possible attack farther along the line, troops were sent to western regions of Canada to occupy fresh places. Wolseley toured this territory, holding interviews with mayors and corporations, making patriotic speeches to stimulate their loyalty and to try and 'get them to provide as much accommodation for troops as possible at their own expense'.[14]

By March, Fenian sabre-rattling became so alarming that the Canadian Government called out 10,000 volunteers. So great was the response that there was a surplus of 4,000, largely because many discharged men came back to the colours. As the tension mounted, the volunteer force was increased to 25,000. The mother country, pleased by this outburst of loyalty in Canada, promptly complied with the request for two additional regiments to be sent from England.

The Fenians launched their general attack at the end of May; but owing to faulty planning, lack of transportation in particular, the only point where the threat did not disappear was along the Niagara River. Trains laden with Fenians arrived in Buffalo, a city large enough to conceal their activities, at least for a few days, from the Federal authorities. On June 1st, Colonel O'Neil, a former Union cavalry officer, and 800 fighting Irishmen crossed the river in a tug-towed barge and occupied the village of Fort Erie on the south-east tip of the fertile Niagara Peninsula. Here the local American consul joined them and raised the Stars and Stripes to Fenian cheers.

The Canadians were as poorly prepared for war as the Fenians. Though Ottawa had precise information about the impending attack from its spies, it allowed itself to be taken by surprise. Moreover, because economy-minded politicians had withheld up-to-date weapons and provisions for the militia, the cavalry went into the Niagara campaign without carbines, haversacks, blankets, or cooking utensils of any kind. Nor was the militia infantry any better off. If it had not been for the charity of townsmen on the line of march, many would have gone hungry.

General George Napier, who commanded the province of Ontario, was a recognized incompetent. Instead of taking all available forces and marching on the filibusters himself, he sent bodies of confused, ill-prepared volunteers under separate and totally inexperienced officers, many of whom were not even acquainted with the men they were given to command.

Colonel Peacock, in charge of a large body composed largely of volunteers, ignored the railway that ran parallel to his line of advance and exhausted his men by marching them through great heat, with knapsacks, down the wrong road; but then he was unaware that a shorter route existed, for the only map he carried was a corner from a postal map.

Meanwhile, a second force, led by Colonel Booker, landed at Port

Colburne and marched along Lake Erie towards Fort Erie, hoping to effect a junction with Peacock's force, not realizing the latter would be thrown completely off schedule by his roundabout march.

The Fenians, learning of Booker's advance, broke camp and came out to meet them before Peacock's force marched far enough south to be of assistance. The Irish surprised the 'Queen's Own' at Ridgeway. After much skirmishing, the Canadians took the offensive and charged. The Fenians, being mostly Civil War veterans, stood their ground boldly and raked the redcoats with a volley. When the volunteers showed signs of wavering, the Irish counter-attacked. At the same moment, some nervous redcoats sighted a few Fenian leaders on horseback and cried in panic, 'Cavalry!' Instead of forming a square, as they were ordered, the green volunteers stampeded to the rear, chased by the exuberant Hibernians for nearly three miles.

Wolseley was on his way. As soon as the news of the invasion reached Montreal, General Sir John Michel, commanding the army in Canada, dispatched his smart young colonel post-haste to deal with the situation. He was told to 'coach' General Napier 'and prevent him from doing anything foolish'.[15] Arriving in Toronto, Wolseley gave the bewildered general instructions on how to deal with the problem, which were accepted without demur. Then he collected what military odds and ends he could before departing for the scene of conflict.

Detraining at Frenchman's Creek, the colonel took his horse out of its box and rode out alone towards Fort Erie to reconnoitre. As he came towards the village, he saw a United States cutter anchored in the middle of the Niagara with an enormous barge astern of her crammed with hundreds of Fenians. Continuing along the water's edge to where the Irish had camped, he found evidence of surgeon's work, garbage, and broken jugs which smelled of whisky. Though short of other provisions, the Fenians seemed to be well supplied with whisky, which in those days could be bought for as little as twenty-five cents a gallon. A lone, drunken Irishwoman, on seeing an English officer surveying the scene, picked up an amputated leg by the ankle, flourished it like a weapon and bawled, 'God save ould Ireland.'*

In the afternoon, Wolseley and another English officer rowed out to the U.S.S. *Michigan*. They were courteously received by the naval officer in charge and by General Barry, who commanded the

---

* The Fenian Sisterhood never attracted many members. The proposal was made to take them into the Brotherhood at the Cleveland convention of the Robert's wing of the movement, but it was voted down for the simple reason that women were unable to keep a secret.

Buffalo military district. Wolseley learned how the Fenians had returned to Fort Erie after the Battle of Limestone Ridge, as the Irish called it, to fight another spirited skirmish with a small body of Canadians who were brought up by a tug. The redcoats were overwhelmed, while crowds of Americans who had gathered on the other side of the river cheered the Irish on. But finding it impossible to get supplies and reinforcements from Buffalo because of the arrival of the United States' cutter, Colonel O'Neil decided to haul his army back to the friendly side of the Niagara. The *Michigan* captured them in mid stream where they were now being held. The American officers promised Wolseley they would be taken back to Buffalo.

Instead of winning the support of the United States Government, as the Fenians had hoped, the administration now turned its hand against the Brotherhood. President Johnson proclaimed against the Fenian invaders on June 6th and sent General Meade, the victor of Gettysburg, to restore order on the border. Most of the Fenians taken were deprived of their arms and paroled on the condition that they abandon their scheme to invade Canada.

The day after O'Neil's force was captured by the *Michigan*, Wolseley was ordered to take command of a mixed brigade of regulars and militia-men at Stratford, a railway station near Georgian Bay, Lake Huron. By now the British colonel was well known among the soldiers of Canada by his reputation. Stories of his gallant conduct in Burma, the Crimea, and during the Mutiny, and the many wounds he suffered as a consequence, were related around many a camp fire – and, as is common when such tales are told, they were frequently exaggerated. During a parade in which Wolseley was taking part, one spectator was overheard relating to another what he had heard about this soldier: 'Do you see that officer over thar with the cocked hat? Wal, that's the commanding officer, and they tell me that he has so many bullets in him that if you'd shake him he'd rattle.'[16]

The volunteers of Canada soon swore by him. They found him thought-ful and cheerful, yet firm, and declared themselves ready to follow him anywhere.

The Canadian Government followed a strangely vacillating policy regarding the Fenians. One month they would treat the threat of invasion as serious; the next month they would treat it as a ridiculous chimera. Wolseley remained at Stratford only a few weeks and then was ordered back to Montreal to resume his original duties. Scarcely unpacked, he was told he was being given command of a miniature army at Thorold, a village on the Welland Canal, to protect the Niagara frontier and the canal, which the Irish threatened to blow up.

Wolseley was anxious to become commandant of the Camp of Observation, but 'nervous' about some line colonel being given the assignment before the decision became final. Since he had hardly done any regimental duty after 1858, there were those in the army, highly placed, who felt this 'upstart' staff colonel was not well enough acquainted with the regimental side of his profession to assume this important command. He nevertheless got the appointment, for his superiors entertained so high an opinion of his military ability that they invariably decided he should be sent to that point on the frontier where the menace of Fenian incursions was greatest.

If Wolseley should fail as a commander, it would not be from want of application. He undertook his duties with a vengeance, constantly exercising and drilling, especially the new militiamen who passed through his hands. He had two field days a week, and 'one grand one when we have a mimic battle and fire off any amount of H.M. Ammunitions ... It is capital practice for me,' he told Dick, 'as I am so little with troops and I now have such opportunities by learning how to handle men.'[17] He hoped the Fenians would try another invasion. 'Who knows but that I may be Sir Garnet before another six months.'[18] With a 'Sir' before his name, Wolseley reasoned, he should have an advantage when competing with any ordinary colonel.

The Fenians on the other side of the border continued to make terrible threats and exaggerated their numbers, even to the point of claiming that all the boys in the Connecticut Reform School were Fenians. They, too, conducted mock battles at Irish-American picnics by refighting the Battle of Limestone Ridge, which always concluded with an irate Irishman stamping on the Union Jack. The only real fighting they engaged in, however, was between themselves. One sober observer commented: 'The amount of whisky that was drunk was inconceivable.'[19]

With the approach of winter, the Canadian authorities decided the crisis had passed. The camp was broken up, and Wolseley returned once more to Montreal. Then in January the authorities, again alarmed by Fenian activities, called out the army. Great centres of field brigades were set up, fully equipped and ready to march. Wolseley was transferred to Toronto to organize the Toronto Brigade. In case of an invasion, the commander-in-chief in Canada promised him the command. Though the Canadian press invited 'that rabble of chicken-butchering, roost-robbing loafers, the sweepings of Five-Point grogeries and scum of Irish rascaldom' to attack, the Fenians decided not to oblige.

As winter came to an end, so did Colonel Wolseley's term as assistant quartermaster-general. The ambitious colonel was rather melancholy at the prospect of leaving the Dominion at a time when honours were to be won. Rumours of a Fenian raid were stronger than ever right up to the eve of his departure; he pictured himself 'landing at Liverpool and hearing the little boys crying out ... "Great Fenian Invasion of Canada!" '[20]

But once in Ireland, Wolseley heard nothing more of the Fenians and stirring words of war; instead his ears were tuned to the sweet words of his 'beloved Loo', that is, Miss Louisa Erskine. His love for her rekindled and burned more fiercely than before. All the solid resolutions to remain a bachelor suddenly melted away. Several times, it is true, he had been tempted to marry while in Canada. His matrimonial prospects seemed so certain that on three separate occasions hopeful but confused friends sent him annoying letters congratulating him on the 'approaching event'. But, alas, none of the maids had a large fortune and somehow or other he always managed 'to "beat off" that dreadful lee shore!'[21]

Now Wolseley weakened to the point where he decided to wed Miss Erskine. Though she was not wealthy, she was comfortably provided for by her family, and he promised his mother that the 'arrangement about my pension which I have settled upon you shall not in any way be interfered with'.[22]

'Loo', as Wolseley always called her, was not very tall, but prided herself on being the same height and proportions as the Venus de Milo. Others compared her beauty to that of the Empress Eugénie, whom she strongly resembled. She was fair-complexioned, with delicate features and golden hair which she piled on her head in Pompadour style. Her exposed ears were a special source of allure to Garnet, as were the ears of the Empress Marie Louise to Napoleon. And he admired her feet so much that later he had a cast made of her foot which he proudly displayed to his friends. Though her mind usually dwelt with affection on pretty clothing, she was a very clever and accomplished woman, who served as an intellectual companion to her husband. Garnet depended upon her to correct his letters and speeches, and especially his French, for she was quite fluent, having lived in France a long time and having been served most of her life by a French maid.

The wedding itself was postponed when Wolseley was recalled to Canada in September 1867 to serve as deputy quartermaster-general. (At thirty-four, he was the youngest officer ever selected to fill such a responsible position on the staff.) The following year, however, he managed a two-months' leave, and returned home to marry Miss Erskine on his thirty-fifth birthday. He then hastened back to Canada without her; and until she joined him in the following October, he busied himself with military map-making* and the completion of his *Soldier's Pocketbook for Field Service*.

Sir Richard Airey, quartermaster-general of the army, first proposed a practical handbook for the staff to be written by officers of his department; but the War Office, motivated by a false sense of economy, rejected the suggestion. Wolseley, who was one of the officers Airey wanted to employ in its compilation, undertook the entire job single-handed. The result was a treasury of useful information answering all possible questions that might arise in the field. It successfully augmented the *Queen's Regulations* and the *Field Exercise*, which were designed primarily for times of peace. There were concisely written articles of an original nature that described surveying, reconnoitring, and other duties of the staff officer. Besides the usual subjects of military law, tactics, etc., he instructed the private on how to clean his accoutrements and brew a pot of coffee; the 'non-combatant' officer on how to write and indent forms for stores; the general on how to manœuvre his army. There were tables of weights and measures, formulas for trigonometry, designs for filters, menus for Irish stew, exchange rates for foreign currency; even poisons and their antidotes were tabulated. Drawing on his wealth of experience, he advised on the care and feeding of elephants; told of the importance of singing on the march; described how a charge of gunpowder dissolved in water is a 'good and safe' emetic; and cautioned against improper burial at sea, reminding his readers how in Egypt at the beginning of the century the army experienced the horror of watching hundreds of bodies being washed ashore.

Being the first book of its kind to prepare soldiers for war and duties in the field, it became an immediate success. It was regarded as a standard authority in army matters, and passed through numerous editions. The War Office later decided to buy him out and distribute the work as an official publication.

The *Pocketbook* demonstrated publicly for the first time Wolseley's propensity for candid and dogmatic statements, for he deliberately used it as a medium to broadcast his advanced military views. They were not altogether popular. He offended the non-military by urging that soldiers 'be taught to despise those in civil life'. He shocked moralists by suggesting

---

* The need for a more accurate survey of the frontier area was revealed during the Fenian 'scare'. One regiment, trusting to a local map, was lost for three days in the Black Creek Swamp country north of Toronto.

that soldiers should 'not be brought into contact with the softening influences of old men and respectable women', and that false news should be given deliberately to journalists so as to deceive the enemy. The gentlemen of the press, in turn, were angered when he implied that they were a nuisance in a military campaign and often less than gentlemen. Imbibers were annoyed when he advocated temperance throughout the army.

Most of all, this presumptuous young colonel, who made no attempt to disguise his intellectual superiority, trod on some gouty toes by suggesting there were official deficiencies, and by criticizing the conduct of the British officer. This heresy was further deepened by the argument that it was not enough for an officer to be a master at drill and memorize the 'Queen's regulations'; he must have some knowledge of how men were to live as well as die. Countless lives could be saved in a campaign by tending to the creature comforts of the soldier. Too long, Wolseley insisted, had the army fought 'in the cold shade of aristocracy', as Sir Charles Napier once put it. It was essential for the officer to understand ways of providing for shelter, good health, suitable clothing; he should be a teacher, a mechanic, a cook, an amateur physician – even a father to his men.

No doubt Wolseley went too far in his denunciation of the old soldier and in rejecting the merits of rigid discipline, but he was impatient to create a better army. He made unseen enemies with his *Pocketbook*, but he was also recognized by the reformers as a leader who would fight for progress in the army at a time when it was in a dangerous state of stagnation.

# CHAPTER SIX

# REDCOATS ON THE RED RIVER

I T was a time of almost universal peace. Newspapers were never so dull. The illustrated journals, pressed for action stories, ran pictorial biographies of dead heroes, etchings of prize-winning pigs and many sketches of the newly-built Suez Canal. In Britain, economy-minded legislators spoke of drastically reducing military spending. They argued that chances for conflict had grown remote. In rebuttal Wolseley made a speech in Toronto in November 1869, pointing out that there never was a peace that lasted and that such talk by 'dreamers' could be dangerous. As if to lend support to his thesis, news came out of the great wilderness of the North American continent that there was an insurrection at Fort Garry in the Red River country.

In the late 'sixties the Red River Valley, fertile heartland of Manitoba, became the target in a confused controversy between the Hudson's Bay Company, the Dominion Government, the home Government, and the settlers. The Hudson's Bay Company held undisputed right over the territory by virtue of a charter given by Charles II. But the time had come for the company to make way for civilization. Upon the completion of schemes for federation in 1867, Dominion statesmen began to negotiate for the transfer of this land to Canada. They contended that if emigrants and capital did not come from Canada, they would press up from the United States, separated as it was from the territory by only an imaginary line drawn across the prairie. Should this occur, the newly-created Dominion could lose all the great lands of the North-West. The home Government, also concerned with the American threat, regarded the Company as an anachronism and played the role of go-between during the negotiations. Under pressure from London, the Company agreed to accept its death-sentence for £300,000 and turn these many acres, larger than all of Europe, over to the Canadian Government.

The transfer was bungled by tactless politicians. Some 12,000 settlers of the Red River region, left in the dark regarding their future, grew restive. No one bothered to explain their status or guarantee their possessions and rights. They heard only disquieting rumours of being reduced to the position of the colony of a colony, of being bought and sold 'like dumb driven cattle'. Settlers noted with alarm that English-speaking surveyors were spreading over the territory and were in an off-hand manner running chain lines across farms to which they could show no written title.

Most of the British settlers decided to await developments, trusting that their rights would ultimately be recognized under English law. But the metis half of the population, more excitable, less educated, and suspicious of change, were not so confident. During the confused interregnum between Company rule and that of Canada, the discontent of the half-breeds, whose French-Canadian forefathers had contracted alliances with squaws, flamed into rebellion. A provisional government under the eccentric leadership of Louis Riel was proclaimed at Fort Garry on November 2nd, 1869. The surveyors were run off the land, and the newly-appointed lieutenant-governor, William McDougall, whose autocratic decrees preceded him, was turned back at the border. The metis were prepared to fight the Canadians, these predatory foreigners with fancy legal papers and ploughs, until their rights were guaranteed.

Though the Canadian Government made some progress in negotiations with the rebellious metis, time was running out. To allow the situation in the Red River country to remain unsettled invited the danger of intervention from the south. Riel's secretary was a Fenian,* and there was evidence from various sources that the Americans were prepared to detach the whole Hudson's Bay territory. Sir John MacDonald, head of the Dominion Government, basing his opinion on confidential reports from Washington, wrote that 'the United States Government are resolved to do all they can, short of war, to get possession of the western territory and we must take immediate and vigorous steps to counteract them.'[1]

Once force was agreed upon, Ottawa sought the support of the home Government. MacDonald favoured a mixed expedition of British regulars and Canadian militiamen because the area was still technically under the jurisdiction of the Company and, most of all, to show Washington that Canada and Britain were acting in accord in retaining the great North-West under British sovereignty. Moreover, it seemed likely that the insurgents would surrender to a mixed British force rather than one entirely Canadian.

Lieutenant-General James Lindsay was sent out from England to replace the retiring commander, Sir John Michel, and take charge of the

* Riel's flag displayed a fleur-de-lis and a shamrock on a white field, a compound of French independence and Fenianism sewn by the nuns of a near-by convent.

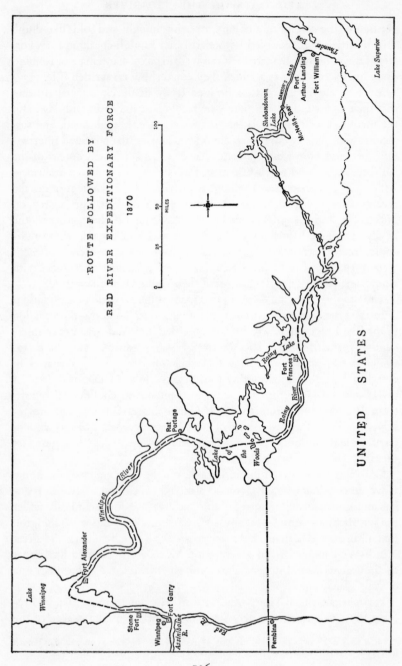

ROUTE FOLLOWED BY
RED RIVER EXPEDITIONARY FORCE
1870

preparations for the force. On the day of his arrival, April 5th, he designated Colonel Wolseley to command what was to be the last British military expedition in North America. The appointment was at first kept a secret. The Government veiled its arrangements to send a punitive force lest 'it appear they are preparing for war whilst they are professing to treat with Riel', whose delegates were on their way to the capital.[2] When the news of Wolseley's appointment was finally released, it was greeted with approval by the press and public. His earlier connections with the volunteers had made him a popular figure, and patriotic societies in Ontario, such as the 'Canada First' organization, worked energetically to stimulate public opinion on his behalf. His selection, they insisted, ensured success.

Wolseley took a keen interest in Red River affairs from the very beginning and worked to secure some sort of appointment. When he learned that commissioners were being selected to treat with the metis, he asked his friends to use their influence on his behalf. MacDonald, however, decided it would be imprudent to send a high-ranking officer on a peace mission with an 'olive branch in one hand and a revolver in the other'. Rejected as an agent of peace, Wolseley began to write reports on the requirements of a Red River force, which he circulated among the military and high-ranking politicians. His eagerness to be appointed head of these troops was no secret. Wolseley quivered with anticipation at the thought of being given his first independent command.

After much deliberation, the strength of the expedition was fixed at 1,200 men. The imperial quota consisted of the 1st Battalion, 60th Rifles (373 officers and men), a battery of the Royal Field Artillery (four 7-pounder mountain guns), a detachment of Royal Engineers, and a portion of the Army Service and Army Hospital Corps.

The officers of the 60th Rifles were an outstanding lot. Among them was Redvers Buller, destined to become one of the greatest heroes of the Victorian age and the brightest jewel in Wolseley's ring of talented military associates. At the time of the Red River expedition, Buller was only an obscure lieutenant, but Wolseley was quick to read his capacity. The colonel's attention was immediately drawn to his skill with the axe and the paddle. The country-boy from Devonshire, who spent his leave-time in Canada's woods, was a perfect outdoors man with all the attributes of an ideal Boy Scout. Wolseley, however, discovered a little-known side to Buller. Behind the blood-and-iron jingo legend was a kindly, genial man with intellectual tastes. He never began a military campaign without a miniature edition of Bacon's *Essays*. Here was a soldier who impressed all with his brusque, blunt manner, but in private, among friends, would wax eloquent about pines and quote Virgil.

The Canadian militia contributed two battalions, the 1st Ontario Rifles and the 2nd Quebec Rifles, of twenty-six officers and 350 men each. They were divided, like the 60th Rifles, into seven companies. All were armed with the new Snider rifles recently invented by Jacob Snider, the Dutch-American wine merchant with an aptitude for things mechanical. The battalions were organized under Lieutenant-Colonel Fielden in Toronto where each volunteer was first given a very strict medical examination. Those regarded as less than robust for the strenuous undertaking ahead were rejected. General Lindsay also insisted on a healthy attitude. No one was to be signed on who was seeking revenge for the death of Thomas Scott, an aggressive Orangeman executed by Riel because he challenged his authority.

Many an officer from afar, hankering after active service, sought a berth with the redcoats* going to the Red River. Few were lucky enough to be selected. One such officer was Lieutenant Hugh McCalmont. Taking leave from the 9th Lancers, he made his way across the Atlantic to Port Arthur, the Lake Superior base of the expedition, to present a letter of recommendation from Sir Hope Grant. As Sir Hope's orderly officer he had won high praise, owing in no small part to the fact that he accompanied his musical chief brilliantly on the piano. But Wolseley, who had more than enough officers, turned the soldier-pianist down flat. McCalmont, not so easily put off, insinuated it was a big country and he could always paddle his own canoe. He slept that night on the counter of the Company's store. Whether it was Mrs Wolseley, who befriended the young Lancer on her trip across Lake Superior to say good-bye to her husband, or Sir Hope's words that finally moved the commander, is not known, but the following morning Wolseley summoned McCalmont to him and asked if he knew anything about boats. When he replied that he had been a 'wet bob' at Eton for four years, Wolseley told the young Anglo-Irishman to join a party of militia.

The personnel of the force was completed when Mr Dawson, an officer of the Public Works Department, hired 100 teamsters and 400 voyageurs (skilled boatmen). Of the voyageurs, the Iroquois Indians were the best. Many of the others had signed on just to make the trip and knew nothing

---

* Soldiers in the Queen's service were called 'redcoats', but in a literal sense that term did not apply on this campaign. Only the Royal Engineers wore scarlet. The Canadian battalions were dressed in black tunics with scarlet facings. The 60th Rifles on this occasion also wore black with scarlet facings. The Royal Field Artillery dressed in their usual dark blue, as did the Military Train.

about managing the boats. They had to be weeded out. Seven men were employed as guides, and they were considered invaluable until it was discovered they were totally ignorant of the route!

The route normally taken from Canada to the Red River settlement passed through the United States, Fort Garry being only sixty miles from the border and 100 miles north of a railway line connecting with St Paul, Minnesota. It was manifestly out of the question to send troops through a foreign country where anti-British feeling was still running high. The American press raved about 'manifest destiny' and demanded the Monroe Doctrine be applied to the North-West territory. Senator Chandler of Michigan, an old friend of the Fenians, offered an insulting resolution in Congress to annex the Red River country. Thus the alternate route by way of Lake Superior, following an old canoe trail west through small lakes and rivers, was decided upon.

The overall distance confronting Wolseley's expedition was 1,200 miles. The men would be carried by rail from Toronto to Collingwood (94 miles) on the Georgian Bay; boarding a steamer, they would proceed across Lakes Huron and Superior to Thunder Bay (524 miles); the next lap was by Dawson's Road to Lake Shebandowan (48 miles); the last stretch was by boat to Fort Garry (550 miles). The last 600 miles would be the hardest. The force, carrying all its supplies through an inhospitable, primeval wilderness of rocks and poor timber, would have to work their way up a watery trail of foaming rapids and pathless lakes. Unnavigable portions, called portages, of which there were no less than forty-seven between twenty yards and a half-mile in length, demanded the additional labour of carrying all the material and dragging the boats behind them. Time was limited, for the regulars had to be back in Canada before the winter approached. Frost could be a deadly enemy. A quarter of an inch of ice could rip open the bottom of a boat crunching its way through.

Everything needed, from food to cannon, must be carried in the boats. The country was destitute of resources, and no supplies of any kind could be shipped in from the outside world. The Indians themselves starved in this land and cannibalism was not unknown. Nor could the sick and wounded be transported to safety; they must be left on shore to the mercies of the elements and the Indians.

What might appear as a gay outing on a grand scale to the ordinary civilian, could be a logistic nightmare to the man responsible for its planning. An expedition such as this required a nicety of organization beyond the comprehension of a person who had never studied military history. Wolseley spent weeks making all the necessary calculations, applying himself with exhausting thoroughness to the multitudinous details – and no detail was too small to be ignored. He knew that success depended upon organization, and experience had taught him that many more men were lost as a result of privation and sickness than from lead and steel.

Careful attention was given to the boats. They must have sufficient strength to withstand the wear and tear of dragging, yet they must be light enough not to fatigue the men unnecessarily. Birch-bark canoes, the only boat employed on this route until now, did not have sufficient capacity. Under the direction of Mr Dawson, who organized the Boat Transport Service, upwards of 200 boats were specially constructed in shipbuilding establishments in the Dominion. The wooden boats varied between twenty-five and thirty feet in length, and were fitted with masts and sails in addition to oars. The crew was to consist of from eleven to twelve soldiers and two or three voyageurs. They had a capacity for cargo of up to four tons. Each vessel was a self-sufficient unit, carrying its own tools, tents, blankets, and sixty days' provisions, though Wolseley hoped to reach Fort Garry in thirty days. Wolseley thought out the contents of each boat with exactness and decided to save freight by leaving all spirits behind.

Wolseley was neither a professed temperance man nor a teetotaller, but his experiences in India taught him that men cut off entirely from liquor for months were healthier than when they received their daily ration of grog. The fallacy that spirits were good for the men before, during, or after the march was clearly demonstrated to him by the military efficiency of the liquor-free army of General Lee. He conceded that an occasional nip was helpful on cold or rainy days until he discovered that Canadian lumberjacks, often wet and cold, drank hot tea rather than spirits. Strong drink, if anything, he was told, impaired their effectiveness.

The 'noble experiment' proved an unqualified success, though many older officers and medical men asserted that it would fail. In four months, not one tea-drinking soldier was listed as 'sick'. At the close of the campaign, Wolseley refused to consider recommending the senior medical officer for promotion on the grounds that 'he had nothing to do, there not having been any sick for him to cure'. It was a unique medical record for that time. And to the absence of alcohol was attributed the almost total absence of crime. Prohibitionists applauded his efforts and hailed him as a hero. Some soldiers, however, took a less enthusiastic view and eventually gave him the nickname of the 'tea-pot' general.

Nor was there any provision made for smokers. What tobacco was taken had to be carried by the men in their own packs. Smoking, moreover, would be permitted only about the camp fire. An uncontrolled fire in the woods could lead to a holocaust. Wolseley even limited himself to a small number of cigars, which he had freely indulged in since the Crimean War when the tobacco habit came into fashion among officers as well as privates.

Wolseley personally tested and examined all the equipment for strength, efficiency and lightness – everything from axes to cannon. It was in this way that he discovered that the regulation field axe was useless for felling trees. He had them replaced with more serviceable axes of the double-edge pattern: a pattern later adopted by the army generally.

During the second week of May 1870, an army came to life at the Crystal Palace of Toronto, whose buildings and grounds had been turned over to the military. Hundreds of denizens of the Toronto area came out daily to watch their citizen-soldiers drill and gradually take on the appearance and bearing of professional fighting men.

There were unnecessary delays arising from divided responsibility. The politicians were not willing to allow Lindsay and Wolseley a free hand in making all the arrangements. After all, the interest of patronage must be served. Contracts were assigned by officials of the Government on the basis of political complexion rather than the promise of prompt and efficient service. As the time for departure drew near, Wolseley went on to Collingwood to arrange for marine transport across the lakes to Thunder Bay and personally examined the capability of every steamer for the conveyance of the troops and supplies; but an Ottawa Minister refused to sanction the favourable terms they had arranged with the owners. The politician insisted on chartering the ships himself and paying far higher prices as a result. The accommodation of the vessels subsequently hired completely upset Wolseley's careful calculations. The change in plans and protracted negotiations that resulted from the Minister's intervention, caused a week's delay in the start of the expedition.

Wolseley interpreted these political snags as deliberate sabotage. If sufficient delay accrued, the expedition would be stillborn. This would come as no disappointment to those in the Government who continued to hope until the last moment that force would not be necessary. When Sir George Cartier, the leader of the Quebec Conservatives, temporarily took over the reins of government on May 6th from the ailing Prime Minister, Wolseley began to feel the coils of intrigue tighten. Not that he doubted the Minister's loyalty or honesty, but as the leader of the French Canadians, Cartier would have 'to bow down before their bigoted and ignorant priesthood, for whom in his heart he had little love and no respect'. And, in order to maintain his political position, 'he had to resort to gross jobbery'.[3]

The Americans were also in a position to place a serious obstacle in the path of the expedition. Steamers leaving Collingwood on Lake Huron could reach Lake Superior only by way of the St Mary River, a broad channel of some fifty miles which divides the United States from Canada. Three miles of the river were unnavigable because of the rapids known as Sault St Marie (called the 'Soo'). The only way of by-passing it was by canal on the American side. Naturally, Wolseley never contemplated transporting British troops over American soil, but would the United States permit stores and military equipment to be carried through? Confident Dominion officials assured him that there would be no difficulty, since their Government had allowed war material – even a gunboat – of the Federal forces to be sent up the St Lawrence through their canals and into the lakes during the Civil War.

Wolseley, however, put little faith in political gratitude. As soon as Lake Superior was clear of ice early in May, he sent a ship free of all war goods through the canal. With a steamer on the Superior side of the 'Soo' he was at least in a position to take men and supplies around the three miles of rapids and place them where they could be transported across the vast lake. Five days later he sent a second ship, again minus troops and supplies of a military nature. This time the Americans were not taken by surprise. They closed the canal to all Canadian ships. While the governor-general dispatched protests to Washington and requested that ordinary cargo at least be allowed passage, the quick-thinking colonel managed to charter a second ship, an American steamer, on the Superior side, so as to eliminate what might prove a fatal bottle-neck. The dollar-loving American captain, on his own, concealed his intentions by making an affidavit before United States authorities that his ship had absolutely nothing to do with the Red River party. (The Americans eventually relaxed their embargo and permitted ordinary supplies to go through.)

The Red River party left Toronto in mid May. When Wolseley arrived at the 'Soo', he found the American 'cousins' civil and obliging. The colonel and most of the troops soon boarded the two ships above the rapids and sailed out into Lake Superior, which was so enormous that it resembled an ocean in storm or in rest. One member of the party remarked that the whole of Ireland could be dropped into it with a fair-sized lake left over. Sometimes, he added, he was tempted to wish it could be!

The country surrounding Thunder Bay was gloomy and unsmiling.

A few days previously a great fire had swept through the land, replacing the green with a forbidding black. Dense smoke still hung over the charred logs and blackened racks as lighters approached the stony beach. Port Arthur's Landing, which Wolseley named in honour of the Duke of Connaught whose regiment was then serving in Canada, became a miniature Balaclava. But the method and regularity made it unlike its prototype.

Wolseley hovered over the landing party like a *deus ex machina* ready to solve every difficulty. When informed by the chief control officer that owing to an oversight all the tent poles had been left behind, the commander, instead of cursing the blundering fool responsible, laughed and inquired if the axes had been left behind, too. On receiving a negative reply, he pointed to half-burned trees and said simply, 'Then you can help yourself to as many tent poles as you require.' When a young officer's efforts to cook a meal of salt pork failed, the ubiquitous colonel was soon at his elbow to show him the rudiments of the art of cooking. Wolseley's gay manner in tackling every difficulty gave his men confidence and inspired them to exert themselves to the utmost.

The following day, while the stores were being unloaded and forwarded, Wolseley inspected the corduroy road (constructed with logs laid side by side transversely) to Lake Shebandowan where the troops would embark in their boats for Fort Garry. The farther he went, the greater was his disappointment. He found a narrow, rough road with many stumps remaining to be removed. The recent fire had burned a number of culverts and bridges. What the fire had not destroyed, the incessant rains had washed away or flooded. The last eighteen miles of road still remained to be cut through a virgin forest. Before he left Toronto, Wolseley had been given the solemn assurances of the Canadian Government that the road would be open for traffic by the end of May. From the way it looked now, they were not likely to get through before the end of August.

Disappointment turned to vexation when Wolseley inspected the men of the Land Transport Service. They were for the most part a worthless lot picked up anywhere with little regard for their qualifications. Knowing little about the care of horses, which were splendid animals to begin with, they abused them and thereby greatly reduced their efficiency. When out of sight of their station, they would engage in pranks and race the beasts to the point of exhaustion. Wolseley soon taught them the meaning of discipline by making an example of the worst-behaved.

The gentlemen of the Public Works Department were equally unfitted for their job. Except for Mr Dawson, the hard-working executive officer whose only fault was in being over-sanguine, the men were loafers, hangers-on forced upon Dawson by the Ministers. Some were hopeless drunks sent out by well-meaning friends who hoped to see these 'decayed gentlemen' rehabilitated in a land where no whisky was to be found. At one of the stations, Wolseley asked a young man who was acting as the book-keeper what his former occupation was. He replied quite frankly that he had none in particular; he had merely joined the expedition to see his brother in Manitoba. His uncle, the Minister of Public Works, had engaged him for the staff of that department 'so that he might be taken there in one of our boats without expense to himself'.[4]

Wolseley suspected another political scheme designed to injure the expedition. He was now convinced that Cartier and Langevin, the Minister of Public Works, and the rest of the 'priest party' were working on behalf of Riel. Undismayed, he was resolved to complete the road so as to reach Fort Garry and return before winter. Fatigue parties were detailed from the volunteers, voyageurs, and regulars to fight against time. Soon the whole available strength of the expedition was pitted against the wilderness. It was arduous, painful labour.

The Thunder Bay area was well named. Each hill, with true American individuality, seemed to boast its own peculiar kind of storm. And it stormed with uncomfortable regularity. When it rained two or three days together, bridges were washed away and parties were trapped, unable to advance or retire. It was easy to understand how this land gave birth to the Red and St Lawrence River systems.

Large rocks often barred the way and could not be budged. Borrowing a page from Livy, Wolseley did as Hannibal did when crossing the Alps. Great fires were built around the obstinate boulders until they were extremely hot. Instead of drenching them with cold wine, however, icy water was used. If there had been any spirits about, it would have been put to other purposes. It was not the congenial work which the volunteer expected before leaving Toronto. They expressed their sentiments in one of the songs of the expedition:

'Twas only a volunteer that I left my abode,
I never thought of coming here to work on a road.

To keep up their morale, Wolseley arranged for boat races, foot races, and other sports after a hard day's work. Competition was also held in fancy dancing on a specially built platform.

Everyone was impressed by Wolseley's cheery optimism. He was the first man up each morning, wearing a broad smile. His strong voice, suave and jolly, but always tinged with authority, was to be heard throughout the camp. When affairs looked black, he never seemed to lose hope, to fret or worry. Despite the threat of a fatal delay to the expedition, he radiated confidence. But Wolseley dissembled. He wore a mask carefully contrived to conceal his true feelings. Confiding to his brother, Dick, he wrote, 'I have always made it a rule through life, no matter whether it was in the danger of battle or any other position or circumstance when men of ordinary characters are likely to be *glum* to appear jolly – and the consequence is that everyone thinks I am of that happy sort of disposition.' But there were times when he was in such low spirits, he could 'sit down and cry like a schoolgirl'.[5] This was such a time.

The English press as well as the French press in Canada hinted that the road would never be built in time and that the force would be recalled. Men of the Hudson's Bay Company and others well acquainted with the route now 'laughed in our faces when we talked of going to Fort Garry, and returning by the end of September.'[6]

The commander was resourceful. When he learned that Lake Shebandowan was connected with Lake Superior by the Kamanistiquia and Mataway Rivers, he decided to explore the possibility of employing a water route as a supplementary road. Officials of the Company were amused and declared the rivers were absolutely unnavigable except for light canoes. They told how the wild-rushing rivers with their rocky bottoms would destroy the boats, and there were rapids and falls – one over 120 feet in height – requiring laborious portage. Wolseley insisted upon making the experiment and detailed a party to make the attempt. After ten days of stupendous effort, they forced their way up fifty miles of churning water to a level 800 feet above Port Arthur. A delighted Wolseley now ordered the boats up these rivers to relieve the strain on the Land Transport Service. The availability of the rivers saved the expedition between a month and six weeks, thereby rescuing it from failure.

After nearly two months of unremitting, back-breaking labour, the force had pushed and pulled, paddled and poled over 150 boats and two months' supplies to a depot at McNeill's Bay on Lake Shebandowan. Here they paused to repair the bruised boats and barrels. Wolseley, who moved his headquarters to the depot on July 14th, was himself in need of repair. Overwork and dysentery had deprived him of much of his customary energy. But his spirit was relieved. Having overcome almost insurmountable difficulties, he had proved to himself he was capable of independent command.

July 16th was set as the date for departure from the sandy beach at McNeill's Bay. The weather, which had brought twenty-three days of rain since the landing at Thunder Bay, made one last mighty effort to impede them on the night of July 15th. A violent thunderstorm of unparalleled fury shook the earth and drenched the bivouac. One flash of lightning nearly struck the commander as he tried to sleep. The tempest, as if to announce their final departure, swept through the whole of Canada, killing a great number of persons and cattle.

The following day dawned clear, warm and auspicious. Companies of the 60th Rifles, accompanied by the Royal Engineers and the Royal Artillery, were scheduled to leave first. Each company of fifty men was to form a brigade of from six to eight boats. A brigade was to be dispatched each day after the first three departed on July 16th. The 60th Rifles were to be followed by the 1st Ontario Rifles, lastly by the 2nd Quebec Rifles, until all twenty-one brigades were afloat. The case of follow-your-leader was necessary to prevent a jam at the portages. These portages would now be negotiated more easily, thanks to the hardships met coming up from Thunder Bay. Moreover, the experience gave Wolseley a chance to test the voyageurs. Many who masqueraded under the high-sounding name were rejected as a result and left behind, much to their disgust.

That first day of departure was one of bustle and excitement. Wolseley himself was there to supervise the advance of the foremost brigades. The embarkation was delayed until five in the evening owing to winds that chaffed the face of the water. Suddenly the west wind died down, and calm prevailed. As the lead flotilla paddled across the mirror-like surface of the now placid lake, Wolseley was reminded of the bands of Viking freebooters who centuries ago set out from such secluded bays in search of plunder and adventure. And like the ancients, these ships were propelled by oar and sail. It occurred to him that his force would soon be as many miles from the nearest telegraph office as Julius Caesar was from Rome when he sent a messenger back to herald his landing on the shores of England.

The commander's musings over historical associations were shattered by the bustle of the present. 'For Fort Garry!' shouted someone in the first boat. A chorus of British cheers resounded across the silent lake, which was answered by their comrades on shore. The witty, punning chaplain gave the expedition its motto that evening: 'Arms, men, and canoes.' (A very free translation of the words in the opening stanza of the *Aeneid*, '*arma virumque cano*'.)

The Red River party hoped to fight, but Wolseley had issued a pro-

clamation before leaving the Thunder Bay area, in which he declared,
'Our mission is one of peace; and the sole object of the expedition is to
secure Her Majesty's sovereign authority.'[7]

The last brigade left on August 1st. By then the first brigade had
arrived at Bare Portage, 150 miles beyond. Arrangements had been made,
however, for close communication up and down the extended force.
Wolseley, with Mr Irvine, his soldier-servant, and eight voyageurs, left
McNeill's Bay on July 23rd in a swift bark canoe. He passed freely along
the column, ready to assert leadership wherever difficulty arose. The
biggest problem was for the boats to thread the right road through island-
studded lakes with numerous deep bays that might easily become culs de
sac. Consequently, many brigades proceeded slowly so as not to go astray.
Wolseley, meanwhile, usually tried to keep ahead of the leading detachment, and at every doubtful turn blazed the trail by scoring the trees
with his axe. He was the heart and soul of the undertaking, the master
spirit that kept it forging ahead, the strong backbone that held it together. Though he had but one eye, it missed very little. As Words-
worth's naval showman said of Nelson:

> One eye he had, which, bright as ten,
> Burn'd like a fire among his men.

Of the forty days allowed them to reach Fort Garry, one day's toil was
like another; only the scenes of the untravelled wilderness changed with
each passing day. Reveille and the shout 'Fort Garry' sounded before
dawn to rouse the men out of their well-earned rest from under a blanket
or buffalo robe. Their clothes, in which they slept, would steam as the
fires were lit. The summer of 1870 was a wet one, and the men soon became amphibious, rarely enjoying the luxury of dry clothing. Their
working clothes consisted of flannel shirts rolled up at the sleeves and
white duck trousers, which before long took on the appearance of Joseph's
coat of many colours as patches were made from canvas and bean bags
to cover the worn places. As true woodsmen, they wore moccasins,
night-caps, and a broad belt from which dangled a tin cup and sheath
knife.

After a hot cup of tea, they hopped into their boats and pulled hard at
the oars. A halt would be made at eight for breakfast and another at one
for dinner, frequently at some pretty little island on the way. Their fare
was indistinguishable from one meal to another – salt pork, beans, and
hard tack. Occasionally they were treated to a piece of dog-choke, a pan-
cake made of flour and water and fried in pork fat. At a Company

post they could look forward to sturgeon, boiled bear or porcupine. Cold black tea was always available, since it was carried in each of the boats.

Navigating their boats across countless lakes and down cork-screw streams, they accompanied the splosh-splosh of their paddles with the songs of voyageurs or those of past wars, from 'John Brown's Knapsack is Number 95' to the fifty verses relating the deeds of General Santa Anna. But the danger was sometimes great, and accidents were not infrequent. Boats were caught in whirlpools or turned turtle in rapids. Most feared of all was to be caught in a sudden squall far off shore. As they strained on their oars, 'some would quake and mutter a silent prayer, others would "damit".'[8] There were many hairbreadth escapes and boats were destroyed, but no man lost his life.

When Wolseley passed along the line, he usually succeeded in creating rivalry between companies. To ensure greater effort, he would tell the men of one company how another crossed a portage with remarkable speed. The regulars in front were told that the militia were close behind, while the militia were informed that the regulars were pulling way ahead. Wolseley believed the spirit of competition would lighten their load.

Fort Frances, roughly the half-way point to Fort Garry, was reached the nineteenth day out, August 4th. The Company post hardly qualified for its high-sounding name, being a collection of wooden shacks surrounded by a palisade. Here Wolseley was to receive an intelligence report from Captain William Francis Butler, who had been sent ahead by way of the United States to discover the affairs at Fort Garry. Butler, who had arrived some days before, on hearing that the commander was coming up the Rainy River, paddled out to greet him. It was not long before he spotted the great canoe skimming along with the full swing of eight Iroquois paddles whose strokes were timed to an old French chant. It was several moments before Wolseley, sitting foremost in the canoe, recognized the bewhiskered Irishman. He then called out 'Where on earth have you dropped from?' 'Fort Garry, twelve days out, sir,' was the reply.

Butler reported that he had not only succeeded in getting to Fort Garry, a bold deed in which he risked his life, but had had an interview with 'President' Riel himself. He described conditions as anarchical. The settlers were in a state of panic. The French and English settlers were afraid of each other, and both dreaded the possibility of an uprising among the Indians who had grown unruly because of untoward conditions. All messages the captain carried from local well-wishers were of the same tenor – 'Come as quickly as you can, for the aspect of affairs is serious and threatening.'[9] Riel, Butler related, was changing his mind daily about whether he should submit, fight, or run. His power had diminished since the passage of the Manitoba Bill which satisfied nearly all the half-breed's aspirations, but he still commanded a large armed force capable of stout resistance. Fearing the hangman's rope for the murder of Scott, he hoped for amnesty, which men like Cartier were anxious to obtain for him so as to preserve the gains already won for the rebellious metis. As Wolseley listened to this man of action and poet – resourceful, hot-tempered, expansive, courageous – he found it difficult to decide whether Butler was more Irish with sword or pen.

The information Wolseley received at Fort Frances induced him to hurry along up the Rainy River. In the few days he allowed himself at the fort, he arranged for the establishment of a hospital and field oven to serve the brigades fresh bread as they came up. A company of Ontario Rifles was left as a garrison. He held a lengthy and boring powwow with the mangy and mendicant sons of Hiawatha. The local chief, Crooked Neck, so-called because his head was all on one side, dressed in little more than yellow paint and a ring through his nose, gestured and talked for hours. Wolseley was not quite sure what they wanted, but he gave them food and clothing, which seemed to please them.

The region of the Rainy River, some seventy miles in length, was the only fertile area along the entire route; it was also the most dangerous. It was the most likely place for an ambush by Indians. Not that the expedition feared their numbers, but it would have been madness to pursue them in this land of woods and water. It was well worth a few trinkets to keep them happy. Moreover, the river formed the boundary between the United States and Canada, and if the Fenians were to attack them, this would be the logical place. Butler, however, after scouting through Minnesota, assured his chief there was nothing to the loud rumours of an attack by the Brotherhood along this line. Not that Wolseley ever took these rumours too seriously for the Irish would have to go through miles of wilderness to get at them, 'and they have been often enough in the woods', he wrote to his brother, Dick, 'to know how difficult it would be to arrange for their transport, etc.'[10] Nevertheless, since their arms were packed in chests, Wolseley took no chances. The brigades were passed quickly along the river without pause.

The Rainy River flows into the Lake of the Woods, which measures about seventy miles in length and breadth. It resembled a vast bowl of pea soup in colour and consistency. The water was impossible to drink unless carefully strained, and then it tasted like mustard. When Wolseley arrived, a gale was blowing, so all that day and the next his party took shelter on what was named 'Detention Island'. Wolseley retired to his tent to play 'patience'.

As the party waited anxiously to get under way, a canoe reached them with mail from Fort Frances. The most significant news was that France had declared war on Prussia. There was much talk of betting on the outcome, but no one would back Prussia. But when Wolseley learned that the 'misfit' Montauban (now Count de Palikao) had been named Minister of War, he turned to the men about him and said simply, 'Then it is all over for poor France.' Later he had the unpleasant task of telling his voyageurs of the defeat at Sedan and the capture of Napoleon III. At first they refused to believe that France, the greatest nation on earth, had been vanquished. They lay down that night and wept.

Soon large Company boats approached from the opposite direction, carrying letters from Captain Fielden at Rat Portage, on the other side of the lake, and from Bishop Macrae of the Red River settlement urging the need for sending a small force to the Red River as quickly as possible. Chafing at his delay, Wolseley decided to disregard the warnings of the Indians and venture out across the lake in a gig without a guide. It was a foolish move dictated by frustration. For two days the commander of the expedition was lost. His party blundered hopelessly through the maze of islands and inlets on the northern shore. It was a baffling Chinese puzzle to which there was seemingly no solution. Not until the night of August 14th did the lost party in the gig come into Rat Portage famished and fatigued to the point of collapse.

At Rat Portage the expedition began its grand detour down the Winnipeg River, into the lake of the same name, and up the Red River to Fort Garry, which was actually only a little over 100 miles due west of Rat Portage. The guides at Rat Portage told Wolseley it would take three weeks to descend the 163 miles of seething Winnipeg, providing they survived the numerous surging rapids and boiling eddies in those outlandish boats. The brigades covered the distance on an average of ten days by travelling as far as they dared on the white waters and making as many as eight portages in one day. It was a marvel that not one life was lost in navigating the turbulent stream, though two boats were completely wrecked. Success was due in large part to the loyal settlers on the Red River who sent a fleet of large Company boats manned by dexterous voyageurs to assist them.

Running the tumbling waters gave the force its greatest thrill. Wolseley called it a 'delicious exciting pleasure'.[11] At one of the fiercer rapids, the Iroquois guides decided to test the courage of the young leader of the 'pale-faces' by deliberately taking the canoe out into mid stream where the current was swiftest, and then paddling as close to the brink of the waterfall as they dared without falling into the roaring abyss below. Every fibre in Wolseley's frame felt the strain. The Indians searched his countenance for some sign of weakness. But Wolseley showed them that a Briton could be as stoical as a red man.

On reaching Fort Alexander near the mouth of the Winnipeg River, Wolseley heard that Riel had issued a call to arms to which 600 followers responded. It looked as if the half-breeds meant to fight. Wolseley waited only long enough to collect all the regulars, and on August 21st pushed on to Fort Garry by way of the 'back door' (from the north). An imposing fleet of fifty boats, with a favourable wind at their back, sailed swiftly along the shore of Lake Winnipeg and entered the Red River the following afternoon. As they pulled slowly up-stream, every man was excited by the thought of a fight.

The force was treated to the best of all possible scenery – civilization. Not since leaving the Soo had they glimpsed neat farmhouses in the midst of cultivated lands. Church bells rang out, women waved handkerchiefs and men fired guns. The Swamp Indians, whose reserve was located near by, manifested the greatest exuberance of all. They were now a few miles below Stone Fort (Lower Fort Garry). As Colonel Wolseley pitched his tent, Chief Henry Prince came to pay his respects to the 'white chief' who represented the 'great Queen'. The chief told him how surprised everyone was to see their boats: 'They had no idea that the expedition had left the boats coming around the point opposite their wigwams.'[12] Wolseley continued to take every precaution to keep the enemy in ignorance.

'On to Fort Garry!' sounded louder and earlier the next morning. A few hours later they arrived at Stone Fort itself, twenty miles north of Fort Garry. Here final preparations were made for an attack. Rifles were distributed. Superfluous stores were placed ashore, and only four days' rations were taken on the lightened boats. All available ponies and carts were commandeered and Captain Wallace's company (B) was mounted. Their efficiency, however, was questioned by some cavalrymen like McCalmont, who watched several soldiers mount from the wrong side. With two signalmen carrying flags to enable them to communicate with Wolseley's gig leading the advance of three lines of boats, the mounted men moved along either bank to prevent anyone from going on to the fort and giving away their presence. Strong currents and head winds made it impossible to reach the 'president's' headquarters that day, so the force bivouacked six miles short of Fort Garry.

A heavy downpour continued all that night, and turned the whole land into black, sticky mud by morning. Wolseley was forced to abandon his plan for a triumphal march on the rebel stronghold. Once more the redcoats, looking like drowned rats, took to their boats. 'Our enemies would have pitied our plight,' opined their commander.[13] The torrents, however, succeeded in masking their approach. Spies who slipped into Winnipeg during the night came back with reports that the petty Napoleon was still unaware of their presence. Rather than Wolseley, Riel expected Archbishop Taché, who was labouring on his behalf, to appear any hour with an amnesty. Nevertheless, the half-breed leader was ready to do battle. Ammunition had been distributed among his rabble, the gates were locked, and the cannons were loaded for action.

At eight on the morning of August 24th, 1870, the bedraggled men of the flotilla effected a landing at Point Douglas, two miles from the fort by land. Loyal parties riding out from Winnipeg told how Riel was still in the fort preparing to resist. A column was hastily organized, skirmishers were thrown forward, and scouts moved out to the flanks. Ammunition and hospital supplies were neatly placed in readiness. Colonel Wolseley and his staff mounted ponies. The signal was given and bugles sounded the advance. With the rain beating into their faces and the mud sucking at their feet, the little army tramped across the prairie with a couple of brass cannon on carts trundling along behind.

It was Wolseley's intention to skirt around, with the village of Winnipeg to the left, and approach the stone fort from the west, thereby cutting off Riel's escape. As the advance company came into sight of Fort Garry, they saw the northern gate shut and several gun muzzles peering grimly out through embrasures. The word was passed along the line, 'Riel is going to fight!' The rebel leader rose in their estimation tremendously. The redcoats expected the gun over the gateway to open fire at any moment. But their hopes for excitement vanished as they came within rifle range and saw no sign of life within. 'By God! He's bolted!' someone shouted. Or could it be a trap? Wolseley, annoyed by field-glasses rendered useless by the rain, rose in his stirrups and strained his good eye to ascertain the meaning of this silence. He turned to his staff and said, 'Will somebody go and see what's on the other side?' Galloping round to the south gate, his officers found it open and the fort abandoned. A half-naked, drunken Indian was the sole occupant.

Only a quarter of an hour before, Riel and his henchmen had sat down to breakfast when they were interrupted by the bugle-sounds of an approaching army. Leaving the table untouched, they mounted, and fled across the crude pontoon bridge over the Assiniboine. As Wolseley suspected, Riel had been bluffing all along and would flee when confronted by force. Personally, Wolseley was happy that Riel had escaped. If he had surrendered without a fight, it would have been impossible to hang him!

The rain-drenched troops were marched through the south gate and on to the muddy square where they formed up. The Union Jack was hoisted on the flagstaff from which the rebel flag had flown for nine months. A royal salute was fired from the fort's guns. Three cheers were given for the Queen, which was caught up and echoed by the inhabitants of Winnipeg who had followed the troops at a respectful distance. Solemnly watching the ceremony from across the river was a short, stout, round-faced man, Riel (the lily), and a taller, slimmer, uglier man, his Fenian secretary, O'Donoghue (the shamrock). Wolseley made no attempt to arrest them, since he had not been invested with any civil authority. Besides, it would only have further complicated Canadian politics.

The authority of Her Majesty had been restored in the land of the Red River after a bloodless campaign. No shot had been fired from beginning to end. Many soldiers were left with a sense of frustration. Having endured so much, they had no opportunity to avenge themselves on the rebels. Buller remarked bitterly that he was 'disgusted at having come so far to hear the band play "God Save the Queen".'[14]

Riel, O'Donoghue, and Lepine (another confederate), whose horses were lost or stolen the following night, extemporized a raft by lashing together logs and fence rails with their braces, neckties, and O'Donoghue's trousers. In this strange contraption they paddled furiously to reach the border. Actually, there was no need for haste, for there was no civil authority to send constables in pursuit.

The troubles of Colonel Wolseley did not end with the flight of Riel and his cronies. Pandemonium reigned that night. After a long dry campaign, soldiers, voyageurs, and Indians with several weeks' pay in their pockets piled into the town in search of strong drink. And, as if by magic, the shabby settlement, a mere collection of some fifty houses built at all angles to one another, produced more saloons than any community several times its size. Selling the vilest intoxicants suddenly appeared to be its main industry. All night long there were screams, shrieks and curses as they celebrated 'the restoration of law and order'. Had Riel been captured that day, he would have been lynched.

Wolseley, surprised that some of the soberest of men made the worst drunks, got the soldiers under his discipline the following morning. The civilians, however, continued their drunken orgy, and some of the loyalist bigots began to bully the metis in the neighbourhood and clamour for reprisals. The colonel, not having been invested with civil authority, was powerless. Had he acted on his own and placed the town under martial law, the political repercussions would have been felt throughout Canada, even in London. Wolseley finally persuaded Mr Donald Smith (in later years Lord Strathcona), the senior officer of the Hudson's Bay Company, who had accompanied him from Fort Alexander to be responsible for the conduct of civil affairs until the lieutenant-governor arrived. Under no conditions would the colonel allow his soldiers to be converted into policemen; but he did agree to detail strong pickets to patrol the city and co-operate with Mr Smith's special constables. It was the moral effect created by the presence of these troops, and the assumption that they were prepared to quell any serious disturbance, that prevented the situation from becoming more serious. Only after the whisky ran out three days later was the brawling and lawlessness ended. On that third morning men were found lying stretched out on the prairie in every direction 'like the killed and wounded after a sharp skirmish'.[15]

On August 28th the advance-guard of the militia battalions arrived to take over garrison duty at Fort Garry, and the next day the Royal Rifles departed for Eastern Canada to be re-embarked at once for England. Their departure was delayed, however, by the Iroquois voyageurs who were still drunk and refused to get into their boats for some time.

The new lieutenant-governor was installed on September 2nd, and Wolseley's mission to the North-West was completed. He thanked the regulars before their departure and remained long enough to deliver an emotional and flattering valedictory address to the Canadian militiamen, of whom he was truly proud.

The commander deserved the most credit. Men of long experience in the West were astonished that such a force should have passed through the wilderness in safety in so little time. Wolseley's consummate skill as an organizer, his fertility of resource, had produced success. He exhibited for the first time his special talent for reducing a military campaign to a mathematical problem, one that could be solved with careful attention to detail, and which allowed him to predict with unusual prescience the time involved. Wolseley arrived at Fort Garry within hours of the forty days he predicted would be necessary to cover the distance from McNeill's Bay.

Wolseley liked to compare his Red River expedition with that of Sir Robert Napier into Ethiopia three years before. Napier marched only 400 miles, through a country where supplies were obtainable, at a cost to the nation of £900,000, while Wolseley's force travelled over 600 miles, carrying all their own supplies, for an outlay of £100,000, only one quarter of which was to be paid by the British taxpayer. The success of his efforts, above all the saving in money, Wolseley attributed in large part to the War Office, which was too far away to meddle in the organization.

One man of the Red River force returned by way of the United States, Lieutenant McCalmont. Wolseley entrusted him with the traditional honour of carrying home dispatches announcing the close of the campaign. An officer selected for such duty was customarily given promotion or a pecuniary reward. On reaching the civilized city of St Paul, McCalmont decided that the United States Post Office was a reliable institution, dropped the precious documents into a letter-box, and went on to New York to board a steamer for England. It was the greatest *faux pas* of his career. General Lindsay and his staff in Montreal were scandalized. Wolseley, suspecting a practical joke, was furious. McCalmont was given no reward of any kind. On Christmas Day, thirty-nine years later, he received, as did other survivors of the expedition, a medal for the Red River campaign.

Journeying back to Britain, Wolseley felt as if he were the most important man in the army. The lavish praise bestowed upon him at the banquet arranged in his honour by the citizens of Montreal still sounded in his ears.* However dazzling his accomplishment, the attention of his own countrymen – of all the civilized world – remained fixed on the Rhine where two nations were engaged in a fateful struggle. Not one home newspaper bothered to herald his success or sing his praises. Nevertheless, a grateful government did not fail to acknowledge his services, past and present. On his return to England, he rose up before his Sovereign Sir Garnet Wolseley, Knight Commander of the most distinguished Order of St Michael and St George.

---

* Mr Smith, to show his gratitude, named the Hudson's Bay port at the north-west corner of the Lake of the Woods, Fort Wolseley, and another at the mouth of the Winnipeg River, Fort Louisa, in honour of Mrs Wolseley.

# CHAPTER SEVEN

# FROM INKSHED TO BLOODSHED

AFTER the Franco-Prussian War all the world went to school in Germany. It had been the custom for nineteenth-century warriors to look to France for military fashions, like women shopping for a dress. Within the space of a few months, the Prussians, striking swiftly and with deadly precision, brought France, paragon of all things military, to her knees. The Germans compelled observers to recognize warfare as a science; everything from their short-service system to spiked helmets would soon be imitated.

The question of military preparedness and possible invasion was now thrust before the British public. The catastrophic defeat of France and such widely-read pamphlets as the *Battle of Dorking*, which described a hypothetical invasion in nightmare terms, rudely awakened them to a sense of danger. A feeling of insecurity provided a powerful impetus to reform the army along lines made popular by the Prussians.

Reform had long been overdue. The lessons of the Crimean War had never been fully learned. The rusted sword of England, the result of peace madness and neglect, was obviously unable to withstand the strain of modern warfare as conducted by Prussia. The sword must be forged and sharpened. The armourer of Britain was Cardwell, a refined and timid civilian, whom Gladstone none the less selected with great confidence to become his Secretary of State for War.

Cardwell, a thoughtful and coldly methodical politician, was prepared to face the task of reform squarely from the moment he assumed office. With the full tide of public opinion behind him in the summer of the Franco-Prussian War, he introduced the Army Enlistment Act of 1870 which provided short service.

The long-service system had never adequately met the needs of the army in times of national strain. Possessing no reserves, it was necessary during emergencies to rely on short enlistments from two to five years in length, or for the duration of the conflict, to keep up the nation's fighting strength. The Prussians, indebted to the genius of Scharnhorst, demonstrated that through a short-service system with a large reserve a nation could have a small peacetime army capable of rapid expansion to great strength. By putting their whole force into the field from the very onset, and striking blows as they did at Sadowa and Sedan, the Germans reduced war to a matter of weeks. Modern states could no longer afford the time to fill the ranks with raw and untrained recruits.

Cardwell proposed a short-service system of six years with the colours and six years in the reserve (later modified to seven and five years). Aside from providing a large body of men always available in an emergency, it possessed certain additional advantages. More men would be attracted to short enlistment. There never were sufficient numbers of recruits for a meagre army where chances for survival, even in peacetime, were poor. Battalions sometimes remained abroad in deadly tropical regions for up to twenty years. The few who returned from such long service were prematurely aged, or broken down, and no provision was made for their return to civilian life. The act further promised to rejuvenate the army by providing for the discharge of the 'worthless' and 'incorrigible'. The army would no longer offer a berth for the worst and most desperate characters. Finally, it was more economical. Huge sums once spent in bounties and levy money to promote enlistment and re-enlistment would, for the most part, be saved. Pensions would also be less frequent, and the wastefulness of drunkenness and desertion reduced. Under Cardwell's system, the younger, cleaner, and more sober soldier was to enjoy a popularity unknown in former times.

The worst that could be said of the short-service soldiers was that they were 'mere children', and that only maturity and years of seasoning could transform them into effective fighting men. This was denied by reform-minded officers such as Wolseley. Having seen Lee's army, he maintained a short-term soldier could be equal to the best, provided he was taught the practical side of war rather than pirouetting on the barrack square.

To assist him in working out the details and preparing further reforms, Cardwell relied on Lord Northbrook, an able under-secretary, and Sir Ralph Knox, for many years accountant-general. Above all, with the senior officers arrayed against him, he sought the advice of distinguished young iconoclasts who, as the avant-garde of the army, devoted themselves to the study of and preparation for modern war. Among them were Captain Baring (later Lord Cromer), Sir Robert Biddulph, Cardwell's private secretary and Wolseley's old tent-mate in India, and Sir Garnet Wolseley, whose invaluable experience of war in all its varied aspects was recognized by Cardwell as second to none.

Sir Garnet's unique career was hardly appreciated by the army leaders who allowed him to languish on half-pay on his return to England. The *Soldier's Pocketbook*, with its highly damnable doctrines, still caused a rise in blood pressure among soldiers of the old school. Before he was called by Cardwell, Wolseley kept busy writing several articles on the Red River expedition – a mere excursion into the woods, according to his critics. His candour was unsparing in its treatment of the Canadian Government and its agents; and the articles were not well received by certain Dominion politicians. They alleged he was nettled into an abusive attitude when the Ottawa Government failed to appoint him lieutenant-governor of Manitoba.* Wolseley, however, was never reluctant to stir up controversy by relating what he believed to be the truth. The articles also served the purpose of providing him with much-needed additional funds. And, as he confided to his brother Dick, they helped to keep his name before the public. Though written anonymously, there was never any doubt as to their authorship, and writing about himself in the third person afforded an advantage in publicizing his virtues.

On May 1st, 1871, Sir Garnet was appointed assistant adjutant-general, discipline branch, at the insistence of Cardwell, who was to regard him as his chief military adviser. To Wolseley it was the opportunity of a lifetime. Ever since his experiences in the Crimea, he had been appalled by the shortcomings of the military system. With each succeeding campaign a gnawing impatience for reform grew in him, but he enjoyed neither social position nor official support. His lively vocabulary and jabbing pen served only to antagonize his tradition-bound superiors. If it had not been for the unexpected support of Cardwell, Wolseley was sure that 'his enemies would have contrived to have him honourably deported to some command at the Antipodes where his tiresome brain would have ceased to worry the War Office.'[1]

Strangely different in so many ways, the politician and the soldier developed an intimate friendship and worked efficiently as a team – Cardwell with the blue-prints and Wolseley giving them practical shape. The fiercely zealous colonel was given a desk at the army staff headquarters in the Horse Guards building where his days were crowded with committee meetings and ponderings on sweeping reforms that would convert a worn-out, anachronistic military organization to a technically advanced one. Wolseley became a familiar figure at Westminster, usually in the company of Cardwell: always dressed in the latest fashion, and looking

* Prime Minister Macdonald, shortly before his sudden illness, told Lady Wolseley he intended to appoint her husband to the post. Cartier knew of the Prime Minister's preference but appointed one of his friends instead.

spruce and debonair; a man of the world as well as a soldier. Members of the Government were most impressed with his alert and decided manner, accentuated by a sharp glance. He had a handsome, youthful face, though his hair was completely grey, including his waxed moustache. (Wolseley shaved off his pointed imperial beard after the fall of Napoleon III.)

One indispensable reform basic to others, whether enacted or proposed, remained to be accomplished: the abolition of the purchase of commissions. It seems incredible, an indefensible anomaly, that rank could still be bought as one buys beef in a market. Such a system could no longer be tolerated. The army, Cardwell told the House of Commons, was 'in pledge' to the officers. Purchase hindered expansion and reorganization of the regiments, which virtually belonged to the officers, and blocked the selection and promotion of worthy officers through a merit system. Wealthy young men, utterly unfit for the duties of their rank, could buy their way up to the rank of lieutenant-colonel in the infantry or cavalry, whereas the deserving officer with unlined pockets grew old in junior ranks. Sir Henry Havelock always complained that he had been purchased over by 'three sots and two fools'.

No one opposed purchase more vigorously than Wolseley, one of the rare officers to enter the army by way of a favour and rise to the rank of lieutenant-colonel through merit, not cash. He was ruthlessly impatient with the attitude of the average officer, who thought courage and devotion were sufficient in war, and the mastery of a few routine field exercises and parade movements sufficient to discharge his duties in peace.* They hardly knew their men by sight, leaving all bothersome details to the N.C.O.s. Guards officers, dressed like expensive dolls, were known to take a hansom cab to Hyde Park to join their battalion there for drill.

Having known too many bad officers in the field, Wolseley insisted that officers take an interest in every soldier under their command and set an example with study and hard work. War was a serious business and soldiering a profession, not a pastime for dilettantes. The days of playing at soldiers was over. Education in the army, still at a dangerously low ebb, should permeate through all ranks. Throughout his own career, he tried to stimulate mental alertness and instil a desire for learning. Wolseley was always vexed by officers who would state: 'I would much prefer to lead into action a company of men who can't write their own names.'

* Some did not tax their memories that much. One soldier testified that he knew a colonel who had to write all the commands for battalion drill on a card, and one day when he lost his card he had to dismiss the parade.

To his way of thinking, an educated soldier was a better soldier. And it was possible for an officer to excel at polo or cricket and also pass through staff college. The elimination of purchase would weed out the unfit and pave the way for the professionally responsible officer who prepared intellectually for war.

Wolseley felt it was his mission to introduce change. No one on Cardwell's team worked harder or with such absolute enjoyment and delight. Snapping his fingers at the powerful conservative interests, Sir Garnet, never known to be indiscreet in spoken or written words, rattled the dry bones of the British army with his Irish impetuosity. His opponents would never deny that he had an outstanding career – certainly his own frank disclosures made him sound like Othello; but they were not modern Desdemonas to be seduced by a hero's radical opinions that would make soldiers into bookworms.

The strongest foe of army reform and Wolseley's personal *bête noire* was Prince George, Duke of Cambridge, commander-in-chief of the army. The Prince was always close to the throne. Born shortly before his first cousin, Victoria, he was for six weeks the first of the grandchildren of George III in order of succession, and as a young man he was a strong candidate for consort to the Queen. Though Victoria married another, she was always very fond of cousin George. After the Crimean War, where he commanded a division, she induced the Government to appoint him head of the army to stress the fact that the military was under the control of the Sovereign, and not of Parliament. Prince George shared with his Queen a dislike for change, and maintained a steady opposition to all military reforms. He laboured hard to keep the army as it was under the Duke of Wellington. Full of reactionary dogma, parade drills were his most delightful chore and extravagant field days his pleasure. A martinent and stickler for order, even to the practice of keeping a separate toothbrush for every day in the week,* he had enormous capacity for the minute and the unimportant; the supreme test of a regiment's efficiency lay in the spotlessness of its appearance and the smartness of its formal evolutions in drill. Wolseley, on more than one occasion, had the impertinence to suggest to the Duke that while the regiments were dressed as cockatoos and paraded like robots, 'it would be little short of murder to pit them against a really military foe ... '2

Royal George, as he was irreverently called, was ordinarily a genial, bluff man full of good-humour, but when crossed he was full of bluster and bad language. And no man in his long career would try his temper

* By examining his wash-stand, a host could always determine the length of his stay.

more than Wolseley, 'that cocksure young bookworm'. The latter had an uncommon knack for enraging the old warrior with his 'new-fangled ideas'. The Duke detested the studious young colonel from the first day he walked into the War Office. That 'radical Cardwellite', he would say, would do what Napoleon failed to do – wreck the army that won the Battle of Waterloo. Little did they know, these two men, one stubbornly clinging to the cherished traditions of the past and the other demanding modernization, that they were destined to battle over the same ground for the next twenty-five years. On the Duke's behalf, it should be noted that he had the welfare of the soldier of all ranks close to his heart, and in his own way he worked to improve their lot. As a result, he was generally popular throughout the service.

The Bill to abolish purchase rallied all the defenders of the old system. On this issue they drew up their biggest guns and made their most determined stand. Purchase, after more than two centuries, had become deeply embedded in the dead weight of prejudice. In no other country were custom and privilege more treasured, and in no other profession was conservatism more pronounced than in the military. The aristocracy regarded the army as its private preserve, and influential families throughout the kingdom closely identified themselves with the interests of its officers. It was always held that the very foundation of the army rested on officers who were gentlemen of good birth and easy means.

The battle raged in the press, in drawing-rooms, in mess-halls. Tongues and pens stated and restated in fury every reason, prejudice and sentiment against abolition. Never were the outdated expressions of the Duke of Wellington so frequently quoted. A deep-murmuring Duke of Cambridge repeated what by now had become a slogan, 'Leave well alone.' A bitter Queen denounced Cardwell as unfit for his present office. Parliament, where the struggle waxed hottest, resounded with loud clamours, recriminations and denunciations. *Hansard* affords a poor reflection of the heat generated by the debates. An insulting chorus of condemnation was heard from the Opposition 'parliamentary colonels'. They were not only loud but strong, for there were 178 service members in Parliament, men who had combined soldiering with politics. A clever campaign of parliamentary obstruction was undertaken, and all sorts of petty motions and amendments were introduced and obscure questions asked during tedious all-night sessions. Cardwell developed the habit of taking Wolseley with him to the debates to provide information upon any difficult point raised by a soldier member.

Never was a Secretary of War more thoroughly abused by the

politicians, the army, and 'Society'. Holding to the principle 'that the officers should be made for the army', Cardwell refused to yield ground. Meanwhile, party discipline began to crack among the Liberals and the firmness of the Cabinet itself was threatened. But Gladstone continued to give him his unqualified support. In the summer of 1871, after months of acrimonious debate, the 'Liberal-lawyer's' Bill passed through the House of Commons. The House of Lords, however, rejected it. The reformers were not to be denied. Gladstone suddenly changed his tactics: since purchase had been legalized by royal warrant rather than statute, it could be cancelled by the Sovereign. The Prime Minister persuaded the Queen, who was anxious to avoid a dispute between the two Houses, to abrogate the system. The opposition growled treason, and shouted 'unconstitutional', but purchase was legally damned and buried.

The reformers did not come off unscathed. Cardwell, later raised to the peerage, went to an early grave, his life shortened by the strain of conflict and overwork. And Wolseley was on his way to being the most disliked figure in the army. He enjoyed some measure of popularity with the public and the young officers, but the Court distrusted him as a revolutionary, and the old school of officers harboured an undying hatred for this 'self-seeking radical and democrat'. The epithet 'democrat' made Wolseley wince, for he abhorred democracy. It was his aim to make the army representative of the entire nation, and above all, an effective weapon adjusted to the particular needs of the Empire – not a democratic institution. Cardwell, who held his assistant in great esteem, shielded him time and again from the machinations of his enemies.

After the purchase struggle, Wolseley busied himself with working out the details involved in the problem of regimental reorganization, another of Cardwell's sweeping reforms. The old regiments of the line (known by number), which were scattered about the Empire 'without any regard to military organization or ideas' (according to Wolseley), were woefully undermanned with no particular recruiting territory; and were incapable of developing organic links with such auxiliary forces as the militia and volunteers which were territorial – i.e., which had a well-established recruiting district. Wolseley advocated a standing army that in peacetime should be an organization for producing soldiers and not a costly receptacle for veterans.

Most officers, however, hotly objected to having their distinguished unit converted into a nursery for some sorry regiment. The opponents were so vehement that Cardwell hesitated and compromised. Not until the Liberals came back into power years later and Wolseley returned from a series of adventures abroad was the reorganization completed under Wolseley's direction.

As a reward for his services in resuscitating the army from the suffocating effects of prejudice and tradition, Cardwell arranged for Wolseley to command the military expedition to be sent against the ferocious Ashanti in West Africa.

In the nineteenth century the Ashanti were to West Africa what the Prussians were to Europe. With an army based upon universal conscription and tactics patterned after the remorseless, unconquerable army ant, their monarchs pursued a successful policy of 'blood and iron'. Neighbouring tribes were welded into a powerful confederation, and with these accretions, Ashanti power was felt far and wide. The coastal tribes, or Fanti confederations, were invaded, and the English colonial authorities who sought to protect them were kept in a perpetual state of terror.

If a nation ever deserved to be punished it was that of the bloodthirsty Ashanti. The cruelties perpetrated by such predatory tribes as the Ashanti were well known to every Sunday-school child of Victorian England. West Africa, as King David would have put it, was one of the 'dark places of the earth, full of habitations of cruelty'. Their bloody rites of fetish called for human sacrifice. When a person of high station died, a position commensurate with his or her rank in this world was assured in the next by sacrificing victims in proportion to the social status of the deceased. There were kings whose burials resulted in the death of thousands. Nor was this the only occasion for killing. Every three months the king performed his devotions and honoured his ancestors by smearing the blood of a score of men on their bones in the dreaded mausoleum at Bantama. The harvest festival and the frequent desire to propitiate the gods called for more human blood. Abolition of the slave trade ironically increased the evil. Where one captive was executed before, ten now died, for there was no longer a large market for slaves. What was once a valued article of trade became a cheap plaything. Kings began to take the throne on the condition that its steps should always be moist with human blood.

The sanguinary offerings that attended every festival or funeral were witnessed with enthusiasm by the populace of Kumasi, the metropolis of murder. Executioners became public idols. Having once thrust a knife through the victim's mouth from cheek to cheek, thereby transfixing the tongue so as to prevent a curse on the king, the headsman would practise his trade with pride. One official tormentor won great popularity by slicing a pinch of skin from the middle of the victim's back then, holding it before the wretched slave's eyes the moment before he was to die, the executioner exclaimed: 'The last thing you will see is this, and you see it for the first time!'[3] The spectators were convulsed with laughter.

The Gladstone Government had hoped to avoid sending an expensive expedition to the Gold Coast. Such expeditions in the past had never been popular, and Gladstone had no desire to increase the disfavour that had developed with army reforms. The truth was that if the expedition suffered a reverse, the Liberal party might find itself occupying the benches on the Opposition side of the House. But the time for feeble and half-hearted efforts had clearly passed. Lord Kimberley, the Colonial Secretary, was determined to follow a programme of prompt and powerful measures. Cardwell, who as a former Colonial Secretary had considerable knowledge of Gold Coast affairs, gave him his full support, and knew just the man for the job of pacifying the Ashanti. He told Wolseley in confidence that he would work for his appointment to head an expedition and advised him to submit a military plan. Burying himself for days in stacks of official papers, Wolseley emerged with a memorandum that covered the situation in great detail. The War Secretary sent it to Kimberley with a note saying: 'Sir Garnet Wolseley, who so successfully went to the Red River, is now ready to capture Kumasi.'[4]

Wolseley's original scheme called for a force of 'about 1,400 picked English soldiers making their way up the rivers', Red River-fashion. But the Duke of Cambridge considered the enterprise too hazardous for white troops. Moreover, the request for a unit of specially selected officers and men was rejected on the grounds that it violated the traditions of service and disrupted the regimental system. Wolseley's final plan, modified to please the authorities, called for his immediate departure with a group of specially selected officers to survey local conditions and to organize a force of friendly natives to drive the Ashanti back over the Prah. Should the native levies prove inadequate for a final thrust across the river to Kumasi, two first-rate white battalions, held in a state of readiness at home, would be sent out upon request to complete the work. Because of the deadly climate, Sir Garnet promised to use these men with all possible speed during the best season between December and February. A good road would be constructed to the Prah beforehand, with suitable shelters erected at each halting place. Once King Kofi had been forced to terms, or his capital at Kumasi destroyed should he resist to the end, the white troops would be hurried back to the transports. Wolseley promised to settle the whole business for less than £150,000.

A final decision was made at a meeting in the War Office on August

13th, 1873, which was attended by high-ranking military and naval authorities. Wolseley was asked if he was prepared to take over civil as well as military authority. If he answered 'yes', he would not be expected to remain in Africa after settling the Ashanti affair. To this he readily, happily, agreed.

But the decision was by no means unanimously supported by the military or by the Ministry. Naval sentiment, supported by at least one minister, favoured a continuation of gunboat diplomacy. It was a simple operation. When the governor on the West Coast was annoyed by some savage potentate, he requested the senior naval officer to drop a few shells on a collection of mud huts held by the enemy, as a punitive measure. It was a cheap way of impressing the coastal tribes with 'the greatness of the White Sovereign beyond the ocean who claimed them as her subjects'. But these measures had only a temporary effect, and the victims were usually innocent women and children. Such rough-and-ready tactics would hardly suffice to intimidate the Ashanti. Nevertheless, the navy by now began to feel that all expeditions to West Africa fell exclusively within their province. Kimberley, irritated by inadequate counter-proposals inspired by the Admiralty and exasperated by the cross-examination of a colleague, finally lost his temper. Thumping a table, he declared in a firm voice, 'Either this expedition comes off, or I cease to be Colonial Minister.'[5]

The navy, however, was not left entirely out of the effort. In August the Colonial Office accepted the offer of Captain Glover, R.N., the Clive-like administrator of Lagos, to organize the eastern tribes and 'cause a diversion in the rear of the Ashanti and threaten Kumasi'. Wolseley had no objection to this roving commission, so long as Glover adhered to his instructions to harass and alarm the Ashanti so as to force their retreat from the Protectorate, or at least to improve prospects for the success of a frontal attack; but he suspected the explorer-captain's 'chief aspiration was to open out a new, an easy route for trade into the interior of Africa by the hitherto unexplored Volta Valley'.[6]

The announcement that the Government had resolved to send a force to West Africa under Sir Garnet Wolseley, who was invested with the local rank of major-general, thus becoming the youngest general in Her Majesty's service, caused considerable comment. Many a silver-haired soldier complained that the undertaking required the services of a veteran general, not a mere youth. There was muttering about a political pay-off. The younger officers and the public generally, however, approved his appointment, though some thought 'Chinese' Gordon better fitted.

The General was limited to the selection of thirty-six staff and special service officers. In making his choice from among the many volunteers, he looked for thinking soldiers who had more than a fair share of courage. He naturally gave priority to those whose qualifications he had tested in Canada, such as Colonel McNeill, and Captains Buller, Butler, McCalmont and Huyshe. Colonel Wood, Major Baker Russell and Lieutenant Lord Gifford appealed to him because of their reputation for daring. Majors Home, Colley, and Captain Brackenbury owed their selection most to their military writings. The studious Lieutenant Maurice, a brilliant young instructor from the Royal Military College at Sandhurst, was at first appointed military secretary, but when the War Office objected to so important a post being given to a subaltern, Wolseley made him his private secretary.

This was the 'Ashanti ring'. It was a splendid staff of able, and in some instances, brilliant men. As Augustus Anson complained, Sir Garnet was 'using the finest steel of our army to cut brushwood'. But Wolseley believed the surest way to succeed was to surround himself with the very best officers he could obtain.

Wolseley's thoroughness in planning the campaign would have won the admiration of the unapproachable Prussians. Since the Intelligence department of the army was in an incipient stage and could give little help, Sir Garnet gathered all pertinent data himself. He digested stacks of unromantic blue books. Official reports of early expeditions were read and re-read, and those who participated in them were consulted. No page was left unturned, no potential source of knowledge ignored. All information was carefully sifted and collated. And for the first time in the history of the British Empire, a general appointed to command an expedition sat down to a table at the War Office with the Secretary for War, the Secretary for Colonies, the First Lord of the Admiralty, and the heads of various military departments to discuss the necessary arrangements.

News of the departure of Wolseley and his staff for West Africa on September 12th aroused little general interest. As they boarded the African Mail Company's steamer for Cape Coast, the Mayor of Liverpool delivered a polite and perfunctory address to the general, but there were no brass bands and not one cheer, even from a street boy, to speed the future conqueror of the Ashanti as his carriage wended towards Prince's Landing.

It was a merry party that started from the Mersey. There was the atmosphere of a holiday excursion among the officers, not one of whom was over forty. But the *Ambriz* quickly damped their festive spirits, and made the passage memorable for its discomforts. The steamer had been purchased recently from the White Star Line, and she was no bargain. Unfortunately she had been bought too soon before the start of her voyage to be properly fitted. The cabins had been repainted only twelve hours before they were slept in. The smell of paint mingled disagreeably with the foul odour of bilge-water which oozed over the cabin floors. She was not only badly caulked, but she flooded from above owing to the absence of bulwarks. In heavy seas she pitched so heavily that watches were thrown out of waistcoats and slumberers out of their bunks. The food downed between spells of seasickness was miserable.

For the use of the staff on the way out, the general bought dozens of books on the history and geography of West Africa. Maurice helped in the search by making a compendium of the various works. These were distributed among the men, along with a table of advice on health written by the chief medical officer. Each day Captains Huyshe and Brackenbury put their notes in shape and lectured the officers on tribes and terrain.

While the officers studied their lessons, their leader carefully studied them. Wolseley would constantly explore their personality and talents, and he would sometimes test them with an assignment or an incisive question, or spring surprises on them, to observe how they reacted in an unexpected situation. His judgment was carefully recorded in a little black pocket-book which was consulted when he needed a man for a specific job. Wolseley called his team 'a bag of tools'. Like a skilled workman, he felt he had the correct tools to complete an assignment with speed and precision.

Take Brackenbury, for example. Most commanders would have passed over the bookish soldier in organizing a staff for active service. Brackenbury himself was a little surprised by Sir Garnet's selection, for he had always been regarded as a writer, a teacher, a theorist. Except for a few months' duty as an artillery officer during the Mutiny, he had spent most of his military career at a desk. He first came to Wolseley's attention as an ardent backer of the Cardwell reforms, which he supported with his abnormal gift of expressing profound thoughts in a clear, logical manner. 'Brack', as Wolseley and his associates (he had few friends) called him, proved tireless and thorough, and soon demonstrated that he was a superb staff officer and an ideal military secretary, thereby vindicating his chief's estimate. At the close of the campaign, he was to write a two-volume, 800-page, definitive history of the Ashanti War in two weeks! 

Henry Brackenbury would never have gained appointment on either

167

his looks or social gifts. In uniform he appeared to be a businessman in disguise. In or out of uniform, he was ugly: with a pasty yellow face, an unkempt black moustache, and bulbous nose, which Lady Wolseley – who detested him – described as looking like a squashed strawberry. She and others were annoyed by the disgusting way he had of clearing his throat loudly. His sonorous, informing voice was clothed in the absurd, comical 'haw-haw' accent of the Victorian 'swell' – a lisp, usually affected, sometimes real, by which 'r's' were pronounced as 'w's'. Hence, 'Brack' would describe the Rifles as 'weahwing gween jackets'. Out of his mouth his own name became 'Whackenbaywe'. His lisping conversation was interspersed with a hectoring or exclamatory 'haw, haw'.

The *Ambriz* reached Sierra Leone on the African coast on September 27th. All were struck by the picturesqueness of the scenery; the bold outline of the majestic Lion Mountains towering over waving palms, the blue waters and whitewashed houses. Could this be the land known as the 'white man's grave'? The land and its people seemed so full of life. Yet the story was grimly told by a large graveyard, the principal feature of the capital, Freetown.

Sierra Leone had a unique origin, being originally set aside as a haven for manumitted slaves. The experiment, a colonial freak, began in 1787 when 400 slaves rescued in mid-passage by the navy were settled on this shore, along with thirty white prostitutes thoughtfully provided from London slums. It became a colony of semi-civilized children – often naughty, vicious children. Henry Morton Stanley, who accompanied the expedition as a representative of the *New York Herald*, declared it was an example of 'how wild and how rank a colony of negroes can become when left to their own sinful and wicked devices, unchecked and un-curbed by the hand of law ... '[7]

Before the *Ambriz* dropped anchor, the childlike citizens of the land boarded the ship in a friendly invasion, armed only with smiles and laughter. Many were dressed in black silk hats, paper collars and spurs. All looked and acted like fugitives from a minstrel show as they swarmed ex-citedly over the deck, jumping, shouting, gesticulating, scrambling over one another, laughing all the while at themselves and one another like people possessed. They carried everything before them. Soon a chair came crashing through a cabin skylight on to a breakfast table. A sur-prised colonel almost tumbled after the furniture, but he managed to hold his ground with an umbrella. Not until the passengers made for shore and porters were assigned to the luggage did the hubbub subside. These same jolly people who welcomed Sir Garnet and his party to Africa would a few weeks later light bonfires to celebrate the rumour of the white chief's defeat and death.

That morning Sir Garnet and his staff, all dressed in their serviceable Ashanti uniform, stepped ashore. Wolseley went to Government House to see Berkeley, the governor, and to arrange affairs connected with the expedition. Since the new commander of all West African territories was also civil administrator of the Gold Coast, it was agreed that Berkeley would not make any embarrassing visits to the place while Wolseley was there, so as to avoid any difficulty involving civil authority.

After a busy day, the general returned to his ship exhausted, mostly from the close, damp heat that left all newcomers dripping. There was no fury about West African heat; the thermometer rarely soared to the heights it did in India. It was an enervating steam bath with constant sweating, night and day, that seemed to bleed the sap of energy from the victim's every pore.

At Sierra Leone Sir Garnet began recruiting. Two officers were sent by dispatch boat north to Gambia, the poorest, smallest, and oldest of Britain's African colonies, to enlist fighting men from among the native Moslem tribes. Another officer remained behind in Freetown in an effort to recruit volunteers, especially pensioners from the West India regiments, who would be of value as drill instructors among the native levies. They would be joined with two entire West India regiments scheduled to take part in the campaign. These regiments had been originally recruited from ex-slaves rescued from slavers, somewhere on the Atlantic, to serve in those areas where mortality was high among European troops.

While in Freetown Wolseley applied to the governor to have his agent at Sherboro enlist the warlike cannibals of the Kosso tribe and send a message to Lagos to bring 150 Haussas to the Gold Coast capital. The latter were the best fighting men to be had in West Africa – tall, strong, daring, and marvels of discipline. It was said of them that 'if their complexion were white instead of black, they would have been nothing unlike Europeans'. They were followers of the Prophet, fanatic fatalists who came originally from a region close to the shores of Lake Chad. The tenets of Islam, however, never fully penetrated their superstitious hearts, for they celebrated the appearance of the new moon with hideous chanting and drumsongs; nor would they, like devout Muslims, abstain from strong drink. Known locally as 'cut faces' because of their practice of furrowing their cheeks with deep scars similar to the ancient Huns, these Haussas, armed with desperate courage and Sniders, could be relied upon to cleave a path to Kumasi for glory and palm wine.

With such military bric-à-brac, Wolseley hoped to build an army. The pay, however, was too small to raise many soldiers in Gambia or Sierra Leone, where only a couple of hundred entered the Queen's service. In Freetown the better element were disappointed that more undesirables were not taken south, for they made the tropic night unbearable with their yelling, dancing, singing, and tum-tumming in the streets.

Some bearers were obtained from among the industrious colony of Kroomen when the *Ambriz* anchored again farther south at Cape Palmas, Liberia. Though as strong as Hercules, they eschewed the smell of gunpowder. Great numbers of these thrifty, itinerant Krooboys were employed on board ships, especially warships, where they were given such names as 'Bottle of Beer', 'Tar Bucket', and 'Pea Soup' by inventive sailors.

On the morning of October 2nd the *Ambriz* arrived at Cape Coast Castle, one of several prison-castles dotted along this slave coast from which hundreds of thousands of Africans were once sent to labour in the Americas after being plucked out of the jungle by tribes like the Ashanti. Beyond the ghastly white old castle stood a squalid town of crumbling huts. The officers at first believed they were viewing the bombarded remains of a town until they were told that the dilapidated appearance was the result of the heavy rains whose season had just passed. Nevertheless, to Sir Garnet and his men it was the Land of Promise. For an armed adventure, it combined the excitement of exploration (for hardly a half-dozen men had travelled the trail to Kumasi) with tales of golden riches about the Ashanti; and this was overlaid with the soldierly thrill of danger that awaited them in a jungle infested with hordes of cruel and cunning savages.

# CHAPTER EIGHT

# FIRE LOW, FIRE SLOW

I F the Cabinet believed they could win Sir Garnet's co-operation by
sending him out as a major-general without an army, they did not
know their man. Wolseley soon forced their hand. In public dispatches
home, he dwelt on the humiliating position in which he found himself:
commanding a worthless body of native auxiliaries who were incapable
of striking a telling blow against an enemy so insultingly close by – only
a few hours' march from Cape Coast. His weakness and embarrassment,
he announced, in turn shamed the English nation. A campaign once
undertaken could not be abandoned until victory was won. Was the
British lion, he asked, so pusillanimous as to turn tail before a few hostile
savages? Even the Duke of Cambridge, a staunch opponent to proposals
that would send his brave soldiers to fight in a deadly climate where there
was little chance for glory, could not resist the pressure.

Sir Garnet beseeched Cardwell to send the two infantry battalions the
Government had agreed to hold in readiness for him. By the time the
troops arrived at the end of the year, he promised a good road, furnished
with sites for encampments, constructed to the Prah; complete preparation of the transport for the advance; and the best organization that could
be attained among the native troops and carriers. During the march, every
recognized sanitary precaution would be observed. Wolseley vowed that
not one man more than was essential to success would be disembarked, and
no soldier would be detained one hour longer than was absolutely necessary. As an afterthought, he requested a third battalion consisting of
picked officers and men to act as a reserve.

Once Cardwell received the application for troops, he acted with
exceptional speed. He obtained Cabinet approval for his decision to send
British troops, and then he sat up all night making arrangements with the
authorities at the War Office. In a matter of hours, the troops – the 2nd
Battalion of the Royal Welch Fusiliers, and the 2nd Battalion of the Rifle
Brigade – were ordered out to sea, along with a battery of field artillery
and a company of engineers. A third battalion from the 42nd Highlanders,
rather than one of specially selected soldiers as Wolseley requested, was

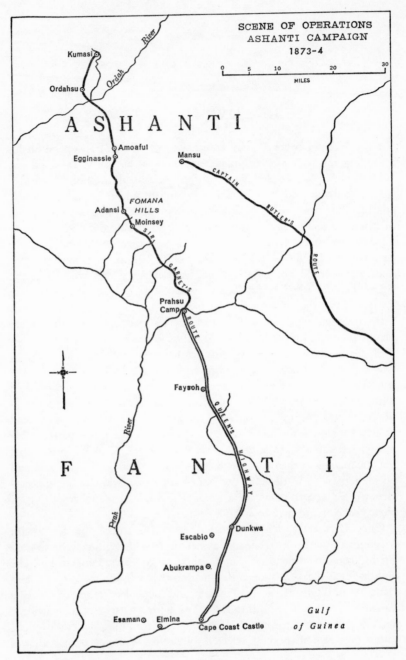

SCENE OF OPERATIONS
ASHANTI CAMPAIGN
1873-4

0    5    10         20         30
MILES

Kumasi

Ordahsu

Ordah River

A S H A N T I

Amoaful
Egginassie          Mansu

CAPTAIN

BUTLER'S

FOMANA
Adansi    HILLS          ROUTE
Moinsey

SIR

GARNET'S

Prahsu
Camp    ROUTE

QUEENS

Faysoh

HIGHWAY

F    A    N    T    I

River

Escabio    Dunkwa

Prah

Abukrampa

Gulf
of Guinea

Esaman    Elmina
Cape Coast Castle

also prepared for African service. The force would arrive off Cape Coast sometime in December.

On the same day that he wrote to Cardwell, Sir Garnet penned a message summoning the King of the Ashanti to withdraw all his warriors to the Prah by November 12th. He was to release all his captives at once and make guarantees for the payment of compensation to those he had abused. Once these conditions were met, the governor would treat him 'in a friendly spirit'. The Ashanti reply came not from the Kofi, who was busy adding to his harem of 300 wives,* but from his commander-in-chief at Mampon, Amanquatia, who intercepted the message. He stated that they had no quarrel with the white man; he was merely punishing vassal tribes who refused to serve their rightful monarch. Amanquatia closed his message with the affectionate phrase, 'I send my love to you.'

The governor was not in a loving mood. The very day he sent his summons to the King, he moved to make his first assault on the Ashanti who threatened Wood's force near Elmina. Wolseley had briefly played the role of diplomat merely to satisfy the authorities at home. He knew the Ashanti could not be influenced by threats. They had no awareness of Britain as a military power. Sneeringly they would ask, would these white men, who were carried about in hammocks like aristocrats, know how to fight in the jungle? When Colonel Wood invited the chief of Esaman, an ally of the Ashanti, to come to Elmina, he replied with insolence: 'Come and get me; white men dare not go into the bush.'

Wolseley decided to go into the bush and destroy Esaman and several neighbouring towns. It would serve not only as a signal chastisement of the Ashanti and their allies, but it would cut off the invaders from their supplies, including armaments, which came up from coastal areas. Buller's effective intelligence efforts clearly demonstrated that Esaman, some four miles north-west of Elmina, was the nodal point of enemy communications. The Ashanti would be forced to begin a retreat that he hoped would not terminate until they reached the Prah.

Only a half-dozen officers were taken into Wolseley's confidence. The Ashanti had an excellent spy system. Should they learn of the proposed attack, Amanquatia would come down on them with his entire army. To deceive the enemy, Wolseley let it ooze out at breakfast, in the presence of correspondents, that Glover was in danger of being surrounded and that he might go to him to see if he could be of any help. At breakfast the next

* Though polygamy was allowed to any extent in his land, the King was restricted by law to 3,333 wives.

morning, he announced that the situation was desperate and he was going to the Volta to assist Glover. That evening (October 13th) the general, his staff, ninety rifles of the 2nd West India, and only two undeceived correspondents, boarded a gunboat and sailed for Elmina instead of the Volta. Wolseley was immensely pleased with the way his ruse had misled the specials. The correspondents who missed the first battle of the war were less than pleased. In defence Wolseley would quote the great master, Napoleon: 'In war all is moral.'

Daylight comes quickly to the tropics. It was sun bright by the time the column of half a thousand soldiers, nearly half of them European, landed and got under way. McNeill, chief of staff, led the way with Haussas dressed in loose, flowing, blue serge tunics and red turbans. They marched with a showy, devil-may-care air, though they were green troops unused to their officers and their rifles. They learned to operate their Sniders, which they 'tenderly nursed like well-loved babies', during the journey from Cape Coast. Close behind, sometimes alongside, were the West Indians, barefooted and wearing ill-fitting white tunics and turbans – a fine wiry-looking body of men, but their white officers, unfortunately, soon proved 'worse than useless'. Then followed the 'blue backbone' of the force, a detachment of sailors under Captain Freemantle ('Little Free') two companies of marines and one of marine artillery. Interspersed between their ranks were naked labourers under Buller and industrious Kroomen dragging a 7-pounder, a rocket tube, ammunition, and hammocks for the wounded. Bringing up the rear was the bulk of the West Indians and a couple of hundred native carriers. Up and down the line passed the European officers in their sombre grey homespun. The constitutionally nervous Wood was in command, but Wolseley, carried about in a great chair, was conspicuous. He wanted to impress the natives with the fact that he was a military commander as well as an administrator.

A string of men followed a swampy path for nearly an hour, sometimes wading knee-deep in black water. Farther on they entered a ten-inch wide path with a jungle wall on either side. Approaching Esaman, skirmishers were sent out, Haussas to the front, marines on the flanks. A few thousand yards outside the town, the invisible enemy opened fire at point-blank range, one Haussa being mortally wounded by a musket that touched him. The battle was on.

The Haussas ran back a short distance, turned, and then fired wildly into the air and at imaginary foes in the bush. The West Indians were infected with their bad example and became almost uncontrollable. The marines in turn became excited, firing without aiming. The main body came up on the double with 'Little Free', bringing the gun and rockets which soon played on the enemy.

The bush obscured the sight of battle but intensified its sounds. From the Ashanti side was heard the thumping noise of tom-toms and the dull sonorous sound of the enormous, overloaded Danish guns and blunderbusses scattering pebbles, rusty nails and bits of lead. Ashanti warriors going into battle chanted, 'If I go on, I shall die; if I remain behind, I shall be killed; it is better to go on and die.' The advancing column contributed to the concert of battle with the sharp crack of Sniders, the screech of rockets, and the occasional deep, throaty roar of the 7-pounder. The tremendous yelling chorus of Haussa men, invoking Allah and his Prophet, drowned the whimperings of the carriers cringing on the ground and even the shouts of officers who bawled: 'Steady, Marines! ... Take ground to the left! ... Don't throw away your shots, lads!'

The officers were discernible through the smoke of battle, dashing about and making emphatic gestures. The staff and special service officers, performing under the critical eye of their chief, sought to justify his choice by freely risking their lives. Prime targets for Ashanti fire, several fell. Buller was saved from a severe wound by his compass case which stopped a slug. O'Neill came rushing back towards Wolseley, supporting a torn arm with all the tendons, muscles, and sinews standing out 'like strands of an unravelled rope's end'.[1] He bellowed from anger, not pain, having lost all chance of seeing further action in West Africa.

The general could no longer restrain himself. He jumped down from his chair and took over the command from Wood, somewhat to the latter's dissatisfaction. By now the troops engaged had lost all formation and the fight was resolving itself into little knots of men led by officers. A few of the native troops fled to the rear and the rest were in danger of being stampeded. The general and his staff, 'with a lively audacity', led the column forward. The enemy fled before them. Esaman and its stores were abandoned.

Captain Brackenbury and Lieutenant Charteris, Wolseley's noble-looking aide, with a handful of marines, were first to enter the deserted town. The only inhabitant was an abandoned infant which was saved from the flames. On the way back the marines argued over who should 'carry the kid'.

The casualties were trifling. Two were killed and twenty-three wounded. Unreported minor wounds were bandaged with turbans and pugarees. The enemy's old flint-muskets, into which gunpowder was loosely poured without wadding, rarely pierced the skin at more than fifty yards. The slugs merely bounced off with a sting.

After a brief halt, the force turned round to destroy the coastal villages which were already being bombarded by the warships. Sir Garnet and his staff returned to Cape Coast that evening.

Wolseley called the little fight at Esaman the turning-point of the war. He had shown his enemies and his friends on the Gold Coast that he could take Europeans through the densest bush with comparative ease. The myth of Ashanti invincibility had been shattered. At once a new attitude prevailed along the coast. The present generation of Fanti, accustomed to a desk-bound administrator, were encouraged by the sight of a fighting governor. The Elmina, braver than most Fanti, deserted their Ashanti allies and joined Wolseley's army. The governor expected large bodies of men from the other tribes to join his forces soon.

Aside from the moral value, the fight at Esaman was a rehearsal for future battles which proved to Wolseley that little could be accomplished without European troops. No reliance could be placed on native troops in a fight; they would never become a thoroughly disciplined body. Furthermore, because of the dense cover in the jungle, where an officer can exercise control over only a few men, he asked Cardwell that a ratio of at least one officer to every twenty men be established in the small European contingent he requested.

The victory at Esaman may have broken the Ashanti habit of victory, but it left unaffected the fear most Fanti had for them. Instead of a heavy enlistment following his victory, as the governor anticipated, an absurdly small number responded to his frequent appeals. Only 2,000 came forward, and most of these were of doubtful value.

As recruiting agents, the women of Cape Coast did their best in ferreting out able-bodied males, becoming more determined in their pursuit and more outrageous in their behaviour every day. In the fore were those whose husbands had already joined. They dabbed themselves with white paint on the face, shoulders and breasts, but abstained from the usual practice of stripping naked, in deference to the feelings of the many Europeans in the town. Going about in groups, dancing, yelling, clapping and acting like Bacchantes, they searched for the lagging men. When the women found their quarry, 'insults and abuse were freely poured upon them – even blows were not wanting – and the breech cloths were pulled off them in token of contempt.'[2] Cape Coast had the highest rate of enlistment among the towns of the Protectorate.

Scarcity of labour owing to the demands of the engineers and transport officers caused the enterprising British to experiment with women carriers. They soon had good reason to congratulate themselves. Girls, some as young as twelve, cheerful and willing, could put the Fanti men and the Sierra Leone men to shame. The women carried loads on their heads weighing from fifty to sixty pounds, often with a baby slung behind their back on a cankey, or bustle-like cushion. Always in good temper, they kept up a stream of chatter, and if not talking, they were singing 'like so many English schoolgirls'.

On November 1st, Sir Garnet deputed Captain Butler to raise the chiefs of Akim, the hereditary enemies of the Ashanti to the east, and march them to the Prah to cut off the retreating Ashanti. Though Wolseley would miss the lively conversation of the great Irish raconteur at his table, he decided to put his eloquence to use among native chiefs. If anyone could win the Akims to the English cause, it was the fast-talking Irishman. Butler left two days later with a few supplies, two Union Jacks, a small boy interpreter, a bag of gold pieces and great expectations.

As the Ashanti continued their retreat, the general sent out strong reconnaissances to keep contact and worry them. They withdrew not as a beaten army but as warriors still confident of their strength to meet and defeat anyone who dared to oppose them in the bush. Before returning to Kumasi, Amanquatia swore he would take Abrakrampa and burn it. It was said he had a special 'crow to pluck' with the King of Abra. Sir Garnet consequently strengthened the garrison under Major Baker Russell at Abrakrampa so that he had nearly a thousand men. Shelter trenches were dug, houses were loopholed, the Wesleyan chapel was converted into a citadel, and the jungle was cleared for 100 yards all round the town. But the cry of 'Wolf!' was heard so many times at Abrakrampa, that the general finally decided the Ashanti would not attack and called for the withdrawal of the Haussas and marines. They were lined up to depart on the afternoon of November 5th when the Ashanti made their long-awaited attack. With drums beating, ivory trumpets blaring, and thousands of voices chanting in unison, they attacked the fortified town. Heavy losses, however, kept them from venturing too far out of the bush and into the cleared area.

When the general in Cape Coast learned an attack had actually begun, he made no preparations to assist Baker Russell, confident he could easily repulse the enemy. Wolseley regarded him as one of his finest discoveries. The dashing cavalryman of the 13th Hussars, whose dictum to all troopers was 'look pretty in time of peace and get killed in war', was a soldier by instinct. He ignored the drill book and danger. His decisions, usually prefaced with a booming 'By Jove,' were quick and intuitive. And right or wrong, he carried them through with dash against the foe, whether in the field or at the War Office.

A little past two on the morning of November 6th, a half-awake Wolseley was informed by a messenger from a near-by post that Abrakrampa was under vigorous attack. The general departed quickly and furtively before dawn with reinforcements.

The forced march was a severe strain on the relieving force. Much of the distance was destitute of shade, and many of the men were without sun-helmets. Giddy from sunstroke, they reeled and fell under the powerful rays of the sun. As soon as they dropped, Dr Home, the principal medical officer of the expedition, had them drawn into the shade where they were fanned and given water and stimulants. By the time the column reached Iscabio (ten miles out) about noon, a third of the force was literally strewn along the way. Though heavy firing could be heard at Abrakrampa, Wolseley rested his exhausted men for four hours, sufficient time for many who had recovered to catch up.

At sundown Sir Garnet, with half of his original column, was escorted by the King of Abra and his warriors into Abrakrampa, which they entered unmolested. Sir Garnet was greeted at the entrance to the beleaguered place by Major Baker Russell and many of his officers, whom he warmly congratulated on their admirable defence. A number of jokes were exchanged about the 'siege of Lucknow'. Soon the Ashanti fire continued as heavy as before, but as night fell it died away. The next morning the noisy but harmless fire was renewed. At noon it stopped altogether and it was assumed the Ashanti had fallen back.

Tardily the general ordered pursuit, not with his best troops but with the cowardly Cape Coast allies who had come up that morning under Wood, declining to engage the enemy as ordered on the way in. A thousand levies were paraded facing the bush. The governor told them that he would give them a last chance to redeem their honour. A pathetic, ludicrous display of cowardice followed. Units in the British army usually quarrelled for the position to the right of the line; these Fanti Allies crowded to the left, the point farthest removed from where the Ashanti were believed to be. Behind them stood their chiefs with whips. And behind them were placed the ferocious Kossos with drawn swords, which they preferred to rifles; they declared they had come to the Gold Coast to die. When the order was given to advance, the Fanti allies stepped forward a few paces and then stopped, 'Like children afraid to go into cold water'.[3] The chiefs moved up, swinging their whips. The Kossos took a malicious delight in belabouring them with the flat of their swords. Officers of the general's staff rushed up waving sticks and umbrellas; some kicked the natives with their heavy boots. Nor were the chiefs spared; one had his ears boxed. Nothing could induce them to budge.

At last some Haussas and King Abra's men were ordered forward with the Kossos. Passing over the Cape Coast levies, they found the enemy camp abandoned. They had obviously surprised the Ashanti and frightened them off. A few prisoners were taken and a number of Fanti captives released. One Ashanti was shot in the act of cutting a mother's throat with her infant still on her back. Along with war drums, heads severed by Kossos and other trophies, the pursuers brought back the sacred stool of Amanquatia, who was said to have been so drunk he had to be carried away to avoid capture.

The action brought glory to Baker Russell and his officers, but not to Wolseley. He had thrown away an opportunity to hurt a fleeing and disheartened foe. Baker Russell had urged the general to attack at dawn with the large force of whites and good negro troops at his disposal. They certainly could have cut the Ashanti army to pieces. Instead, Wolseley waited until two in the afternoon and then ordered out his poorest troops. The next day Sir Garnet, who planned to return to the coast with most of the Europeans, ordered strong reconnaissances with the same timid mob of Cape Coast levies supporting the Kossos and Haussas.

That morning, while the general was marching out of Abrakrampa, a reconnaissance party made contact with the Ashanti rear-guard. They turned about and mauled their pursuers. The Cape Coast men lost their heads and fired on one another, killing over a score of their own people. Rushing to the rear, they knocked over the Haussas, drowning one man as they trampled him into a stream. They did not stop running until they reached home. For three weeks all sight of the Ashanti was lost because none of the Fanti allies could be persuaded to approach the retiring enemy. Unmolested, the Ashanti army retreated slowly; a great wounded beast dragging itself to its lair, trailing blood and dripping disease.

The general was not himself. He seemed to have lost his characteristic vim and his ability to think clearly. The day the Ashanti retreated from Abrakrampa, Reade of *The Times* watched him post a 7-pounder in the clearing and carefully point it away from the enemy position! Then he enigmatically sat with his staff staring anxiously in a direction opposite from that of the enemy. Though he refused to admit it to anyone, the enfeebling hand of fever had touched him. Back in Government House he

179

collapsed. Dr Home diagnosed his condition as 'ardent fever', induced by his prolonged exposure to the sun on the march to Abrakrampa.

For the best part of November, Sir Garnet struggled to live. To improve his chances of recovery, Dr Home ordered him removed to the hospital ship, the *Simoom*, a converted troopship ill-fitted for the purpose. When Wood visited him, he came away doubting he would reach Kumasi. As second in command, 'that ambitious little red-headed colonel', as Wolseley called him, began to think in terms of taking over the expedition.

Wood saw him on one of his better days. Much of the time Wolseley was delirious. At times he believed he was going mad. Over and over again he dictated to himself a letter of resignation to Cardwell, expressing his regret at being forced to do so. Then his puzzled brain tried repeatedly to work out a quadratic equation which no amount of transposition could solve. The nights brought even more impossible problems to his fevered mind while the surf pounded jarringly out of harmony with his quickened pulse. He speculated irrationally on how the unused force of sea power could be harnessed to work all the spinning jennies of Lancashire until he suffered such torment that perhaps only the pen of Edgar Allan Poe could describe them adequately.

By his side, night and day, was his devoted nurse, Lieutenant Maurice, who did not take off his clothes for a fortnight. To him and Home, he owed his life. For the rest of his days, he remained fiercely loyal to Maurice.

Lord Derby described the expedition as 'an engineer's and doctor's war'. Upon the services of these men, he contended, its success depended. After the retreat of the Ashanti, the construction of the seventy-three-mile road to the banks of the Prah and the preparation of the camping grounds proceeded far more quickly. Major Robert Home and his sappers cut a path through forest and jungle, varying from eight to twelve feet wide; 237 bridges were built, and innumerable swamps were corduroyed so that the troops would remain dry-shod all the way. A telegraph-line was strung to the Prah, and eventually beyond, which helped to relieve the look of barbarity. The Ashanti believed this to be a powerful fetish. Not to be outdone, they took white thread and intertwined it among the trees from the Prah to Kumasi.

At intervals of from seven to twelve miles, encampments were constructed to accommodate 400 men and officers. To ensure the health of the troops, each station had a hut for infectious cases. A rapid transport system was created whereby the sick and wounded would be quickly removed on cots or in hammocks to hospitals at Cape Coast, Mansu and Prahsu. Eventually all patients were to be placed on hospital ships, fitted with all modern conveniences. Arrangements were made to receive many of them at Gibraltar rather than send them home in the middle of winter.

Instead of an engineer's or doctor's war, it should have been called the Control's* war, for the greater includes the less. The talents of the engineers were indispensable; but they required labour to fell trees, construct huts, and to set iron telegraph-poles. The skill of the surgeons was vital; but they could not function without labour to carry medical panniers, stores of medical comforts, and, most of all, their patients. It was the function of the Control to supply this labour. Thus, it became the mainspring of the whole expedition.

Labour difficulties commenced early. The natives were difficult to induce to work at a shilling a day. When they were hired, they often proved shiftless and insubordinate and deserted by the thousand. Sir Garnet, who was deeply concerned with the problem from the first, complained that handing men over to the Control 'is like pouring water into a sieve'.

The pressing urgency of the situation led Sir Garnet to adopt extreme measures. After the disgraceful conduct of the native auxiliaries at Abrakrampa and their subsequent flight to Cape Coast, he disarmed nearly all 3,000 of them and turned them over to the Control to labour. In mid November compulsory service was introduced. The police were instructed to seize any male in Cape Coast who was not employed by the Government or carrying a special pass stating he was exempt from military service. It was like the press-gangs of old: a casual visitor, a schoolteacher, a small storekeeper all found themselves moving up country with barrels of pork on their heads and policemen with loaded rifles at their sides. Wolseley wrote to the Duke, 'I cannot afford to allow the Expedition to come to a standstill through a rigid observance of English law.'[4]

On December 22nd, Sir Garnet took a somewhat revolutionary step by taking the transport department out of the hands of the Control and turning it over to combat officers under Lieutenant-Colonel George Pomeroy Colley, who had just arrived from England. By this time there were 6,000 carriers working between the coast and the Prah. But the problem of desertion was by no means solved.

The period from Sir Garnet's return from Abrakrampa to the landing of

---

* A civilian rather than military organization that represented an awkward amalgamation of the purveyors, commissariat, transport and paymaster departments.

European troops at the beginning of the year was called 'the quiet time' by the correspondents. It became increasingly difficult to obtain news because of Sir Garnet's distrust of the press. The general's reluctance to talk about his mission and his intentions was imitated by his staff. They carried it to such an extent that Stanley compared them to 'a lot of wise-looking owls'. When information was passed along to them, the correspondents sniffed at it with suspicion, suspecting one of Sir Garnet's little tricks.

Reporters, desperate for copy, began to write about local customs. They told fantastic yarns about how 'prisoners of war were eaten, but not women, because they were tough'.[5] The irascible Henry Morton Stanley, who considered the whole business 'a one-horse affair', pondered on ways to promote civilization and commerce in this benighted part of the continent. Being accustomed to native ways, he taught the other 'gentlemen of the press' how to flog their servants to get the most out of them. If they had no stomach for the job, he obligingly carried out the sentence for them with 'no gentle hands'.[6] Mr Livingstone would have been shocked.

Sir Garnet dreaded inaction. The press was a capricious monster: 'If I am forced to do nothing for a couple of months,' he wrote Dick, 'the press may turn round and abuse me as soundly as it has previously lavished unmerited praise upon me.'[7]

Wolseley did not realize for some time, for it took nearly a month for news to reach him from home, that public opinion was now solidly behind his expedition. The general's confessions of embarrassment and weakness had their desired effect. 'The British people, though averse to combat,' wrote one newsman, 'like to fight it out; when once arms have clashed and blood has been spilt they want no parleyings.'[8] It was a time of national humiliation, for English prestige all over the world had slipped in the past few years. They had allowed Prussia to become master on the Continent 'by falsely betraying France'; they had sumbitted 'to a gross violation of bad faith' by permitting Russia to remilitarize the Black Sea, thereby sacrificing the most important advantage gained from the Crimean War; they had accepted a 'fraudulent bargain' in the Treaty of Washington by agreeing to pay tribute to the United States.[9] Here was a powerful incentive for imperialism: the opportunity to regain a lost reputation by whipping a mob of arrogant savages. The press began to clamour for the speedy dispatch of regiments from home.

Arriving early in December, the European troops came at the wrong time. They were too late to defeat the Ashanti while they were still close to the coast, and too early to attack them on the other side of the Prah, for the 'Queen's Highway' to the Prah, with its eight camps strung out along the way, would not be ready before Christmas Day. Wolseley, determined not to expose them to the deadly climate any sooner than was necessary, ordered them on a cruise until the first of the year. It was no holiday for the bored and cramped troops who wanted to get down to business as soon as possible. Everyone wanted to get into the fight.

When it was learned that certain officers in different units were of necessity to remain behind and would not take part in any attack, bitter remarks and grumbling was to be heard. Some nearly went mad with anger and disappointment. One officer threatened to send in his papers and go along as a civilian. Others disobeyed orders, and went forward on their own. Many volunteered to forgo rank and serve as non-commissioned officers with the native regiments. More serious was the fact that many who were selected to go, deliberately concealed an illness, fearing they would be confined to a hospital ship if they sought medical attention. Some officers later died as a result. The men displayed a similar spirit.

Wolseley's plan was to invade Ashanti territory on January 15th from as many directions as possible, with the lines of the advancing columns converging on Kumasi. The main body, composed of the Europeans, the Naval Brigade, Wood's and Baker Russell's natives, and Rait's Artillery, was to advance directly on the main road from Prahsu to the Ashanti capital. On the extreme left, Captain Dalrymple with a force of Wassaws and other native allies. On the extreme right, Glover's men moving from the Volta. A connecting link between the main force and Glover's was to be a body of Western Akims raised by Butler. The 1st and 2nd West India were to act as a reserve and guard the line of communications for the main body. Wolseley was later criticized by students of war for violating the first principle of strategy by dividing his force. Actually he never planned to use the columns of native auxiliaries for anything more than a 'diversion in favour of the main attack'.[10]

If the invasion had been contingent upon the movements of the other three converging columns, it would never have succeeded. Butler expended all his ready eloquence and energy in a vain effort to induce the Akims to fight the Ashanti. After heart-breaking delays that would have vanquished a less indomitable nature, he neared Amoaful with 1,400 Akims on January 30th. Suddenly realizing they were deep in Ashanti-land, the entire body was seized with fear and vanished. Dalrymple's errand was no more successful. But Buller later estimated that the presence of Butler's force alone diverted 10,000 Ashanti from contesting the advance of the main body.

The Glover force actually represented a rival expedition. Glover was under Wolseley's orders, but it was understood that the former retained a certain independence of action. Wolseley could neither remove him nor interfere with the details involved in his command. The captain was a servant of the Colonial Office, while the general, though his dispatches as governor went to Lord Kimberley, was the agent of the War Office.

Actually, Glover, anxious to open an easy avenue of trade into the interior by way of the Volta, regarded the suppression of the Ashanti as a minor part of a grander project. Therefore when Wolseley ordered him to take his force and cross the Prah on January 15th, he seemed surprised and complied with reluctance; but Glover promised he would be there with an army of not less than 16,000 and possibly as many as 30,000. It was Wolseley's turn to be surprised on Christmas Day when Glover reported that he could not possibly reach the Prah for forty days because of the hesitance of the chiefs upon whose co-operation he relied. But the general could not alter his plans; further delay could defeat his projected invasion. Armed with the information that the dilatory captain was under more stringent orders from London to obey his instructions, Sir Garnet sent a peremptory order to Glover to comply with his original request, taking what Haussas and native troops he had. Otherwise, as far as being of any service to him in the war, Glover was told he 'might just as well be operating on the Zanzibar coast of Africa'.[11] Thus, the stocky little captain marched with a column of 800 natives and a few white officers to Kumasi and fame, though he did so under protest, and formally declined to accept any responsibility for the undertaking. Both men always denied that there was any lack of cordiality between them, but a perceptive reporter was convinced 'that they both wished each other at the devil'.

Sir Garnet left Cape Coast for the front on December 27th seated on a light buggy drawn by six strong Fanti. He hoped this conveyance would spare him some of the pain he was suffering from his old leg wound.

Before leaving Cape Coast, Sir Garnet issued a general order for the information and guidance of the white troops, into whom he hoped to inspire confidence. He pointed out that if ordinary precautions were observed, there was no real danger from the climate during the few weeks they would be ashore. As to fighting in the bush, he compared it to fighting by twilight, and called upon the men to be steady and self-reliant. To implant a feeling of scorn for the enemy, the general reminded them that with their breechloaders they were equal to at least a score of the enemy. The Ashanti, on the other hand, were so poorly armed that their slugs did little harm except at very close range. He reminded them that Providence instilled in the heart of the black man a superstitious awe and dread that prevented him from meeting the white man face to face. He stressed the importance of being kind to the native carriers, upon whom they must rely for food and ammunition. And the general warned that all plundering and unnecessary destruction of property would be strictly repressed. The order closed with the celebrated direction, which in his *Pocketbook* he urged should be fixed in the mind when meeting an enemy: 'Be cool; fire low, fire slow, and charge home; and the more numerous your enemy, the greater will be the loss inflicted upon him, and the greater your honour in defeating him.'

When the young general approached Prahsu, inside a great bend of the Prah, he found a sylvan town with streets laid out and squared by the compass, and large barracks constructed according to the latest dictates of military science. One of the first buildings to be completed was the hospital, over which was a sign reading 'THE FORLORN HOPE'. In the centre of Prahsu was a great square, along one side of which stood a line of huts for the staff, and over the general's dwelling floated the Union Jack. No one was idle. Long lines of men, mostly Wood's and Baker Russell's, wound in and out of the trees through the streets carrying equipment and rubbish on their heads. Others were cutting brush, digging holes, planting stakes, etc. In one corner infantry officers were drilling their companies; in another, artillery officers were teaching Haussas of Rait's Artillery how to aim. A large body of engineers was occupied with bridging the dark, turbulent stream. They all paused long enough to greet the general with 'a hoarse murmur and deep hum of joy', as he made his way to the square to be received by Wood, Baker Russell, and other officers.

Within an hour after Sir Garnet arrived, a gold-badged Ashanti envoy, escorted by Buller, appeared with two letters from his king to the governor. Writing in his customary ambiguous style, Kofi assumed an aggrieved tone and asked for an explanation of these unjust assaults on his people. He defiantly repeated his earlier demand that certain Fanti tribes be recognized as coming under his authority, and his demand for money which would buy the release of his European prisoners.

The governor replied that he was about to invade his kingdom from four different directions. To avoid the destruction of his power, the Ashanti king could have peace on the following terms: 1. All prisoners, European and African, must be released at once; 2. the payment of 50,000 ounces of gold; 3. a treaty of peace to be signed at Kumasi after the delivery of hostages for the safety of the general and his escort.

Meanwhile, on New Year's Day the disembarkation of the European regiments began. In the unpicturesque Ashanti uniform of Norfolk grey, the Europeans moved out half a battalion each day. On the fifth day, the advance was deadlocked as hundreds of carriers deserted all along the highway. When the news reached Prahsu, the general immediately transformed Wood's regiment of blacks and the West Indians into carriers and sent them back along the road to bring up loads from down-stations. The Highlanders volunteered to carry their own baggage in the enervating climate and made a trip or two until the general heard of it; he forbade their exertions, which in this climate could wreck their fighting capabilities.

To delay in Africa is to invite death. Desperate for carriers, Wolseley cast all forms of legality aside. Kidnapping began on a large scale. Nearly 3,000 short of the 8,000 required, Colley asked permission to burn villages where the deserters had their homes, and to employ more women and children as carriers. Wolseley approved. Similar drives were made by other officers. The navy also participated. The commandant of Accra, with a man-of-war at his disposal, went up and down the coast collecting carriers. If the chiefs were unco-operative, a party of sailors would land at night, surround his village, and carry off the entire adult population, leaving only a few old women to care for the infants. In Cape Coast, Brigadier-General Sir Archibald Alison, the one-armed commander of the white brigade, placed a cordon of troops around the town and combed it for deserters and men who were not exempt from service. All public works were stopped, and with the permission of merchants, their employees were drafted into the transport work. The Wesleyan Mission contributed 150 women and girls.

These vigorous measures had the desired effect. Carriers came in by the thousands and the advance was renewed. A fortnight after the mass desertions began, Colley reported the carrier problem completely solved with an excess of 2,000. He reorganized the carriers on a tribal basis with an interpreter attached to each unit. Moreover, they were paid regularly, and one day's rest was allowed after four days' work. The system he evolved began to function with mechanical exactitude.

Colley had a powerful mind and an extraordinary facility for hard work. He had been regarded by the advanced school of officers as 'a coming man' in the army. During the Ashanti campaign he 'arrived'. His vast theoretical knowledge (his staff examination was the most brilliant on record) was proved in practice. In a crisis, the sober theoretician became a man of action. He rushed about the country, persuading chiefs and beating up villages at all hours, but always returning with carriers. In an incredibly short time he had long lines of blacks, hurried along by perspiring, unjacketed officers, carrying food and ammunition. His unflagging zeal won the admiration of all. Everyone began to say, 'What should we have done without Colley.' As Sir Garnet expressed it, 'He brought order out of chaos.'[12]

The land of the Ashanti was pierced on January 5th when Baker Russell's regiment crossed the Prah. The sharp point of the advance was represented by Lieutenant Lord Gifford and his guides who kept in touch with the enemy, dogging his movements, noting his position, capturing the unsuspecting so as to provide Captain Buller with vital intelligence. The lean and handsome Gifford held the most honourable and most hazardous post in the army. Unassisted by any other white man, the young baron risked his life daily. More than half of his brave little band were killed in this dangerous work. 'Every day,' said Wolseley, 'I expected to get a letter saying that Gifford had been shot.'[13]

As trackers, some of the guides were as good as North American Indians. At a given command, they would dash forward, darting to the right and left like a set of well-trained spaniels. Many of these men were cannibals. Now and again a ghastly whisper would circulate among the Europeans that the Bonnys or Opobos had eaten a prisoner. The less credulous scoffed at such rumours, but Boyle of the *Telegraph* noticed that by some strange coincidence an Ashanti prisoner with a disabling leg wound disappeared at the same time the Opobos' butcher was absent without leave for six hours.

Close behind Baker Russell's slow-moving native regiment was Wood's, and behind them Colonel Webber and some West Indians. Taken together, the force was called the 'black brigade'. Their officers were enjoined by the general to avoid an engagement; Gifford's scouts were ordered not to fire unless fired upon so as not to prejudice the negotiations.

But there was little shooting beyond the Prah. Within ten days, the black brigade occupied a range of steep truncated hills called Adansi, or Fomana, which stood half-way between the Prah and the Ashanti capital, a total distance of sixty miles. From Prahsu to these hills there was hardly a sign of life, animal or human. This broad tract of thirty miles of desolate wilderness had never been colonized by the Ashanti conquerors. Like the Suevi in Caesar's time, they preferred to keep a belt of wasteland around their country. Yet, evidence that the Ashanti were always close by was provided by fetishes and cruel charms staked out in the middle of the road, or hanging from some tree. Slaves, men and women, were mutilated and impaled, sometimes found with their flesh still quivering. Thus the Ashanti propitiated their gods and left a terrifying message to the invaders: 'Regard this body, white man, ye whose feet are hurrying on to our capital, and learn the fate awaiting you.'[14]

The white brigade commenced the passage over the Prah on January 20th. The five-day delay caused by the transport failure was counterbalanced by the rapid, uncontested advance into Ashantiland.

King Kofi needed time to collect his armies. Once more he relied on diplomacy to slow the advance of invading feet that for the first time trod on Ashanti soil. The day after Sir Garnet arrived at Moinsey, Kofi's white prisoners suddenly appeared with a message from the King urgently entreating the general to halt his army. He promised that the disobedient Amanquatia would be made to pay the indemnity.

Immediately after Kofi's message arrived, Sir Garnet sent a telegram to Her Majesty's Government:[15]

ALL THE WHITE PRISONERS ARE NOW IN CAMP. THE KING ACCEPTS TERMS I OFFERED, AND SAYS HE WILL PAY THE INDEMNITY DEMANDED – £20,000. I HALT TOMORROW FOR A FEW DAYS AT FOMANA, 30 MILES FROM COOMASSIE. ALL GOING ON WELL.

Believing that Parliament was about to assemble, Wolseley was eager to have the news of his bloodless success reach a grateful Gladstone Government in time to adorn the Queen's Speech. Not a minute was to be lost. A special runner was selected and promised a large reward if he reached Prahsu on the following morning. From there his words were taken to the nearest telegraph station six miles south. The message reached the coast at ten-thirty a.m., and that evening the swiftest ship carried it to Gibraltar where it could be cabled to London. The news reached home in less than ten days at a cost of £7,000. But it arrived too late, for Gladstone's Government had resigned and a general election was in progress. The message had been sent to be included in a Queen's Speech that was never given, for the opening of a Parliament which never sat, to proclaim a promise of peace that was never kept. It did little more than 'shed a brief and delusive gleam' over the last days of Mr Gladstone's ministry.[16]

In his reply to the King on January 24th, Sir Garnet required as a preliminary to the conclusion of peace the release of all native prisoners, and half the gold indemnity to be sent with important hostages such as the Queen Mother and the heir-apparent. Wolseley never realized that the terms could not be met by the King, for the six hostages he demanded were together more powerful than he.

Two days later the general moved his headquarters to the deserted village of Fomana, beyond the Adansi hills, where he waited to allow the transport to catch and establish a supply depot. The unavoidable delay served the purpose of appearing as a concession to the King's request so that he might arrange for complying with the general's demand.

While waiting at Fomana, where he occupied the home of the King of Andasi, Wolseley inspected the various units of Alison's brigade. The ranks were already sadly thinned by sickness. Of the 1,800 Europeans on shore, 218 had already become ineffective from illness. Wolseley also learned that his good friend, the sweet-tempered Captain Huyshe, was stricken. The fever turned his brain, and he attacked his servant with a sword and sliced off his ear. A few days later he was dead.

After a night of monotonous and defiant tum-tumming that did little more than frighten sleep, the little army had an early breakfast and advanced in column. It was to assume a large open-square formation as soon as they met the enemy so as best to oppose the invariable flanking tactics of the Ashanti. The front face under Alison, consisting of the Black Watch and Rait's Artillery, was to extend 300 yards to either side of the path, with Home's engineers helping to clear the way for movement and firing. The flank columns – Colonel McLeod on the left with Baker Russell's Foot and half the Naval Brigade, and Colonel Wood on the right with his native force and the rest of the Naval Brigade – were to cut paths diagonally outward, and then march parallel to the main path, keeping contact with the Highlanders if possible. The rockets were to take up a position at the front angles of the square. The Rifles were to form the reserve or rear face, if needed. In the hollow of the square would be the general and his staff with a company of Fusiliers. The square represented a total force of 1,509 Europeans and 708 Africans. A party of the 2nd West India, along with some of the native soldiers, remained behind to guard the baggage.

The Battle of Amoaful began at eight five a.m. as Gifford and his guides dashed into Egginassie, driving the enemy scouts back on the main army beyond. When the Black Watch took the lead on the far side of the village, they were greeted by a heavy fusillade. The battle was now fought in earnest as the Highlanders advanced company after company in skirmishing order on the concealed enemy, and the sailors and native levies moved to defend the flanks. The brunt of the fighting was borne by the Highlanders as they descended into the ravine, but they were greatly aided by Rait's booming little 7-pounders which were continually pushed in line with the leading scouts by enthusiastic Haussas. Months of assiduous drill now showed its value. After fourteen or fifteen rounds of slaughtering discharge, in addition to the crushing volleys of the Black Watch, the enemy was swept back. Heaps of dead and wounded lay mutilated by the shells and tearing wounds of the Sniders. The shocking execution of fire was followed by a spirited charge of the Scots against a shaken foe. After securing twenty yards or so, the pattern was repeated, and bit by bit, the obstinate Ashanti were driven back on Amoaful. But there was no respite in the roaring fire of the enemy. Alison claimed he never came under heavier fire in India or the Crimea. The slugs hummed all around them, rattling trees, stripping the bark, and bringing down 'the leaves in a rustling shower suggestive of a gusty autumn morning in England'.[17]

The struggle surged noisily to the sides of the square as Kofi's warriors resorted to their favourite tactics of enveloping the flanks. They came forward in great numbers, their naked bodies sliding through the bush, determined to demolish utterly this force that dared to approach their fetish-guarded capital. On the sides of the square it soon became impossible to keep pace with the Highlanders because of the dense mass of bush penetrated by only a few narrow lanes. The soldiers clearly did not enjoy fighting in the jungle and looked forward to getting the enemy in the open. There was a feeling of helpless uncertainty as parties lost their sense of direction in this baffling maze of hedge. The disadvantages of advancing in parallel columns through dense jungle became manifest. Owing to the nature of the resistance – human and vegetable – or the caution of an officer, they would progress at different speeds and cross lines of fire as one party converged and another diverged. The Highlanders complained that the Naval Brigade fired upon them, and the same complaint was made by the sailors against the Scots.

After several false starts and sanguinary delays, McLeod's column on the left began to make progress. The sharp edge of his force was a party of Opobos who cut a path, one half firing into the bush as the other half slashed at it with their knives. A large clearing was eventually made, rockets were brought into play, and the rest of Baker Russell's men drove the enemy before them in an effort to restore contact with the Highlanders.

Wood's column on the right had less success. His force was so hotly engaged by a very large body of bold Ashanti that he directed his men to make a clearing, lie down, and engage in a duel – rifles against muskets. Wood himself caught the head of a nail in his chest, immediately over the heart. Their progress arrested, a serious, ever-widening gap developed between the advancing Highlanders and the right face of the square. As the enemy poured into the angle, some of the Rifles and Fusiliers moved up to close it.

With violence storming all about him in this hide-and-seek jungle, Sir Garnet with his staff and the surgeons occupied the village of Egginassie – the calm eye of the hurricane. Home's engineers made a great clearing around the village, but the general would not allow the houses to be loopholed, lest such a defensive precaution cause the men to assume that he considered the possibility of falling back.

Wolseley retained an air of perfect calmness, speaking and acting with the greatest composure, mindful that all eyes were upon the general and that courage, like fear, could be infectious. He paced up and down in 'quarter-deck' fashion, deliberately puffing one Havana after another. At times, he whistled a merry tune. With sounds of battle his slight figure seemed to attain greater proportions and exude the promise of victory.

By three converging roads reports came in from his commanders, all telling the same story: 'many wounded ... hard pressed ... would like some support.' Wherever the Ashanti threatened to break through, reserve companies were marched to the critical point with the order, 'Chin straps down, open out, and push on through the jungle.' Wolseley received all news with an easy indifference. His orders were clear and definite. Buller was kept trotting up and down with these orders until it was feared he would collapse from the warm work. Brackenbury remained close by the general's side, assisting him 'unremittingly by the sagacity of his suggestions'.

Early in the afternoon, the enemy made one final, reckless effort to break the face of the square and recapture Egginassie. The scene at the centre suddenly became exciting. The Ashanti came to within 100 yards of headquarters. Slugs began to fall all around. The surgeons momentarily stopped their probing and bandaging. Everyone was up on their feet. The armed guard and reserve of Rifles faced about in the direction of the assault, firing low and firing slow, sending their bullets skimming a few feet from the ground until they struck a tree, an Ashanti in his lurking place, or possibly a chief seated on his stool beneath an umbrella far to the rear. Some of the Ashanti were shot out of trees.

The correspondents were all armed, some with double-barrelled shot-guns. As the enemy made an ugly rush, Wolseley's attention was drawn to the plain-clothed Stanley, who was as 'cool and self-possessed as if he had been at "target practice" '. Time and again, he watched him drop to his knee and ply the advancing foe with never-failing aim. Wolseley's prejudice against this haughty, gruff journalist-explorer evaporated in the smoke of Amoaful. He would never forget the 'unflinching manliness of that face'.[18] Though he was not aware of it, Stanley's fierce black eyes were taking full measure of him. Grudgingly, he admired 'the calm, proud air of the General'.[19]

After nearly an hour, Ashanti fire slackened. Sir Garnet sent word for the line to advance, 'swinging around from the rear so as to drive the enemy northwards before them. The movement was admirably exe-cuted.' The Kossos, who had fought in silence on the defence, began to sing their shrill war-song, 'and slinging their rifles, and drawing their swords ... dashed forward like so many panthers let loose.'[20] The Rifles at their side stalked forward quietly, searching every bush. Meanwhile, the left column cut its way into the main path behind the Black Watch, who had already driven the Ashanti before them. Around noon, after nearly four hours of struggle, the whole line of Highlanders swept into Amoaful. Wild cheers of victory mingled with the most strenuous notes of the pipers. 'What a pity we didn't have our kilts and bonnets,' observed one of the victors.

The Ashanti, who had fought magnificently, were in retreat but not in flight. The rest of the day the reinforced enemy made desultory attacks on the flanks and even menaced Amoaful. The most sustained effort was made towards evening on the line of communications to the rear. The West Indians and Rifles moved back to hold the line, but not before a great deal of baggage was lost. Firing on the road continued until night closed in.

Through the night, science and tenderness were applied to relieve the injured. The surgeons, all of them picked men, were to be seen hard at work with their sleeves rolled up and saturated with blood. The stifled groans of sufferers were to be heard as their limbs were being taken off. Chums knelt beside them, holding their hands and muttering soothing words. The casualties amounted to four dead, 194 wounded; some died later. Several slightly wounded natives, being cared for by their com-rades, were not counted in the official list. The Highlanders suffered most, with two killed and 113 hurt. Most tragic was the case of a wounded Scot who evidently lost his way in the thick bush. Discovered by a party of

Ashanti, he was overpowered and decapitated. His head was their only trophy of the day.

Since the Ashanti removed most of their casualties, their losses were difficult to compute. It was estimated they lost between 800 and 1,200 killed, with as many wounded. Amanquatia was slain, shot in the back as he was being carried to the rear. It was a great victory, and many officers predicted they would march to Kumasi without further resistance. But the general warned, 'They will certainly fight again.'

At dawn on February 2nd, the entire body continued the advance from Amoaful. Baker Russell's Foot were in the van, brushing aside weak ambuscades and the slight resistance encountered at each village on the way. Everywhere the road bore signs of a defeated enemy: the abandoned stores and empty litters, the large dark stains, and the grass and plants that had been flattened by rushing throngs. On reaching Ajimamu, six miles from Amoaful, the army made camp.

Napoleon declared, 'the secret of war lies in the communications'. And to protect a line of communications passing through a densely forested land is the most difficult operation of all. Reports kept coming forward of attacks on posts and convoys all along the line, with frightened Fanti carriers bolting in every direction. Shortly after reaching Ajimamu, Wolseley heard the enemy had made a determined attack on Fomana that day. Only the timely arrival of Colley saved the hospital and store supplies from complete destruction. The timid carriers were so thoroughly frightened by the vigour of the attack, that nothing could persuade them to leave for the front with provisions. Colley reported it would be impossible to move any large load of supplies for several days. The Ashanti proved more of a threat after their defeat than before. Broken up into marauding parties, they harassed the line of supply which was as vital to the existence of Wolseley's force as blood is to the life of a human being.

Thus, sixteen miles short of Kumasi, with an ever-increasing number of soldiers reported sick, the general was faced with a protracted halt. It would be nearly a week before sufficient supplies could be brought up. Even then their progress would be slowed by having to detach units to protect the provision columns. Wolseley always held that in conducting a war against savages, nothing was so disheartening or unsettling as an unremitting offensive. If you stop, the courage of your enemy is restored, for he always assumes you halt from fear.

Deciding delay was the greater enemy, Wolseley prepared a bold dash on Kumasi by deliberately abandoning the long line of communications he had so elaborately prepared. He had but four days' rations for his troops. To capture Kumasi and return to Ajimamu, where Colley promised they should find food in a few days, would take five days, possibly six. The captains of the companies were instructed to ask their men whether they would agree to take four days' rations for at least five days' work. To this they all cheerfully agreed. Preparations were made at once to convert Ajimamu into a base of operations with strong entrenchments. Left behind with the heavy baggage was a garrison composed of all the weak and wounded.

Carrying only their great coats and ammunition, the flying column advanced on Kumasi on the morning of February 3rd by the western and longer road, which was believed to be superior. Gifford's scouts and Baker Russell's men, with the Rifles in support, were in front shooting their way through one ambuscade after another on the narrow road. Mounted on a handsome mule, the general moved up and down the column, his eager eyes revealing his inquisitive nature and indomitable energy. Having recovered his health, Wolseley looked as bright and vigorous as he did those first days after he landed. Courteous, communicative, and smiling, he seemed in no way to distrust his fortune or his men. His staff was all around him, 'and in the beaming faces of the officers you see reflected the good hope and perfect contentment which possess their chief,' remarked Stanley.[21]

The invaders marched on unmolested to the Ordah, which they reached at three p.m. Russell's men waded across the sixty feet of water to build an entrenchment on the north side so as to cover Home and the sappers as they worked through the rest of the day and into dark of night constructing a bridge over what the Ashanti called the sacred river. The main body, meanwhile, cleared the south bank for their bivouac. A prisoner captured late in the day told of 10,000 Ashanti still south of the river; another 10,000 were believed to be to the north. Precautions were taken against a night attack, though the enemy was never known to attack at night.

The next day, the immediate objective was to take the village of Ordahsu, where the army would leave its impedimenta under guard before the final thrust. At Ordahsu the order of battle was in single column. The advance guard, under McLeod, was formed by three companies of Rifles, and the native regiments. The Opobo company of Wood's Foot was in the lead. The wounded Wood himself was at their head. The rest of the Rifles, Rait's Artillery, and 23rd and 42nd Foot formed the main body under Alison. Wolseley and his staff followed. The Naval Brigade was to wait until the baggage crossed the river and then close up the rear of the column 'like an iron shield'.

The column was scarcely in motion when Ashanti pickets opened fire. In a quarter of an hour the advanced men were heavily engaged. The Ashanti style of fighting, however, had changed somewhat since Amoaful. Instead of pressing in close to deliver their fire, they hung back, firing volleys at forty yards and more, trying to conceal their dusky bodies behind every inch of cover. Their fire was also more accurate. The bullet-headed Opobos, to the intense annoyance of the general, behaved badly, falling flat on their faces and firing into the air without raising their heads to look for human targets. Their officers, 'employing much more than verbal persuasion', tried to induce them to fire steadily from a kneeling position, but without much success. The native troops, who had fought well until now, seemed to lose their nerve as they found themselves close to the capital of their dreaded enemies. Since their conduct was giving the Ashanti confidence, Wolseley ordered the Rifles, supported by a single cannon, to take the place of the black troops at the head of the column. Slowly, very slowly, the advance continued as the opposition stiffened. McLeod soon asked for reserves to be pressed forward as quickly as possible. Meanwhile, as was his habit, McLeod, 'Old Jack', went about placing a copy of the Book of Psalms in the hands of wounded officers. One seriously wounded officer had such a laughing fit at the sight of the good colonel, he later claimed it stopped the bleeding from his wound and saved his life.

At a little past nine, after nearly two hours of unabated fighting, the Rifles gave a cheer and made a short rush which carried the village. But the Ashanti rapidly recovered from the successful thrust into Ordahsu. At eleven o'clock the village clearing, which was widened and held by the Rifles, was enveloped with steady fire from all sides. The enemy was determined to retake the village. Transferring his headquarters from the vicinity of the bridge to Ordahsu, Wolseley found the position a raging inferno. The Ashanti fired as fast as they could load, and at times pressed boldly up, yelling and cheering, but 'steady volleys from our Sniders', observed Wolseley, 'stopped and silenced them.'[22]

The general, sitting on a small stool, took little notice of the enemy attacks as he consulted with his staff seated on the ground around him. As the roar of musketry briefly swelled, Baker Russell leaned forward to shout something in the general's ear. Suddenly Wolseley was up-ended and rolled into the dust by the great force of the slug that struck his helmet. The staff jumped to their feet and Colonel Greaves (who had replaced O'Neill as chief of staff) emptied his revolver in the direction of the enemy. When Wolseley recovered his feet, he laughingly suggested they find better cover. The thick folds of an Indian pugaree saved him from serious injury, but he suffered from a severe headache for the rest of the day.

About this time, the main column parted to either side of the road between the bridge and the village to create what Wolseley called his 'covered way', which afforded protection to the Fanti bringing up reserve stores. Hemmed in by files of sailors and soldiers so they could not bolt, the panting, terrified carriers were forced to run a gauntlet of whistling slugs fired by thousands of Ashanti lying on both flanks. Many fell, but not an instant's delay was suffered nor an article lost as officers relentlessly drove the baggage-train forward.

The instant all the baggage was in, the audacious general prepared to renew the advance on Kumasi, six miles away. Because the Rifles were heavily engaged all about Ordahsu, the honour of leading the advance fell to the Highlanders. Under cover of artillery, they were ordered to smash right through the centre of the Ashanti force and make straight for their capital, disregarding all flank attacks. The remaining troops would follow as soon as the attacks on the village slackened and it was safe to leave the baggage with a small garrison. As Rait's guns ripped the road to open the way, the Black Watch, now greatly reduced in numbers – from the original 656 to 340 – were drawn up in double file at the end of the village by McLeod. Briefly he surveyed his men and said, 'The 42nd will fire volleys by companies according to order. Forward!'

As they ventured into fearful gaps in the forest, the enemy fired upon them from behind an immense silk-cotton tree that had fallen across their path. Six Scots were knocked over. But the men of the 42nd, firing in rapid succession, rapidly carried the ambuscade. Without stop or stay the Highlanders rushed right on through the enemy as the air filled with the music of battle. Soon the bagpipes joined in with the warlike music of Scotland. The men cheered and the whole regiment broke into the double. At a rattling pace, they carried ambuscade after ambuscade, and village after village. The Ashanti were bewildered. Running and shouting past ambuscades, disregarding flank attacks, and leaving the foe behind them was out of all precedent. Surprise gave way to fear and the Ashanti broke and ran.

While the Highlanders were sweeping everything before them, the counter-attack on Ordahsu continued without let-up. The Ashanti fought well, for the King himself was looking on, seated on his golden stool, swearing he would decapitate any chief who from cowardice deserted his post. A little before two p.m., a message was received from Alison, who accompanied the advancing 42nd, saying that every village except Karsi had been taken and that they would be in Kumasi that night. The general communicated the message to his soldiers, who raised such ringing cheers that the Ashanti immediately ceased firing. The enemy seemed to know instinctively that the day was lost. They withdrew in silence. The King had already left.

Leaving a sufficient garrison in Ordahsu, the general ordered a rapid advance of the whole force upon Kumasi. Heaps of baggage and knots of men were disengaged and strung out for the march. Sir Garnet himself soon passed to the front with the Rifles. Overtaking the men on the march, he smiled and said, 'Come on, my lads, you will have a house to sleep in tonight, perhaps a palace.'[23]

Just before dusk, the Highlanders reached the celebrated moat-like swamp that insulated Kumasi. In this pestilential black marsh were to be seen the floating skulls and rotting flesh of sacrificial victims. While crossing, Alison's mule stumbled and threw him into the nauseous mass of human putrefaction. It took no little effort to extricate him.

The city was taken without a shot being fired. Forty-five minutes later, at six-fifteen, on February 4th, the day he designated before leaving Cape Coast, Wolseley entered Kumasi mounted on his mule, escorted by a body of Rifles. Alison had drawn up the Highlanders in the great market-place where they received the general with a general salute. Taking off his hat, the general at once called for three cheers for the Queen, which were given with such heartiness that the wondering citizens looking on ran in all directions.

On entering Kumasi, the brigadier had thrown out pickets and placed artillery so as to sweep the streets leading to the market-place, but there was no show of resistance of any kind. Now that they had been beaten the Ashanti accepted their defeat philosophically. They now confidently sauntered forward to shake hands, or offer a drink of water. Every Englishman was greeted with the words 'Thank you, thank you' – the only English words they had learned. Crowds of Ashanti, curious to see white men for the first time, stood about laughing and uttering cries of delight and amazement; it was as if the appearance of the European troops had been arranged as a spectacle for their enjoyment.

Uppermost in the mind of the general was the conclusion of a peace with the King. As the political leader of the expedition, he hoped to pluck the diplomatic laurels of victory. On entering the capital, a party was sent to find Kofi. It was soon learned that the King had fled to the north, and that all other persons of importance had disappeared. Later messengers appeared who agreed to carry a letter to the King.

In his letter, Sir Garnet asked Kofi to come in and make peace on the terms originally proposed. If he did not wish to send his mother or brother, he would accept any other hostages of rank. He promised the King that he and the members of his family would be treated with all honours and be allowed to return in safety. The general then told the messenger that if the King accepted his offer and if any of the royal family came to Kumasi to treat with him, the town and the palace, which was guarded, would be left exactly as he had found it. On the other hand, Kofi was warned that at the first sign of treachery, or if a single shot were fired against his men, the city would be destroyed, and all inhabitants would be put to death without hesitation.

There was no rest that night in their well-earned beds for the general and his weary men. Under cover of darkness the released Fanti prisoners, Kroomen, and native levies began to loot and set fires. One lurid blaze after another blossomed all over the town, followed by deafening explosions, for nearly every house contained powder. The palace itself came close to being burned. Sir Garnet, having promised the King he would protect his capital, was greatly vexed. This destruction might discourage the King from coming in, for the glow could be seen for miles. Home's engineers spent much of the night tearing down dwellings to prevent the spread of fires. Those who were caught pillaging were very severely flogged. One of the Fanti policemen, who had just come off duty, was caught red-handed stealing a cloth. He was summarily hanged. The screams of those being punished were heard all through the night. The most harrowing cries came from the condemned policeman. The victim's suffering was unnecessarily prolonged because the bungling executioners had failed to tie his hands before hoisting him up; the half-strangled Fanti was able, therefore, to prolong his torture with his own hands.

The next day Kumasi resembled a city of the dead. The wide, straight streets and well-kept houses were deserted. During that night of looting and flames, when the white man's fetish seemed to call for a human sacrifice on the street, between 30,000 and 40,000 inhabitants departed from the city. Though a guard was said to have been posted over the palace, Reade of *The Times* claimed that when he arrived in the morning, the King's slaves were occupied in removing the treasure, and had obviously been at the job all night. Certainly no gold dust and few golden objects were found inside. Only after Sir Garnet made a visit to the palace later that morning was a guard of 100 Rifles posted as sentries.

It was no simple matter to guard the palace, consisting as it did of a large irregular-shaped building in Moorish style surrounded by ten or twelve courts leading one out of the other. The courts were now empty but for a few birds of gorgeous colours and some of Kofi's pet cats. The main stone building, which alone could have quartered fully a thousand men, was more of a disorganized museum than a dwelling-place. There were enormous state umbrellas and litters covered with silks and velvets along the corridors. Each room held heaps of chests and coffers containing articles of value and curiosity – silks, gold and silver bells, glass goblets, porcelain and chinaware, old European swords and uniforms, books in many languages, and many objects representing native crafts. As Wolseley walked through the apartments, he was reminded of scenes from the Kaiser Bagh and the Summer Palace.

Other things of a wholly different nature were to be seen, which filled the general with disgust. There was the great Death Drum decorated with human skulls and thigh bones, which was struck three times whenever a human was sacrificed. There were the concave wooden stools, swollen thick with the coagulated blood of countless victims. They were always kept wet and still showed great fresh clots from those recently put to death to appease the soul of some ancestor. Dense clouds of flies arose as Wolseley interrupted their repulsive repast. Sickened by the sight, he cut short his tour.

Those with stronger stomachs than the general went on to search for the Garden of Death, a carrion bower where most of the sacrificed were placed. The gruesome hollow was found a short distance from the market-place, concealed from the main road by a patch of reeds. As they approached, the smell became so suffocating that handkerchiefs were produced to prevent the stench from overpowering them. It impregnated the entire city with the odour of death.

On this charnel field, over an acre in extent, lay thousands of skeletons and corpses in every stage of decomposition. More recent headless additions, among them women and children, were found bloated and discoloured, 'the whole mass living, writhing, with worms that feast in corruption'. Blood was plastered like pitch coating over the trees and ground. Here vultures never ceased to hover and swoop. They hung upon every branch of gaunt trees. Their number astonished even those who had visited the Spanish Main. No wonder none of this gorged flock attended the banquet that was laid out for them in the jungle around Ordahsu.

The massacre of humans was said to number a thousand a year. Stanley calculated that since the capital was established here a little over a century before, 120,000 were slain and left to rot in this receptacle or in the streets. It was a sight which the soldiers felt should have been witnessed by all at home who defended the Ashanti and protested against the dispatch of an expedition to Kumasi.

Early on the first morning in Kumasi, the general received a messenger professing to be from the King, who said that his master would come in before noon. The King did not come. Another message arrived saying he would come later. Sir Garnet sent messages back urging the King to meet with him, saying the palace was still at his disposal. They waited much of the day without any sign of the royal coming. The general and his staff, kept in a state of readiness to receive him, grew impatient and fidgety. It became evident to Wolseley that he was the victim of a policy of dissimulation when Kofi's messengers were discovered later in the day passing out arms and powder from the town. They were arrested on the spot and all persons of any consequence were ordered to be seized and confined.

An angry general circulated a report that since the King had failed to keep his word, the troops would push on the next day in pursuit of him. At the same time, it was given out that any Ashanti in Kumasi after daybreak the next day would be shot. (This was to ensure the departure of all inhabitants before the town was committed to flames.) The officers and correspondents, wise to Wolseley's ways, concluded the real order would prove to be 'right about face'; this was merely Sir Garnet's final effort to frighten the Ashanti ruler into submission. Surely the general would not be so foolish as to chase Kofi from one village to another. To do so would add failure to what had so far been an unqualified military success.

Privately, Wolseley had decided to leave early the next day when Baker Russell, having marched off that morning with all the wounded under escort, sent back word that the bridge over the Ordah was over a foot under water. It appeared that the rainy season had come early. If so, the roads of retreat would soon be rendered impassable.

The first night in Kumasi was one of fire; the second was one of water. There was a succession of violent storms that swept the city and the rain came down with merciless force. Again it was a sleepless night for most. Wolseley in his alcove fought a losing battle to keep dry with his umbrella. At the palace, Major Home and his men worked through the night arranging mines so as to collapse the thick walls in the morning. Inside the apartments, Buller and other prize agents were sorting the loot by the light of two feeble candles. Limited to thirty carriers, tons of valuables were to be left behind.

Promptly at six in the morning, the troops formed in the market-place of Kumasi, wet and discouraged at the thought of another march. But when they learned they were going home, 'every face brightened'. The sailors marched off first. The Highlanders remained as a rear-guard to provide cover for those engaged in the work of destruction. At every block of houses stood the burning parties with torch in hand. The sappers waited at the palace for the word to touch off the mines. As Sir Garnet passed out of the city, the signal was given, and the torchmen rushed through the city. After some delay, 125 kegs of powder were exploded and the palace became an unsightly ruin. Dense columns of smoke arose to create a funeral canopy for Kumasi.

While the column continued its march to the sea without further incident, Sir Garnet paused at Iguamu to write official dispatches announcing the fall of Kumasi. These were sent to London with Lieutenant the Hon. H. Wood, A.D.C. As a present from the troops to Her Majesty the Queen, he carried with him the state umbrella of King Kofi; and for the Prince of Wales there was a handsome carved stool looted from the palace at Kumasi. Travelling night and day, Wood was the first to arrive at Cape Coast. Arriving second and third were Reade and Stanley, who raced each other to relay their stories home.

By the time Sir Garnet reached Fomana on February 10th, a singular piece of news overtook him from King Kofi, saying that he was anxious for peace and ready to accede to all demands. This willingness to conciliate an enemy that was now leaving his kingdom was explained by the request accompanying the royal messenger: please order Captain Glover, who was approaching Kumasi from the east, to halt his forces. The general told the messenger that the terms of a treaty would be arranged immediately if the King sent him 5,000 ounces of gold in proof of his sincerity before the general left Fomana. Only then would Captain Glover's forces be sent back across the Prah.

Knowing the destruction of Kumasi had already loosened the ties between him and the feudatory chiefs, the King could not run the risk of having Glover's presence encourage them to show greater independence. Therefore on February 13th, Kofi's envoys came into Fomana with 1,000 ounces of gold which appeared to be masses of broken-up bracelets, necklaces, and plates. They explained that the King could not produce more at such short notice. Another forty ounces of gold was then shaken out of the envoys, which they had concealed in the folds of their clothing. Though the amount fell far short of that which Wolseley demanded, it was of little significance, so long as the King recognized his defeat by making his submission. The messengers were given a hastily composed draft of what was to be known as the Treaty of Fomana to take back to their monarch to sign.

By the treaty, which the King signed with his mark of two Xs in pencil, he renounced all claims on the Protectorate; recognized the independence of the Adansi and other tribes formerly subject to the Kingdom of the Ashanti; agreed to open the country to trade and maintain a good road to the Prah; promised to pay 50,000 ounces of gold to make reparation for past misdeeds; and forswore the practice of human sacrifice. British prestige in West Africa was never higher.

The arrival of Sir Garnet at Cape Coast on February 19th touched off the greatest celebration ever known on this dismal coast. As the general passed through a triumphal arch festooned with flowers, guns of the fleet and castle saluted, and the excitable populace went wild with enthusiasm. Bonnys and Opobos, dressed in ladies' hats with feathers and patent-leather boots, danced like maenads. A bride, just married, was deserted by the groom, bridesmaids and guests. The women were most con-spicuous wearing white paint and waving green branches. Jostling, sing-ing, perspiring, screaming, they snaked around the conqueror of the Ashanti, and began to throw themselves in heaps on the ground before him. With unintelligible words of gratitude, they tried to clasp his hand, or brush his feet with their heads. The general, not knowing how to re-ceive this unexpected ovation, for once lost his British air of self-assur-ance. He smiled uncomfortably and was obviously relieved when he passed out of their company.

There was sadness in this hour of triumph. Of all his staff, only Captain Brackenbury was well enough to march with Wolseley through the streets to Government House. Most were stricken with fever. Some would never march again. At the grand reception held in the dining-room at Government House, but four of the brilliant staff were to be seen at the table, and they were 'dreadfully altered and pulled down'. Wolseley, who looked uncommonly fit himself, thought, 'How the brave who fell would have exulted now.' Poor Charteris! Where was that cheerful face that was always at the head of the table? Where was McNeill with his soldier-like frankness? Huyshe with his almost feminine courtesy? McCal-mont with his comedy? Buller with his arguments? Butler with his wit?

When someone spoke of the missing, Wolseley said with feeling: 'Don't talk of it.'[24]

While the European troops rapidly took to their ships and the native regiments were disbanded, Sir Garnet busied himself with a variety of problems, not the least of which was the selection of a successor. He had undertaken the expedition with the understanding that he would not remain at Cape Coast after the close of military operations, and nothing could induce him to remain – even the offer to name his own terms if he remained but for three months more. The governorship was in turn offered to Alison, McLeod, Greaves, and Colley, and refused by them because of the climate. From the very beginning, the failure to get first-rate men to accept the office had been one of the major factors behind the mismanagement and lack of progress on the Gold Coast. Sir Garnet finally made a special trip to Accra, where he persuaded Colonel Maxwell of the 1st West India regiment to take over the government of the colony. Within six weeks Maxwell, harassed by the climate, was dead.

Bidding goodbye for ever to the Gold Coast, Wolseley embarked on March 4th with all that remained of his staff. In sixteen days they hoped to be in England where they could once more enjoy milk in their tea.

# CHAPTER NINE

# CHAMPAGNE AND SHERRY DIPLOMACY

THE Ashanti War made Wolseley a celebrated general and a popular figure. The press and public hailed him as a national hero. Praise was lavished on him without limit. The fall of Kumasi filled the penny papers with more print than a dozen Waterloos might have produced in an earlier age. Leading statesmen of the day vied with each other in eulogizing the achievements of this outstanding soldier. The Queen herself seemed reconciled to his sudden rise to national prominence and hence more favourably disposed to his person.

Wolseley, at his request, had the time and place of his arrival kept a secret so that he might be spared the ordeal of a popular ovation. Dressed as a civilian, he took the first train out of Portsmouth to London where he was greeted at the railway station by his mentor, Sir Hope Grant. The next day, March 22nd, he was commanded by the Queen, who had already cabled her congratulations to the general at Madeira, to proceed to Windsor. Victoria found the hero of Kumasi 'thin and grey, but well', and ' ... a very smart, active, wiry-looking man, full of energy, and calm and decided-looking.'[1] Wolseley found the Queen 'gracious and sympathetic', and told her 'all sorts of amusing things about the Gold Coast that made her laugh'.[2] He spoke of cannibal Kossos going into battle with swords between their teeth, of the courage of the Fanti women, of the peculiar law of succession through the female, and of how one officer slept in the executioner's hut in Kumasi without knowing it.

The Queen reviewed the general's little army in Windsor Great Park on March 30th. After the inspection, the Ashanti force formed a hollow square. Sir Garnet dismounted and came forward to be invested by Her Majesty with the Grand Cross of the Order of St Michael and St George, and of a Knight Commander of the Bath. Sir Archibald Alison and Lord Gifford then came forward to be decorated and presented to the Queen. The Duke of Cambridge expressed Her Majesty's gratitude to the assembled troops; after which Sir Garnet led the parade before the Queen, who was stationed beneath the royal standard. The ceremony concluded with the victorious general raising his hat in the air and calling for 'three cheers for the Queen'. She was radiant with delight.

That evening Sir Garnet was received in the Houses of Parliament, where the benches and galleries were crowded with the nation's leaders. The halls rang with such words as 'exemplary skill ... distinguished courage ... perseverance'. The leaders of both parties moved a vote of thanks in the Upper Chamber. In the House of Commons a similar vote was asked for by Gladstone and Disraeli, who in this rare moment of agreement tried to surpass one another in their encomiums.

The rewards of the state for the successful soldier were above politics. Before Wolseley's dispatch reporting his success arrived in England, the Liberals had resigned as a result of their defeat in a general election. Nevertheless, as a token of his appreciation, Gladstone sent Sir Garnet and Lady Wolseley a small enamelled china vase. Disraeli inherited the task, which he described 'as never very easy or pleasing', of ascertaining what the general expected, or wanted, as a reward. He met Sir Garnet privately and described him as 'a little man, but with a good presence, and a bright blue eye, holds his head well, and had a lithe figure'.[3] The general was given a grant of £25,000, approved unanimously in the House of Commons, and promotion to the rank of major-general 'for distinguished service on the field'.

Pressure was put upon Wolseley by the Government and the commander-in-chief to accept a baronetcy, but he rejected this 'honour', which he regarded as one reserved for common people, such as the Duke of Devonshire's gardener who had been lately named a baronet. Sir Garnet wrote to his mother, 'I don't wish to have my name inscribed with such people.'[4] If it had not been for the untimely fall of the Gladstone Government, he was sure that he would have been offered a peerage and become known as 'Lord Wolseley of Kumasi', or some such title.

After his return from Africa, Sir Garnet expected to leave for India where he would be adjutant-general to Lord Napier, but in June he was attached to the War Office as inspector-general of the auxiliary forces. He undertook his work with characteristic energy. The organization of English volunteer regiments was a subject of great interest to Wolseley after his experiences in Canada. He was a staunch advocate of placing the militia and volunteers directly under the Crown, and thereby, into the army. His work with the auxiliary forces did not get beyond the planning stage when he was called upon by the Government in February 1875, to go to Natal and take temporary command of military and civil affairs.

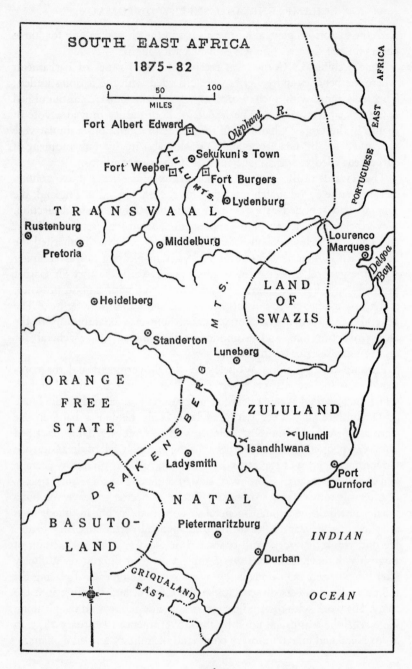

SOUTH EAST AFRICA
1875-82

0        50        100
MILES

Fort Albert Edward
Sekukuni's Town
Fort Weeber
Fort Burgers
Lydenburg
ZULU MTS.

Oliphant R.

PORTUGUESE EAST AFRICA

TRANSVAAL
Rustenburg
Pretoria
Middelburg
Lourenco
Marques
Delgoa Bay

Heidelberg

LAND
OF
SWAZIS

Standerton
Luneberg

ORANGE
FREE
STATE

M T S.

DRAKENSBERG

ZULULAND
Ulundi
Isandhlwana

Ladysmith

Port
Durnford

NATAL
Pietermaritzburg

BASUTO-
LAND

INDIAN

Durban

GRIQUALAND
EAST

OCEAN

N
W    E
S

Lord Salisbury described Britain's programme in the Far East with the happy title: 'The policy of the open door!' A less happy phrase might be applied to her aggressive policy in South Africa: 'The policy of the open sore.' It dated from the accession to power of Disraeli in 1874 and his selection of Lord Carnarvon as Colonial Secretary. The empire-makers had succeeded the empire-breakers. In South Africa a half-century of imperial apathy was replaced by feverish interest; gestures of withdrawal gave way to energetic intervention. It has been claimed that England lost the thirteen colonies because Lord Granville had a penchant for reading and answering his correspondence from America. Lord Carnarvon was that kind of administrator. He reversed a policy of unfortunate neglect, but he was over-confident, impatient, and often without tact when he sought to impose his principles and ideas, the most significant of which was federation. Having fathered Canada in 1867, where the colonists had favoured such a move and taken the initiative, Carnarvon tried to promote federation as a political panacea in South Africa where enthusiasm for political integration had not yet fully matured.*

Mounting tension between white colonists and black tribesmen in Natal afforded Carnarvon an ideal opportunity to remake the Colony's constitution so as to insure Natal's adherence to his programme which would eventually lead to federation. In theory, the home Government could abrogate or revise the constitution but this prerogative had grown weak from want of exercise. Moreover, to pursue such a reactionary policy in a precipitate manner could have serious consequences. A gentler course must be adopted whereby changes would be initiated in the colonial legislature itself and approved by the citizens of Natal. To achieve this purpose, the services of an exceptional governor were required. And Wolseley, the hero of the hour, appeared to be Carnarvon's man. Just to send a man of real eminence to such a remote colony, accustomed to worn and undistinguished governors, would awe and flatter the colonists and, perhaps, make them more amenable to an abridgement of their political rights.

The political task of reforming the administration of Natal was the sort of work Sir Garnet would have been happy to be kept out of. He was prepared to accept a military assignment in any climate under the most difficult conditions, but he had no appetite for politics or diplomacy.

* At this time there was in South Africa an example of almost every variety of colonial government. There was responsible government in Cape Colony, two crown colonies in Griqualand West and Natal, semi-independent native locations at Namaqualand, Basutoland and Kaffiraria proper, and the independent country of Kuti and the Pandoes. In addition to these there were the two Boer republics, the Orange Free State and the Transvaal.

Carnarvon was aware of this prejudice and thought it unlikely that Wolseley would accept the post. But Cambridge, anxious to remove this 'reform-mad' general from England, insisted to the Secretary of State that Wolseley was the man for the job. Sir Garnet was finally 'asked in a way that made it impossible for a public servant to refuse'.[5] The request was sweetened with the promise that he need remain no longer than six months in South Africa, and in no way would this mission be allowed to handicap his military future. His present position at the War Office was to be kept open.

Within the half-year allotted to him as chief administrator, Wolseley was to inquire thoroughly into the conditions of Natal. He was to overhaul the entire system of native administration and bring serious crimes within the scope of the colonial courts. Matters of administration, taxation, military defence, and relations with neighbouring territories, especially the Boer republic of the Transvaal, were to be investigated and reported on. Carnarvon was also anxious for suggestions that would further confederation 'as an ultimate object in view'.[6]

Above all, Wolseley must carry through the uncongenial and delicate work of inducing the colonial legislature to efface its own constitutional powers. Ironically, the Natal legislature passed a resolution a few months before Wolseley's departure requesting a new constitution which would give them responsible government and free them from 'the interference of political parties in England'. There was good precedent for this, for neighbouring Cape Colony had gained responsible government two years before. Of course, the colonists had no inkling of Carnarvon's desire to reduce them to the status of a Crown Colony, Jamaica style, for no public mention was made of his intentions. This was quite in keeping with his lordship's method of doing business. It was to be a period of strange political methods with new ethical standards.

Sir Garnet sailed for South Africa on February 23rd in the company of comrades from the Gold Coast who were to serve as his staff. He had asked Carnarvon to be allowed to have 'a few clever men about me whom I could trust implicitly and would I think be invaluable in soothing away difficulties with fractious colonial members.'[7] Wolseley pleaded for as many as the Colonial Secretary would allow, for it would give him 'a sort of grandeur' which was helpful, he believed, in dealing with colonists. Carnarvon decided that four officers would be sufficient. Colonel Colley was the general's first choice. By the close of the Ashanti War, Wolseley was completely infatuated with the worth of this sober and modest young Anglo-Irishman. He asserted that Colley was 'the ablest officer in the army, and in all respects ... the man most fitted to be a general.'⁸ Next came Major Butler, recently discharged from the hospital, and still carrying a little poison of the Gold Coast in his veins. But in his convalescence he found the energy to write another book, this time about his adventures in West Africa. Then there was the indispensable Major Brackenbury whose extraordinary capacity for business was such that Wolseley attributed most of the success of his political mission on the Gold Coast to his efforts. His dispatches to the War Office were so outstanding that they drew warm praise from Lord Cardwell. And, finally, Captain Lord Gifford whose name had become a household world in the army after it was told, and retold, how he bravely led his scouts through labyrinths of the Ashanti forest with thousands of savages before him. Never in the history of South Africa had an official of the Crown gone out to the colonies with a retinue of such illustrious men eminent in war, administration, letters, and daring.

The Secretary of State added a fifth member to the party, Mr Napier Broome, a former writer on the staff of *The Times*, who would fill the post of Colonial Secretary and probably succeed Sir Garnet as governor. Wolseley knew nothing of his background, and argued that in his opinion Colley, who had some experience in dealing with Kaffirs when in South Africa in 1859–60, was better suited to the post. Carnarvon thought otherwise.

The *Windsor Castle* provided a comfortable twenty-four-day passage to Cape Town for the governor and his party, except for 'Brack', who suffered greatly from sea-sickness; he turned the colour of verdigris the first day out, and spent much of the voyage rolled up in rugs on the deck.

At Cape Town, Sir Garnet was entertained by Governor Barkly. After several days of official receptions and sightseeing, Sir Garnet boarded the handsome frigate, H.M.S. *Raleigh*, which had been placed at his disposal by the Admiralty so as to lend an air of proper importance to his mission.

The landing at Durban took place on the morning of March 30th, 1875, and the incoming governor was received with the usual honours and considerable enthusiasm. He told them in his first official address that his mission was to establish 'a firm Government that shall guarantee perfect security to the white settler, both in life and property, whilst the great native population within your province shall feel that their interests are not forgotten.' No one was quite sure what this meant, but they cheered anyhow.

It became readily apparent that the hero of Kumasi was about to take the colony by storm. One leading citizen described him as the 'Strong

Arm of the British Army and the Long Arm of the British Empire'. His party of polished and clever assistants were quickly nicknamed the 'brilliant staff'. All were impressed with the soldierly appearance of the governor and his party. It was impossible to look into the face of the governor, where a sparkling intelligence animated every feature, without feeling that the man who stood before them was one possessed of more than ordinary ability. A few minutes of conversation confirmed this impression.

Two days after his arrival in Natal, the impatient governor and his staff boarded an open brake with four horses and raced on to Pietermaritzburg, doing a distance of fifty-four miles in less than seven hours. This was an extraordinary feat over a road full of ruts and holes. Normally it took two days. Somehow, after Wolseley appeared on the scene, all the clocks in Natal seemed to run a little faster.

An escort of volunteer cavalry, which had awaited the governor's appearance outside the town, galloped with them into the capital. Pietermaritzburg, Maritzburg for short, or more disrespectfully 'P.M. Burg', was little more than a village of thatched houses surrounded by flowers. The buildings were low, single-storeyed, and uniformly ugly. The government offices were housed in a structure described by one contemporary as a 'dilapidated barn on a bankrupt farm'. Wolseley found it in a state of 'unmitigated barbarism' when contrasted with the civilization he found at the Cape. Its sleepy, grass-grown streets were illuminated only on particularly dark nights when there was no moderate starlight.

Sir Garnet was inaugurated as governor on the day of his arrival, and he immediately called for a meeting of the Executive Council on the next day. His first objective was to capture the principal executive offices. Broome was appointed Colonial Secretary. Two officers of the Council were given leave with full pay, and their places were filled by Colley, who was nominated Acting-Treasurer and Postmaster-General, and Butler, who became Acting Protector of Immigrants. Together with the Secretary of Native Affairs (Shepstone) and the Attorney-General (Gallwey), these officials sat as the five nominated members of the twenty-member Legislative Council. And when these same five met with the Commandant of the troops and the Chief Justice, they composed the Executive Council, which was presided over by the governor. Brackenbury was named Clerk of the Executive Council.

The remaining fifteen members of the Legislative Council were elected by 4,000 electors from the counties and boroughs. The preponderance of elected members made it possible for them to dominate easily all the divisions of the Council, thwart the Governor, and reject the votes of the nominated members. The chief difficulty with such a system lay in the presence of 300,000 natives who had absolutely no representation in a Legislative Council selected exclusively by white voters whose interests were diametrically opposed to theirs. The home Government could not divest itself of the responsibility of governing these natives. To give European colonists too great a power over the natives, which had proved so disastrous in New Zealand, could provoke another Kaffir War. Should this occur, British troops would have to be employed and the home Government would again foot the bill.

The first impulse of the soldier-governor was to abolish the constitution altogether with a stroke of his pen, but when legally advised that not even Carnarvon could do this, he tried to work out a programme that remained within the bounds of the existing constitution. This meant introducing a measure that would strengthen the official, or nominated, element in the Legislative Council.

Wolseley fixed May 5th for the first session of the legislature and prepared a Bill which would increase the number of Government members in that body from five to fifteen so as to balance the elective elements. To achieve victory by arts of peace rather than war would not be easy. The settlers of Natal took pride in being 'English' in their origin and in their political instincts. To ask them to perform an act of political sacrifice by parting with their cherished legislative independence would be unpopular. It was most probable that such an autocratic request would excite considerable opposition.

To win the colonists over, Sir Garnet resorted to social means, lavish hospitality and public flattery. Where he could not coerce, he would cajole. Balls, good food and wine became his weapons. As a witty local judge later commented, he 'drowned the independence of the colony in sherry and champagne'.[9]

The social life of the somnolent little British colony was suddenly elevated to the level and atmosphere of Victorian England. The tempo was even more accelerated. Formal dinner parties were held every night, and fashionable balls, which had been rare, occurred at least once every fortnight. Every last yard of silk and every pair of white shoes was bought up in the colony. The balls of the previous administration had taken place in a confectioner's rooms, but Governor Wolseley insisted on creating a ballroom in Government House.

Until now, Maritzburg's official circles had favoured the slow and stately quadrille to the slightly undignified waltz, but Sir Garnet put his guests on three-four time. It caused a great sensation and became the rage at parties. He also introduced the polka, and was only too happy to provide instructions, if necessary. Its popularity caused a sudden rash of advertisements for 'polka hats', 'polka jackets', and 'polka-dot ties'.[10]

Each member of the governor's staff was expected to participate in the continuous round of entertainment. Lord Gifford was created Master of the Household, an office of no small importance, considering the nature of Wolseley's mission. It was his duty to introduce the guests in the newly-decorated reception room, supervise the arrangement of paper lanterns, and cool the champagne which Sir Garnet had imported in large quantities from Cape Town. The governor himself avoided drinking the liquid when he learned it was made from coal oil.

Popularity carried an expensive price-tag. Sir Garnet spent money without stint, and insisted upon defraying charges imposed upon his staff. His first month's bill exceeded £1,400. At that rate, his annual pay of £5,000 did not cover expenses. Moreover, he wrote to his brother Dick that he found it necessary to subscribe 'to every dirty little race meeting and association in the country'.[11] One race held for the Kaffirs came to an embarrassing end when a competitor dropped his only garment. Too excited to go back and pick it up, 'he rushed past all the young ladies at the winning-post as naked as he came into the world.'[12]

Nor did the governor neglect Durban. There were thirsty electors to be won, and an imposing ball must be provided for their wives and daughters. It turned out to be the largest ball in the history of the colony, with over 600 guests. The Corporation of Durban gave him a banquet in return. The Governor's hand began to suffer from all 'the pump-handle work'. One old lady squeezed it almost to the breaking-point as she bade him good night in a very incoherent manner.

After the first ball in Maritzburg, and now in Durban, the ladies were completely won over to the governor's side. Many of the men were not far behind. It was difficult to resist the fascination of this charming young general. He was famous, masterful, and self-assured, yet no governor had been more accessible, frank and pleasant.

Before leaving Durban, Wolseley made a speech revealing his programme for reducing some of the constitutional privileges the colony had enjoyed for nearly twenty years, ever since it had been reluctantly granted a Royal Charter in 1856. He reasoned that the time had come, before the novelty of a new governor had worn off, to rally those parties that would give sympathetic support. Opposition to the governor's proposed Bill was rather general throughout the colony. Broome reported to Carnarvon that the citizens were 'rather aghast at this announcement and everyone is still looking his neighbours in the face.'

Having announced his policy, Wolseley worked harder than ever to be popular. Candid and pleasant to his critics, nothing seemed to disturb his good temper, his excessive amiability. His seeming confidence of the success of his mission became contagious, not only to those who supported him, but even those who were in opposition to him. An amused Broome told how he 'frightened these small folk with his amazing energy and decision'. The Mayor of Maritzburg, after dining at Government House, confided to Broome that he felt as though he 'had been put through a cullender'.[13]

It was Wolseley's good fortune that the two leading politicians of Natal, who would most stubbornly oppose his programme, had conveniently left the country on a furlough. Mr Barter, a member of the Legislative Council and the most outspoken among those who demanded responsible government, had left for England, assuming that it would be two or three months before the new governor got down to business. 'He does not know me,' observed Wolseley, 'and has exactly played my game. I would have willingly paid all the travelling expenses during his tour out of my own pocket as an inducement for him to have done what he has now carried out without its costing me a penny.'[14] Mr Foss, another Council member and likely to be no less ardent a foe of Wolseley, was off on an extended vacation, confident that he could return to Maritzburg before the opening of the legislature. But Sir Garnet resolved to push his Bill through the hastily convened body before either of them returned.

As the legislators came into the capital for the opening of the Council, the governor singled them out for special attention. Private meetings were held at Government House to disarm their hostility and overpower them with his charm. Sir Garnet possessed a great shrewdness; he knew when to wheedle and when to browbeat. At one moment he would try to persuade them that by surrendering their political power now, they would eventually gain more. Then, if necessary, he would bluster and warn that if they did not give way, they would be forced to do so by an act of the imperial Parliament. He adroitly enticed five or six members from the coast, who represented the sugar and coffee interests, with a promise of government assistance in importing coolies from India to work on the plantations. If they were unco-operative, he hinted that Delagoa Bay might be developed instead of Durban. Members from the upland and midland area, however, resisted his charm and subtle threats.

The lights never seemed to go out at Government House where the governor and his staff worked, played, entertained and slept. Wolseley always rose early, sometimes before dawn, and worked for hours before breakfast. Brackenbury, pursuing a different regimen, worked through much of the night. The governor had an enormous capacity for hard work. When engaged in serious affairs involving grave responsibilities, his youthful ardour was sobered by the trust reposed in him by his Government. But once the work was put aside, at about five in the afternoon, his buoyant spirit burst forth. Colley told how he would 'run upstairs three at a time, singing like a schoolboy, and turn us all out for a game of tennis or a gallop.'[15]

His staff were devoted to him. Butler believed him to be the ideal leader 'on whom command sat so easily and fitly that neither he nor the men commanded had ever to think about it.'[16] Unpretentious and incapable of even the slightest display of patronage, Wolseley had a way of lifting men to a level with himself to share his conceptions. Colley, who five years later would preside as governor over this same household, told his sister that nothing seemed to bother him: 'Work, play, difficulties, annoyances, all seem to be the same fun that a good run is to a hunting man.' It made Colley feel twenty years younger to be with him, and he confided to her 'that if I work long with him I shall lose all calm judgment of his character and abilities in their fascination.'[17]

On May 5th a cannon sounded to salute the governor as he approached the new (1871) building that worthily sheltered the Legislative Council, as well as the judges of the Supreme Court and post-office officials. On hearing the explosive report, the members filed in to take their places. Concerned with observing the forms and trappings of Parliament, the neighbouring Presbyterian church was illuminated 'in humble mimicry of St Stephens, Westminster'.[18] The band struck up 'God Save the Queen' as the governor dismounted. Followed by his uniformed staff, His Excellency entered the crowded Chamber, where all rose and remained standing until he bade them be seated. Brackenbury handed Wolseley a weighty manuscript from which he read his opening speech, hissing out every syllable where he had anything of significance to say. He spoke exclusively of the need for modifying the constitution, and promised that the measures he proposed would hasten the time when complete self-government would be possible in Natal. These measures would remove the feeling of insecurity that now prevailed, and create confidence in the outside world that would provide capital and a fresh influx of white settlers to their shores. The speech was handed to the Speaker, and Sir

Garnet departed in the same state in which he had arrived. Cannon were fired once more to announce that His Excellency had opened the council. As a soldier, Wolseley had a disdain for politicians. Those of Natal were 'pettifogging ... self-seeking ... and about as ill-conditioned a lot' as he had ever met with, but he hoped their sense of loyalty to the colony and the empire would transcend their selfish instincts.[19] Instead, his speech from the throne rekindled the Opposition and seemed to make them more unyielding than ever. The general feeling was expressed by Mr John Akerman, a member of the Council, when he made the gloomy prediction, 'this is to be made a black Colony'.[20] Before that would happen, the whites would fight.

In reality, Wolseley feared those politicians whom he pretended to despise. They could bring disaster to his mission. His well-concealed anxiety was at complete variance with his public utterances and his posture of aplomb. Wolseley's parliamentary moves were to betray his doubts and uncertainty. The governor's strategy was to rush the Bill through its readings 'lest its opponents find time to swing public sentiment against him'.[21] Discussion in the Council upon the Bill began at once.

With Colley and Butler speaking in the Chamber, the deliberative body of the Colony attained new heights of excellence. The other legislators responded admirably to the occasion. A surprised Butler found these 'ambitious Hampdens and journalistic Vanes' far more able than representatives of much larger colonies, such as Canada.[22] Unluckily, nearly all the clever men were to be found among the Opposition. The best speaker was without question John Robinson of the *Natal Mercury*. Wolseley and his staff continued to work hard to win him over, but failed. The Opposition, Wolseley complained to Carnarvon, operated well together, while his own supporters could not be induced 'to work cordially as one team'.[23]

And at the worst possible time, Broome was damaging the governor's cause with his offensive manner. Wolseley attributed it all to his 'inordinate personal vanity'. When Broome answered public questions in the legislature, he did so 'with his nose in the air and with a sharp disagreeable voice'.[24] Being a handsome man, he assumed that he was irresistible to the ladies. Many women complained to the governor about how he squeezed their hands. Their men didn't like it. Finally, he was black-balled from the local club. To Wolseley it was most unpleasant that the chief officer of his government 'should be actually turned out, I may say, of a little wretched club'.[25] The fact that he was disliked by the people of the Colony did not seem to penetrate his conceit.

It soon became evident that most of Sir Garnet's staff was engaged in hand-squeezing – and perhaps it was more serious than in Broome's case, for none of the women complained. Dependent upon the good will of the men as the women, these balls could be damaging. This was true, also, in a literal sense. Sir Garnet held a Club Ball in the middle of May and the floor was 'so slippery that men and women were tumbling about "promiscuously", one girl being ... badly hurt.'[26]

Bismarck advised there were two things that should never be witnessed: the making of a sausage and the making of a Bill. But when Wolseley's Natal Bill reached its critical second reading, all Maritzburg seemed eager to watch the process. It promised to be the most dramatic event in the Colony's brief legislative history. The Chamber had a reputation for 'robust combat', and was accustomed from the beginning 'to bitter attacks on the executive officials'.[27] Everybody who was anybody, had been – or aspired to be – somebody, used his influence to gain admission to the galleries on Tuesday, May 20th.

It was like a popular performance at the theatre as the long, bare Council Chamber with its whitewashed walls and no ceiling (the roof was open to thatch) was thronged with important-looking gentlemen and gaily-dressed ladies. The galleries above were soon packed with spectators, and every spare foot was occupied on the floor around the horseshoe table with its cane chairs. The table was overlooked at one end by the Speaker's chair, covered for the occasion with a square rug of skin, such as native blacks often wore, and above it was a shield bearing the royal coat of arms. The Speaker, who was in his place, was curiously dressed in a tailcoat and tartan trousers under his silk gown. Dress among the legislators was largely a matter of personal taste; some wore gowns and others not. One clerical member indicated the importance of the debate by appearing in his cassock. Stranger still was a deaf member who appeared with an enormous ear-trumpet which, when assisted by a neighbour (Robinson), allowed him to follow the proceedings. It was an embarrassing duty that sometimes suspended the course of a debate.[28]

The lights of the adjacent church were turned on. After several introductory speeches, Colley arose to deliver the main address in support of the Bill. Respected and popular, he had an appreciative audience, 'and his leading opponents greeted his rising with cordial cheers'.[29]

Colley was a great hand at making speeches. As he marshalled his abundant notes, not a person doubted that the cynosure of the governor's team would discharge his parliamentary undertaking with great credit to himself and the governor. He began his speech with measured tones amid deep silence. All went well for a few minutes; then he paused, looked down at his notes, and then at his listeners. There was a flutter of friendly applause as he rubbed his brow as if to 'dispel the mist that had obscured his memory, and then murmuring gently, "Mr Speaker, excuse me, I cannot proceed," he sat down, and, with his head resting in his hands, remained in gloomy silence as the debate proceeded.' It was a painful experience for his listeners as well as himself. They seemed to share his embarrassment. The arrested speech was sympathetically applauded as if he had finished it in style. The reason for Colley's conduct remains a mystery. Robinson suggested that being a high-minded Irishman with a strong sense of justice, the task of depriving a people of their political rights was 'so repugnant to his instincts' that he found it impossible to perform his duty.[30]

The stormy debate lasted for three nights with eloquent, caustic, and sometimes humorous words supplied by Butler. Great excitement attended the voting. One member of the Opposition, because of poor health, had to be carried into the Chamber. Another highly intelligent opponent became so flustered that he voted in favour of the Bill by mistake. The alteration of the constitution was carried by a vote of eleven to seven, though not entirely in the form originally proposed. During the debates, the Government had to submit to a compromise whereby the number of nominees would be reduced from fifteen to thirteen. Wolseley apologized to Carnarvon for his incomplete success, but to have gained thirteen nominees was far more than he actually expected.

The tension continued, for there was still a third reading attended by vexatious delays. There were elements of uncertainty that worried Wolseley. An indignation meeting was called to protest against the Natal Bill and abuse the governor on the week-end before the third reading came up the following Monday. It turned out to be a failure in respect of numbers, and the speechmaking came to an abrupt end when a youthful orator, anxious to allude to the fact that the social season was over at Government House for the present, began his speech by saying, 'Now that Sir Garnet has got rid of his balls ... ' There were 'roars of laughter which drowned out all further talking, and the affair broke up with three cheers for Sir Garnet.'[31]

The third reading, where the vote was ten to seven, went off quietly and, Wolseley observed, 'people seem to have suddenly awoke to the belief that the change I proposed was not such a dreadful thing after all.'[32] The antagonism that had developed quickly subsided. Basically, the colonists were too loyal to carry their opposition, beyond a few angry words, to a Bill which had the support of the home Government. After all, it was home Government that built railways, provided efficient administration, and kept a watchful eye on the Zulus. As good citizens of the empire, they were prepared to give the constitutional experiment a fair trial.*

'No man in England could have got more out of the Council than I did,' Wolseley asserted proudly and privately to his brother Dick; 'it was the prestige of my name' and 'an admirable staff' that did it.[33] It was an unpleasant task carried out with an absolute minimum of friction. Carnarvon expressed his sincerest thanks for the tact and ability Wolseley displayed in getting the Bill through, and he hoped that the change effected would give him 'a very fair base of operations as regards other questions of South African policy'.[34] Regardless of his success, a political life was more repellent to Wolseley than ever. In his correspondence he kept reminding Carnarvon of his promise not to delay him in South Africa.

While Wolseley was labouring to enlarge the powers of the Crown by altering the constitution, he devoted much time to a study of the basic problem, a great human problem, the eternal African native. Ostensibly the object of his political mission was to prevent the recurrence of repressive acts against the native, which in the eyes of the home Government violated the spirit and letter of English law. This was, after all, the principal source of difficulty between the mother country and the Colony.

It was by now an old story in imperial affairs; distant England, the colonists argued, had only the vaguest notion of local domestic problems. The benevolent policy of the Colonial Office conflicted with the settlers' concept of security and their labour requirements, for nearly everyone in Natal had a vested interest in the farms, and resented the system of native locations where the blacks wasted the soil with primitive agricultural methods. They charged that the native was encouraged to be lazy and, at times, impudent. The colonists were eager to draw labour from these 'social backwaters'. The home Government kept them from fulfilling their needs. Hence, there was a perennial demand by Natal politicians for what they called 'sponsible government'. Only Bishop Colenso, an outspoken champion of the blacks, and a small knot of sympathizers were irritatingly out of step with the great majority of settlers.

On the native question, the new governor made an effort to maintain 'an evenly balanced position' between hostile parties. In a way he suc-

---

* As an effort to strengthen the power of the Crown in the legislature, 'Sir Garnet's Nominees' Chamber' was not altogether successful. The octave of newly nominated members proved 'independent' in a way that was not anticipated by the authors of the Bill, for they frequently voted against the Government.

ceeded, for each side accused him of favouring the opposition. To men with Colenso's temperament, a policy of neutrality was interpreted as open hostility. Wolseley, knowing the latter's reputation as the *enfant terrible* of Natal, feared him. To a practical politician anxious to win over the colonists and still please his chiefs in Downing Street, an outspoken, meddling, self-righteous ecclesiastic, who advocated the inexpedient precept that what is morally right is politically right, could become a real menace. 'The Bishop is mad upon one subject,' Wolseley told Carnarvon, 'and he thinks that unless everyone sees as he does, they are cruel oppressors of the black man.'[35]

The dynamic governor and the fanatical bishop were quickly estranged. When Wolseley learned that Colenso, who never wearied of doing good, was acting as 'the Supreme Chief of the Natives' by sending emissaries about the country to explain the intentions of the home Government to Kaffirs, he was angry. The indiscreet views spread by the interfering prelate, he complained, were not only erroneous as regards Carnarvon's policy, but excited the natives; and this excitement was in turn communicated to the colonists, who became nervous, and imagined the Government was planning to convert Natal into a black settlement. The Governor's entire mission was unnecessarily complicated by 'this self-appointed agent of the Colonial Office'.

Colenso would have been the first to admit that he was the protector to whom the native must look for justice, and that it was his role to see to it that the Colonial Secretary's wishes were correctly interpreted. He, in turn, complained that instead of coming to him for advice, the governor and his staff treated him with marked coolness, and sought the company of his enemy, Mr Theophilus Shepstone, Secretary of Native Affairs in the Natal Government. Wolseley regarded Shepstone, who had lived among the Zulus from his childhood, as the greatest living authority on the natives. The two men were frequently seen together, and they were to have a great influence upon each other.

Caught between a hostile Council and an agitating bishop, Sir Garnet attempted to introduce changes in native affairs tactfully so that a native war might not result. Taking no chances, however, he applied to the home Government to increase the size of the local forces to a full regiment with a battery of light mountain guns. Downing Street, aware of the risk his reforms incurred, directed a troopship, the *Adventure*, returning from the Orient with a battalion of marines, to stop at Durban for orders.

Repeatedly, Wolseley warned Carnarvon that Natal 'was the weakest and most dangerous point in the Empire'. The preponderance of natives in the Colony – they outnumbered the whites twenty to one – coupled with the fact that there was a powerful Zulu nation on its frontier under a despotic ruler, Cetewayo, who had the gunpowder and ambition to make his reign celebrated, could lead to a fearful catastrophe, if not the destruction of the entire Colony.

It was a policy dictated by high philanthropic sentiment based upon the belief in equal rights for all human beings, he bluntly told Carnarvon, that had led to this dangerous situation. If the settlers had been permitted to deal with the Kaffirs as the Boers did, he concluded, the Colony would have been purged of most of its blacks, so that only a manageable 100,000 remained, completely disarmed.

The native problem, as Wolseley saw it, was not merely internal and social, but rather external and military. The solution lay beyond Natal borders. Zululand must be annexed, he advised the Colonial Secretary. The time had come to take sword in hand and cut the Gordian knot. Shepstone, he related, had assured him that a thousand men could cross the Tugela River and depose Cetewayo without difficulty. The Zulus themselves, many of whom hated and feared their cruel chief, would welcome the Union Jack in the hands of Shepstone, whom they esteemed above all other white men. Zululand could be converted into a new Kaffir province, superintended by white magistrates, which could easily accommodate the surplus natives of Natal and thereby provide a sort of safety valve. The scheme had the additional advantage of providing an easy solution to the 'disputed territory' question which disturbed relations between Zululand and the Transvaal, a question which the home Government had asked Wolseley to look into with a view to annexing the territory to Natal. Such a move, Wolseley assured Carnarvon, would put an end for ever to the barbarous cruelties of Cetewayo, and be hailed as a blessing to humanity. Annexation, he argued further, was inevitable. The time to strike was while Cetewayo was still relatively weak.

Carnarvon, the cautious politician, was at first a little frightened by the bold soldier-like solutions suggested by Wolseley, and he refused to be a party to such drastic action. But as South African affairs became more tangled, the temptation to adopt a more forceful policy, as advocated by Wolseley then and later in private conversations, increased. It was Wolseley more than any man who caused the impatient Colonial Secretary to think in terms of a summary approach.

The tragedy that developed from the Zululand situation was that the annexation, as Wolseley pointed out, was inevitable and could easily have been accomplished at that time. Thus, the disastrous Zulu War that occurred four years later, with its terrible toll of human life, could have been avoided.

The longer Wolseley remained in the Colony, the less confidence he had in the colonists to run their own affairs. The introduction of responsible government would not only aggravate the native problem, but it would increase the difficulties of administration. 'I am as sensible as anyone can be,' he told Carnarvon, 'of how unfitted these people are for framing laws that should in any way whatever affect the interests of the Kingdom ... '[36] In the various departments of government he found a serious lack of energy and grave irregularities, with the suggestions of corruption in high places. Publicly Wolseley continued to flatter the Colony's officials; privately he doubted whether there were enough men with 'sense and ability in Natal ... to fill the offices of government'.[37]

A Committee of Public Departments, consisting of Broome, Colley, and Brackenbury, was created to reform the public services. Colley, in taking over the treasury, found confusion and a shocking disregard for regulations. Estimates were improperly prepared and revenues seriously under-estimated. It would take an accomplished embezzler, he believed, to straighten out the books. Butler, meanwhile, tried to work out a more efficient land policy that would stimulate immigration. The colonists were astonished by the zeal, the efficiency and the thoroughness of these talented men.

To the hard-working staff, the land of labour became the land of romance. Butler and Gifford moved from one love affair to another, and most of Wolseley's team had some slight flirtation on their hands at one time or another. The worst offender was Brackenbury, seemingly the least likely target for Cupid's arrows. Wolseley discovered to his amazement that being in love was his 'normal state', but then he reasoned that 'really his wife is so dull that I am not surprised he is glad to be away from her'.[38] Nevertheless, he thought that 'Brack' would at least be discreet enough not to become romantically involved with a woman who had a very jealous husband. Yet he had to admit that the object of his adoration was 'really a pretty woman with plenty of fun and wit'.[39]

When Gifford revealed that he actually intended to marry the girl he was currently courting, Wolseley became alarmed. The governor learned from a 'female source' that the lady in question was a 'designing' woman who did not love the young lord, but wanted the advantages that went with being Lady Gifford. All Wolseley's efforts to dissuade his amorous aide from marriage failed.

To keep the female situation from leading to a 'serious explosion', Sir

Garnet looked forward to taking his staff on a trip up-country in mid June while the Council was not in session. 'This short separation', Wolseley scribbled to his own 'dear little spider', 'may do some good.' Keeping 'Brack' out of Natal for several weeks would 'prevent accidents'.[40]

Having put the government departments 'on a better footing', Wolseley undertook his tour of inquiry and observation round the hinterland. This part of Natal had been shamefully neglected and ignored by previous governors, none having gone as far up-country as Ladysmith, only 100 miles from the capital. To this fact, Wolseley attributed the general antagonism of the up-country people towards the Government. Not one of the members of the Council from these districts had supported his Bill to pack the legislature with nominees. A governor of Natal, Wolseley reasoned, should be a man of physical energy, capable and fond of travelling to all parts of the colony, and if possible a sportsman; having a first-hand knowledge of the country is an asset to any politician.

Besides the lovesick pair, Gifford and Brackenbury, the governor took with him Shepstone and Butler. Colley was sent ahead on a semi-official visit to the Transvaal to sound the Boers as to their sentiments regarding confederation. Butler was later detached from the main party to undertake a similar mission among the Boers in the Orange Free State.

The party travelled South African style in a large and roomy 'buck-wagon' drawn by eighteen oxen. The wagon, which carried the supplies and baggage, creaked along over the rough country, averaging between five and ten miles a day. The only mishap occurred when the giant vehicle slid down a bank and turned over, smashing the cases of champagne and sherry, an event which somewhat handicapped Sir Garnet's diplomatic efforts.

Late June and July was a time of midwinter in Natal. The air was dry, and sudden clouds of dust whirled up on the rough roads. The days were clear and the nights frosty. Evenings were magical as the sun set behind the blue Drakensberg with its white-capped peaks, black gorges and sparkling waterfalls. The weather was perfect. The staff reminded one another how a year ago they were struggling through the dreary, equatorial regions of Africa.

It was a time for refreshing relaxation. True, the innkeepers charged exorbitant rates for their 'dirty accommodations', the speeches of welcome by townsmen were unvarying and tedious, the ritual of war dances by the natives became tiresome, and the missionaries were a trifle irritating, but it was an immense relief to get away from the complexity of political life in the capital and the formalities imposed by social events. The latter made Wolseley feel like a dog forced to walk around on his hind legs.

After six weeks of trekking, Sir Garnet and his staff returned to the capital to prepare for the new session of the Council. Twenty-five Bills were drafted, touching almost every question that affected the welfare of the Colony. Some did not pass without difficulty.

Having taken a retrograde step in putting Natal's house in order, Wolseley concentrated on the forward step of confederation. He was one of the first to recognize that South Africa's future prosperity was linked to unification. More than any other man of his time, he foresaw the coming struggle for African territories by European powers and cautioned his Government to prepare for the international jostling and pushing that was rapidly approaching. And Wolseley continued to explain the unsound military state to his Government, but it had no visible effect at the time.

In his letters to Carnarvon, Wolseley also urged upon him the necessity of having a new governor arrive by August so that he could be home early in September. The desire to leave was prompted by more than the attractions of home. Brackenbury and Gifford, on returning from the trek up-country, became more enmeshed with their women than ever. 'Brack's love reached a state of 'red heat'. Wolseley told his wife that he 'can be got out none too soon'.[41] As for Gifford, that 'silly goose' refused to listen to reason, and insisted on remaining in Natal with his 'designing' woman after Wolseley departed. And what a woman! On investigation, Wolseley found that she had an uncle who was said to have stolen money in Maritzburg and run off to Mauritius to escape imprisonment. Her parents were Jewish, and the mother was 'a hard drinker', having once been carried out of a London place 'dead drunk'. 'Worse still,' Wolseley declared, 'the brothers and sister used to deliver milk daily in Durban.'[42]

The young lord was unaffected by these shocking revelations. Wolseley swore he would never have Gifford on his staff again; a man who makes 'such an ass of himself throws discredit upon his general'.[43]

'It is high time I get out of this place,' wrote Wolseley, 'for I seem to live on a female powder magazine.' The women seemed to grow bolder. They began to show affection towards the governor himself, 'in a very demonstrative manner'. 'Indeed, greyheaded as I am,' confided the faithful husband, 'I might have had a *rare high time* of it here ... '[44]

At last Sir Henry Bulwer, whom Wolseley had suggested as a successor, arrived at Durban on August 27th. 'I feel like a schoolboy,' Wolseley wrote, 'just told that I may go home for the holidays.' A final farewell dinner was held in Maritzburg by the 13th Light Infantry. The next morning he left the capital as he had first arrived, at full gallop with a change of horses every eight miles. In Durban, Wolseley immediately called upon Bulwer, whose entire staff, he commented, 'consisted of a leggy-looking youth, not long, I should say from school, who seems the picture of weakness and dullness. He little knows what is before him if he thinks he can get on in Natal with such help alone.'[45]

There was one more ball in Durban and an overwhelming number of addresses and deputations – even the Opposition press displayed unusual affection, and praised Sir Garnet's work. Wolseley suspected that there were also a good many husbands of pretty wives cheering the departure of the ex-governor and his staff. Broome did not accompany the general. He remained behind to assist the new governor, and Bulwer was welcome to him as far as Wolseley was concerned. Colley was to travel in another direction and rejoin his regiment. Gifford, after much last-minute persuasion by Wolseley, had a change of heart and boarded ship. On September 3rd, Wolseley embarked 'for home and beauty' – that is, his 'dearest little porpoise'. There was a brief stop at Cape Town, time enough for a banquet, a reception, a parade, and a grand ball.

At the close of summer, decked with fluttering flags from stem to stern, the *Windsor Castle* (which sank a few months later) sailed into Portsmouth with Sir Garnet and his staff. They landed with hearty cheers being raised on all sides and quickly made their way to London.

After several weeks' holiday, Wolseley resumed his duties at the War Office as commander of the auxiliary forces. He was given an office in the mass of makeshift old buildings in Pall Mall that were connected by three-step doorways and devious stairways. These confused structures in which the administration of the British army 'was then carried on was quite typical of the confused work itself'.[46]

Most of Wolseley's time and energy was dedicated to reform. His major effort at this time was to establish an adequate reserve force. The authorities did not share his enthusiasm, and treated his labours with indifference. Angry, he wrote a strong memorandum on the subject which his superiors tried to persuade him to withdraw. Wolseley spoke of resigning rather than withdraw the memorandum.

But so long as the Disraeli Government appreciated his talents, Wolseley never seriously contemplated resignation. The Colonial Office was delighted with the results of his efforts in Natal. Carnarvon continued to look upon the ex-governor of Natal as one of his chief advisers on South African affairs. But Wolseley's insistence on a bold programme seemed out of place, for an unusual quiet settled over South Africa. It was the proverbial calm before an impending storm.

# CHAPTER TEN

# A MODERN OTHELLO

THE marriage of the only daughter of Tsar Alexander, and the grand-daughter of that old enemy Nicholas I, to H.R.H. the Duke of Edin-burgh was a momentous and unique occasion, for never in history had the ruling families of England and Russia been drawn so closely together by family ties. It was expected that this royal marriage would improve relations between two nations that had been estranged. But the next year, 1875, persecuted peasants in the Balkans engaged in one of their chronic rebellions against their oppressive Turkish masters, and the prickly Eastern Question was reopened. Soon big brother Slav went to the rescue of his co-religionists and resumed his march towards Tsargrad (Con-stantinople), which had been arrested in such a humiliating fashion by the Crimean War. The honeymoon was over.

Disraeli ordered the fleet to proceed to the Turkish capital, and asked for a supplementary £6,000,000 for naval and military expenditures. There was talk of sending an expeditionary force. Hostilities appeared imminent. Wolseley prayed for war. 'Nothing short of war with Russia,' he confided to Dick, 'can re-establish our "honour" or save our great interests in the East from serious injury.'[1] Being a soldier, however, he dared not express his views openly lest it be said he wanted war for per-sonal reasons.

These were busy days at the War Office. Everybody seemed chained to his desk, save for a few Intelligence officers who took a sudden 'vacation' to enjoy the scenery of the islands in the Levant, hunt snipe along the Suez Canal, or, perhaps, take a journey through Asia Minor 'for the sport of the thing'.[2] Wolseley privately advised the former members of his Ashanti staff to be prepared to join him at a moment's notice, for he ex-pected 'to play a very important role' if war should come.

It was announced in February 1878 that Lord Napier of Magdala would command any expeditionary force that might be sent to fight Russia, with Sir Garnet acting as chief of staff. This choice was enthusiastically approved by the public.

Napier was called in from Gibraltar by Disraeli for preliminary consultation with Wolseley. Owing to differences over army reforms, Napier and Wolseley had little affection for each other. The old field-marshal had a distinguished record, but Wolseley enjoyed poking fun at him, as did the other 'Cardwell boys'. He whispered that the commander-in-chief was an incompetent. One of Wolseley's favourite stories about Napier, which was repeated with delight by the members of his staff, told how his lordship was asked to attend a meeting of the Cabinet where the subject under discussion was the possible dispatch of the force to the East. The ministers were soon looking at one another in shocked dismay when it became painfully apparent that the commander-in-chief did not know the Dardanelles from the Bosphorus! A few hours later, Wolseley chanced to go into one of the rooms of the War Office where he found his old friend of Ashanti days, Colonel Robert Home, standing, pointer in hand, before a large map of the Near East, giving a lecture in elementary geography to the officer designated to lead the British army in the event of a war with Russia.[3]

In the end, the Tsar pocketed his pride, as Disraeli expected, and agreed to a congress to take place in Berlin that summer. At the Berlin meeting, where a somewhat feeble Disraeli downed tumblers of port at frequent intervals to keep going, the British Prime Minister, nevertheless, found sufficient strength to lead the other powers into forcing Russia to tear up the Treaty of San Stefano. The 'great Jew', as Wolseley called him, returned to London to receive a hero's welcome, and from the steps of Number 10 Downing Street he offered the phrase 'Peace with Honour' to a cheering crowd. Only a few 'high-souled jingoes of the purest water', as Wolseley described himself, deplored the peace. To the Queen, Lord Beaconsfield offered his last gift, another addition to the empire – Cyprus.

Cyprus was to become Britain's great *place d'armes* in the Near East. That is to say, it would become a station where troops and munitions could be collected for future advance. This was the chief object of the Convention of Defensive Alliance signed in great secrecy between Great Britain and Turkey on June 4th, 1878, a few days before the opening of the Congress of Berlin. Under this agreement the Sultan, Abdul Hamid II (the Damned), assigned the island of Cyprus 'to be occupied and administered by England' so as to enable her to carry out a pledge to defend the Asiatic domains of the Sultan against further aggression by Russia.

That Britain's efforts to bolster the Ottoman empire were not a matter of friendship but an attempt to create a bulwark of her own against expansionist-minded Russia was disclosed with cynical frankness by the Queen's ministers. More culpable in the eyes of the Turks was the unauthorized revelation by the enterprising *Globe* that five days before the Cyprus Convention was signed, the British had secretly concluded a working agreement with Russia which ensured peace.* It was now apparent to the deceived Turks that Disraeli had deliberately fostered the impression that Russia would probably renew the war so as to gain their approval in securing Cyprus as a base. Thus, the Turks had bartered away part of their empire in exchange for a promise to fight that Disraeli would not have to redeem, at least not in the immediate future. Anglo-Russian relations were never quite the same after Disraeli worked his cunning diplomacy on the Turks. But then, in digging down to the roots of empire, one cannot always expect to find them clean.

Disraeli's trickery had only begun. He took this skillet-shaped island that lay in a dead angle of the Mediterranean, gilded it with a lustre it never possessed, and dished it up before the believing eyes of a dazzled and delighted public who acclaimed his diplomatic feat a masterful *coup*. Enthusiastic jingoes could throw their hats in the air and crow.

The general ignorance of the English people about Cyprus was bottomless. As *Punch* said, the average Englishman had a vague idea that from the reign of Venus it passed to the Venetians, when a certain Governor Othello smothered his wife, Desdemona. That was about all, except perhaps that schoolboys who had learned their history remembered that Richard the Lionheart interrupted his crusade to marry Princess Berengaria of Navarre on the island. The public, however, was eager to learn more. Daily journals, periodicals and hastily-written books tried to satisfy this desire by describing the island as an earthly paradise. The popular mind was further excited by opportunities of profit painted in glowing terms. Companies were soon begun in England with millions in capital to be invested in developing the island's abundant resources.

Early in July, the Wolseleys were on a brief holiday up the Thames when he received a telegram telling him of an important letter awaiting him at his home in Portman Square. The urgent message was from the Secretary of State for War, the Right Honourable E. Stanley, asking him to call on him at once, but in such a manner as not to arouse suspicion. (The Cyprus matter was still a state secret.) Later at the War Office, Wolseley learned that he was to become Her Majesty's High Commissioner and commander-in-chief to the latest jewel fitted to the imperial crown. There was no question of his acceptance, though Wolseley did not relish the role of governor after his Natal experience. As a soldier, he had

* The unexpected disclosure appears to have been part of a Russian plot to embarrass the British.

looked forward to succeeding General Staveley in the Bombay Command at some time in the autumn.

Stanley tried to handle the appointment as delicately as possible, for the gruff old Duke of Cambridge, who had just returned from Malta, was angry over not being let in on the Cyprus secret – and then the selection of Wolseley was made without his knowledge or consent. More irksome still to Royal George was the body of officers selected for the staff. It was the same old game of follow-the-leader with the Wolseley 'ring' – Greaves, chief of staff; Baker Russell, military secretary; McCalmont and Gifford, a.d.c.s; Dormer and Brackenbury, assistant-adjutants and quartermaster-generals; Biddulph to command the Royal Artillery; and Dr Anthony Home, the principal medical officer, etc. Some were unavailable, like Butler, Colley, Maurice and Buller; and Wolseley knew better than to ask the Duke's assistance in gaining their services. In fact, so that the Duke would not recognize Wolseley's handwriting, Stanley carefully burned the list of names of those he had selected. But the commander-in-chief could hardly be misled; Wolseley's hand in the selection of officers was obvious. Knowing the Duke's mood and fearing that Wolseley might become embroiled in controversy, Stanley advised a hasty departure to avoid unpleasantness. Wolseley, after some pleading, was given two days to prepare and he was thankful that his departure would fall on Saturday rather than Friday. He was superstitious about undertaking any new venture on a Friday. It was an Irish trait, he confessed, and the only one he possessed – he hoped.

Wolseley would need all the luck he could get. In parrying a forensic thrust by Lord Granville in the course of a parliamentary debate, Lord Beaconsfield pompously declared 'it was a great error to suppose that the Government decided on this step of the occupation of Cyprus without the possession of adequate information.' But if the Government possessed such information, it was carefully kept from the future governor. Rarely has an administrator been assigned to a post with so little previous information. Wolseley's only official source of information was a digest of consular reports compiled by Home's Intelligence department, documents which in themselves were fragmentary, irrelevant, and out of date. The only good map came from a French source. Wolseley knew infinitely more about West Africa before sailing for Cape Coast Castle than he knew of Cyprus. Deprived of all essential information relating to population, climate, terrain, and system of government, it was more of an expedition of exploration than of occupation.

This decision to take Cyprus was something of a bad joke to Wolseley.

It was made early in 1878 by Disraeli, owing to the advice of Colonel Robert Home. Though Wolseley recognized the need for a base in the Near East, he looked upon Cyprus as a poor choice. Egypt, Wolseley argued, was the logical place of arms. In British hands, an uninterrupted flow of soldiers to India would be guaranteed, and 'the fellah', he predicted, 'well-disciplined under English officers, would enable us to economize the use of the British soldier in the East.' Disraeli was unimpressed with this view and continued to rely instead on the advice offered by Home. The curious part of it was that Home, though a brilliant officer who had thoroughly mastered his profession, had one great failing that was always a source of amusement to Wolseley and other officers who knew him – he habitually exaggerated.* It was his extravagant claims that had sold Disraeli on Cyprus.

Weighed down with imperial impedimenta – camp-beds, pith helmets, hampers from Fortnum and Masons – Wolseley and his staff departed from Dover on July 15th. As soon as he boarded the Channel steamer to Calais, the general, made weary by the peevish Duke's last-minute demands that he attend to some petty, time-consuming details, found a bench and instantly went to sleep. His ability to sleep at will, Wolseley later explained to his fellow passengers, was a characteristic he shared with Napoleon.

While 'the Chief' slept serenely and the ship sailed through pale patches of drifting fog, the staff went to work in the saloon. Archibald Forbes, ace war correspondent of the Daily News, who journeyed with them to Cyprus, was amazed by the way they met, blended and worked out administrative details. The general merely resolved, directed, and then retired, for 'he was sure of his machine; it was of his construction; he had selected every cog and pinion of it; he had tested its efficiency both in parts and as a whole.'[4]

The Cyprus party, on landing at Calais, quickly made its way to Brindisi and then Malta, except for Brackenbury, who 'disappeared when passing through Paris "to dine with some friends" ', as Wolseley facetiously described 'Brack's' latest little romantic escapade.[5]

Wolseley spent a day in Malta making last-minute preparations with the local governor, mostly regarding the transfer of troops to Cyprus. Three battalions were to accompany him on the Himalaya, and three Indian battalions were to follow a few days later.

---

* During the Ashanti War, for example, Home claimed, with a straight face, that he made possible the capture of Kumasi by cutting down the timber and placing the piers that bridged the rapid Prah *with his own hands*!

Approaching Cyprus, Wolseley began to feel that there were 'great days ahead'. He remembered the words of poets of all ages in describing this diadem of the sea – Cyprus the 'salubrious ... the delightful ... the glorious ... the blest'. The birthplace of beauty, of Venus, the goddess of love. He could visualize Botticelli's artistic masterpiece depicting her advent to this playground of the gods, a rapt presence that had sprung from the silver foam. He imagined, he told Salisbury, he was to govern 'a land flowing with plenty, a land of orange and myrtle groves, interspersed with picturesque-looking oriental cities, abounding in palatial residences ... '6

At three p.m. on July 22nd, 1879, Wolseley stepped ashore at Larnaca in full dress, surrounded by his very strong staff. Taking over the island from Admiral Hay, Wolseley swore himself in as Lord High Commissioner. Stout Greaves, the chief of staff, perspiring profusely in the intense heat, then stepped forward to read the Queen's commission and Sir Garnet's proclamation, telling of the Queen's wishes for the island's prosperity, etc. After the proclamation was read in Greek and Turkish, as well as English, the people cheered. Some of the eager young officers were grievously disappointed that the people received the English with open arms rather than with arms.

An Irish doctor who came out to Cyprus remarked that the island reminded him of pictures of the moon 'which show there is neither water, vegetation or even atmosphere in it'.7 The trip the governor made north from Larnaca to Nicosia on the last day of July confirmed this impression. It was a depressing journey. Cyprus may have been a garden spot when Aphrodite and her beloved Adonis frolicked here long before the Turks got hold of it, but the goddess of love and bloom left very little of her beauty behind as a legacy to the modern-day inhabitants. The land in midsummer was desolate, brown and arid. Not a tree nor a shrub added variety to the landscape. Now and then a gaping peasant was to be seen obviously speculating as to the meaning behind the governor's appearance. Did it mean fresh taxes? Would there be some new, onerous law? Could it possibly mean a lessening of his load?

Twenty-seven miles out of Larnaca, the governor and his party came to Nicosia, girded by Venetian ramparts and dominated by a Gothic cathedral flanked by towering minarets that marked its conversion to a Muslim mosque. It was a medieval city with narrow, tortuous streets. The sanitary arrangements were disgusting. To Wolseley, it was one enormous cesspool into which the filth of ages had been poured.

As governor of Cyprus, Wolseley had entertained notions of residing in some luxurious Venetian palace, like a modern Othello. Instead, he was forced to pay an exorbitant rent to a private citizen to house himself and his staff. Fleas and bugs of every description were everywhere. His Excellency's dignity suffered. One day his attention was drawn to his trousers, 'which, below the knee, were literally covered with a mass of jumping fleas!'[8] His collars were a disgrace, for no one understood the art of starching. (Wolseley later imported a washerwoman from Malta.) Then on a state visit to the ex-governor, his horse fell, throwing him into the filthy street.

In mid August, Wolseley could bear it no longer and decided to move from this impossibly dirty city with its high rents. The seat of government was temporarily established under canvas some two miles outside the city, near an old monastery. With the weather unbearably hot in the daytime, some of the many cells of the monastery were used as offices by the governor and his assistants.

The climate was treacherous. The temperature would rise to over 120 degrees in the daytime and turn to a chilling cold at night, dropping as much as fifty degrees in a very short time.

The staff, at first, taking their cue from the chief, pretended to the world that Cyprus was the place that a person would select if he sought a residence that combined the comforts of home with the glamour of an oriental life. One indiscreet colonel, however, tersely summed up the island's attractions by saying: 'It was like Cape Coast Castle, without the castle.'[9]

Then came the fever, severe chills and sometimes death. The soldiers began to drop off like sheep. Their constitutions were shocked by the contrasting heat of day and the coolness of the night. In the daytime, they were gasping from the heat. At night, they lay their heat-filled bodies on a rapidly cooling earth, for their mattresses had been left behind. They were without comforts, with few duties to carry out, 'and no amusements to distract their attention from thinking who might next be seized by fever'.[10] The Indian troops, children of the sun, suffered no less than the British. Even the hardy Gurkhas seemed to have the steel taken out of them.

Everything seemed to go wrong. An alarming telegram was received by Wolseley warning him not to serve out lime juice to the men. Disinfecting fluid had been put into the bottles by mistake. The error was discovered in Malta when some fifty Punjab troops began to roll and writhe in agony on the ground.

Even interment brought its share of confusion. Some had to be burned, some buried, for various religious ceremonies had to be observed – Hindu, Muslim, Sikh, Catholic, Protestant, and Orthodox. At one funeral, a groggy member of the firing squad managed to shoot another soldier in the eye.

The staff miraculously escaped illness. McCalmont claimed it was because they lived more or less on champagne.

Once again the press began to harass Sir Garnet. His Excellency was startled to learn that *The Times* correspondent had telegraphed home that women were shamefully being sold in the market of Nicosia. After consulting with Turkish authorities and the Greek archbishop, Wolseley learned that no slave had been openly sold on the island for many years. Evidently the newsman, in search of a story, mistook some women sitting about the market-place as slaves on sale. Then the clever Mr Forbes of the anti-government *Daily News* vividly described the whole story of sickness and death to the readers at home. The Queen herself telegraphed to inquire if the men who were stricken could be sent on a cruise.

Wolseley branded these newspaper reports 'exaggerated'. The climate of Cyprus, he told Salisbury, would not be 'one whit more unhealthy than Malta when the men have good barracks built for them!'[11] Even the doctors misrepresented the true facts, complained Wolseley. He wrote to the Duke that 'the doctors seem to take a gloomy pleasure in painting the health of the men and everything here in the blackest of colours', and prophesied that one day Cyprus would 'become a favourite station in the Mediterranean'.[12]

When on August 15th Forbes wired home an accurate report that in all about twenty-five per cent of the whole force were down with fever, and that about two-thirds of the medical staff were also down, the matter became the subject of a great national debate. Newspapers began to take sides, and the very next day questions were put in the House of Commons. The Government indignantly and stoutly denied the truthfulness of these statistics. The War Secretary quoted a telegram from Sir Garnet which stated that only six per cent of the soldiers were in the hospitals. This was literally true, for they could not accommodate any more! The official version was accepted, and the Government took pride in this 'airy little jibe'. When Lord Beaconsfield confided to Lady Bradford that he preferred to select those men who were 'not too scrupulous', was Wolseley to be included among them?

The Indians were hurried back to their homeland, leaving behind them their roomier, thicker and more serviceable tents for the British soldiers. Sir Anthony Home, in charge of medical affairs, sent out experts to search for a sanatorium somewhere in the highlands. After a month's exploration, a site was found at Dali where 'the fever demon might at length be exorcized'.[13] A regiment marched thither, somewhat slowly, for the Maltese carts had been sent out without linchpins and were for some time quite useless. Sir Garnet and Sir Anthony breathed a sigh of relief. Not a very long one, however, because the new camp site at Dali was as harmful to the soldiers' health as the condemned camp at Chifflick. The number reported sick continued to stand at one-fourth of the entire force on the island. In a few months the Disraeli Government withdrew all but a few companies of redcoats.

But Sir Garnet stubbornly refused to concede that the climate was something less than desired. He pretended that there was nothing wrong with the island. 'Who takes quinine?' he declared to those around him. 'Never heard of such a thing! Splendid climate!'[14] But it was common knowledge that the general had been and was still taking a two-grain pill every morning for years.

Publicly and privately, Wolseley continued to defend Cyprus and boast of its great future. His 'private letters' to friends were used as testimonials which were published in leading publications. But in his letters to his wife, Wolseley could not conceal his disenchantment. However, he cautioned her: 'Don't allow anyone to think I am disappointed with the place – tell them I write most cheerfully.'[15]

Meanwhile, the British press, with effusions of delusive articles, caused thousands of Britons to flock to Cyprus where fortunes, it was said, might easily be made. Since it was believed that great military and naval bases were to be established, fortifications, barracks, and government buildings would surely be constructed in profusion. Great profits, it was alleged, were also to be made in agriculture. Along with pictures of voluptuous-looking women, maps were reproduced showing zones of cultivation – a zone of cotton, of the orange, of the grape, of tobacco, etc. Editors printed the most preposterous stories without inquiry or research. A mysterious Mr Zealous Williamson, posing as a former consul in Cyprus, had his letters published in a leading article which told of large chunks of gold washed down daily from the hills by mountain streams.

Larnaca became a boom town. The streets teemed with soldiers, sailors, merchants, and representatives of those nations noted for their commercial instincts – Armenians, Hebrews, Syrians, Maltese, non-Cypriot Greeks, etc. Most conspicuous were the English dressed in white – white suits, white canvas shoes, and white helmets or pulp hats.

The governor and his administrators became concerned when speculators and questionable characters came to the island. Cyprus was becoming a place in the sun for shady people. Dozens of bars were opened in the thirsty climate. A club was established and a music hall was opened by a French woman of easy virtue from Egypt. There were games of poker and brag, cricket and horse-racing. There was swearing, fighting and singing. And always there was drinking, with 'Dizzy' sharing the toasting honours with the Queen.

Drinking led to frequent mishaps. The former British consul's son reeled over a low railing and broke his neck. The chief accountant of the Government shut himself in with a couple of cases of champagne to help him balance his books. His 'assistants' proved false. His accounts became so muddled that a scandal ensued which led to his being sent home. The 'tea-pot' general was disgusted.

The visitors came as sellers and exploiters, and they found no buyers and nothing to exploit. The Government decided not to establish a naval station. The troops were withdrawn. Farming was obviously unprofitable. The metallic wealth of the island had been exhausted by the ancients. The island was rich only in pestilence and fever. To remain would be a form of commercial suicide.

Within two months the Cyprus bubble had burst. The newcomers departed as suddenly as they had come, many having to sell their few remaining possessions to pay their passage home. Merchants closed their shutters, rents fell, and the music hall grew silent. 'The rush to Cyprus had been a spree, a bean-feast over the water,' reported one disillusioned participant. 'When it was over, Larnaca, save that a slight increase in population rendered the place a trifle more lively, practically resumed its normal aspect before the act of occupation, which events proved to have been a mere squib in the air.'[16]

The strategic value of Cyprus was now more carefully examined. Of what value was it to the Straits, it was asked, when Malta was the same distance to the Dardanelles and every article of stores shipped to Cyprus had to pass through Malta? Malta was also closer to Alexandria than Cyprus. How would its possession enable England to defend the Sultan's domains in the East? Lord Northbrook sarcastically observed that 'to undertake hostilities in the right rear of the enemy was not precisely the way to defend a country'. If Russia began to move towards the Euphrates Valley, a couple of English regiments in Cyprus could not 'even be the fly on the wheel of her chariot', wrote Archibald Forbes.[17] Was this the treasure 'Dizzy' had won by his astute tactics?

The press, shifting its sights from *coup* to fiasco, sketched more accurate pictures, minus sensuous women, which made the island look less like the seventh heaven promised by Mohammed to the faithful. New maps were drawn with zones of disease rather than of cultivation. Enteric fever, malarious fever, aguish fever, and dysentery were all represented. It was no longer a place fit for a gentleman. Behind the walls of clubland, good Conservatives confessed there was not another such cursed hole on the face of the earth. Lack of confidence on the part of the Government itself was indicated by reports that public works projects had been abandoned and the soldiers removed; even the sailors were not permitted to land when the fleet paid the island a flying visit.

Worse was yet to come. The fine print of the Convention stipulated 'that England would pay the Porte whatever is the present excess of revenue over the expenditure in the island; this excess to be calculated upon and determined by the average of the last five years'. Turkish statistics demonstrated that the average surplus was about £100,000, so the tribute was set at £92,686, an impost of 10s. a head on every inhabitant of Cyprus. Only after the British occupied the island did they learn that they had been tricked by the foxy Turks. The revenue they had expected to collect had been placed too high and the expenditure under-estimated, so the British Exchequer was compelled to meet the deficit after the tribute and cost of administration had been paid.

'Dizzy's' boast that the island would be no burden to England was sheer fantasy. The popular verdict was that the nation had been 'hoodwinked'. It was said by critics that the English occupied Cyprus not as proud owners but as tenants, paying £92,000 a year 'for the ruined house, and leaving ourselves no balance from the revenue for the necessary repairs'.[18] And if evicted, the tenant would not even be allowed to claim compensation for improvements.

The realization came quickly to Wolseley that Cyprus was so heavily mortgaged that the tribute would absorb most of the revenue and the cost of administration would barely match the surplus allotted by the Convention. Moreover, when the expenditures of governing the Turkish province were published, no one seemed to take into account the unwritten custom of allowing public officials to complement their pitifully low fixed salaries through bribes. No British governor, however, could tolerate an evil that corrupted officers of the customs, excise, and police. Wolseley, using Warren Hastings' reforms in India as a model, felt strongly about sufficient emoluments that would ensure the independence of the civil servant. With this increase in salary for native officials, there was little money for much-needed improvements. By the end of Septem-

ber, Wolseley, having estimated the revenue, discovered that after sub-
tracting the expenditures and the tribute, he was left with a net balance
of £3,000 to make essential improvements. Despite his slender financial
resources, Wolseley continued to speak bravely of converting the island
into 'a model province'.

It has been said an Englishman's first idea is improvement. If this be
true, Wolseley was no exception. He came to Cyprus a conscientious
military administrator eager to lift the island out of Turkish misrule and
make it a success through good government: at once strong, just and
tolerant. He would make it a province 'to which all men in Asiatic Turkey
shall point as what a Turkish province may be converted into when
removed from the influence of Constantinople intrigue.'[19] The Turks
would soon recognize the moral of a contented province with a constantly increasing revenue.

Relentlessly, Wolseley applied his extraordinary capacity for hard work
to rescuing the island from its feudal stupor. It was a task from which the
most seasoned administrator would shrink. A mixed commission had to
be established to define the lands that were alleged to be the property of
the Sultan. Complicated legal battles had to be fought with foreigners
accused of wrong-doing who sought the jurisdiction of consular courts
authorized by capitulations, or by treaty. Locusts, an annual plague, had
to be exterminated. Dispensaries had to be established throughout Cyprus
to curb disease. English shillings and pounds had to be introduced as the
currency of the islands. In his spare time, Wolseley supervised the planting
of 20,000 eucalyptus trees.

The main source of revenue was the tithe, accounting for one-third of
the total. The Turks had sold the tithes to rich farmers, and corruption
flourished. Wolseley abolished the system of farming out taxes. Operating
on the theory that ex-smugglers make the best customs officials, he
appointed the most successful tax-farmer to be his chief collector of
tithes, placing him under the scrutiny of the auditor and accountant-
general. He in turn advised in the selection of all superintendents and
agents. Justice was served and the tithe was collected almost in its entirety,
an event without precedent in the history of the Ottoman empire.

Tithes, locust abatement, tree-planting – Wolseley and his officers
pined for soldier's work. As the British prepared to invade Afghanistan in
November, Wolseley wrote: 'All our thoughts here are now turned to the
Afghan frontier, and I long to be in the saddle leading our men through
those passes which former wars have made so familiar to us in history.'[20]
Colley, now military secretary to the Viceroy, caused his old chief to

curse his bad luck when he informed him that had he taken the Bombay
Command instead of going to Cyprus, he would in all likelihood be in
charge of the southern line of advance into Afghanistan. Now he was
condemned to remain on this forsaken island. It was impossible for him
to leave Cyprus, even for a brief visit, without special leave from the
Queen. Everyone around the general knew he was bitterly disappointed,
but they never heard a word of complaint from his lips.

One by one, Wolseley's officers began to search for duty elsewhere.
Though he made no effort to stop them, he was hurt by what he regarded
as an act of disloyalty. When Greaves left, complaining that anyone who
went to Cyprus was a fool, Wolseley wrote him a letter of reproach:
'You have gone through hardships here! I confess I don't think so: we
had champagne every day and ice most of the hot days since we landed.'
When he selected officers to join him in Cyprus, Wolseley continued, he
believed he 'was paying them a great compliment and professionally
doing them a great service ... apparently the whole army was anxious to
get here.'[21] Wolseley would miss Greaves's mordant wit and his amusing
stories, proper and otherwise.

Life was not altogether dull at headquarters. The general insisted upon
vigorous exercise and sport for himself and the staff. There was tennis,
which some considered a new-fangled sport; horse-racing, which created
great interest; horse-play, with McCalmont and Baker Russell playing
practical jokes on each other.

There were few parties and official receptions at headquarters. The
governor did not feel obliged to woo his subjects as he did in Natal. Nor
could he afford it. In September, he used the first day of the Muslim
festival of Bairam as the occasion to proclaim his appointment of a
legislative council. His Excellency and staff appeared in full dress for the
first time, 'mounted on ponies and attended by a swarm of Turkish,
Greek and nigger ragtag and bob-tail in all sorts of garments, by way of
escort'.[22] Under the direction of the head butler, sweets, coffee and
cigarettes were served to the notables in a large, well-ventilated tent lined
with dark green felt like that of an Indian prince. That evening a special
guest was entertained from Constantinople, Rifaat Pasha, whom the
Sultan had sent out to supervise the removal of cannon and munitions of
war. After dinner, Sir Garnet offered his distinguished guest a cigar. The
Turkish gentlemen promptly filched fifty and rolled them up in his nap-
kin, which he likewise appropriated, as His Excellency looked on with
unbelieving eyes. McCalmont hoped they would not be called upon to
entertain many more specimens of this acquisitive type, or there would

be nothing to smoke and no table linen left in the place.[23] To Wolseley, it was an example of how bold and corrupt a Turkish official could be.

When British rule was extended to the island, the Greek Cypriots were far more enthusiastic in their welcome than the native Turks. Under the administration of a great Christian and liberty-loving people such as the English, they expected an amelioration of existing conditions and looked hopefully to eventual Enosis. Union with Hellenic Greece seemed a logical step in an island that numbered three-fourths Greeks out of an estimated 150,000 inhabitants. The day Wolseley stepped ashore in Larnaca, the Bishop of Kitrion in his address of welcome said: 'We accept the change of government inasmuch as we trust Great Britain will help Cyprus, as it did the Ionian Islands, to be united with Mother Greece, with which it is naturally connected.'[24] At Limassol, before starting for the capital, a Greek deputation expressed the hope to the English governor that Britain would follow the precedent established in the case of the Ionian Islands.

Napoleon said: 'Scratch a Russian and you find a Tartar.' The Cypriot Greek might have said: 'Scratch an Englishman and you find a Turk.' Before reaching Nicosia, Wolseley decided to do everything in his power to quash Hellenic aspirations. When petitioned to make Greek the official language, he gave them a verbal answer which amounted to 'Certainly not!' He told Salisbury: 'If the administration here is not to be English, I hope it will be largely Turkish.'[25]

Wolseley feared that if the Greek element prevailed, it would become a perpetual thorn in Britain's side. They would demand costly improvements of all kinds, as in the case of the Ionian Islands, and then demand Enosis. Wolseley was anxious to have 100,000 Muslim refugees from the Balkans located on the island, which would ensure its remaining a British possession. When this plan fell through, Wolseley (with Salisbury's backing) began to work on the possibility of settling Maltese immigrants on uncultivated lands that were known to have yielded revenue in the past. If successful, such a move might thwart an irridentist movement among the Greeks. (The colonization scheme was never carried through because of the fall of the Conservative Government early in 1880.)

The Greeks' criticism of Sir Garnet's administration began to grow. It was said that the arbitrary and vexatious system of taxation that existed under the Turks was still enforced by his administration. The courts employed the same civil and criminal code used by the Turks, and the same Turkish officials, who were prejudiced against the Greeks, were kept in service. Ordinances were passed which created a system of forced labour and decreed that only Turkish and British subjects would be allowed to purchase land. Wolseley ignored his opponents.

The matter took a more serious turn when charges emanating from Limassol and taken up by the facile pen of Mr Jassonides, a Cypriot residing in Oxford, became a subject for debate in Parliament. Politicians like Sir Charles Dilke found this 'evidence' politically useful in attacking the Conservative Government. Cyprus soon afforded 'a fertile theme for the wit and invective' of the Opposition from Gladstone downwards.[26] It was alleged that churchmen were degraded. Greek newspapers were suppressed. Men were flogged in front of a commissioner's home, and others were forced to work in chains on public projects. Conditions were so oppressive, it was claimed, that Cypriot Greeks were emigrating.

Called upon to explain these charges, Wolseley told Salisbury they were 'based upon untruthful reports' inspired by ecclesiastics embittered by his refusal to collect their tithes and by trouble-makers who sought to spread Hellenic ideas among the people. The ringleader, he added, was the Enosis-minded Bishop of Kitrion who was very much aggrieved when forced to pay taxes like everyone else, and suffered the indignity of paying a fine for contempt in the court at Limassol.[27] Most of the agitators, he assured the Foreign Office, 'could be silenced by employment under the government, but this would only encourage others to act in the same manner.'[28] Contending that he dealt fairly with all his subjects, Wolseley refused public answer to these baseless accusations. In fact, to do so would play into the hands of the 'newspaper scribblers'.

A public investigation nevertheless followed in Limassol with Judge Lushington Phillips, Wolseley's friend from Natal, presiding. But many of the leaders of the Greek community, including the archbishop, refused to support the charges of his critics. The testimony of the Greek vice-consul in Larnaca contradicted the charges relating to emigration and the suppression of the press. And in the end, the Bishop of Kitrion admitted that he preferred British rule, conceding that the government was very good in most districts, except for Limassol and Famugusta.

The critics of Sir Garnet's administration painted a false picture, combining certain half-truths with fanciful imagination. But there is no denying that his commissioners were often heavy-handed. Wolseley himself became concerned over their arbitrary acts, for the sake of public opinion, if nothing else. He wrote to Commissioner Warren, who was in charge of the politically sensitive Limassol district: 'We soldiers are apt to be blunt and outspoken – we are in fact at times too honest and straightforward in dealing with men in civil life, and too prone to disregard the arts of pleas-

ing and to despise the power which men can obtain over others by
geniality of manner and by the creation of a sympathetic feeling between
us and those in civil life with whom we are brought in contact.'[29]

Months after its acquisition, Cyprus remained a subject of interest to
the English people, the press, and the Parliament of England. The conditions and prospects of this latest addition to the empire were widely discussed and many eminent persons went to see for themselves this 'land
famous in all ages ... the rosy realm of Venus', as Disraeli described it.

They were greeted by the warm-voiced governor, 'cheerful and genial
as if in the midst of the London season'.[30] He invariably spoke of the
island as possessing a great future, punctuating his statements with a sweep
of his walking-stick. He continued to describe the climate as being
'simply delightful', though some suspected he was affected by the heat.
The staff, by now, made no effort to hide the fact that they were sick of the
place. Even the 'plucky Gifford' could not find a good word for Cyprus.
Brackenbury grumbled about living in a cell like a celibate monk. (Wolseley thought it a welcome change from his Natal days.) McCalmont concluded that 'nobody but a born idiot would stop in such a place if he
could live out of it.'[31]

Lady Wolseley arrived at Christmas-time with their six-year-old
daughter, Frances, to occupy their new home. They soon found that the
new Government House provided little shelter from a climate that now
'alternated between freezing cold and unbearably hot'.[32] They shivered
round stoves after the sun went down, and even when dressed for dinner,
Her Excellency found it necessary to wear a fur coat.

Other wives made the journey to Cyprus. Soon there were so many
wives on the scene that Mrs Scott-Stevenson reported that it was impossible 'to get above the gossip and evil speaking which overshadow the
small society of the place: there is so much envy, hatred, and malice.'[33]
The wives all shared one idea: to get out of Cyprus as soon as it was
decently possible.

On January 23rd, Sir Garnet with part of his staff were scouting in the
direction of Mount Troodos for a new summer camping-ground. As they
cantered along the track, the conversation turned to the war in Afghanistan. Dejected, the Chief said: 'I have put my hand to the Cypriote plough
and must hold it until the furrow is finished.'[34] The same morning, Lord
Chelmsford was moving the remnants of his main column out of the
wrecked camp at Isandhlwana in Zululand, where disaster had struck:
some 800 European and 500 native soldiers had been wiped out by Cetewayo's Zulus.

Cyprus was not favoured with a news telegram service, and it was not until February 18th that the terrible news reached the out-of-the-way island. Wolseley's first thought was to make available to the War Office the notes he had prepared in Natal for the invasion of Zululand, notes which he had hoped to use some day as the commander if, or rather when, war came. On second thoughts, he would much prefer that the authorities recognized his availability after Chelmsford's failure. Communicating his anxiety to the Duke of Cambridge, he told him how he longed to be at the scene of action. 'If required,' he said, 'I could at any time reach Natal from Cyprus sooner than anyone could get there from England, and as I know the people and the country well, I think I might be of use.'[35] Yet Wolseley must have realized that if the Duke had any say in the matter, he would do everything possible to keep him in Cyprus.

At the same time, Wolseley wrote to the Foreign Office. Too tactful to suggest openly that he supersede Chelmsford as commander, Wolseley hoped to cultivate the idea in Salisbury's mind. First, assuming the role of expert, he advised that operations should be undertaken in Zululand before the end of May, and not prolonged beyond September 10th. Then he warned that if war were carried out 'in Horse Guards* practice the result may be a failure'. Assuredly, failure or not, he told the economy-minded politicians, the war under the direction of Cambridge's men on the Horse Guards staff would be enormously expensive. Finally, he told Salisbury that former wars in South Africa 'were conducted chiefly by men ignorant of their trade who took their inspiration from books of regulations, and who seemed to think that everything was all right as long as they guided their conduct according "to Act of Parliament". Of course, when it is a question between failure and success, England can never pay too much to avoid the former, but she may, I think, pay too highly to secure the latter.'[36]

When Wolseley heard that a new commander was to be selected for South Africa, he telegraphed to Salisbury a message much more to the point, 'Will you send me?'

The appointment that Wolseley so fervently prayed for did not come. McCalmont wrote that the Chief seemed to 'be living on the hope ... of being sent to Natal, and I think the anxiety is almost too much for him sometimes.'[37] To relax his nerves, Wolseley went on a picnic to the hills, which were green at this time of the year. The ancient castles that crowned the peaks of the Kyrenia range had an ethereal quality that made them

---

* Meaning the military authorities in charge of the army, namely the Duke of Cambridge and his staff, as distinct from the civil authorities under the Secretary of State for War.

look like something out of a fairy tale. (They later inspired Walt Disney's architectural creations for *Snow-white and the Seven Dwarfs*.)

Returning to the newly-built Government House on April 27th, Wolseley found a cipher telegram ordering him to leave Cyprus and report to the War Office. The naval dispatch boat placed at his disposal was appropriately named the *Surprise*. It looked now as if he would be sent to South Africa after all. Hoping never to see Cyprus again, he packed all his belongings, most of which were to be sent after him. The government was handed over to Biddulph, whom Wolseley recommended as an admirable successor.

Travelling by way of Brindisi to Paris, Wolseley arrived in London on May 21st. He went to the Foreign Office, where he made his last report on Cyprus to the Foreign Secretary before taking another command.

As governor of Cyprus, he had established order under the most trying conditions and demonstrated, if nothing else, that he was a thrifty, cautious and shrewd administrator. But his heart was never in his work.

# CHAPTER ELEVEN

## CATCHING CETEWAYO

THE official reason given for Sir Garnet's recall to England at the end of April was that he had been selected to join a committee appraising the short-service system with relation to small wars, such as was then being fought in South Africa. The true reason, which Wolseley suspected, was that the Ministry wanted him to clean up the mess in Zululand, but for the time being they believed it prudent to conceal their choice from the Horse Guards.

When Wolseley reported to the hostile military leaders in Pall Mall on May 21st, he had 'a rough time of it', though for the sake of peace he 'had to be conciliatory'.[1] The Duke of Cambridge took advantage of the deplorable situation in Zululand to deliver a severe reprimand on short service. The Duke sternly informed Sir Garnet that 'his damned new-fangled methods' had wrecked the fine army with which he (Cambridge) proudly served in the Crimea, and was at the bottom of the present difficulties in South Africa.

While the Duke scowled and expressed his disapproval, Wolseley found the War Secretary and the rest of the Cabinet smiling and full of compliments. He met Disraeli on the very afternoon (May 22nd) that the Cabinet discussed sending him to South Africa in the double capacity of governor and general. The Prime Minister did not reveal what was in store, but Wolseley by now fully expected the appointment. The next day, after three consecutive meetings, the final decision was made. The Cabinet agreed to supersede immediately both Lord Chelmsford, the inept commander, and Sir Bartle Frere, the aggressive High Commissioner in South Africa whose actions had provoked the Zulu War. They selected a soldier-administrator who boasted of unbroken success and considerable knowledge of South African affairs, Sir Garnet Wolseley. Appointed to the local rank of general, he was invested with supreme power as commander of Her Majesty's forces in South Africa and High Commissioner for South-East Africa. Chelmsford was to remain as second in command, while Frere was to continue to serve as High Commissioner of the Cape Colony and its dependencies.

When Disraeli imparted the news to Wolseley, he asked how soon he could start. 'By the four o'clock train this afternoon if you wish it,' was the characteristic reply. It was decided, however, that Sir Garnet and his staff would leave on May 29th.

No choice could have won greater popular approval. Politicians and journalists had brought Wolseley's name forth with increasing frequency since the calamity at Isandhlwana. They expressed satisfaction with his appointment and wondered that the Government had not made the change long before, knowing that Sir Garnet was eating his heart out in Cyprus. The Opposition acted as if he were their man all along. The bare announcement of his appointment brought a feeling of relief to the nation. With Wolseley on his way to Zululand, the public seemed assured that all difficulties would now vanish. *Punch*, playing on the similarity between his name and that of the Duke of Wellington, expressed this sentiment:

When Wolseley's mentioned, Wellesley's brought to mind;
Two men, two names, of answerable kind:
Call to the front, like Wellesley, good at need,
Go, Wolseley, and like Wellesley, greatly speed.

The Queen, however, saw no resemblance whatever between that ambitious thruster, Wolseley, and the great Duke. The change in command greatly displeased Victoria and the royal family. From the beginning of the crisis, they made no secret of their sympathy for Chelmsford and Frere. On hearing of the reverse at Isandhlwana, the Queen sent a precipitate message to Chelmsford expressing condolence and confidence. The Prince of Wales openly exonerated him from all blame. And they believed Frere was treated unfairly and should be supported and encouraged, rather than censured. An angered Cabinet would undoubtedly have recalled Frere, who resentfully kept insisting that he had been right and the Government wrong, if Disraeli had not spared him in his desire to mollify the Queen. The Prime Minister told her that it was with much difficulty he secured an arrangement whereby Frere would be kept at his truncated post in South Africa. The Queen was nevertheless 'much annoyed' and strongly protested what she regarded as a public mark of want of confidence in Sir Bartle. She would 'sanction the proposal' to send Sir Garnet to Africa, 'but she would *not approve* it'.[2]

Certainly, of the 488 generals on full pay in the British army, no more irritating choice could have been made in the eyes of the Court than that of General Wolseley. The Queen thought him unconciliatory and boastful.

Disraeli, who had great confidence in Wolseley, defended him to the Queen by admitting: 'It is quite true that Wolseley is an egotist, and a braggart. So was Nelson ... Men of action,' he explained, 'when eminently successful in early life, are generally boastful and full of themselves.'[3]

The Duke of Cambridge, most responsible for poisoning the Court against Sir Garnet, did everything in his power to prevent the appointment. He stood loyally by Chelmsford, though he frankly never agreed with his strategy. When it was apparent the Cabinet would no longer tolerate him in command, the Duke tried to promote the candidacy of Lord Napier of Magdala. But it soon became obvious that the Cabinet would accept no substitutes. Owing to the counter-proposals of royalty, they met six times in eight days, which Disraeli believed established a record, but refused to give way on Wolseley's appointment.

The drooping Prime Minister told a friend that Sir Garnet was going to South Africa, though 'the Horse Guards are furious, the Princes are raging, and every mediocrity is jealous as if we had prevented him from conquering the world'.[4]

His enemies at the Horse Guards would not give way gracefully. They criticized his plans. Cambridge remonstrated against that detestable 'gang' of officers – Colley, Brackenbury, Maurice, Baker Russell, and Co. – that Wolseley had selected for his staff without bothering to consult him, his superior. Only after the War Secretary applied pressure was Colley, the designated chief of staff, given the rank of brigadier, and the four aides, to which Wolseley was entitled, approved.

Wolseley was glad to receive the appointment, but arriving so late on the scene, it would be full of difficulties. No doubt he would be too late to revise Chelmsford's plans, in which he had absolutely no confidence. And he disliked the responsibility of answering for officers and schemes not of his choosing. Sir Garnet told Dick that the chances of penetrating the centre of Zululand before the end of the season seemed very slim, because 'the Staff arrangements are utterly bad ... the transport and commissariat department are a disgrace to our nation'.[5] He realized that if the war were not brought to a conclusion soon, it would destroy the Ministry. But, after all, they richly deserved it for not having removed Chelmsford immediately after his first blunder.

Wolseley's one great fear was that Frere might resign when he learned he had been superseded. He had no desire to take on his responsibilities; he wanted nothing more to do with confederation schemes. Frere, however, refused to resign, much to the delight of Wolseley – and the Queen.

There was a great send-off for the general, his staff, and the large number of special service officers going to South Africa. Swarms of people came down to Paddington Station. When Sir Garnet arrived, a crowd gathered in the street and gave him an ovation. Hicks Beach, the new Colonial Secretary, boarded the special train and accompanied the general as far as Didcot Junction so as to give a few last-minute instructions. At all the stations to Dartmouth there were large crowds cheering and waving their hats. Wolseley hated demonstrations of this kind *before* the event, and tried to sleep through it all. At one station he was startled by an enormous body of well-wishers who besieged his carriage and pressed against the glass of his saloon until he thought surely it would break. What he did not know was that McCalmont and his clowning comrades had conspired not to disappoint the crowd, so they dressed one of their group, Major Bushman, to look like the general. The enthusiastic crowds went wild as the counterfeit commander appeared in a second saloon, waving a sword and making grandiloquent statements on everything from punishing the Zulus to taking off all duties on tobacco when he returned.

Sailing out of Dartmouth at midday, the *Edinburgh Castle* was accompanied by every small ship and yacht in those waters. The ancient castle at the mouth of the harbour was black with people wishing them godspeed. The shouting and horn-blowing was more than a measure of Sir Garnet's popularity: it was an expression of the public feeling that all would now go well. This feeling gave rise to the phrase 'All Sir Garnet', which is still occasionally heard in England. It was a synonym for 'everything's going well', and roughly equivalent to the American saying, 'The marines have landed and the situation is well in hand.'

In Cape Town Wolseley learned that Chelmsford had begun a second invasion of Zululand on June 1st with three times the force he had commanded in January. The advance was divided into two main columns: a southern force under General H. Hope Crealock (brother of Lieutenant-Colonel J. N. Crealock) operating along the coast, and a northern column under General Newdigate (to which Chelmsford attached himself) that was to make straight for Ulundi. This time Chelmsford did not undervalue the fighting qualities of the enemy. All the precautions that had been ignored before were scrupulously observed. As a result, progress was exasperatingly slow. Archibald Forbes sneeringly called the advance 'perverse pedestrianism'. Another reporter likened the British army to the children of Israel wandering aimlessly in the wilderness. Chelmsford's dawdling march prompted his own brother to write: 'For God's sake do something. Wolseley supersedes you.'[6]

As his lordship ploughed his way through Zululand, Wolseley hoped to overtake him before an important engagement took place. He left Cape Town the next day, stopping at Port Elizabeth barely long enough to send messages to Chelmsford and Crealock which were deliberately stiff and peremptory so as 'to wheel them into line'. He insisted upon full information from his lordship and told him that all preparations for peace must be referred to him. Both generals were asked not to correspond with the authorities at the Cape or in England, except through him. Three days later, Wolseley informed Chelmsford that he did not like his plan of campaign: 'I regard this separation and independent action as extremely dangerous.'[7] Wolseley told his fellow passengers that he feared on his arrival in Durban there would be word of another set-back, possibly a disaster!

Four days out of Cape Town (record time), Sir Garnet arrived at Durban where the harbour was decorated with bunting and the citizens turned out to cheer him. 'What is the news from Zululand?' Sir Garnet asked. He was told that Chelmsford, with most of his army, was now only seventeen miles from Ulundi, the Zulu capital. There was still time, thought Wolseley, to deliver the *coup de main* himself.

After receiving and replying to civic addresses of welcome by the mayor, Wolseley visited old friends who declared he had not altered in the slightest in appearance since he left Natal. A quick trip was made to the hospital to see the sick and wounded. After a few words of sympathy, Wolseley invariably asked the convalescent how many Zulus he thought he had shot. Later in the day, the general boarded a special train which was prepared for him and sped on to Botha's Hill, where he transferred to a post-cart to complete the journey to Maritzburg. Rattling along at breakneck speed, Wolseley arrived at Government House long before he was expected. The guard of honour had not yet formed up, nor was Sir Henry Bulwer buttoned up for the welcome.

Sworn in as governor of Natal, Wolseley now united the chief civil and military authority in the neighbourhood of the seat of the war, and thereby cut through 'the knot of dispute' that had arisen between Bulwer and Chelmsford. Necessary conferences were held with General Clifford, commanding the line of communications, and his bright new assistant, an old comrade, Major William Butler. Bishop Colenso, not happy to see Wolseley in the role of governor again, privately muttered about the legality of his acts. Despite Isandhlwana, the good bishop's sympathies were still with the Zulus.

Two days after his arrival, a prearranged meeting was held with some seventy native chiefs summoned from all parts of the Colony. Wolseley hoped to win their co-operation in carrying provisions for his army. Surrounded by much pomp and ceremony, Sir Garnet, standing with legs apart and his hand resting on the hilt of his sword, told them in strong language that he had come to put an end to the war, adding that if necessary the Great White Queen could send one army after another until the Zulu king was overwhelmed. The meeting was a success.

At the time, Wolseley was more worried lest Cetewayo overwhelm Chelmsford. Betraying his justifiable anxiety, he sent a message from Maritzburg to Chelmsford: 'Concentrate your force immediately and keep it concentrated. Undertake no operations with detached bodies of troops. Acknowledge receipt of this message at once and flash back your latest moves. I am astonished at not hearing from you.'[8]

Wolseley was no less concerned about General Crealock. He knew the old-school martinet well, having served with him in the Crimea, India, China and Canada, and regarded him as a hopeless incompetent, totally unfit for command in war. Cambridge was candidly advised that Crealock's cleverness should be restricted to peace manœuvres. In private, Wolseley spoke of him as a loudmouth 'who is enough to sink a ship'. As for the younger brother on Chelmsford's staff, his lordship's 'evil genius', he was even worse. 'They are both snobs,' he wrote to Dick, 'and as they were not born gentlemen, they cannot help it.'[9]

On arrival in Natal, Wolseley heard all kinds of fantastic stories about General Crealock's outlandish behaviour. Dressed like a guest at an artists' ball, he wore a sombrero with a long peacock feather and an imitation pugaree tied on one side, in what he believed to be picturesque, artistic carelessness. At a time when transport was at a premium, he had one wagon designed as a movable hen-house so that he might have fresh eggs for breakfast. He even telegraphed for six milch cows to be sent forward so that he might not be deprived of milk in his tea while campaigning. The major in charge of supplies telegraphed back, 'Must draw the line at milch cows.'[10] Nevertheless, Crealock eventually requisitioned his milch cows.

Conducting the war half as a campaign and half as a picnic, Crealock's column crept into Zululand so slowly, with many halts between the creeps, that his men, who detested him, called him 'General Rip Van Crealock'. And it was mischievously related that his rise in the army was owing to his talent for caricaturing, which so amused the headquarters staff in the Crimea that he was promoted.

The trip to the capital was felt by Wolseley to be a waste of valuable time. He had hoped to proceed overland by way of Rorke's Drift and overtake Chelmsford's force before it reached Ulundi. But rather than wait any longer for the horses he had purchased in Cape Town, Wolseley decided to double back to Durban on the morning of July 1st, board a ship, and land at Port Durnford on the Zululand coast, close to where General Crealock had his headquarters. With the Coast column he would move on to Ulundi and unite all his forces. As far as the war was concerned, Wolseley complained to his wife, 'Crealock's column might just as well have been in England'.[11]

Egging the train engineer on with a heavy wager, Wolseley broke the record for speed he had established coming in. Taking perilous curves at high speeds, one soldier passenger exclaimed he 'did not think anyone alive was ever in greater danger'.

Port Durnford was misnamed. It was a port only in exceptionally good weather. Normally a heavy surf pounded the open beach. When the *Shah* arrived the next morning, the surf was so violent that Captain Bradshaw persuaded Sir Garnet to put off landing until the morrow. The following day the signal 'good beach' was received from the commodore on shore. Sir Garnet and his staff were bundled into a tug and then transferred into the hold of a small lighter just outside the breaking rollers. Thirteen men were battened down in the small, dark hole, and for two hours a desperate struggle was made to tow them ashore. The commodore finally signalled that the surf was too heavy for a landing, and they were towed back to the *Shah*.

Cursing his luck as he paced the deck of the *Shah*, His Excellency began to receive strange messages from Crealock, who had opened heliographic communications. The sybarite Crealock informed him: 'I have got two milch cows for your Excellency.' Wolseley, who despised luxury in the field, refused to vouchsafe a reply. A second message was sent: 'I have a marquee for your Excellency.' This time Wolseley shot back a prompt reply: 'All marquees should be at the base: send it back!'[12]

In the night, the sea became so rough that the captain began to fear for the safety of his ship so close to the shore. Moreover, he told Wolseley, the sea might be in this state for days. Thereupon His Excellency decided to return to Durban and enter Zululand by wagon. Butler, anticipating his possible return, had horses and wagons ready for the general and his staff. This false movement cost Wolseley six valuable days and a chance to lay hold of Chelmsford's force at a most critical time.

News of the arrival of Wolseley had the effect of spurring Chelmsford on in his movements towards Ulundi, but not in replying to the new commander's urgent messages. Chelmsford completely ignored Wolseley's authority over him, though he received messages from every direction announcing that he had been superseded. He turned a deaf ear to Wolseley's order, received on July 2nd, to concentrate his forces, for he believed he was in a better position to judge the military situation. Contrary to Wolseley's orders, he opened negotiations with Cetewayo when the latter made overtures of peace, and communicated directly with the authorities at home informing them about his plans and policy. Not a word of this reached the new commander.

The Zulu chief's peaceful protestations were merely a ruse to gain time in gathering upwards of 20,000 of his trained warriors at Ulundi for another such massacre as Isandhlwana. It might well have been another disaster had the Zulus attacked the night before the battle. As the British and their native allies lay tense and tired listening to the chanting of weird war-songs, native guards mistook the shadow of a cloud in the moonlight for the advance of a Zulu impi. As they fired, their comrades, believing it was an attack, jumped up and ran back towards the British. The Europeans in turn, in their excited imagination, thought the 'naked devils' rushing among them were the enemy. They left their beds and sprinted for protection in the laager. In a frantic effort to get inside, some clambered over the wagons, while others crawled underneath. Behind the wagons, incompletely trained boys, many of whom had never fired a bullet before embarkation, huddled together and sobbed pitifully like children. Seasoned veterans, heeding their officers, stood their ground and vigorously thrust their bayonets into the whirlwind of howling humanity. Demon panic produced scenes that were ludicrously disgraceful. One high-ranking officer left his bed crying, 'Lord help us,' and stumbled into a bush. Pricked by a thorn, he cried, 'I am assagaid! I am assagaid!' It took some effort to hold him, and assure him that there was no danger and that he was uninjured.[13]

The next morning, July 4th, while Wolseley was being defeated by the surf, his army was being marshalled by Chelmsford in the form of a great square, with sides four deep, braced at intervals and angles by Gatling guns and artillery. The 4,000 British, with 1,000 native allies, advanced slowly towards Ulundi.

The Zulu strength was in the attack. Out of the circular kraal the impis swarmed like angry hornets, led by unmarried regiments roused to violence by the heat of their celibacy. Undaunted by all the appliances of civilized warfare, they flung themselves on the quick-firing lines of infantry, leaping and shrieking, pausing only long enough to hurl an assagai or fire slugs and pieces of cooking-pot legs from their museum pieces. As they dashed forward, a war correspondent overheard Chelmsford say to his troops, 'Men, fire faster; can't you fire faster?' He could not help contrasting his words with Wolseley's in Ashantiland, 'Fire low, fire slow!'

The brave blacks came within nine paces of the square. They would have come closer had they remained true to their old tactics of closing ground at once and stabbing, instead of pausing to fire. Once the attackers began to waver, a gap was made in the square and Drury Lowe, with the 17th Lancers, galloped out upon them. Cetewayo's whole army turned and ran, having first displayed what Aristotle called the greatest of all virtues, valour.

When Chelmsford told Archibald Forbes that he did not intend sending a courier with the important news until the next day because of the absence of some minor details, the latter was moved by 'angry impulse' to exclaim hotly, 'Then, sir, I will start at once!'[14] As a reporter, he wanted not only to be first with the news, but he knew that his friend, Sir Garnet, was eagerly awaiting the tidings of the day. It was a decision Forbes had cause to regret several times as he rode continuously for seventeen hours through an area alive with armed Zulus. Staggering into the telegraph-station at Landman's Drift, he had the satisfaction of knowing that his was the first news to England of a great victory. His words were given the honour of being read in Parliament.

Meanwhile, having returned to Durban, Wolseley raced overland towards Ulundi in the company of Colley, who had just arrived from India. At Fort Pearson, Wolseley and his officers paused to rest for the night. During mess, they held a cheerless discussion about the military situation. The Chief had difficulty in concealing his gloom. He had never embarked upon an expedition with less enthusiasm. There was a general feeling that Chelmsford would pull some 'death or glory stunt', now that he knew that Wolseley was on his way. As the long-faced diners pondered the possibility of another Isandhlwana, the Chief was handed a telegram giving Forbes's brief description of the action. Having read the contents, Wolseley smiled and announced: 'This is indeed the best news I have read for many a long day. Tonight, gentlemen, we may sleep peacefully, for Lord Chelmsford has been engaged with the army of the Zulu king, and has thoroughly defeated it.'[15] Being only human, however, the news was not altogether welcome. As professional soldiers they had come to South Africa to fight. Without hearing a shot fired or seeing an assegai hurled, the war was virtually over before they reached the scene of action.

Wires began to hum as Wolseley congratulated Chelmsford, thanked

Forbes, and told the Government, 'The war is over.' Orders were sent directing reinforcements which were on their way to return to England. Under Colley's direction, preparations were made to move the great bulk of the army to the coast and embark for home. All the generals – except Clifford – and their staffs were asked to pack up and join them, for Wolseley decided that the responsibilities of these 'worthless generals' could be discharged more efficiently by his own lieutenant-colonels. On reaching Port Durnford, it was all Wolseley could do to speak to Crealock, whose manner was 'so repulsive'.

Critics censured Sir Garnet for his haste. The colonists were alarmed. The Duke of Cambridge was surprised by his opinion of the 'distinguished generals' and feared that if there was any fight left in the Zulu race, 'this hurried withdrawal of troops and staff must tell very greatly in its moral effect against us.'[16] Wolseley's military intuition, however, told him that 'the Zulu reputation as a military power had been a bubble' that had burst at Ulundi.[17]

After the battle, Chelmsford did not remain to reap the fruits of his triumph. No effort was made to capture Cetewayo (Chelmsford expected he would come in to surrender), or to pursue his shattered impis. It is true that the Zulus made no attempt to rally, but no precautions were taken to prevent such a move. Once the Ulundi kraal was burned, the British army returned to camp and prepared for a withdrawal. The failure to take Cetewayo, whose royal hut was occupied only by bottles of champagne and gin (which were executed on the spot), prolonged unnecessarily the pacification of Zululand. Chelmsford was widely denounced for committing an 'irremediable blunder'.

Chelmsford tried to fix the blame for his hasty retreat on Wolseley by claiming that he gave him no instructions before the battle on how to act in the event of a victory; the distant new commander only told him what to do if he suffered a defeat. Disraeli, who could never forgive Chelmsford for the predicament in which he had placed his Government, investigated the allegation that Wolseley was responsible for the precipitate withdrawal and declared it unfounded. The Prime Minister told the Queen that Chelmsford's retreat from Ulundi 'was his last and crowning mistake'.[18]

Wolseley, however, was not entirely without fault. Chelmsford was right when he claimed that he received no orders either before or after Ulundi to pursue the defeated enemy.* Too pessimistic to believe in

---

*Wolseley's telegrams at this time support Chelmsford's contention; but, when a Blue Book treating with the Zulu War was published in February, they were left out.

victory before the battle, Wolseley became over-optimistic after the battle. His chief adviser on Zulu affairs, John Dunn, a colonist who had gone native and acquired a profound knowledge of the Zulus as well as an assortment of wives, assured him after Ulundi that an offer of 5,000 head of cattle and an independent chieftainship to the king's rival brother, Oham, would succeed in effecting his capture. Thus, Wolseley himself decided against sending a force of Europeans on a wild chase after Cetewayo into the remote and rugged country, into which he had disappeared. He fully expected the chief to come in, or be brought in by his people – or maybe 'some kind friend will run an assegai through him'.[19] Not until mid July did it become obvious that Cetewayo would have to be hunted down. Only then did Wolseley begin to complain bitterly of Chelmsford's failure to remain at Ulundi and order pursuit; only then did he express the fear that the enemy was given a certain amount of renewed confidence by a hasty withdrawal that gave 'a semblance of defeat'. He told his wife: 'It is now I realize Chelmsford's stupidity in not staying here after the fight.'[20]

But would Chelmsford have acted differently if he had received specific instructions on how to conduct his operations after a victory? He disregarded practically all Wolseley's other instructions before and after Ulundi. By his own admission, he refused to recognize Wolseley's authority in South Africa until he received a much-delayed telegram of his appointment from the Secretary of War on July 5th, at which time he asked to be relieved. Even then, he continued the fiction by maintaining it was his understanding from the War Secretary's message that Wolseley merely replaced Frere as High Commissioner and commander-in-chief (purely a courtesy title), and that he was not to interfere with his position as general commanding the forces in South Africa, except to regulate the overall campaign. Acting upon this incredible assumption, he actually refused to forward his report of the action at Ulundi to Colley, the new chief of staff, as Wolseley ordered, but sent it directly to the War Office.

Chelmsford and Wolseley met at St Paul's mission station on July 15th when the latter rode out with his staff and an escort of mounted men. There was no unpleasantness. Wolseley found it difficult to be unkind as he looked into the retiring commander's gentle, stag-like eyes. Basically, Chelmsford was a chivalrous gentleman and good fellow, thought Wolseley, as he 'studiously avoided all subjects upon which there could be any difference of opinion'. [21] But God forbid, he observed, that such an officer ever be given command of soldiers in the field again.

At this time the chief found pleasure in greeting and congratulating his old comrades, Wood and Buller, who had served with Chelmsford. 'You two,' he declared, 'are looked upon as the heroes of the war, whose actions have pulled us through the mess and redeemed the reputation of the army.'[22] But for Wood and Buller, Wolseley said repeatedly, Chelmsford would never have reached Ulundi. He delighted in writing his friends a riddle that was current in camp: 'Why is it that the men of Lord Chelmsford's column cannot be regarded as Christians?' Answer: 'Because they made an idol of Wood and did not believe in the Lord.' Wolseley urged the Duke to make Wood a general, but Royal George strongly deprecated 'too early promotion'. Wood, along with Buller, was received at Balmoral by Victoria who was greatly impressed and found him to be 'extremely agreeable'. Wood became a great favourite of the Queen.*

Moving on to Ulundi, Sir Garnet received the submission of virtually all the principal Zulu chiefs. Speaking through an interpreter from the centre of a large circle, Sir Garnet told the chiefs that the war, which would soon be over, was never waged against the Zulu people but against Cetewayo, who was now deposed. And though England could annex Zululand, he promised she would not do so. Neither land nor property, only their arms, would be taken from them. To prevent the re-establishment of a military system, he intended to divide their nation into districts, each governed by an independent chief, who in turn would be subject to the control of European supervisors.

His words were favourably received, and another meeting in Ulundi was arranged with the Great White Chief for August 12th. By then, Sir Garnet hoped Cetewayo would be in his hands.

After a brief visit to Maritzburg where his presence was required as governor, Sir Garnet and his staff returned to Zululand in August to organize the capture of Cetewayo. At Rorke's Drift, the general ordered a parade of two companies stationed there, and medals were dispensed on the very spot where they had been won. Crossing the Tugela, a visit was made to Isandhlwana. British officers and men who had fallen on that fatal day had been buried long before, but Zulu skeletons were still to be seen. As Wolseley paced about and spoke of Chelmsford's plan as being 'a hideous mistake', one of the officers slipped off and busily engaged himself in extracting teeth from Zulu skulls, souvenirs for his many inamorata.

They travelled over undulating grassland, broken by rocky eminences,

* Equally winning in her manner was his sister, Kitty O'Shea, whose illicit romance with Parnell wrecked a brilliant political career.

furrowed by deep ravines, and shaded occasionally by clumps of trees. It was beautiful country. The nights were cool and the days were warm, sometimes a trifle sultry. 'By Jove!' the staff exclaimed. 'It's nearly as hot as Cyprus.' Time and again they expressed their joy at being off that 'wretched little island'. Letters from their comrades stationed there told of 'a general stampede' from the place now that attacks were made almost daily in Parliament on 'Grandma' Biddulph, as Wolseley called him, and his commissioners. Wolseley explained that the row really began with the cutting of the hair and beards 'of some filthy Greek priests', and then the civil administrators made a serious error by inserting 'the *whole* truth' in their official correspondence. 'Dispatches should always be strictly true,' was Wolseley's advice, 'but unpleasant truths that can be made use of by the opponents of the Government you are serving should be reserved for our private correspondence with Ministers.'[23]

Several times every day throughout the ten-day trek, McCalmont asked the chief, 'Do you think, sir, Cetewayo will fight again?' It was a question that was on everyone's mind. The colonists insisted that the cruel, tireless monarch would fight again; Wolseley thought otherwise.

It was soon learned that Cetewayo had sought refuge somewhere in the dense Ngome forest beyond the Black Umvaloxi River, some thirty miles north of Ulundi, and it was reported that he still had some 3,000 men with him. Wolseley, therefore, established a cordon of redcoats, colonists, Swazis and other friendly natives about the general area, and formed an advance camp at Ulundi with direct communications to all fortified posts. Established in a good central position, well garrisoned and provisioned, with his military net carefully laid, Wolseley reasoned it would be just a matter of time before Cetewayo and his men were captured or exterminated.

After a few days, Cetewayo offered to come in under certain conditions. But Wolseley refused to negotiate.

Patrols went out daily, travelling light, often living off the country on Zulu beer and Zulu beef. By degrees, they caught his horses and servants, but not Cetewayo. They did slow him down. Being a big man, he became so footsore he could no longer move quickly from place to place. For the pursuers, who hunted through the most difficult country, each day was filled with hard work. The English cavalry horses soon became exhausted, and the chase continued with colonials and natives on foot. Often they were hot on the fugitive's trail, only to have him slip through the patrols. Meanwhile, the fallen king's subjects and virtually all his lieutenants came in to tender submission to His Excellency, thereby demonstrating that Cetewayo's cause was a hopeless one. Pressure was brought to bear on those who might know where their leader was hiding, but they either did not know or refused to play the role of informer.

As the days extended into weeks and his patrols encountered disappointment on every side, Wolseley became apprehensive. He began to dread lest the pursuit should have to be carried on into the rainy season, and all the while his presence was urgently required in the Transvaal. What would the Ministry think of his failure to conclude the Zulu War? What would his enemies at home do if he continued to fail in his efforts? Wolseley began to regret his policy of unconditional submission, guaranteeing 'that accursed Cetewayo' nothing beyond his life.

On the seventeenth day of the king-hunt, shortly after dawn, Wolseley heard the clatter of hoofs outside his tent. As the general, wakeful in his anxiety, drew back the flap of his tent, a tired and dusty dispatch rider dismounted from a foam-covered horse and shouted, 'They've caught him, sir.' Wolseley could feel his heart jump within him.

It was Gifford's relentless persistence that finally cornered a completely worn-out king, only to have Major Marter stumble on the fugitive's whereabouts by accident and seize him from under Gifford's very nose. Nevertheless, Wolseley recognized it was Gifford, with the assistance of Maurice, who created the opportunity for Cetewayo's capture. As a reward, the Chief allowed Gifford to carry home the dispatches and receive the sum of £300.

The celebrated captive aroused great interest among his English captors. They saw not the cruel-looking, bloated savage portrayed by press illustrators; instead they saw a fine specimen of manhood, tall, huge in limb, with a grand chest-development. His grizzled hair and scant beard set off a face that was pleasing and intelligent. When one of Marter's men seemed inclined to guard him too closely, he looked at him with fearless eyes and said in a strong deep voice, 'Hands off, white soldier!' Fearing further humiliation, he announced proudly, 'Shoot me here at once. I wish to die.'

Drawing himself up with dignity, Cetewayo slowly and deliberately marched to Ulundi, a large escort all about him. Arriving at British headquarters two days later, he made an impressive entrance, walking very erect and looking 'every inch a king', though he wore only his moucha and a red table-cloth around his shoulders. 'By Jove,' exclaimed one officer, 'he is a fine-looking nigger.' To prevent eager sightseers from getting too close, Sir Garnet had him pass through flanking parties with drawn swords, thrown out 100 yards on either side, and Dragoons were

I

sent out to the front and rear of the procession. Unfortunately, it added a stateliness to the ex-king's arrival in camp which Sir Garnet had not intended.

The British commander took no official notice of his royal prisoner, treating him as a mere fugitive from the law rather than as a captured king. Cetewayo was kept in a tent under heavy guard while his departure was prepared for the following day. Through the interpreter, the only person (except for the general) allowed in his tent, he protested that he had always wanted peace, but that war was forced upon him. His remarks were interspersed with tears which failed to move the general. Sir Garnet lectured the delinquent monarch for almost an hour about his misdeeds and broken promises made on this same spot exactly six years before when he was crowned king by Sir Theophilus Shepstone.

At a distance, Sir Garnet and his staff witnessed the departure of their important prisoner who was to be confined in Cape Town Castle. The melancholy Cetewayo took few of his possessions with him; among those he left behind was his necklace of lions' claws which Wolseley kept as his only prize. The general sent the keepsake home with Gifford with instructions to have the individual claws mounted and engraved, 'CETEWAYO, 28 AUGUST 1879', and then distributed as a little 'charm' to certain prominent ladies, such as the wife of the War Secretary, Lady Cardwell, etc.

With the capture of Cetewayo, Sir Garnet was confronted with the weighty problem of making a political settlement that would guarantee the stability of the conquered land. It was an uncongenial assignment to which he brought neither temperament nor talent. After he divided the kingdom among thirteen princelets of his own selecting, Wolseley borrowed a political idea from Shepstone, by placing some of the tribes under the scions of families which had ruled before the Zulus imposed their military system. Where this was not possible, he appointed special chiefs, among them the polygamist renegade, John Dunn. The scheme was seriously weakened by the absence of a controlling European authority. Instead of establishing a protectorate, as Hicks Beach later intimated, Wolseley stuck to his initial orders and established a Resident who was to offer his advice and act as the 'eyes and ears' of the British Government, but was expressly forbidden any active interference whatsoever. Missionaries, moreover, were not allowed to return unless specifically invited by the individual chiefs.

The Cabinet gave its blessing to Wolseley's settlement, but Frere and his supporters argued a policy of direct control through a British Resident. Frere feared a revival of Zulu power and was irked by Wolseley's refusal to consult him about what he proposed to do. The earliest information Sir Bartle could get about these important arrangements was from the newspapers. Wolseley defended himself to Hicks Beach by associating Frere with what he and Bulwer privately called the 'anti-black' party in South Africa, which assumed that the land belonged to the white settler and that the native was his servant. Wolseley boasted that his settlement would last for generations, provided Frere did not upset it with his well-meaning interference. Under no conditions should he be allowed to intervene.

Wolseley's arrangements, based upon 'Zululand for the Zulus', satisfied the Colonial Office and pleased the penny papers. It was said to have realized the description of the land as written by Tennyson in 'Locksley Hall' –

Never comes the trader, never floats an European flag,
Slides the bird o'er lustrous woodland, swings the trailer from the crag.

But there was a howl of unpoetic disapproval among the colonists. Persons of very different opinions in the colony emphatically denounced the scheme. Most favoured Frere's policy of strong control. The missionaries and their supporters, who were to be excluded, felt betrayed by Exeter Hall's toleration of heathenism. The Natal press examined Wolseley's record and questioned his qualifications. And they attacked the character of the chiefs he had selected: one was a Basuto, a foreigner, who took part in the invasion; another was a drunkard; a third was, by Wolseley's own admission, 'of a time-serving disposition'; and there was that renegade scoundrel, John Dunn. And how was peace to be maintained, they asked, among 'Kilkenny cats'?

It was a well-conceived scheme of reconstruction, arranged with great skill, but as forecasted the absence of a central control caused a break-down. As the colonists predicted, it was only a matter of months before the thirteen chieftains were squabbling and warring. After the Transvaal won its independence a year later, the independent princelets became tempting bait to filibustering Boers. Nor could the Zulu national sentiment be easily dismissed – many were still unmistakably devoted to the banished king. So in 1882, the British Government recalled Cetewayo from exile and restored him to his throne under very strict conditions. Before returning to Zululand, Cetewayo was brought to England where he might be duly impressed with the power of the conquerors. The Queen gave him a silver goblet and the Prince of Wales made him a present of a walking-stick. The Zulu king, half-tyrant and half-child, delighted thousands of Britons, from the M.P.s he visited in the House of Commons, to the waving nursemaids of Kensington who watched him appear each morning on the balcony of his house in Mebury Road.

The reception the restored monarch received from his jealous chiefs was far less enthusiastic. He was soon to be defeated in battle and driven from his royal kraal, which was looted of all the mementoes he had received while in England a few months before. Cetewayo remained a fugitive for some time and died of poison in February 1884. To end the trouble and disorder in Zululand, it was annexed to the British Crown in 1887, and ten years later it became part of Natal.

# CHAPTER TWELVE

# TAMING THE TRANSVAAL

W HEN Bismarck wrote in 1879 'of those unruly wasps that annoy the British lion in some of his dominion', nowhere were the wasps more disposed to sting than in the north-east corner of South Africa. While the British were subduing the Zulus, a troubled situation in neighbouring Transvaal was moving towards a dangerous climax. The discontented Boers agitated for independence, and Sekukuni, the pugnacious chief of the Bapedi tribe, openly challenged Britain's authority. It was a task that once more called for the services of England's ace trouble-shooter, Sir Garnet Wolseley, who was stamping out the last embers of Zulu resistance.

That portion of the complex map of Africa lying between the Vaal and Limpopo Rivers, known as the Transvaal, was inhabited by a million blacks and 40,000 self-reliant Boers. The latter were pastoralists – Boer means farmer – conservative, quiet, homely, bigoted, and devoutly attached to the stern, unadulterated doctrines of John Calvin. With great powers of endurance, living a life largely in the saddle, with a rifle across their knees, these hardy frontiersmen established a home insulated from the 'verdoomdt Englischman'* by hundreds of miles of wilderness. But not for long. Their lack of knowledge in the science of government and continued difficulties with Cetewayo, Sekukuni, and other natives gave the British an excuse for intervention and annexation under Shepstone in 1877.

At first, stunned by Shepstone's *coup* and soothed by his promise that they would 'enjoy the fullest legislative privileges', the protests of the Transvaalers were feeble. Only after the dull Boers realized how precious their lost liberty was and that Shepstone's promise was meaningless, did they bellow in protest. If a truly generous financial settlement and a constitution guaranteeing responsible government had followed annexation, the Boers might have settled down quietly as British subjects, and certain

* To the pious Boer, the expression 'damned Englishman' was not profanity but a truthful utterance. The British, according to their creed, were a condemned race, children of darkness. Being himself a saint, the Boer felt his sanctity soiled by contact with the disciples of Beelzebub.

bloody pages in South African history might never have been written.

By the time of the Zulu War, the Boers had waited two years for a constitution which had been pledged by Shepstone and endorsed by the Colonial Office. Their patience was coming to an end. Meeting followed meeting, protest succeeded protest, memorials were signed praying for independence, and delegates were sent to London only to be treated by Whitehall with studied aplomb and political coquetry, which hinted much but delivered nothing.

The day after the Zulu War began, a congress of Transvaalers, having heard the negative results of their delegates' visit to England, entered into a solemn covenant to recover their independence by every constitutional means available. As for the Zulu War, the Boers refused to support the British against their old enemies; some hotheads even advocated joining Cetewayo against those who suppressed their freedom. Frere, in the midst of his Zulu troubles, tried unsuccessfully to conciliate the surly Boers with soft words and promises of eventual self-government.

When Wolseley was appointed to overall civil and military command in the eastern part of South Africa, the disaffected Boers assumed that the appointment of this man of action meant that a new era would be inaugurated, far different from the line followed by Sir Bartle Frere. They were right: a new era was to follow, but one vastly different from what they had expected. If the Boers were disappointed by Sir Bartle, they were to be even more disagreeably disappointed by Sir Garnet.

In air thick with rumours of a Boer uprising, Wolseley decided early in September that his presence as High Commissioner was required in the Transvaal. The general's remaining movements in Zululand were necessarily abrupt. A commission was quickly appointed to settle the boundaries of the thirteen independent kinglets, and a general inspection was held at Ulundi prior to breaking camp.

Because of his haste in getting to Pretoria, Wolseley's line of march over the vast plateau of grass and scrubby bush was direct and untravelled. Many of the wagons, as a result, came to 'unutterable grief' manœuvring over the difficult terrain. In the lower undulations of the tableland, where water flowed down from the hills, towns and hamlets were to be found surrounded by pastures and cultivated strips. At each of these settlements in his path, Wolseley addressed gatherings, which seemed to hang back at first as if awed by his august presence. Knowing that these 'infernal Boers' were requisitioning powder in Cromwellian fashion, Sir Garnet boldly told them they must realize that annexation was irrevocable. As the Boers listened in quiet and indignation, he assured them in his strong, stern voice that the sun would cease to shine and the Vaal would flow backwards through the Drakensberg Mountains before the British flag would be hauled down in this land. His rhetoric curled many a lip, but Wolseley believed it gave courage to loyal men who might hold back lest they be punished by the disloyal after he left.

A strong government bred loyalty, was Wolseley's argument. Force, not concessions, was the answer to Boer discontent. No political reforms, he advised Hicks Beach, should be undertaken so long as armed men roamed about the country uttering seditious nonsense about fighting British soldiers. Only after the Boers decided to behave should they be given a free constitution. The failure of the Government 'to put its foot down and make its power felt', he wrote his wife, 'had encouraged the idea they would give up the Transvaal'.[1] To stamp out this notion that encouraged sedition, Wolseley asked Lanyon (who had replaced Shepstone in Pretoria) to repeat his words, 'that so long as the sun shone the Union Jack would never be taken down'. Frere, too, was asked to say it. He then advised the Colonial Secretary to write it into his dispatches, to announce it in Parliament, 'and not to falter in making it known that nothing could affect the permanency of the British occupation ... Until then the Transvaal Government would live as upon quicksand.'[2]

Before reaching Pretoria, the shocking news that Sir Louis Cavagnari and his escort had been massacred in Kabul overtook Wolseley and his party. It meant a renewal of the war with the Afghans. Having no personal military adviser, the Viceroy requested the services of Colley. Unselfishly, Wolseley authorized his departure, though he would 'miss Colley's good sense and sound judgment *very much*'. Colley, in his opinion, was by far the ablest officer he had ever had, 'and any sensible commander-in-chief would make him a general. H.R.H. does not come under that category.'[3]

Wolseley feared the disaster in India would bring 'Gladstone and Co.' to power, which would mean handing back Cyprus, withdrawing from the Transvaal, granting Home Rule, and reversing Indian policy. And Wolseley prayed the Disraeli Government would survive long enough to reward him properly for the troublesome assignments he had undertaken for them. No 'wretched G.C.B.' such as was given to 'that failure Chelmsford' would be acceptable. A peerage with a good pension, for they knew him to be a poor man, would be satisfactory. After all, how could the present Ministry deny him what they freely gave to head clerks in public office? Perhaps his clever little wife could arrange to have a hint dropped in the right place and 'devise some plan for it'. In this respect,

Wolseley observed, Sir Bartle was well served by his wife, who mani-
pulated the Queen. Perhaps his 'little snipe' could study 'old Mother
Frere's' technique 'and see how she helps her husband out in this sort of
work'.[4]

The fear that Sir Bartle Frere, or 'Sir Bottle Beer' as Wolseley irreverently called him in private, would resign, never ceased to plague him.
He suspected the Government might commit some 'monstrous' act such
as offering him a peerage to induce him to resign, while he was 'left out
in the cold' without a peerage and forced to remain in South Africa to
take his place.[5] Frere also annoyed the general with a barrage of angry
letters and dispatches, some of which were downright venomous, for
Wolseley's independent action and refusal to co-operate vexed Frere.
He saw the general as taking a perverse delight in playing the role of a
naughty youth before his elders. It is true that on one occasion Wolseley
mischievously sent Sir Bartle a dispatch by way of Whitehall. It was a
fatuous political arrangement that allowed the common good and needs
of South Africa to be eclipsed by the clash of views between two High
Commissioners enjoying exclusive powers.

Sir Garnet was welcomed to Pretoria by crowds waving banners and
petitions for independence. He replied with more 'sunshine rhetoric'
about the British flag flying over the Transvaal; he uttered threats one
moment and friendly, peaceful proposals the next. To the Boers, Sir
Garnet's movements and gestures were quick; he seemed to run rather
than walk. His examinations were so hasty, they seemed to confirm
what he already knew by means of some strange prescience. The High
Commissioner's actions gave credence to the rumour that he had bet his
friends he would straighten out affairs in this land soon enough to be
home for Christmas dinner.

And Wolseley did expect to eat dinner with his family in England
before the end of the year. He wrote to Lady Wolseley that there was 'no
use in doing governor's work here for the few weeks more I shall be in
the country'; indeed, it would hurt the feelings of 'Billy' Lanyon, who
was doing a good job, and seriously lower his position in the eyes of the
colonists.[6] Moreover, it was work which he thoroughly disliked. He despised these 'half-civilized Dutchmen'. If they meant to fight, he would
be happy to oblige them, but Wolseley doubted their courage to face a
test of strength in anything more than wordy warfare.

After being sworn in as High Commissioner, Sir Garnet lost no time in
proclaiming the creation of an Executive Council whose members,
selected by the governor, were to serve in a purely advisory capacity.

The Legislative Council, the voice of the people, would be arranged for at a later date. It was an act that ignored the promises of Shepstone and Frere, and would hardly satisfy the political aspirations of the Boers who grew more restive by the day.

In Middelburg, a centre of unrest, some fifty Boers prevented the law from taking effect on a farmer who had abused a native. Furthermore, when they heard that the High Commissioner gave orders that no permits to buy ammunition would be given unless the applicant could prove payment of his taxes, they formally resolved not to pay anything to the 'foreign' government and in a riotous manner seized ammunition from the local stores. Sir Garnet immediately sent out a troop of cavalry from Heidelberg. The agitators dispersed as soon as the troopers arrived. Though there were occasional, isolated flare-ups throughout the Transvaal, the discontented Boers remained largely passive in their resistance. More serious, at the moment, was the defiant attitude of Sekukuni.

Sekukuni, the chief of the Bapedi, ever a fighting people and related to the Basutos, controlled a triangular-shaped territory in the north-east corner of the Transvaal, comprising some 250 miles of thorns, sand and rocks. Through the middle of this land ran the Lulu Range, which rose sharply from the surrounding plain like an enormous ant-heap. In the centre of these steep and rugged mountains was an almost inaccessible stronghold, Sekukuni's 'town', built on a mountain-side, and his Fighting Kopje,* defended by some 4,000 men with muskets and rifles. The entire area was protected by thick stone walls, one behind the other, dug-outs, thornbush zaribas, and even beehives strategically placed so that they could be upset in case of attack. The Fighting Kopje itself was honeycombed with caves and crevices that concealed warriors and war stores of ammunition and grain. Even the distant approaches to Sekukuni's natural fortress were protected by deep, winding ravines overgrown with bush and ideally suited for ambush, the Bapedi's favourite mode of warfare.

The Bapedi chief resembled a robber-baron of medieval times. He attracted to his mountain fastness all the lawless turbulent spirits of the surrounding territories. This was their 'sanctuary' from which they could issue forth against neighbouring kraals and Boer farms to massacre and steal cattle and women. Abortive attempts by Boer and then British forces to subdue him caused Sekukuni to boast that he had never been defeated.

The Bapedi continued to give trouble to the British during the Zulu

* A kopje is an isolated mass of rocks and boulders attaining heights up to 600 feet.

War. Because of his sympathies, Sekukuni was called 'Cetewayo's dog'. Until troops could be spared, the British were content to hold on to their dreary little forts and engage in an occasional patrol to run down raiders in this wild and unfriendly land. When Lanyon took over from Shepstone, he began to scrape a force together for an assault. He was ready to take the field in July, but his advance was halted by orders from Wolseley when the latter arrived at Maritzburg. The general wished to avoid the possibility of another inglorious retreat which would further convince Sekukuni of his invincibility.

Wolseley hoped that war would not be necessary. 'I think he is beginning to fancy himself as a diplomatist,' wrote McCalmont.[7] Hating the idea of fighting a 'filthy little war' at a time when the Republican element was beginning to assert itself, the High Commissioner sent Major Clarke with a conciliatory message to Sekukuni at the end of September. If the Bapedi chief paid a fine of 2,500 cattle and agreed to the establishment of a military post on his mountain as an outward sign of British supremacy, Wolseley stated he was prepared to permit him to live in peace. He felt sure that 'Cetewayo's dog' would give in after he learned the fate of his 'master' in Zululand. In the meantime, preparations for military operations were begun in case they became necessary. All available troops from Natal and Zululand were concentrated in the Transvaal. Even if Sekukuni accepted his terms, Wolseley reasoned, this sizeable force would serve the purpose of overawing the Boer malcontents.

Puffed up by his long string of victories, Sekukuni scorned Wolseley's terms. He declared he would fight to the last. Wolseley now regretted that he had ever wasted valuable time by seeking a peaceable solution. A great deal was at stake. Success would restore British prestige in the Transvaal. Native chiefs everywhere would be persuaded to pay their taxes, and the Boers, who had twice failed against Sekukuni, would be properly impressed with British power. Failure could touch off a major rebellion of Boers and blacks. And how certain jealous gentlemen at the Horse Guards would rejoice, thought Wolseley, to hear of a terrible disaster when he was in command!

The Transvaal Field Force, as it was officially called, would consist of 1,400 British infantry, 400 colonial horse, and nearly 10,000 natives. It would be the first offensive battle fought by these British soldiers, for unlike the Zulus, the Bapedi preferred to fight on the defensive, shooting from caves and from behind rocks. With the short-service system on trial once more, Wolseley told the Duke he was 'curious to see how the much-abused young British soldiers will do when *attacking* a very strong position under a heavy fire'.[8] He had confidence in them so long as they were well led by their officers.

Brackenbury, who took Colley's place as chief of staff, lavished meticulous care on the preparations and displayed without question that he was the most able administrator in the army. Supported by such brilliant staff work, Wolseley could confidently describe his future operations to the War Office like a time-table, fixing the exact dates when his men would arrive at given points in the campaign. He boasted that on the afternoon of November 28th he would sip his afternoon tea in Sekukuni's hut – and he did.

In the middle of October, the general decided to move his headquarters to Middelburg to superintend personally the organization of the main column. The day before he took his departure, he reviewed the troops left under the command of his old comrade, Colonel Harrison, who would be responsible for the defence of the capital, the chief base of supplies. After the review, McCalmont and St Leger Herbert, civil secretary to Sir Garnet, gave a picnic for all the unmarried women of the town. Both had a great reputation with the ladies, and 'Sanky' Herbert had a habit of constantly referring to women he had been successful with, or was at the moment making love to. Such conversation disgusted the high-minded Maurice, irritating him to the point where Wolseley feared they might come to blows. The general was happy to leave the capital with its mischievous females, insatiable office-seekers, sulky Boers, and drunken servants, who on the night of the picnic were so intoxicated they lost the officers' horses.

At Middelburg, on October 23rd, Sir Garnet reviewed the main column under Lieutenant-Colonel Baker Russell, whose staff officer was Captain Herbert Stewart, before they marched on to the advanced base at Fort Weeber the next day. Wolseley had decided to give 'poor Baker' complete charge of tactical operations so that he might have a chance of writing a dispatch announcing success, though he privately expressed the fear that his friend had lost some of the dash and daring he had exhibited against the Ashanti.

The men looked smart and ready for active service. The British troops were in their normal red serge with white helmets; the colonials wore brown cord and the staff were in blue. Nearly all the officers wore on their head-dress what was called the Sekukuni button, a meercat's tail carefully fashioned into a button.

The natives were rapidly collected – Swazis, Knobnoses, Rustenburg levies, Mapock's Kaffirs, blacks from Zoutpansberg, etc. Of greatest

value were the Swazis, natural enemies of the Bapedi and great in-
fighters. Acting as High Commissioner, Sir Garnet sent a message to
Captain Norman MacLeod, Special Commissioner and British Agent
for Swaziland, requesting him to raise as many warriors as he could without delay. It was hoped he would bring no less than 2,000. (MacLeod
raised 8,000.) They would be permitted to keep the cattle they might
take from the Bapedi and to share proportionately in whatever fine was
levied against them. The Swazis wanted girls, too. But they were instructed not to make war on women and children, and that while in
friendly territory, they must behave in an orderly manner.

The general and his staff followed the Transvaal Field Force to Fort
Weeber, where they arrived on October 28th. On investigating the state
of supplies, Wolseley found that discouraging delays had occurred. Some
of the contractors had exhibited a want of energy; and a great number of
the native drivers, anxious to get home after the Zulu War was over, had
deserted. Many of those who stayed on 'were nearly always drunk'. The
situation was further complicated by heavy storms and swollen streams.

Though his head ached and his leg throbbed from an old wound, out-
wardly the general drew on what seemed to be an inexhaustible source of
energy. He quickly provided for the present emergency and arranged for
the future, imparting confidence to all those around him. Where other
commanders might be 'fussy and solemn' under similar circumstances,
observed one officer, Wolseley would be 'chatty and amusing', and even
render 'the most dry of official details interesting by his remarks'.

The transportation snag eliminated, Wolseley reconnoitred the area
ahead to get some idea of the nature of the mountains and of the problems attending an advance. Then he rushed back eighty-six miles with
McCalmont to see to affairs in Lydenburg. Travelling through violent
thunderstorms, they made the journey in twenty-six hours. Descending a
steep mountain-side, the general's bad leg gave out. Though he scorned
the notion of carrying any sort of stimulant, 'he was uncommonly glad to
partake of a generous nip from my flask,' noted McCalmont.[9]

At Lydenburg, the general discussed the advance with Major Henry
Bushman, who was to command a second column assembled there con-
sisting of Swazis, two companies of the 80th, two of the 94th, a few local
Mounted Rifles, and assorted natives.

On the hasty ride back, the weather cleared and the two riders saw a
sight they had missed coming in: the hills were crawling with fierce-
looking savages, still neutral, but ugly enough in appearance, according
to McCalmont, to 'turn the devil's hair grey'. The general complained

there was more to fear from his aide's cooking, which was the greatest filth he had ever tasted!

Sir Garnet decided on his plan of operations after gathering every last scrap of information about the enemy. His chief sources were the Reverend Merensky, the German missionary-explorer and expert cartographer, who knew more about the Bapedi than any living European, and Colonel Ignatius Ferreira, the daring Boer leader who acquired an outstanding record engaging in every military enterprise in South Africa since he was old enough to shoulder a rifle. Rather than take any of the paths leading directly over the mountains from the west, which according to the experts were too rugged for horses and insufficiently supplied with water, the main column would march up the valley of the Oliphant River, swing around the northern tip of the Lulus and descend a small valley, some twenty miles long, running north and south between two great ridges, and attack Sekukuni's town at the southern end. Simultaneously the town would be attacked from the east by Bushman's column, based on Fort Burgers, after marching along the eastern slopes of the Lulus.

The campaign was undertaken at a distance of over 500 miles from Durban, the sea base. No supplies could be bought within 100 miles; the closest farm-house was fifty miles away. All the grain fields and groves of tropical fruit were abandoned. And as a consequence of the menacing behaviour of the Boers, the supply lines in the Transvaal had to be protected as if they were campaigning in enemy land. An additional burden was thrown upon the supply officers when Wolseley created a second supply line along the bush veldt road from Pretoria to Fort Oliphant close to his advance post at Mapashlela's Drift, where Fort Albert Edward was built. Supplies, however, soon began to arrive in the forward area far in excess of consumption.

The advancing force faced many obstacles as it crossed the more or less open veldt. The days were hot and sultry, for this was the South African summer. The nights were shiveringly cold at 5,000 feet above sea-level. Intermittent thunderstorms – not entirely unwelcome because of the scarcity of water – slowed the progress. Several men were killed by lightning and others 'were a good deal shaken'. Horse-sickness took its daily toll among the steeds of officers and colonials.

Arriving at Fort Albert Edward on November 23rd, Sir Garnet decided sufficient supplies were concentrated to enable the troops to enter the long valley to the south and attack the stronghold. Colonial volunteers would lead the way. Baker Russell had already formed an advance post seven

miles beyond, named the 'Seven-mile Post', and actual fighting commenced that day with a successful assault by Ferreira's men on the kraal of
Umkwane, one of Sekukuni's trusted followers, situated on a mountain
opposite the post.

At daybreak the following morning, leaving only a small garrison at
Fort Albert Edward, the main column entered the valley. The next day,
the volunteers, supported by a few regulars, took the Water Kopje without opposition three miles from the citadel; Sekukuni by now had called
in all outlying detachments for the final stand. In the meantime, Herbert
Stewart had ridden to the east, across the mountains, and found Bushman's auxiliary column at an entrenched post, Fort George, with adequate
supplies and ready to advance.

Escorted by men from Ferreira's Horse, Sir Garnet rode forward to
reconnoitre the battle-area. He examined the approaches to Sekukuni's
mountain, and came within 250 yards of the Fighting Kopje. Through his
telescope, the general saw that the latter position was thick with blacks,
but not a shot was fired at him. After finding a good camp site and an
excellent position for the guns, Sir Garnet rode to Fort George to inform
Major Bushman of the plan of attack. The mountain would be hit first,
while the Fighting Kopje was shelled and contained by regulars. Once the
defenders on Sekukuni's mountain had been destroyed or driven off, the
isolated rock fortress would be assaulted from all sides. Bushman was
given verbal orders to have his men in a position to attack from the
eastern end of the mountain at four-fifteen a.m. on November 28th.

Nature takes sides. Violent storms of rain and hail harassed the advancing column until the narrow old Boer road, already partly overgrown
with dense bush, became almost impassable. Wagons stuck and oxen fell
as the heavens thundered and lashed out with strong winds. The curses
of the drivers and the crack of their cruel whips resounded through the
valley. Men of the 21st and the 94th, under arms for nearly twenty-four
hours, marched in rags that had been turned many colours by mud and
rain. As Billy Russell watched them stumble towards the camping ground
during the small hours of November 27th, he told the readers of the
*Daily Telegraph* that he was frankly uneasy about their fitness for action
the next day. His doubts were not dispelled the following morning as he
looked at the grim mountain which hid and protected its vicious children.
But the general, who had great faith in his young soldiers, had no qualms
about their ability to take either Sekukuni's mountain or the Fighting
Kopje.

For the first phase of the battle, which would secure possession of

Sekukuni's flat-topped mountain, with its town and his personal kraal (or lower town) on the western slopes, Baker Russell divided his main column attacking from the west into three parts. The right attack (to the south) that would begin the assault, hence the position of honour, was assigned to Colonel Ferreira and his dismounted commando, backed by native contingents. They were to take the kraal. The left attack (to the north) was entrusted to Major Carrington and the rest of the colonials, supported by other native contingents. They were to clear the town. The central attack was given to Colonel Murray and the 21st (the Royal Scots Fusiliers), the 94th (later designated the 2nd Battalion, Connaught Rangers), detachments of the 80th, the Royal Engineers, the four guns of the Transvaal Artillery and the Rustenburg contingent; their mission was to act as a reserve and keep down the fire of the Fighting Kopje, which they would eventually storm. Baker Russell relied on Bushman and the Swazis to ascend the mountain from the eastern side during the night, so as to reach the summit and begin descent upon the town in the morning, thereby co-operating with Ferreira and Carrington from above.

With scant time to rest themselves, the men were quietly roused from their sleep at two a.m., for no bugle-calls were to be sounded that morning. Quickly the tents were struck and the column formed in front of the camp. Marching swiftly across the valley with sufficient moonlight shining at intervals through a cloudy sky to trace the outline of the invincible mountain, the attackers took their selected position. Sir Garnet and his staff moved to a level piece of ground and dismounted. Acting as an interested spectator, the general seated himself under a tree. The stormers waited in the dark silence for the signal. At the first glimmer of dawn a shell was discharged at the Fighting Kopje. Instantly mountain and kopje came alive with enemy fire. War horns and shrill yells sounded to summon Bapedi courage and terrorize the foe charging towards them.

There was a bitter struggle as the colonials rushed the stone breastworks. Stormers staggered and dropped all along the extended line. Leading them ever forward and upward was the inspiring figure of Ferreira. The Bapedi recognized their old enemy immediately and shouted, 'Kill him!' Long ago they had christened him 'Umtakati' – 'he who bears a charmed life'. Hearing their challenge, the redoubtable Ferreira stood up and shouted, 'Forward!' Bullets whistled and assagais hissed, but none touched him.[10]

The advance moved in fits and starts, and then hesitated and seemed to falter as the resistance stiffened. Fearing that Ferreira's men might be driven back, Murray reinforced his command with a company of the

94th. Carrington's party was soon no less hotly engaged by superior forces. Then some of the Bapedi, who had slipped around the chain of mountains to the rear of the camp, fired upon the small detachment of guards and threatened an attack. Time and again the attackers looked to the summit and asked: 'Where are the Swazis?' The general and his staff betrayed their anxiety as their powerful glasses swept the crest of the mountain for some sign.

On the other side of the mountain a no less dramatic scene was being enacted. The Swazis refused to ascend the mountain before daybreak. And when dawn came they still would not budge and sulked in the shadows. Loyal natives told MacLeod that they whispered among themselves: 'Why should we go up the impregnable mountain and fight invisible warriors, and be killed like dogs while the white men steal cattle as they did three years before?'[11] They never forgot how they were deserted by a Boer commando in an earlier campaign. Left stranded on a mountain-side, they had been forced to run the gauntlet of the Bapedi's firing powerful elephant guns on one side, and the fire of panicky Boers who shot at them by mistake on the other. Their witch-doctors warned them that the Europeans meant to desert them again.

Only after the battle was well under way and they were convinced that the whites meant to fight, did the Swazis dash up the eastern slopes and appear belatedly on the skyline which had been so eagerly scanned. There was no vacillation now as they descended with a fierce roar on the surprised defender, slashing and stabbing with assagais, fighting hand to hand on narrow ledges, dragging and dropping one another off the many overhanging cliffs. Soon they drove the Bapedi before them like so many sheep, stabbing those who could not crowd ahead fast enough.

Aroused by the appearance of their black allies, the colonials below surrounded Sekukuni's kraal, penning the defenders in their own stockade and setting it ablaze. Soon the town above and most of the caves were cleared and burnt. The defenders, however, well armed for short-range fighting, continued to take their toll among the officers, who exposed themselves freely. Maurice was shot from the mouth of a cave. Wolseley watched him as he continued to dash up the mountain with a bullet in him, and exclaimed: 'Now I know the value of Maurice – to lead forlorn hopes!'[12] Maurice remained on his feet until he was able to report personally to Wolseley that the victory was assured. He later received the brevet of major for having proved, according to Wolseley, that a bookworm could be as good a soldier as the best of dunces.

After three hours of hard fighting, the mountain was taken and Baker

Russell prepared for the second phase of the battle by mustering every available man on the plain below the Fighting Kopje. So far the barrage of artillery shells fired on the ugly conical heap, armoured by giant rock slabs and grey boulders, had no more effect than rifle fire on a modern tank. Sekukuni's warriors were secure behind their clefts and crannies which formed natural loopholes for their muskets. The ground all round the 'Gibraltar of the Transvaal', as it was called, soon swarmed with colonials and Swazis, while Murray's regulars fixed bayonets and lined up at the base of the hill, the 21st and the headquarters escort of the 80th towards the north and the 94th towards the south. The dense masses of Swazis were a spectacular sight 'in their savage fighting gear, cranes' feathers on their heads and leopard skins over their shoulders'.[13] In addition to assorted charms, they carried hollow bones which they would sound every now and then. All were to wait for the signal of two rockets, the first to make ready and the second to charge.

The first rocket went high over the valley with Sekukuni's flaming town and kraal on one side and his trapped warriors on the other. The men on the floor of the valley became stiff and alert. As the second rocket pierced the calm blue sky, the general's eye flashed and he remarked casually in a soft voice: 'Mark the time. I make it nine-forty-five.' In that same instant all was in motion. Whizzing shells and hissing rockets exploded above as the English infantry sprang forward, led by Baker Russell, sword in hand. Even the staff – Brackenbury, McCalmont, Herbert – were given leave by their general to join in. Only the Swazis remained immobile, as if momentarily stunned by the sight. They wanted to see if the 'red soldiers', who had done little but watch the colonials and native allies attack Sekukuni's mountain, as their witch-doctors had predicted, actually intended now to fight. Seeing them standing there, Wolseley rode over to them, waved his hand towards the Fighting Kopje and shouted: 'Come on, you fellows; come on. Is there no one to make them understand?'[14] They understood not a word, but no interpreter was needed to explain the general's gestures. Obviously the 'red soldiers' meant business, so they moved forward with the High Commissioner himself leading them on right up to the base of the hill.

The Swazis now ran as if death were behind them rather than before them. They answered the English cheer with their own battle-cry and made the same peculiar 'whish' sound by striking their knees against their lowered shields as did the Zulus when they charged. Thousands of knees pounding in unison had the sound of roaring surf. It seemed in harmony with the fusillades, the screams and yells, and the skirls of pipers

– the very breath of battle. The pipers stood at the foot of the hill beating the ground with their feet while playing with fiendish energy. The deep furrow that ran across Wolseley's cheek – a souvenir of the Crimea – grew purple.

The very steepness of the Fighting Kopje, as Wolseley had predicted, gave the men cover as they bounded up the slope over the rock terraces. The defenders proved to be very poor shots, considering that they often fired at point-blank range before they vanished back into their deep, dark holes. Hand-to-hand fighting in the caverns was another matter; many attackers were shot or assagaid. The Swazis, darting about like the Psalmist's rams, overtook the 'red soldiers' and were the first to reach the top. 'But it was not the fault of the British soldier that the Swazis got in front of him,' Wolseley later stated, 'but of his trousers and boots.'[15]

'At ten-thirty,' wrote Billy Russell, 'the "Fighting Koppie", in which Sekukuni enshrined his faith, belonged to Queen Victoria; but inside its stony bowels was still hidden a band of desperate and resolute men, of women and children, of wounded and dead – a fearful combination.' Baker Russell, a resolute and hard-handed man, called upon the engineers to put charges of gun-cotton at the many cave entrances. The noise of the explosions, however, failed to drive them out, except to fire biting, random shots. And in many instances, the Bapedi, having worked in the Kimberley mines, cut the fuses. As the defenders refused to surrender, the stormers were withdrawn and a cordon of men was carefully placed in a trench around the kopje. The Swazis were asked to send some men to sleep on top of the mountain. They refused. They were more interested in pursuing cattle and women.

During the night, as is so often the case after heavy cannon fire, there was a thunderstorm. The weather favoured the beleaguered. While worn-out soldiers sought to improvise some scanty shelter, large numbers sallied from the recesses of the cavernous hill. 'We seemed to be caught in the midst of a human cyclone,' wrote Captain Henry Nourse of Ferreira's Horse, 'with masses of savages charging clean through us, assagaiing our men from all sides, and actually leaping over our heads in their wild efforts to escape from the imprisoned kopje.'[16] The lightning flashed like some ghastly beacon, lighting up lurid scenes of horror and murder. Those trying desperately to prevent the cordon from being broken, might suddenly see a plumed induna with his assagai poised to transfix them. During the uproar many escaped through the tired but watchful cordon; among them was Sekukuni.

Early the next morning about 500, mostly women and children, surrendered after Major Clarke succeeded in communicating with them and promising their lives to all those who might give themselves up. Unfortunately, before they could be restrained by the Europeans, the bloodthirsty Swazis killed a great many who had surrendered earlier in the battle. Thus, an undetermined number still refused to come out of the rock fortress and died of thirst and starvation in its dark, secret corridors. In one place there was a great, yawning chasm, believed to contain water at the bottom. Maddened by thirst, some let themselves down by means of many thongs tied together. Not even a splash was ever heard by their comrades waiting above.

Owing to the great use made of the Swazis, the loss among Europeans was very small: three officers killed and seven wounded; other ranks, seven killed and forty-three wounded (bee stings were not counted). MacLeod placed the Swazi losses at between 500 and 600 killed, and about the same number wounded. As to the Bapedi, it was difficult to estimate the casualties, but it appeared that a good part of the tribe was exterminated. The Fighting Kopje was littered with dead, and an unbearable stench soon came out of the mouths of the caves. Charles IX of France declared that the smell of a dead enemy was always sweet, but if he had stood outside one of those caves he might have had cause to change his opinion. The caves of the Fighting Kopje were later sealed by the engineers.

There was still the matter of capturing the Bapedi chief. Wolseley hoped it would not take as long as it did to capture Cetewayo. When it was learned on November 29th that Sekukuni had been located with a large number of loyal warriors hiding in the mountains about twelve miles away, Ferreira and Clarke, with a small detachment of mounted men, began the pursuit early on the morning of November 30th. The general and his staff joined the posse, but in climbing the steep paths, Wolseley's bad leg gave out and he had to return to headquarters. By noon, after a difficult ascent made more trying by the hot sun and the fear of an ambush, Sekukuni's hiding-place was found. A large body of Swazis, who had been hot on the spoor of the fugitive chief, were already on the scene. The cave in which Sekukuni was believed to be hiding was fired into by Ferreira; the cornered Bapedi fired back. Clarke made an abortive attempt to smoke them out.

A minor siege followed. When Baker Russell arrived, he sent for engineers and infantry to support Ferreira. Between shots, negotiations were shouted. On learning that Sekukuni feared death at the hands of the Swazis, Ferreira ordered his dark allies to withdraw. On the morning of

December 2nd, after Clarke swore to spare his life, the starving chief crawled out. He had to pass between lines of soldiers who began to shout and fire their guns into the air. The war was over.

McCalmont had the pleasure of hurrying back to the encampment near the battlefield and announcing the capture. 'Thank God!' exclaimed Wolseley on hearing of Sekukuni's surrender. 'I shall now be off to Pretoria, and if God will only bless my dealings with the Boers as He has blessed my dealings with Zululand, I may be able soon to get out of South Africa.'[17]

Orders were immediately issued by the general to break camp the next morning. The Swazis, who had fraternized freely with soldiers, as each admired the other's pluck, were sent home. They had captured thousands of head of cattle and a great number of women. Sir Garnet, however, demanded they set the women free, threatening to use force if necessary.

Nearly all Pretoria turned out to see the successful general and his famous prisoner. Escorted by a hundred dragoons, Sekukuni was to be seen seated in a mule wagon surrounded by his wives and daughters – most of his sons had died in battle. He was photographed and lodged in a jail while his conqueror was serenaded by the band of the 80th Regiment. An address of congratulations followed. Two days later, the city turned out again to see Sir Garnet review the troops and present the Victoria Cross. A 'fiercely fought' sham battle followed, much to the entertainment of the onlookers.

Considering the character of the terrain and the great natural strength of the position, the taking of Sekukuni's stronghold must be ranked as a gallant feat by the soldiers and a skilfully managed campaign by their commander, Sir Garnet Wolseley, though he insisted on sharing the honours with Baker Russell, who had amply demonstrated that he had lost none of his nerve and daring. The Queen telegraphed her congratulations from Windsor Castle. The Government at home, whose South African policy so far was extremely unpopular, derived great pleasure from his success. Disraeli told Lady Bradford: 'Sir Garnet has not disappointed me. He is one of those men who not only succeed but succeed quickly. Nothing can give you an idea of the jealousy, the hatred, and all uncharitableness of the Horse Guards against our only soldier.'[18]

The Boers, who laughed and said the British would fail to storm the Fighting Kopje, were impressed by Wolseley's success but as irreconciled as ever to annexation. In fact, having destroyed the military power of the Zulus and the Bapedi, the British were no longer needed. The volume of discontent actually increased. While Wolseley's force was marching back to Pretoria, armed Boers were riding towards Wonderfontein, seventy miles from the capital. Despite the High Commissioner's ban, a great national Boer meeting was held on December 10th, as scheduled. The irreconcilables went so far as to threaten any who should absent themselves. Thus, in a land where the adult male population numbered only 8,000, nearly 3,000 men assembled on the high veldt under the flag of the Republic. The High Commissioner's warnings and the presence of a force of 1,750 soldiers in the Transvaal, rather than intimidating the malcontents, seemed to add spice to the occasion. After seven days of angry talk, resolutions were passed, couched in threatening language, demanding independence and expressing their intention to convene a Volksraad. The Boer committee was asked to take the necessary steps. Before separating, they agreed to meet again in April.

An outspoken minority declared the wish to fight, but most hesitated to take such a drastic step. Had a favourable opportunity presented itself, disaffection might have culminated in open rebellion. Cooler heads, however, were discouraged by the short supply of ammunition for a prolonged conflict and the presence of so many 'rooibalcher', or redcoats, who seemed prepared to act decisively at a moment's notice. The *Volkstein*, a Boer organ in Pretoria, prudently exhorted the discontented not to give the High Commissioner an excuse to order the army out against them; they should go home, adopt an attitude of passive resistance and wait until Wolseley and most of the 'rooibalcher' had returned to England. It was good advice.

The High Commissioner was ready for war. 'Military dispositions were made', wrote Brackenbury, 'to cover the front of Pretoria camp and town with cavalry and infantry pickets, as though in an enemy's country.'[19] Redoubts were built at eight stations, with thirty days' supplies concentrated for the garrisons of roughly one company each. Every possible military precaution was taken to ensure against surprise. Cavalry patrols were sent out night and day. If armed Boers approached soldiers on the veldt or in camp, they were instructed to draw swords and load rifles. However, officers were told to do all in their power to avoid a collision. 'Let them fire the first shot,' Wolseley ordered, 'and having been fired upon, let him use his rifles well.'[20] The High Commissioner, though accused of trying to provoke war, was averse to bloodshed. 'I feel I could walk over them easily,' he told Lady Wolseley, 'but at the same time the killing of them would be ... unsatisfactory work, extremely distasteful to a soldier and would be extremely embarrassing to the Government.'[21]

Having shown them the sword, the High Commissioner concluded that the rebels were sufficiently awed so as not to go beyond 'tall talk'. 'Confidence,' declared His Excellency, 'has been greatly restored throughout the Transvaal.' The expensive colonial volunteers – even a private received five shillings a day – were disbanded as early as December 18th. By the end of the year, some of the regulars were marched off to the coast to board transports. Sufficient troops, however, were kept in the country to garrison well-supplied stations. There was also 'a carefully organized movable column ready to march in any direction, and put down at once any rising of discontented Boers'.[22] Not that Wolseley contemplated the necessity of using force. Each day his contempt for the Boers mounted, while his estimate of their fighting qualities fell. Soon he called them cowards. Another great British general, named Wolfe, made a similar error of judgment during the French and Indian War when he spoke of the Americans with his army as 'the dirtiest, most contemptible, cowardly dogs that you can conceive'.

There was an old saying in the service that 'a soldier would even get tired of Paradise, were he stationed there longer than six months'. Wolseley was already tired of South Africa before he entered the Transvaal. Having lost his bet that he would be home for Christmas, he told his wife that he had an idea that he would be back in England before the opening of Parliament early in February. The Government, however, decided, for the time being, to keep him in South Africa. Hicks Beach spoke of his presence being required until the monster Boer meeting of April 6th was over. Then there was talk of remaining until his successor, Colley (whose place in India was to be taken by Brackenbury), arrived in South Africa, which would not be before the end of May.

Why was he forced to remain in South Africa? Wolseley asked angrily. He had been sent out to conclude the Zulu War and settle conditions in the Transvaal. Now that his mission was completed, the Government kept him tied to a detestable civilian appointment and tried to convert him into a colonial governor. He assumed that he was being made to serve the exigencies of the Conservative party. If there should be trouble here, he told his wife, the Ministry would use him to disarm the Opposition, 'as I am well thought of by the leaders of the Liberals I shall not be attacked by them and so on'.[23]

As he fretted over each day he was kept in South Africa, Wolseley reserved some choice words for 'Mr Hicks Bitch'. He scarcely knew the Colonial Secretary before leaving England, but soon developed 'the most supreme contempt for his intelligence ... He is one of those well-born looking men,' he told his wife, 'with high principle, very little genius and a character of obstinacy and variety which is feminine ... ' If he had only known what he was to be let in for by the Colonial Secretary, he would at least have his sweet Loo spend the winter abroad away from the London cold and fog.[24]

Depressed and sore in spirit, Wolseley complained of his health. He suffered once again from fevers, accompanied by severe headaches; and his digestion was so bad that he was constantly annoyed by heartburn. Looking into the mirror, he felt he appeared sixty rather than forty-six years old, for he was rapidly growing bald. Caesar hid his baldness with a laurel wreath, but his was yet to be won – and that seemed a long way off with the Duke and 'Mr Hicks Bitch' conspiring against him.

Week after week, the High Commissioner reported all quiet in the Transvaal. The monster meeting called for April 6th, at which the Boers threatened to elect a president and set up the machinery for self-government, was postponed. Wolseley claimed credit for putting a stop to it, though it was obvious that most malcontents sat on their farms awaiting the outcome of the British elections and the departure of the present High Commissioner. To put a stop to the rumour that the Transvaal would be surrendered to the Boers, His Excellency asked the Colonial Office for positive and final assurance that Her Majesty's Government refused 'to entertain any proposal for withdrawal of the Queen's sovereignty'. A proclamation was issued to this effect when the Legislative Council opened.

On April 10th, Wolseley wrote to the Colonial Office that his administration had been a success. The Boers had been tamed. Reports from all parts of the Transvaal told him that the people were prepared 'to renounce all further disturbing action, and to return to the peaceful cares of their rural life'. Taxes were being paid and a foundation had been laid upon which in time there might be built 'a fabric of Government in furtherance of the prosperity of the people, and in unison with their sympathies and their wishes'.[25]

Wolseley was firm in the belief that his threats one moment and his cajolery the next, supported by the repeated assertions that British authority would never be withdrawn, had brought peace to the land; and that by rescuing the economy, building a 'party of progress', composed of men sympathetic to the British cause, encouraging immigration to dilute Dutch blood, etc., he had initiated a policy that would preserve the British position in the Transvaal. He asked himself: Could any man in the empire have done a more complete job in so short a time?

Anticipating permission to leave, Wolseley could not shake the dust of the Transvaal off his feet fast enough. He departed from Pretoria a full two weeks before receiving official sanction to go home on April 19th. Together with Major Herbert Stewart, his new chief of staff, he covered a distance of 350 miles in three days by galloping 200 miles of the way, instead of taking a post cart. He came into Maritzburg looking more dead than alive, but when he spotted McCalmont, he shouted cheerily, 'I'll ride you for a fiver.'[26]

Before leaving South Africa, Sir Garnet spent a few days at Government house, Cape Town, to be bored to death by 'that dreadful old snob Mother Frere and by the platitudes of Sir Bottle Beer'. Oddly enough, from this time forward, Wolseley began to soften towards Sir Bartle. He later had the courage to admit that he had misunderstood this 'far-sighted statesman', as did so many of his contemporaries, and expressed his unqualified support when the question of a posthumous peerage was suggested for Frere years later.

In those last few days before leaving South Africa, Wolseley was concerned with his own chances for a peerage. The defeat of the Conservatives at the polls in April, in which the disasters in South Africa undoubtedly played a large part,* brought the whole matter to a climax where Disraeli was concerned, for he would draw up a final list of peers before retiring. Candidate Wolseley had served the Government well in Natal in 1875, in Cyprus, in Zululand, and in the Transvaal. Where the troublesome Boers were concerned, he had succeeded far beyond anyone's expectations. According to Wolseley, he had saved the nation at least one million pounds by disbanding the 'ridiculously large army' that Chelmsford had collected. Had it not been for him, Chelmsford would in all probability 'still be wandering about in Zululand doing nothing except expending millions of public money'.[27] 'Dizzy' would be a fool, thought Wolseley, if he did not avail himself now of 'an opportunity of associating his name with mine' by rewarding him 'in a most gracious manner ... '[28] To make sure that the retiring Prime Minister had not forgotten him, he sent telegrams to his influential friends to help remind him.

When the list of peers was published it did not include his name. Wolseley received no rewards for his services in South Africa. He was gazetted a G.C.B., which he had turned down six years before, and since then, in his eyes, it had depreciated in value 'by having been conferred upon poor, incapable Chelmsford!!!'[29] And though 'that failure Chelmsford' had

* Disraeli had good reason to complain after Isandhlwana that the Zulus converted Her Majesty's bishops, defeated her generals, and destroyed her Ministers.

his local rank of lieutenant-general confirmed, the Horse Guards saw to it that Wolseley's local rank of general was not made substantive. Nor did he receive any decoration for services in Natal (1875) or Cyprus. And the Indian command seemed farther away than ever.

Wolseley learned before leaving Africa that he had been nominated quartermaster-general; but he told his brother Dick, who had just been promoted to brigade surgeon, 'I don't care a straw to be Q.M.G. for I cannot pull with the Duke and we shall have continued rows and he will hate me more than before if indeed that be possible.'[30]

# CHAPTER THIRTEEN

# OUR ONLY GENERAL

IN ENGLAND Wolseley learned that his popularity had reached new heights. In an age of renewed imperialism, he had proved himself master of the small war. When there was a difficult mission, it became the national habit to 'send for Wolseley'. Ubiquitous, all-knowing, unfailing, he was regarded as indispensable to the security of the Empire. After his arrival in Zululand, it seemed to those at home that the war was brought to an end in a matter of hours. The press sang his praises, and in rapturous appreciation the public borrowed Disraeli's fanciful appellation and dubbed him 'our only General'. Gilbert and Sullivan, in their latest nonsensical musical, *The Pirates of Penzance*, satirically tailored the role of 'the very model of a modern Major-General' to fit him. If there was any doubt that the authors had the celebrated soldier in mind when they created the part, it vanished immediately when George Grossmith, the great actor, walked on stage and caricatured the mannerisms and dress of 'our only General'. Wolseley took no offence at the friendly satire. He was delighted by the ludicrous imitation, and in the bosom of his family often sang the part of the 'Major-General' for their amusement.

Being a political asset, this prototype of the new professional soldier was claimed by Liberals and Conservatives alike. Because of his advanced views on military subjects, Sir Garnet was described as a Radical, and it was generally believed his sympathies were, at least, with the Liberal party. Nothing could be further from the truth. Wolseley detested the Radicals; Gladstone and men of his stamp were abhorrent to every instinct within him, 'because they are churchwardens and parish vestrymen more than Englishmen'.[1] Privately he described himself as 'a Jingo of the Jingos', with a great veneration of 'old Dizzy' and a militant sense of imperial mission that bordered on the religious. To him, the victory of the Liberals at the polls was 'a national catastrophe', mitigated only by the fact that their large majority made them entirely independent of the Irish party. Moreover, these 'liberal professors', who were now coming into office, were far less inclined to fight than the National party, and therefore his chances for a command in the field were far smaller under Gladstone than they would have been under Disraeli. He doubted if the former would fight for the Isle of Wight if it were seized by an enemy. Wolseley, however, was too prudent to let these views become public.[2]

But the Conservatives, on the other hand, had not been gracious masters, and were anything but lavish in their rewards. And they eschewed army reforms because it was unpopular with the royalties and their aristocratic backers, whereas the Liberals were certain to take up where Cardwell had left off and to rely on him as their chief adviser. It was, therefore, to Wolseley's advantage to appear as a Liberal supporter.

Because Wolseley worked with the Liberals who were anxious to improve the army, opponents of reform called him a 'political general'. One cynical observer described the expression: 'Once you become a general, never care a damn about the War Office, or Selection Boards. Keep in with the politicians and you will be all right.' Jealous members of the 'old school' of soldiers, less clever and fortunate than he, found the phrase convenient to explain Wolseley's meteoric rise and belittle his success. As to Sir Garnet's military reputation, they declared it was built up from his own and his supporters' talk, sustained by a sympathetic press. Above all, they claimed he was a lucky commander, nothing more.

Though Wolseley had a great knowledge of war derived from fighting in almost every clime and under every condition, his foes – in the Horse Guards especially – denied him the right to pose as an expert on military affairs. Small wars against uncivilized nations were an irrelevance; his experiences under outlandish circumstances could never be applied to an army drilled to fight a European war.

England's 'only General' returned to the War Office a little older and somewhat saddened, but full of fight, prepared to act as a flesh-and-blood battering-ram to break down the wall of prejudice, inertia and stupidity in order to create a more efficient army. It would be difficult. In the army nothing fails like continued success. Continental soldiers learned from disaster – Prussia after Jena, Russia after the Crimea, Austria after Sadowa, France after Sedan – and reformed. The British army suffered only a minor catastrophe in the Crimea, not severe enough to shake the majority of leaders loose from a hidebound system of outmoded traditions and precedents.

And while Wolseley was abroad, a reaction set in against the Cardwell reforms. The short-service system, for example, was exposed to attack by the notorious inefficiency of certain battalions in Zululand, and by the increasing demand for soldiers in India and elsewhere in the Empire, which created a strain on the recruiting system. Moreover, many Irish lads, who had helped to fill out even the Scots regiments, now preferred to seek their fortune in America. Cardwell's scheme of linked battalions remained incomplete because of a strong rear-guard action, and a determined effort was now afoot to destroy it. Wolseley was ready to do battle for what he believed were the best interests of the army, realizing that his task would be far more difficult and less rewarding than any undertaking in the field.

'Wolseley has returned home,' wrote the Duke of Cambridge. 'He seems wild and dissatisfied ... '[3] The Duke hoped to restrict his new quartermaster-general to the limited functions of troop movements and quartering, with occasional ceremonial functions, which he knew the reformer detested. The commander-in-chief was not the least bit interested in the notions that 'our only General' brought back with him from South Africa, notions that seemed to bubble and stew inside him, everything from the construction of new ammunition boxes* to an improved machine-gun. Even at this late date it was fashionable among the 'old school' to disparage the Gatling gun, which at best was 'the automatic representative of ten unskilled and nervous riflemen'.

In his war with the opponents of reform, Wolseley fired the opening shots over the same blood-soaked battle-ground of short service. At a banquet at the Mansion House, he reminded the enemies of short service 'how an army raised under the long-service system totally disappeared in a few months under the walls of Sebastopol'. What difficulties developed under the present system he blamed on the 'pipeclay prejudices' of the Horse Guards, who were not above sabotaging short service. At the Newspaper Press Fund Dinner, he asked for support from the press to enable him 'to put new wheels on the military coach, which by its creaking tells us of its present dangerous condition, and which is only with difficulty maintained in an upright position at all'.

Moderation in statement was an art that Wolseley never bothered to cultivate. Candour in private conversation could be one of his most winning traits, but in public speaking his lack of discretion made him many bitter enemies. He publicly treated with scorn those who stood in the path of progress, rarely bothering to apologize. And he left no doubt in the mind of the public, whose support he courted, that the most formidable barrier to progress was the person of the commander-in-chief.

'Damn his eyes,' exclaimed the Duke, whose position was openly

---

* Ammunition boxes at that time were still screwed down and could hardly be opened fast enough to feed a firing-line that faced charging Zulus.

challenged. At the moment H.R.H. was not in the happiest frame of mind. He suffered cruelly from a crippling attack of the gout and ridicule, which had its origin in a story begun by a comic journalist a short time before. It was common knowledge that the commander-in-chief unfurled an umbrella when it rained during a military review; a reporter therefore related that the Duke had countermanded a field day at Chatham owing to the fact that it was raining and he had no umbrella. In reality, the Duke, fond of his soldiers, thoughtfully called off the exercise in the rain so that his men might be spared several days of scrubbing and cleaning. But the public took up the story, and the Duke of Cambridge became known as 'Umbrella George', much to his chagrin. And he learned that none told the story better than Sir Garnet. Once more he had to contend with this 'very model of a modern Major-General' who offended his high sense of personal authority. The Duke was never more open in his opposition to Wolseley, and he reserved a few choice words for his private estimate of him.

The disagreement moved from short service to the subject of promotion, a perennial source of discord. In and out of season, Wolseley advocated a system of promotion based upon merit; for, despite the abolition of purchase, the old evils were perpetuated by the seniority rule. It was downright criminal, declared Wolseley, to place the lives of gallant soldiers in the hands of officers who were 'deplorably ignorant of their profession'. He begged the Duke not to advance men whose capacity to command troops in war was extremely doubtful; all promotions from lieutenant-colonel and above should be based on selection. 'Give him orders and ribbons,' he pleaded, 'but don't give him men's lives to lose.' In the navy, he pointed out, they were very careful to select the right man to captain a ship; why should not the same care be taken in choosing an officer to command a battalion?

The Duke, who saw no connection between the army and the navy in the matter, clung to the old system with uncommon tenacity. Though a Royal Commission recommended the rule of seniority tempered by rejection, the commander-in-chief, in practice, made it a matter of seniority alone. It was the contention of Cambridge and his supporters that what Wolseley suggested would in reality provide 'a fine field for the cultivation of "backstairs influence"'. Gallant and able officers would be 'passed over by some subtle, smirking, cocked-hat hunter'. Promotion by selection, the Duke held, was the curse of Republican France where a career in the upper ranks of the army was open to intrigue, corruption, and political influence.

The debate grew more heated when it was a question of promoting individual officers of Wolseley's team, for Wolseley never tired of pressing for the advancement of men who had proved their worth in the field under his command. No army, declared the Duke bristling with indignation, could long endure preferences towards very junior officers without damping the energies of the senior officers. This kind of favouritism would destroy the *esprit de corps* of the whole body of officers.

No doubt the 'Wolseley gang' or 'Ashanti ring', as enemies called it, had an unsettling influence on a great number of officers. The very terms implied favouritism, through which friends and followers of Sir Garnet were constantly being advanced, under his generous and faithful sponsorship, at the expense of others. Those outside the favoured circle gnashed their teeth over the fact that all the prizes of the service seemed to go to that select clique of 'mutual admirers and hangers-on'. The members of the 'gang' seemed to serve under a set of rules and regulations entirely distinct from the rest of the army. The 'old school' angrily contended that there were men as good if not better than those who enjoyed a monopoly on all the military ventures of their time. How could they ever learn the tricks of the trade? Think of all the potential talent in the British army that was wasted.

The critics, of course, had a point. If nothing else, the existence of a select band of officers was a demoralizing factor. The most telling retort, however, came not from Sir Garnet but from Archibald Forbes, who spoke for him: 'I know these men of men,' he had Wolseley say, 'and they know me. I selected them originally because of my discernment of character, not at the behest of interest or from the dictates of nepotism. We have worked long together; their familiarity with my methods and my just reliance on them relieves me of half the burden of command. And again, it is obvious that I must ever, as more important commands are assigned me, be widening the pale of the "gang". I never see a man doing good work in the quiet efficient manner that I like, that I do not recruit him into my following. I am always on the alert for capable men, since they are not so plentiful; and, oh! outsider, if you should fulfil my requirements, your turn may come tomorrow.'[4]

Could Wolseley be blamed for thinking in terms of military success, rather than concerning himself with the possible disheartening effects his selection of officers might have upon the professional zeal of those who were not chosen? Few factors in war are more important to the supreme commander than the organization of a body of picked men upon whom he can rely to carry out the details of his own 'generalling'. As Wolseley put it, 'Men don't cut down trees with razors.' One test of a leader is his power to choose able men. Few would question Wolseley's genius for selecting the right men; fewer still realized how sedulously he strove to find the best material available.

From the first campaign in Burma, Wolseley carefully noted those officers who were able and efficient. Each selection was studied, polished and fitted like a precious stone before it became a permanent part of his 'ring'. He carefully distinguished between fighting leaders and regular staff officers. Each had his speciality. One was the ideal scout; another gave added dash to the attack. A third was a positive genius when it came to prompt organizing; while another had an unusual flair for administration. There were those who spoke well, wrote well, or served as experts in legal matters. One officer, Forbes observed, seemed to have no particular gift except for strong language and the pleasures of the table. Not until the fighting began and he drew his sword, did it become clear that Sir Garnet had enlisted 'a veritable god of battle' who drew men into a fight like a magnet does steel. Buller!

To insist that some attained positions incommensurate with their ability because they later failed as independent commanders, or at other jobs, merely proved that the whole was greater than the parts. Every man who served under 'the Chief', as they affectionately called him, recognized that it was his subtle charm of manner, his uncompromising loyalty, his eagerness to acknowledge their value that inspired them to their best efforts. Supremely confident of himself, he gave them confidence, especially because he believed in them. The ultimate test was success in war, and so long as Wolseley passed it, he had the politicians and the public behind him, and there was nothing his opponents could do to break up his 'gang'.

The Duke did succeed in preventing the creation of a General Staff, which was one of Wolseley's pet projects. Cambridge told Cardwell that he was in effect chief of staff. Wolseley had to be content with improving the training of the Staff College, though he met with continued obstruction from the military authorities. The red tab of the staff officer was looked upon by many as a badge of infamy. What intellectual superiority they developed was regarded with contempt. Officers of the Household Cavalry were discouraged from competing for entry to Staff College. The Duke had absolutely no faith in it. The school was a factory which produced more windy doctrinaires, of which the army already had its quota. He seemed almost pleased when they did not turn out too smartly for inspection. When Wolseley later asked for a Staff College officer to fill a vacant appointment, Cambridge was heard to grumble as he studied the memorandum: 'Staff College officer, what does he want a Staff College officer for? I know those Staff College officers. They are very ugly officers and very dirty officers.'*5

Basic to all Wolseley's reforms was an eagerness to fit the army for war, most of all the officers. Striving to get the officers to apply themselves earnestly to their profession and to study it as a science, Sir Garnet was accused by the Duke of attempting to create 'military bookworms'. But Wolseley had no desire to create a bookish soldier. 'Any boy who has mastered the first book of Euclid', he wrote, 'can learn and understand the theories of Jomini and Clausewitz and be a perfectly useless soldier afterwards unless by hard thought he learns how to apply their theories to the ever-changing conditions of war; and how are you going to train a man to think unless you encourage him to read?' To those who held that an ounce of experience is worth a pound of study, he would say, 'The story of every great commander gives the lie to that. It is often said that a man who writes well cannot be a good soldier; most of the great commanders, from King David, Xenophon, and Caesar to Wellington, not only wrote well, but extremely well.'6

Though not a prominent man of letters, Wolseley wrote easily and well, and few commanders in history were so well read. For a man whose life was one of excitement and animation, he spent an enormous amount of time devouring books and scholarly articles. His knowledge of books and authors impressed others as encyclopaedic. It was said he had read everything that was ever written about Swift. This love of reading he attributed to his Irish mother. 'I would sooner live upon porridge in a book room,' he liked to say, 'than upon venison and truffles where books are not.' He enjoyed the companionship of bookish intellectuals, among them some of the leading literary figures of his time, such as Andrew Lang, Edmund Gosse, James Anthony Froude, and most of all, Henry James. They accepted him into their literary circles, never talking down to him, but treating him as one of them. The Poet Laureate, Alfred Austin, was also a close friend. Wolseley, however, derived no pleasure from poetry.

The introduction of the territorial system produced more friction and hard feelings than any single major reform introduced into the British army. To be linked with another battalion, as Cardwell conceived it, was

---

* The Duke's language was often less restrained. The story was told that he once began an address to the cadets of the Royal Military College at Sandhurst with the plain exordium, 'You dirty little bastards!'

bad enough, but to be permanently welded with a subsequent loss of historic numbers, traditions, and exclusive battle honours won with blood
was an intolerable innovation to most soldiers. Even the treasured regimental facings were to be obliterated. Wolseley, however, always believed that soldiers should be dressed for work in the field, not to enrich
tailors or to delight nursemaids. As a practical matter it would be difficult,
if not impossible, to produce clothing stores for mobilization if each
battalion had its distinct dress. The quartermaster-general respected the
regimental spirit that had kept the British soldiery together for two centuries, but he now wanted to see this collection of regiments transformed
into an army.

To avoid offending regimental sentiment any more than necessary, an
extraordinary amount of tact and care was exercised in introducing these
reforms. But some old battalions resented being united with younger
ones and losing their identity completely. Some changes were not only
difficult, but ludicrous, as when the 3rd *Bombay European* regiment was
combined with the 100th *Royal Canadians* to form the *Leinster* regiment.
Four battalions that had nearly forgotten that they had originally been
Scottish, suddenly found their knees bared once more by kilts. There
were a few battalions that would rather wipe the floor with their yoke-
fellows. These unwilling victims of shotgun marriages who saw their
ancient regimental traditions ruthlessly destroyed, including such precious
nicknames as the Springers, the Slashers, the Pompadours, found no
humour in the irreverent observation: 'Whom Wolseley hath joined, let
no man put asunder.'

The territorial system provoked a howl of indignation in the army
from stalwart old war-dogs down to lowly recruits, who as the foundation of all their training were indoctrinated with an almost childlike
belief in the supremacy of their unit. Hugh Childers, the new War
Secretary, who was adamant in his support of military reforms, reported,
'The House is a terrible beargarden.' An alarmed Duke complained they
were playing tricks with the army again, and he made an impassioned
appeal to the Queen to save the glorious regimental system against this
destructive mischief. Her Majesty, realizing it was impossible to revert to
the old single-battalion system, tried to preserve at least their hallowed
numbers and designations. She bombarded Childers and Gladstone with
protests, but with little success.

The traditionalists repeatedly declared that the ill-considered territorial
system, the fruit of an unholy alliance between necessarily uninformed
politicians and certain ambitious soldiers, would finally destroy the *esprit*

*de corps*, which was the life-blood and soul of the regimental system. But to Wolseley, narrow regimental loyalties were a hindrance to simplifying administration, promoting recruitment, and improving short service. He would rather see a wider *esprit de corps* in their profession, such as was found in the navy. According to the 'whining pessimists', as Wolseley publicly called them, all recent reforms were destructive to discipline and *esprit de corps*. The latter expression, he insisted, was a time-worn shibboleth used by a very conservative class of officers to frighten the non-military public, just as the cry of 'No Popery' was once used to inflame the masses politically. When he joined the army in 1852, the military disease of chronic grumbling was no less prevalent among the old soldiers; antiquated croakers then claimed that officers and men were not as good as they had been in their day and that the army was going to the devil because enlistment for life and for twenty-one years was being abolished. Writing for the *Nineteenth Century*, Wolseley told his readers of a group of officers who seemed to believe that the world, as far as military affairs were concerned, stood still; all about them they witnessed 'the most marvellous changes effected by steam, electricity, and mechanical inventions, and they accept them as a matter of course, ignoring or unconscious of the fact that all such discoveries and inventions react upon armies and military science.'[7]

It is easier to attack a man than an idea. In the wrathful storm that developed, Wolseley was pelted with insults and rebukes. The impact of disfavour fell upon him rather than upon Childers, an ignorant civilian, for the quartermaster-general was obviously the mainspring of military reform. Moreover, his cocksure manner and impatience with opposition invited attack. Behind-the-hand whispers were heard from officers in club smoking-rooms that he was a charlatan and a 'duffer'. Vituperators claimed that this iconoclastic self-seeker knew nothing of the practical workings of the regimental system which he flouted, for his own regimental experience ceased twenty-four years before and never exceeded three years.

Wolseley's temperament was such that he refused to temporize, and unlike Childers, he fought back. Setting down his critics as antiquated noodles, he laboured to educate the non-military public, upon whose ignorance the opposition presumed. He advocated in print and word 'the necessity of abandoning fossil futilities in military matters'.[8] His articles and after-dinner speeches provoked his enemies into outcries that were long and loud. The public had only a vague idea of the revolution that was taking place in military matters, though they were inclined to trust the judgment of their 'only General'. Wolseley won, but the struggle exhausted him more than any military campaign.

Wolseley liked to repeat a paradox which he borrowed from Sir William Napier: 'We may not be a military nation, but without doubt we are the most warlike people on earth.' There seemed hardly a time when a tiny force belonging to this great maritime nation was not busily engaged in a campaign; and artists and correspondents delighted the public with descriptions and sketches of redcoats charging or repelling Indians, Dacoits, Zulus, Ashantis and other savage peoples of variegated pigmentations. Yet, at home, the sight of a red coat would cause its owner to be treated as a social outcast.

It was Wolseley's aim to convert this warlike spirit into a military one, military in the best sense, with habits of discipline and respect for lawful command without sacrificing independence of character. Short service and the spread of a volunteer system helped instil a military spirit, but it was only the beginning. He would like to see more young men given an opportunity, on a voluntary basis, of course, to gain a little experience in the service. It would benefit the individual and the nation. Above all, he fought to remove the unpopularity of the military among the classes from which the army must look for recruits. The uniform should become an object of pride such as it was in Germany.

To improve prospects for recruiting, Wolseley advocated improvements in pay, food, housing, recreation, and the abolition of flogging. Childers was in whole-hearted agreement with such a programme. He, too, was disgusted with the 'vulgar prejudice' which still existed against the man in uniform and permitted his red coat in some public place to be regarded as 'a reproach and not an honour'. Because soldiers were often not allowed to sit in certain parts of a theatre, in first-class seats on a train or boat, or sometimes on an omnibus, Wolseley suggested he would finance N.C.O.s to take expensive seats in a theatre, etc.; and should they be refused admission, have the Government prosecute the management. Childers, however, thought he was going a little too far.

Childers did push through the abolition of flogging on active service as well as during peacetime, which had been eliminated by Cardwell in 1869. Military clubs, however, resounded with anguished cries. Senior officers vigorously hurled about the outdated views of the Iron Duke on the subject. The 'cat', nevertheless, soon passed into oblivion. Wolseley declared the soldier could now feel a little prouder of himself and his profession, for no longer would privates wear stripes on their backs as sergeants wore stripes on their sleeves.

An increase in pay and pensions would undoubtedly have attracted better recruits, men instead of boys. Though economy-minded in many other matters, Wolseley urged a rise in pay by fifty per cent, to one shilling and sixpence a day, so that British soldiers might receive approximately the same sum as a recruit in the United States, the only other major power relying on voluntary enlistments. 'We could then pick and choose,' he declared. 'To me it has always seemed the height of folly, the most unbusinesslike folly,' he continued, 'this sweeping into our ranks every year those who are only a little above the blind.'[9]

A niggardly Parliament, however, would never consider such a proposal. It was pointed out that the Duke of Wellington had opposed any increase in pay on the ground that it would make the nation resentful. And it was argued by certain M.P.s that more money in the soldier's pocket would cause him to be more drunken, thereby creating a serious discipline problem. Over the years only the slightest increment in pay was approved. Nevertheless, improved conditions, short service, and the glamour that the 'Queen's Army' began to acquire during the Kipling era produced a steady increase in enlistments, and an equally steady decrease in desertions.

Few did more or cared more for the common soldier than Sir Garnet Wolseley. Yet, unlike Buller, who had a kind of animal magnetism that cast a spell over those who served him, he never won their affection – nor did he want it. Like Kitchener, he possessed the impersonal hardness found in great organizers. Even in the field, Wolseley seemed detached. The flush of enthusiasm he might arouse in a campaign quickly paled afterwards.

Lasting fame is built on legend, and Wolseley had neither the personality nor the inclination to create legends. No one ever suggested a nickname. As one contemporary remarked, because of his aloofness, his intellectual superiority, 'even to think of it was ridiculous'.[10] Some declared he was wholly without sentiment, and looked upon soldiers as mere pawns (as Kitchener did); but all his private correspondence reveals that he actually had a very great affection for the man in the ranks.

Wolseley was less successful in concealing his feelings where the Duke was concerned. There were occasions when he felt like giving him 'a good thrashing'. And never was he more in the mood than when Cambridge contested his promotion to adjutant-general. The post was no sinecure such as that of quartermaster-general, but one of influence that would give Wolseley a greater sphere of authority; he would stand next to the commander-in-chief himself and be in charge of recruiting, training, discipline, and education, with a general control over other divisions of the military department. The post also carried with it a certain dignity from the old days when there was no commander-in-chief, except in time of war, and the adjutant-general was the channel of communication between the Sovereign and the army, a fact which neither the Queen nor the Duke had forgotten.

Wolseley made no pretence at false modesty regarding the appointment. Once Lord Ripon's application to have Wolseley made commander-in-chief in India was emphatically refused, largely owing to the objections of the Duke, Wolseley made known his availability to serve as adjutant-general, a post that would become vacant early in 1882. Moreover, when Childers, who was contemplating new schemes of army reorganization, was informed by Wolseley of the approaching vacancy, he got the idea that it would be essential to his plans to have an adjutant-general who would be co-operative. To make Wolseley's selection acceptable to the Horse Guards, Childers recommended Lord Roberts as successor to Wolseley as quartermaster-general.* (Rather than leave his post in India, Roberts later refused the appointment.)

The proposal deepened the Duke's perpetual frown and clouded his china-blue eyes. 'Uncle George is here,' the Prince of Wales wrote to the Queen from Sandringham, 'but worried to death by the Adjutant-General question.'[11] Royal George warned his nephew that if Wolseley and the band of reformers he headed had their way the Sovereign's control over the army would be surrendered to the politicians. It was no longer a question of dealing with an impertinent upstart advocating revolutionary ideas; Wolseley was a dangerous rival who as adjutant-general would undermine the authority of the commander-in-chief.

Impressed by these dire prophecies, the Prince conveyed the Duke's almost pathetic appeals to the Queen, and added his own strong protests against the appointment. Might not Sir Garnet be of greater service, he suggested, if she employed him as governor-general of Canada.[12] The Queen, whose interest in the army never flagged, shared their fears and was disposed to think of Wolseley as a low Radical whose ambition was to upset everything in the army. An indiscreet courtier told Ponsonby, the Queen's secretary, that the Royal family would like to burn Wolseley, along with other army reformers, at the stake.[13]

It certainly would have given Victoria the greatest of pleasure to keep

---

* Roberts, the hero of the much-eulogized march from Kabul to Kandahar, was a strong opponent of the short-service system.

Wolseley from being made adjutant-general, but she was after all a constitutional monarch. Ponsonby, who personally sympathized with Wolseley (the Duke had also opposed his appointment to private secretary on the ground that he was a Radical), reminded Her Majesty of her position and tried to restrain her so that her meddling in this matter 'might never be suspected'. The press, however, which was becoming very vocal in advocating the appointment, already concluded that certain illustrious susceptibilities had to be overcome. With her private secretary working adroitly to smooth ruffled feelings, the Queen politely and quietly ignored the constant protestations of her son and the old Duchess of Cambridge, the Duke's mother, and sought to take advantage of 'the Duke's occasionally reasonable moods'.[14]

The Duke felt 'pain and distress' when he learned that Her Majesty, in whose affection he felt firmly rooted, thought it undesirable that further opposition to Sir Garnet's appointment should be made, since Childers, with Gladstone's backing, obviously would not budge on this issue. But he made one more direct and desperate appeal. He claimed there was more to this appointment than met the eye. He pointed to an article in *The Times* which told, unofficially, that henceforth the adjutant-general would give advice to and carry out the orders of the War Secretary, the commander-in-chief's functions being completely ignored and set aside. All the attributes of his office, in other words, would be enjoyed by the adjutant-general. 'How *impossible* my position must become,' he complained, 'suddenly to be placed in an inferior and degraded position would be unbearable to myself'.[15]

Ponsonby answered by suggesting that the Duke of Cambridge had never formally stated his reasons for objecting to Sir Garnet. To this the Duke replied that he had done so over and over again to the War Secretary, but never in *writing* because he judged it an imprudent course to follow. However, he no longer harboured such scruples, and would be only too happy to state his objections:

> I consider in the first place that Sir Garnet is *not* the officer I deem at present best qualified for the post ... In the next place I think the Army wants *rest*. Such great changes have been introduced, that time should be given to allow matters to settle down. Sir Garnet Wolseley's great object seems to be to go further and further, and to upset the little that is left of the old spirit of the officer by indiscriminate selection, carrying education to the extremest limit, by letting men go to the Reserve after three years' service, and in a

variety of ways intensifying the sweeping changes that have already been effected. Thirdly I think the mode of his introduction into the office of A.G. would be a slur and imputation upon me, and on the manner in which I have performed my Departmental duty as military adviser to the Secretary of State, and as such a serious insult would be offered to me in my official position. Lastly Sir Garnet's close connection with the Press, and his strong expressions on military matters in speeches and writings, are of that character as I believe would prove most detrimental to the interests of the Army, and would certainly turn military matters into subjects for political discussions ... I fear there is now no alternative left to me but to withdraw from a position which has become unbearable ... [16]

Wolseley gave an amazing performance of suppressing his own rancour during the crisis. He continued to be hurt by the attitude of the Queen, who accepted without question her cousin's estimate that he was a dangerous Radical. Shortly before the crisis, he wrote to his wife: 'I am sick of Royalties and never wish to see one of our Royal family again. I think I used to be the greatest Royalist in England but the cruel treatment I have received from the Queen, I can never either forgive or forget.'[17] He prayed for some signal event which would one day place him in a position strong enough to stand up to the Court party and expose the Duke of Cambridge and the lot of incompetents which he had taken so much delight in honouring.

In the end, the Duke cooled down and Childers had his way. The fear, perhaps, that Childers would resign and be replaced by a Radical like Dilke, caused him to have second thoughts about Wolseley's promotion. Moreover, when Wolseley learned that the Duke angrily believed that certain unflattering articles in the press were written by him, he promptly arranged an interview with H.R.H. and vowed that he had absolutely nothing to do with them. The Duke was satisfied and agreed to accept him as adjutant-general; however, on the condition that he would not write or speak on military subjects, 'and that his [Cambridge's] position was publicly and properly recognized'.[18] Wolseley and Gladstone agreed. And the latter made a public statement on December 1st declaring that the authority and responsibility of the commander-in-chief were unchanged, any previous newspaper announcements on this subject being purely conjectural.

The Duke of Cambridge continued to dominate the army, assured of the enduring confidence of the Queen and secure in the knowledge that he held the affection of the men, which he took more or less for granted. But the new adjutant-general, because of his intense belief that he was right in trying to put the army in a sound state, continued to enrage the commander-in-chief. The Duke tried to keep him busy inspecting cadets, watching them drill, etc.; but with miracles of energy, Wolseley found time to work for reforms. And he soon found it impossible to keep his promise to refrain from writing for publication and speaking his mind publicly on military matters.

Working in the War Office, the new adjutant-general was always in a hurry to get his orders and measures pushed through. With the utmost contempt for 'red tape', which maddened his clever brain, he communicated directly with officials without bothering to employ prescribed channels. Whole departments would be by-passed and confusion often resulted, relations already strained coming close to a complete rupture. To restore tempers all round, some like Maurice or Brackenbury tactfully tried to salve the hurt. To the plodding and orderly commander-in-chief, it often seemed as if his office was turned into a nightmare of confusion. It got so bad, at times, that he was afraid to make a trip or to take a holiday because it meant leaving Wolseley in charge.

Though the Duke, backed by the power of the Queen, worked hard to thwart Wolseley's reforms, Wolseley, single-handed and with uncommon courage, chipped away, bit by bit, at the great boulders that obstructed his way in creating a modern army. He was driven by the fear, as Disraeli once expressed it, that the Horse Guards would ruin England, for if a major war occurred with the commander-in-chief's reactionary generals in command, England would be lost.

A more immediate peril was the construction of a railway tunnel under the Channel which, in Wolseley's eyes, would undermine the island's security and destroy England's cherished insularity. The tunnel scheme had been mooted by various engineers since the time of the great Napoleon, but it was not until the 'seventies that their dreams – and Napoleon's – of a dry road between England and the Continent began to take practical shape in the hands of enterprising capitalists. A British firm, headed by Sir Edward Watkins (the Liberal party whip), obtained approval to sink an experimental shaft near Dover in 1880, while the French began a similar test tunnel on the other side.

Popular approval mounted as the political, social, and moral purposes of the project were extolled. There were rhetorical expressions by prominent personages that promised a blessed brotherhood of nations and victories of peace, a rise in trade and a corresponding decline in unemployment. The Francophile Prince of Wales endorsed it, and Gladstone soon gave it his backing.

As Sir Edward dug, Sir Garnet struck. 'Surely John Bull,' he grumbled, 'will not endanger his birthright, his liberty, his property simply in order that men and women may cross between England and France without running the risk of sea-sickness.' He publicly denied that Watkins's 'mad enterprise' would serve any real advantage, save perhaps to private speculators and company promoters.

In an ably reasoned memorandum, written in June 1882, 'our only General' speculated upon the grave risks involved in destroying an impassable barrier which God had placed between Britain and her enemies, and pointed to the Germans who declared: 'What would not Germany give for twenty miles of water between themselves and France.' In rebutting the argument that the tunnel could be neutralized by treaties with Continental powers, Wolseley asked, what did a Napoleon or Frederick the Great care for such treaties? As to the fortifications constructed in the Dover area, they could easily be seized by a small force employing surprise or treachery; he reminded his readers that from 1700 to the present time, not one war in ten began with a formal declaration. Was the nation, he concluded, prepared to add this new danger, necessarily attendant upon the construction of the tunnel, to those which already existed in England?

Sir Garnet stirred the insular instincts of his countrymen. Editorials reverberated with the words of England's 'modern and scientific general'. To preserve the 'silver streak' and prevent the annexation of Britain to the Continent, *The Times* and the popular *Nineteenth Century* made journalistic history by presenting a memorial against the scheme, signed by the most representative soldiers, sailors, clergymen, scientists, and men of letters; it was an illustrious chain of resistance that extended from Thomas Huxley, Herbert Spencer, and Robert Browning to the Duke of Cambridge and the Queen herself.

As the controversy spilled into the halls of Parliament, the issue rapidly reached a climax. Sir Garnet became the chief witness to testify before a select committee of both Houses, headed by the ardent tunnelite, Lord Lansdowne. The general ridiculed the argument of supporters that in time of danger this Wonder of the World could be quickly and easily drowned, dynamited, or otherwise destroyed. He told how during the Franco-German war the Germans gained control of several railway tunnels through the Vosges Mountains, despite the elaborate precautions taken by the French. It was his contention that 'were a tunnel made,

England as a Nation could be destroyed without any warning whatever when Europe was in a condition of profound peace.'

Obviously impressed by the pronouncements of England's leading soldier, the commissioners voted in July 1883, six to four against the project.

The digging stopped, but not the talk. Periodically, public excitement on the subject, always a fascinating one, waxed and waned. But so long as Wolseley, England's leading military authority, asserted, *ex cathedra*, that it would be impossible to block the entrance of a tunnel or prevent its seizure by treachery – e.g., by Irish Republicans co-operating with an external enemy – it was returned to the limbo of impractical schemes.

# CHAPTER FOURTEEN

# THE COUNTERMARCH OF MOSES

PEACE, which reigned for a little over a year throughout the Empire, was completely shattered by the most significant of the many 'small wars' in which Wolseley was engaged – the Egyptian campaign of 1882.

Difficulties in Egypt stemmed from the wildly extravagant Khedive (Viceroy) Ismail, who bit into the golden hook of the international money-lenders with disastrous results for himself and his subjects. The leech-like coterie of bankers – French, British and German – helped him to mortgage the assets of his country until the National Debt soared from £4,000,000 to £100,00,000. As the financial chaos continued and it became manifest that the revenue could no longer pay even the interest due on the bonds, the money markets of Paris and London pressured their respective governments into establishing a Franco-British condominium to control the Egyptian budget and secure payment on their loans. Though Egypt was still nominally part of the Ottoman Empire, after 1876 its destiny was in the hands of the 'dual control'. When, for example, in 1879 Ismail Pasha began to wriggle and intrigue to escape the bond-holder's net, the powers instantly hauled him ashore, and had the Sultan depose him in favour of his more pliable son, the mild-mannered Tewfik Pasha.

Anglo-French management of Egypt's finances provoked widespread unrest. The country swarmed with foreign officials who introduced unpopular reforms to meet coupons. Enjoying many immunities and privileges, including exemption from taxation, or trial in native courts, these officials seemed to grow fat on lucrative appointments in a land where the peasants, the fellahin, were perpetually hungry and almost naked. Discontent, often fanned by Muslim religious leaders, rapidly spread throughout classes of the population, many of whom suspected 'dual control' was merely a prelude to handing the country over to a European nation as was done in the case of Cyprus and Tunis.

The cry 'Egypt for the Egyptians' was loudest in the army, which was wretchedly underpaid, and where thousands of officers had been summarily

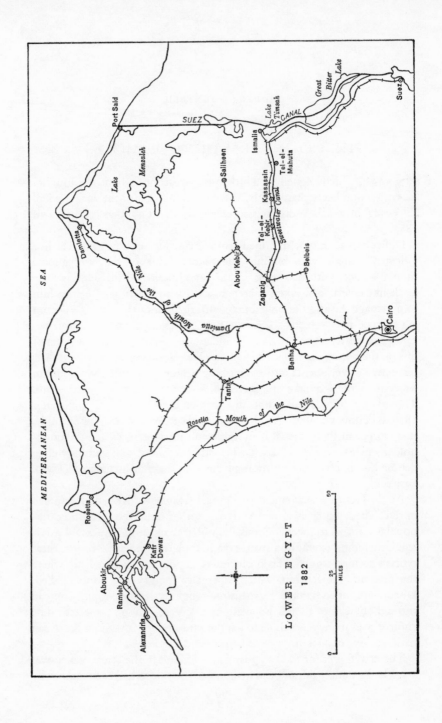

LOWER EGYPT
1882

dismissed as an economy measure. Among them arose a champion, Colonel Ahmed Arabi, by birth a fellah from Lower Egypt. This burly, eloquent agitator with large stern features became the recognized leader of a nationalist movement that soon resembled a crusade against all foreigners. The truculent patriot, supported by the military and acclaimed by the people, wrung concessions from the bullied Tewfik, who in quick succession made him Under-Secretary for War, War Minister, and Pasha. Finally, after a bloodless military revolt in mid May 1882, Arabi grabbed the reins of power and became a virtual dictator, with Tewfik a prisoner of his own Government.

Foreign military intervention became inevitable. Not only were Egypt's foreign debt and free passage through the Canal in jeopardy, but the lives and properties of nearly 100,000 non-Egyptians were in grave danger. When a naval bombardment of Alexandria by the British (the French refused to co-operate) failed to bring about the collapse of the national movement, Gladstone, reluctantly acting like Disraeli, decided on July 20th to send a military force to Cairo.

The announcement that Wolseley was to head the expedition to Egypt merely confirmed public expectation. No one could imagine anyone else in command. The Duke told the Queen that it would be inadvisable to oppose the selection, and grudgingly admitted that Wolseley was 'very decidedly as able a man for the field as we have got'.[1] Cambridge had begun to soften in his attitude towards the adjutant-general. During the Egyptian crisis, Wolseley confided to McCalmont that His Royal Highness actually invited him for a drive one afternoon.

The Duke, however, was soon upset by the appointment of so many of that charmed circle, 'the Ashanti Club', whom Sir Garnet considered indispensable. Rather than rely on untried talents, the Chief called to his side Buller (who had his honeymoon cut short), Butler, Baker Russell, Maurice, Wood, McCalmont, Herbert Stewart, and others. Some were conspicuously absent. Brackenbury was serving as military attaché in Paris. And Colley ... Wolseley still found it painful to think of the loss of his friend, who was killed leading a small British force against the Boers in the Transvaal in 1881.

Men were drawn to the campaign as steel filings to a magnet. To the British, war was still a kind of dangerous sport. A brief contest in the shadow of the Pyramids, rather than rigorous campaigning in some far-off place, was especially attractive. As soon as it was learned that an expedition was being organized, eager soldiers haunted the War Office. The more irrepressible went on their own account, as young Kitchener did, often in the guise of newspapermen or visiting tourists. The lucky ones were given assignments, though the majority were ordered back to England by an unsympathetic commander.

The appearance of such persons who went to the front on their own was most distressing to the Duke. He requested, in some instances without success, that Wolseley send such officers home. Privately, Cambridge asked Wolseley whether he could find a place for his son, George, a major in the 20th Hussars.

Wolseley never had any use for the Fitzgeorges, either the Duke's wife or their three sons.* George, the eldest, to his way of thinking, was a 'horrid snob and I dare say quite useless'. Wolseley considered the request to be 'very unfair', but he dared not offend the commander-in-chief on so sensitive a matter. 'Perhaps,' he sardonically opined to Lady Wolseley, 'old Mother Fitzgeorge would like to come also.'[2]

Even the members of the royal family exhibited a fierce desire to see active service in Egypt. The Prince of Wales, then forty-one, resolved to go on the expedition. He sought out its commander to plead his case. Though Wolseley dreaded the responsibility of caring for the heir to the throne in the middle of a war, he could not find the courage to turn him down. The Queen could. She vetoed the idea, and the Government supported her. Wolseley was only too happy to obey her wishes.

Still drawn to the notion of joining Wolseley after he departed from England, the Prince sought the company of Lady Wolseley who was on holiday at Homburg. On more than one occasion he tried to persuade her to write to Sir Garnet and mention his great desire to be at his side. It was all very embarrassing and Lady Wolseley, still an extremely attractive woman, became concerned lest there should be gossip linking her in a romantic way to this jovial *bon-vivant* who had such a great reputation with the ladies. She quickly instructed her ten-year-old daughter, Frances, on how to behave as a chaperone. Above all, when the Prince came to call on her, Frances was not to leave the room. Even if the Prince were to command it, Frances was to disobey and stay with her mother.[3]

But Prince Arthur, the Duke of Connaught, the Queen's favourite son, '*dearer* than any of the others put together', had his way. However, it was only after many tears and much vacillation that the Queen agreed to let her 'darling, precious Arthur' go. In a way, she was pleased with the idea

---

* As a young soldier, the Duke fell in love with an attractive actress and dancer, Sarah Louisa Fairbrother. After the birth of two sons, he braved royal displeasure by contracting a morganatic marriage. Though Victoria was on the best of terms with the Duke and 'Mrs Fitzgeorge', who led a long and happy married life, she absolutely refused to recognize the legality of this union.

of an English prince going into battle, but she did not want to see him run the slightest risk. For a soldier in war this could be extremely awkward.

Entire units insisted upon being part of the force. Most controversial was the subject of the inclusion of the Household Cavalry. Opponents declared that the Queen's bodyguard were impressively handsome on State occasions but useless in war; these 'carpet knights' who lived in voluptuous indolence were unsuited for active service. The day of the heavy cavalry had passed; light cavalry such as the Uhlans was far more useful in battle. Wolseley himself was inclined to believe that bulky troopers on big horses would be out of place in desert engagements. But in the end, Wolseley, against his better judgment, was persuaded to support their commanding officer's petition. It was decided to form a composite regiment consisting of squadrons from the 1st and 2nd Life Guards and the Royal Horse Guards.

The expedition, owing to Wolseley's arrangements for embarkation, was dispatched with a completeness and speed that was in marked contrast to the occupation of Tunis by the French a year before. The troops sent from England and Mediterranean stations numbered about 22,000; subsequent reinforcements added another 11,000. In addition, 7,000 were sent from India. The grand total of 40,560 officers and men was a small force by modern standards, but it was one of the largest single expeditions ever dispatched by Britain to date. Sixty-one steamers were employed to carry the army and over 41,000 tons of supplies from England to Egypt, some 3,000 miles away.

Those who left by way of Westminster Bridge pier to board four steamers waiting to take them down river were given a great send-off by enormous crowds. The cheers of thousands of well-wishers along the Embankment from Westminster to Blackfriars were deafening as they sailed by. Many people took the train to Gravesend and went on the river in small crafts for a last glimpse of their heroes in scarlet serge Norfolk jackets.

Wolseley had little choice in the selection of his generals. The chief commanders were those originally designated to participate in autumn manoeuvres. He quickly developed a strong dislike for his division commanders, Hamley and Willis, who had 'an overweening opinion of their own importance'. Neither had seen any service in the field since the Crimea. Wolseley's foes suggested it was because neither had won the ear of the politicians who favoured that 'ring of exclusive traders in military glory'. Hamley, nevertheless, had earned an enviable reputation as a first-rate writer on military affairs. On the strength of this, Wolseley, in the beginning, actually argued that he should be given a chance to prove his worth in the field. Wolseley had always had a high regard for Drury Lowe, who was in charge of the cavalry. And he found the white-haired Adye to be a loyal, capable chief of staff, though Adye was somewhat hurt that an officer fourteen years his junior should be given supreme command.

These general officers, along with Generals Earle and Wood, visited the Queen at Osborne before leaving. Sir Garnet spoke kindly of Arthur and of how happy he was to be 'clear of the French', who had declined to support the expedition. The Queen was very much impressed with the officers he presented. The Queen later sent a sympathetic and kindly telegram to overtake Wolseley. Unwilling to forgive past hurts, the general thought this 'Royal attention came a little late'. 'We are loyal in every fibre and every thought to the Crown of England,' he wrote to his wife, 'but it is difficult to forget the Queen's attitude to us both hitherto.'[4]

Originally it was arranged that Sir Garnet and his staff would make a rapid trip overland, via Brindisi, with a quick side trip to Cyprus to inspect the depots; but on his trip back from Osborne to his new home in Hill Street, he caught a cold, complicated by an attack of erysipelas. Prostrated by illness, his physician recommended that he go all the way to Egypt by sea to improve his health.

While the staff proceeded overland and most of the home-based units steamed out on August 1st, their commander quietly drove up to the Albert Docks the next day, bundled up as if it were the middle of winter. He boarded the *Calabria* which conveyed most of the Household Cavalry. The departure was kept secret to avoid last-minute visits. No less a personage than the Prince of Wales, who came to say goodbye, was forbidden to enter his sick room. No remedy could please Wolseley more, for he hated all the fuss associated with leave-taking, particularly at a time when illness rendered him so unsightly. By the time he arrived at Gibraltar, he had recovered his health completely and visited the governor, Lord Napier of Magdala.

The unexpected sea voyage afforded Wolseley the pleasure of Colonel Herbert Stewart's company; he was to be chief of staff of the cavalry division. By now, Stewart had become a favourite and close friend. How fortunate it was for England, reflected Wolseley, that Stewart's clergyman father had failed to discourage his son's martial bent. Indeed, it was a stroke of luck that he had chanced upon a somewhat forlorn captain on the line of communication while casually riding to Rorke's Drift.

A few hours' conversation that day were sufficient for Wolseley to judge his ability. Stewart might have departed from Zululand unnoticed, had not Wolseley telegraphed to stop him and appoint him as his military secretary. In the Sekukuni War that followed, Stewart impressed the Chief with his audacity, his common sense, his swift judgment, and his rare tact which fitted him for diplomatic service as well as soldiering. All these merits were combined with a charming manner that made him a delightful companion.

The *Calabria* made a stop at Malta so that Wolseley might be apprised of the latest developments. The news was not good. That 'clever ass', Arabi, had occupied Nefiche a couple of miles outside Ismailia, which Wolseley intended as his base. Fearing that Adye, who reached Alexandria before him, might be drawn to Ismailia to defend the Canal, thereby spoiling his plans, Wolseley telegraphed his chief of staff, ordering him to stay where he was and not to undertake any action until he arrived.

Wolseley's strategy was simple. To achieve his objective of taking Cairo and defeating the enemy as swiftly as possible, he decided to transfer his base to Ismailia. If he advanced from Alexandria, operating up the Nile Valley as Napoleon did, he would be forced to campaign in the highly cultivated Delta interlaced with countless irrigation ditches at a time of 'high Nile', which would afford an enormous advantage to the defence while inhibiting his own cavalry and artillery, or else move along the edge of the Western Desert with its treacherous soft sand. Taking the Delta in flank by marching west from Ismailia, placed the advancing army in a parallel line with a railway and a canal that would provide him with fresh water. Except for an occasional soft patch, the desert here was hard and firm. It was not merely the shortest distance to Cairo (96 as opposed to 127 miles), but also to the Egyptian main camp, Tel-el-Kebir, in the high open desert. Here he could administer the *coup de grâce* that would end the war.

To deceive Arabi and prevent his destroying the Suez Canal was vital to the success of this plan. After Alison, who had occupied Alexandria subsequent to the naval bombardment, moved forward and established his line on the ridge at Ramleh outside Alexandria, Wolseley directed him to worry Arabi into believing a full-scale attack on the Egyptian position was imminent upon his arrival.

Wolseley reached the new harbour of Alexandria, which had been built with English capital three years before, on the night of August 15th. Taking up his headquarters aboard H.M.S. *Salamis*, the general prepared orders to re-embark all the troops, except for a small holding force. The

305

next morning he conferred with Admiral Seymour, 'the Swell of the Ocean' as he was known throughout the navy, though most visitors on board his flagship could not quite understand the sobriquet, for the corpulent sailor usually went about in his shirt-sleeves. While the bushy-bearded Seymour mopped his neck and forehead with an enormous coloured kerchief, Wolseley revealed, almost in a whisper, his scheme to utilize his nation's superior amphibious strength by grabbing the Canal in one bold move and by secretly transferring the base of operations to Ismailia. To mislead Arabi, a feint would be made in the form of a supposed combined military and naval attack from the sea upon Aboukir Bay, Nelson's old battle-ground.

Once he had settled the details that would lay a sturdy foundation for a rapid advance to Cairo, Wolseley requested that as few naval officers as possible be made privy to the secret. Secrecy to prevent the Canal from being blocked and international complications from developing was so essential to success that neither Sir Edward Malet, the new High Commissioner, who as 'minister plenipotentiary' had precedence over both commanding officers, nor his generals (except Adye) were to be told of the fleet's true destination. Seymour promised his full co-operation.

Arrangements completed, Wolseley made for shore wondering how Caesar must have felt on his first visit to Alexandria. His uniform was more colourful than a toga: blue tunic, brown boots, gauntlets, a solar topee, and enormous black goggles. The High Commissioner took him to see the Khedive, who seemed a well-mannered young man, but the lengthy interview in French was difficult for Wolseley as he tried to avoid complicated idioms. Later he drove out to inspect the British position at Ramleh where he shook hands with the one-armed Alison, who thanked him for including the 1st Battalion of the Black Watch in the Highland Brigade, and the Duke of Connaught, who commanded a Brigade of Guards and was by now 'burnt as brown as a saddle'. Together, they rode about and took a long look at the enemy lines. Wolseley told his wife he acted the role of commander-in-chief in a way 'that would have done credit to Napoleon as he was crossing the Alps'.[5]

Keeping up the pretence of attacking at Aboukir Bay, Wolseley actually put the generals of 2nd Division, Hamley's, to work drawing up the necessary plans. Hamley and his two brigadiers, Alison and Wood, and their staffs, slaved over the elaborate details for co-operation with the advance of the rest of the army after they disembarked at Aboukir Bay. The chief was privately amused as he studied Hamley's programme for a frontal attack on the lines at Kafr Dowar in concert with his own 'flank attack'. Wolseley examined it carefully, made suggestions, and then with a grave air, endorsed it!

Noticing the great excitement his arrival created among the news-hungry correspondents, Wolseley hit on the idea of putting these pestiferous, often mischievous 'drones' to good use, as he did in the Ashanti War. 'The Press has become a power,' he told Lord Minto, 'which a man should try to manage for himself.' Knowing that the city was swarming with Arabi's spies, he employed the press as a medium of misinformation.

Suddenly, on August 17th, the chilling reserve towards the newsmen – regarding operations – maintained by the commander and his staff vanished. A staff officer ostentatiously announced to assembled correspondents that an attack on Aboukir Bay was in the offing which would be in keeping with Nelson's splendid victory of an earlier day. Censorship was removed and the press were invited to send the story to their papers. To mislead the enemy further, Major Tulloch, in charge of Intelligence, telegraphed to the *Standard* under the name of its correspondent to the effect that rumours respecting the occupation of the Canal by the English were false. De Lesseps, builder and president of the Company, with the support of the French Government had settled, he added, 'that the neutrality of the Canal shall be rigidly observed'.

While messengers were galloping to warn the Egyptian command of an attempt to force their position at Aboukir, the British soldiers boarded the transports. Once the 1st Division, Willis's, embarked, the fleet anchored outside the outer harbour. At noon on August 19th, the powerful squadron of eight ironclads guarding seventeen transports, formed in five lines and swept to the east in a long procession of smoke clouds. Hamley was left ashore clutching a sealed packet not to be opened until August 20th, which told him of the fleet's real destination and instructed him to keep the enemy busy with as much shell fire as possible.

It was an imposing sight as the English armada glided before the Aboukir forts to begin the simulated attack. The warships struck their top-masts in preparation for action, while the gunners in the forts stood by their guns, expecting a bombardment at any moment. Wolseley tried to persuade the admiral to deceive the enemy further by firing a few dummy shells. Seymour, however, refused to violate naval customs by making such an unorthodox demonstration.

After nightfall, some small craft moved close to shore and opened fire. At the same time, zealous but overly-credulous scribblers reported hearing 'the great bombardment'. The rest of the fleet, meanwhile, weighed anchor in the pale moonlight and flitted off for Port Said and the Canal. When day broke the Egyptian gunners found that the entire fleet had disappeared.

By the time the fleet steamed into Port Said shortly after sunrise, naval forces had taken command of the entire length of the Canal and all the main points on its shores in a quiet, workman-like manner. The nocturnal and surprise occupation of Port Said was so silent that sailors on board a French warship moored near by were in complete ignorance of what was being done. Sleeping Egyptian sentries were disarmed, and the entire garrison surrendered. A beardless, diminutive midshipman of fifteen took possession of the Company's telegraph-station to prevent any information from reaching the enemy.

Most of the foreign vessels moored in the eastern basin at Port Said remained mute as the stately file of English ships passed by. But when they got abreast of the Americans, 'they gave us such ringing sounds of applause,' wrote one soldier, 'that it seemed as if it would not have taken much to make them join us.'[6]

Wolseley's adroit, delicate, almost bloodless *ruse de guerre* was applauded in Britain. Childers was a little annoyed when he first heard of the move through his colleague at the Admiralty, who learned of it through Seymour; but he sent his heartiest congratulations. The Queen and the Duke added their felicitations, but questioned the unethical means of lying to the press. The newspapers, with few exceptions, quickly forgave a successful general. Hamley, sent on a fool's errand, never forgave.

Ismailia was a man-made oasis on the shore of Lake Timsah, which owed its origin to the construction of the Canal, being the shortest distance between it and Cairo. The sleepy little town, two miles from the great stream of Canal traffic, was suddenly galvanized into life when armed sailors landed at the port's one small pier and the warships bombarded the enemy at Nefiche into flight. Old Ferdinand de Lesseps, who had fêted Egyptian officers a few hours before and publicly declared he would kill with his own hand the first Englishman who dared to land at Ismailia, rushed down to the quay from his palatial residence. His moustache bristling with indignation, he shouted that the 'sacrés Anglais' would land over his dead body. A sailor pushed him aside, saying, 'We don't want no dead bodies about here, sir; all you've got to do is to step back a little.'[7] Resentful, he returned to his home and sullenly refused to have anything to do with Wolseley or his staff when they landed. The next day, the general paid a visit to his house. By now the old man had recovered his temper and received him cordially.

Wolseley and his staff took over the residence of the governor; and the palace, which the Empress Eugénie had occupied while presiding over the opening of the Canal, was soon converted into a hospital. A few natives who had not fled when the shooting began, squatted on the flat roofs or stood passively at the doorways of their parched homes and watched them file by. Most of the soldiers marched dressed in red tunics and Indian mud-coloured helmets, stained to prevent their becoming conspicuous under the bright sun. Every man had his hair cut as short as possible before landing, and most were issued with a pair of dark spectacles and green or blue veils, though many refused to wear them. The troopers had had their swords ground on board; blade, hilt, and scabbard were browned by burning to prevent their glaring in the desert.

The only source of water for the perspiring army about to advance from Ismailia was the Sweetwater Canal. Originally constructed by De Lesseps to bring water from the Nile for labourers on the Suez, it soon served as nourishment for much of the desert and as an artery of traffic. By August 23rd the water began to shrink rapidly. It was soon learned that the Egyptians had constructed a dam and torn up part of the track at Magfar, six miles towards Cairo. A fresh water supply being of 'paramount importance', Wolseley was forced to move forward sooner than he wished; if Fortune smiled on him, he might capture some rolling-stock while moving to demolish the dam. No serious opposition to 'a strong reconnaissance' was expected, for the enemy was assumed to have few men this side of Tel-el-Kebir, thirty miles away.

Before daylight, on the morning of August 24th, Wolseley gathered what cavalry and artillery were available, namely the Household Cavalry and two guns, and moved off to Nefiche where at daylight Brigadier Gerald Graham marched in support with a thousand soldiers and marines, and a company of mounted infantry. The entire party was under the command of Willis, though Wolseley and some of his staff, distinguishable by the pink scarf on their helmets, rode forward with the cavalry, so that the Chief might see for himself what was in front. He expected to ride back for breakfast.

The cavalry under Drury Lowe reached the dam at seven-thirty and drove in enemy skirmishers. The Household Cavalry, enormous bipeds and quadrupeds, were an awesome sight as they charged forward. Wolseley proudly reported to the Duke how in some instances these great, grimy, semi-bearded giants 'with their heavy swords cut men from the head to the waistbelt'.[8] The few prisoners who were taken told of a second dam and a large body of infantry a few thousand yards beyond, at

Tel-el-Mahuta, the spot where Pharaoh ordered that the 'chosen people' should make bricks without straw. (It was generally believed that the British were entering Egypt along the same line that Moses led the Jews in their exodus.)

At Tel-el-Mahuta, Wolseley had to decide whether he, too, should try to make 'bricks without straw'. Ahead were great lofty mounds of sand dotted with many dark figures, 'while to the right and left of them a long, open line of Arab camel-men and horsemen stretched along the skyline far into the desert on either flank'.[9] Behind them were great columns of black smoke rising into the thin, clear desert air, indicating reinforcements from Tel-el-Kebir. For some time the general carefully watched through his telescope as soldiers in dazzling white tunics, wide drill trousers, linen gaiters, and red fezes detrained, formed up and marched forward hugging their rifles. There was no doubt that the enemy, numbering nearly 9,000 with several field guns, were determined to make a stand. In the face of such great odds, should he fight an advance-guard action until reinforcements could be brought up in seven or eight hours, or retire?

Wolseley decided to gamble. The very smallness of his force might tempt the Egyptian commander, Rashid Pasha, to engage him until more British troops could be rushed up to inflict a crushing defeat that might secure for him the Sweetwater Canal and the railway all the way to Kassassin; beyond which point the enemy was not likely to cut the canal because of the nature of the terrain and possible damage to cultivated land. In addition, there was a psychological advantage that a successful first encounter gave the victor. Considerable risk was involved in the decision, for men and horses, recently landed, would be required to undergo the severe strain of racing with short provisions across deep sand during the heat of an August day.

Looking over his shoulder, Wolseley watched his officers gallop back towards Nefiche to hurry up the Duke of Cornwall's Light Infantry, and bring up the Guards Brigade and whatever other military odds and ends of the three arms had already left the transports. And on the horizon, the general saw a long cloud of dust billowing over the sandy plains, showing that a force, Graham's puffing men, was moving up from Magfar to take a position with their left resting on the Sweetwater Canal, near the first dam, and their right extending out into the desert. Echeloned further to the right were the marines, and beyond them, about a mile from the canal, were the cavalry and mounted infantry, alert to any effort by the 'Gypies' to turn the British right. The two guns were placed under the shoulder of a sandhill, between the marines and Graham's half-battalion.

On a hillock above the gun position stood Wolseley, Willis, and their staffs waiting for the enemy to make his move.

A little past nine a.m., the Egyptians – cavalry, infantry, and artillery – moved down cautiously from the high ground they held and began to spar with the British. First contact was made with Graham's well-protected infantry near the canal; but the bark of their Martinis was so menacing, they dared not come too close. The Egyptians, however, continued to move forward and extend towards the right until checked by the accurate firing of the dismounted mounted infantry, every man of which was a chosen sharp-shooter. Their conduct that day afforded Wolseley a great deal of satisfaction. For years he had tried to persuade traditionalists that an army possessing mounted infantry, provided their leaders knew how to use and handle them, 'will have an enormous advantage over an army that adheres exclusively to the stereotyped employment of cavalry, infantry, and artillery'.[10] If only Colley, he mused, had had them with him in the Transvaal.

Wolseley's thoughts were sharply brought back to Egypt by a bronze rifled muzzle-loader. With surprising accuracy, a shell passed only a few feet over his head and burst among the horses behind, killing one of them. The Chief ordered all the horses, a conspicuous target, to be withdrawn behind the hill. Four enemy guns, served with considerable skill, continued to drop shells among the 'brains of the army' until the horses were out of sight. But no further damage was done, for the enemy shells, fitted with percussion fuses, buried themselves deep in the sand before exploding.

Wolseley never seemed more calm or boyishly light-hearted. Feeling that his serene, visible presence was reassuring to the men, he rejected the remonstrances of his staff at least to get out of the full sun. The men all along the line had no difficulty distinguishing the general, for the flat faces of his scabbard reflected the rays of the sun like a heliograph.

The horses out of sight, the enemy guns – now numbering six – shifted to the better target of mounted infantry and cavalry on the hard gravelly flats. At first, Wolseley refused to allow his guns to reply at such great range, hoping to conceal them until the enemy came closer than 1,000 yards. As enemy shells fell with greater accuracy, cavalry and mounted infantry were ordered to fall back. Finally, at ten-thirty, deciding it would be foolish to wait any longer, Wolseley had his pair of guns open up with two rounds of shrapnel which burst directly over the Egyptian artillery. An artillery duel commenced, which became unequal as an Egyptian flanking battery of six fresh Krupp guns were wheeled into an enfilading position on the English extreme right. The enemy guns were supported by considerable numbers of cavalry and infantry. 'What has Arabi got behind the desert ridge?' asked Butler. 'What if the Egyptian puts another ten or twelve thousand men and a couple of brisk batteries on our flank?'[11]

None too soon, a party of bluejackets from the ship *Orion* came up with two Gatlings. Willis made the dispositions to give them maximum protection while replying to the enemy's flanking fire. The gunners' unflagging energy and the firm front presented by the whole of Wolseley's little army seemed to deprive the enemy of resolution. They remained content to continue the duel at some distance. All the while, Wolseley was winning the battle for time. By early afternoon the Duke of Cornwall's Light Infantry had come up to be placed in reserve.

More men dropped under the unremitting Egyptian sun than were laid low by Egyptian fire. The heat came down with terrible force, 'hotter than the furnace of Nebuchadnezzar'. Sunshine was in the very air they breathed. Systematically, water was brought up from the canal and poured over those who fell from exhaustion.

Prince Arthur and the Brigade of Guards, dressed in flannel shirts and needlessly warm woollen trousers, rushed up from Ismailia in the stifling heat. Normally, the English would cheat the scorching sun with sunrise or sunset marches, but there was no time. Though ankle-deep sand burned their feet, and man after man 'was knocked down by the severity of the strain, and by the stroke of the sun', wrote Maurice in his official history, 'all who were physically able pushed on with honest pride and steady discipline'.[12]

General Willis, standing next to Sir Garnet, was one of a half-hundred who collapsed from sunstroke that day before Tel-el-Mahuta. The Chief managed to keep on his feet, but the strong glare from the sand burned the skin from his nose. And he found it impossible to sit for more than a few minutes without baking his posterior.

The sun overhead grew more fierce; enemy guns kept multiplying and shells dropped faster and closer. But the Chief never lost his composure. He had a good word for all who approached him, a keen eye for events to front and flank, and a quick way of judging the officers about him. Willis, for one, he set down as an old woman wanting in nerve. Butler, who had never admired his Chief more, declared 'he personified more than any man I had ever seen the best type of soldier.'[13]

In mid afternoon, when the Egyptians began to press both flanks a little harder, Wolseley told Butler to mount and ride with him to have a closer look at what was happening on the right. Half-way there, when they were concealed from the view of their own men by a sand dune – though still in full sight of the enemy who tried to reach them with their bullets – Wolseley reined up and turned to Butler saying, 'I cannot stand the pain of this leg of mine any longer, the London bootmaker has made the leg of my right boot so tight that when I was dragging it on in the dark this morning the riding breeches got so wedged and crumpled upon the calf of the leg that its pressure has been intolerable for some time past. Can you get it right for me?'[14]

They dismounted and Butler removed the boot and slit the leather. As they rode on, the big Irishman wondered why the Chief waited for such an inopportune moment for him to perform this little service. Then it occurred to him that Wolseley did not want his men to see him 'down', for at a distance, it might seem to them that a surgeon was preparing to amputate the general's leg. Wolseley would rather keep the pain to himself for hours than spread a false and mischievous rumour through the army.

On reaching the cavalry, they saw a shell drop among them and kill a horse. The trooper was on his feet instantly, shouting, 'Three cheers for the first charger in the Life Guards killed since Waterloo!'

Enemy cavalry and guns began to move forward in force as if to attack the right flank. Then they hesitated. The appearance of 350 fresh sabres from Ismailia under Baker Russell, with McCalmont by his side, seemed to have changed their minds. By six, the Duke of Connaught and the Guards arrived. The Egyptians retired to their entrenchments. They had waited too long and lost their chance to destroy Wolseley's small force.

Since it was too late for the English to undertake an offensive movement, Wolseley ordered Willis to prepare for an attack at daybreak; though, because of superstition, he found it highly distasteful to undertake a battle on a Friday. Before returning to Ismailia, the commander-in-chief spent the remaining moments of daylight visiting each of the positions, thanking the men and telling them that few troops had ever stood up to such great odds.

Long before sunrise, August 25th, Wolseley and his staff were in the saddle on the way back to Tel-el-Mahuta. He came up in time to see his troops, after a chilly night sleeping on the sand, move forward in attack formation. They found, to their disappointment, the enemy positions abandoned and the guns withdrawn. It was soon evident, however, that the Egyptians had not fallen back very far.

Wolseley had a plan. He would pivot his force, with the left fixed on the canal near the dam, by swinging his mounted right in a great arc into the desert, and then bring it down on the canal far to the rear so as to cut off the Egyptian retreat. If successful, he might bag the entire enemy force, guns and all.

The Egyptians fired only a few rounds at Graham's men before perceiving the British cavalry moving far out around their flank. They limbered up their guns and boarded their trains without further pause. When Wolseley and staff rode up to the high ridge from which the enemy guns had pounded them the day before, they saw the dust kicked up by retreating men and horses, and several trains chugging up the valley to their left. The Chief called to Butler and gave him a verbal order: 'Gallop to Drury Lowe, tell him to take all his cavalry and Horse Artillery forward and *coûte que coûte* capture one or more of those trains. An engine would be worth a lot of money to me now.'[15] Wolseley kept sending messenger after messenger to hurry the movement of the cavalry on to Mahsama station, some ten miles beyond.

'I have never seen him so eager or so bent upon anything in my life,' observed Maurice.[16] The movement was tardy, for the horses were pumped by the long sea voyage and the fatiguing manœuvres of the previous day. Disgusted, Wolseley remarked, 'There is not at this time in the whole of the cavalry brigade a troop that can gallop.' Nevertheless, the mounted force reached the station at Mahsama in time to seize a fair amount of guns and supplies. There was some show of resistance. While the Horse Artillery took on a battery of seven Krupp guns near the station, Drury Lowe moved to the rear of the enemy camp where a hurriedly formed line of infantry took a stand. They had time to fire but one volley, emptying twenty saddles, before the British troopers had 'a good smack at them' and cut them up in all directions as they threw away their guns and fled for their lives. Numbers who tried to cross the canal 'were picked off like rats'. A body of enemy cavalry drew up in line as if to lunge at the flank of the British troopers; but when the Life Guards wheeled around in their direction, the Egyptians galloped off to safety. It was impossible to overtake the small Egyptian horses accustomed to the climate and country. Equally frustrating was an attempt by Dragoons on panting horses to overtake the last train that hastily departed on their arrival. They fired at the driver but he ducked low and escaped their bullets.

The action at Mahsama was a great success. Seven Krupp guns, large quantities of rifles and ammunition, seventy-five railway carriages laden with supplies and other stores were taken at a cost of five killed and twenty-five wounded. At first, Drury Lowe was ordered to destroy what he could, for it would be some time before infantry could be brought up and his force supplied. However, now that the food problem was solved, Willis ordered them to remain while Graham marched his brigade by moonlight to support the anxious cavalry commander. After dining on Egyptian corn and biscuits, the men slept well that night under captured tents or in railway coaches with sheets and cushions.

After twelve hours in the saddle, Wolseley returned to Ismailia. His last order of the day was to occupy Kassassin lock two and a half miles west of Mahsama, which Stewart on reconnaissance learned had been evacuated. Graham's battalions occupied the advanced point late the next day and the Dragoons were withdrawn to Mahsama. With the lock in his possession, Wolseley had complete control of the water in the upper reaches of the canal – 'no small advantage', commented one observer, 'to an army worked like his on strictly temperance principles.'[17]

Thus by August 26th, fully a week before he expected, Wolseley held the canal, railway, and telegraph lines as far as Kassassin, nine miles from Tel-el-Kebir. This was accomplished despite limited facilities for landing and by marching across the desert in the hottest season of the year. Some additional effort was required, however, to remove the dams. The Egyptian fellah may not have known how to fight well, but he knew how to construct a dam. Moreover, it seemed that Arabi's men had 'played hanky-panky with the canal' before retiring. Dead bodies of men and horses were found floating in the water beyond Mahsama. Decomposing in the great heat, they tainted the air. None the less, thirsting men frequently drank the unwholesome beverage – to which they later attributed all sorts of ailments.

The British paid a price for their successes at Tel-el-Mahuta and Mahsama: they had completely outmarched their commissariat. Graham's hungry men, weakened under the sun by the heavy labour of removing dams and digging entrenchments, had to endure a great amount of discomfort. It was an excellent opportunity for the enemy to attack – and they did.

Arabi himself came out on the morning of August 28th with some 12,000 men and a dozen guns, hoping his presence would give them courage to drive back the invaders at Kassassin. Boldly they advanced upon Graham's strong defensive position astride the canal and then waited out of range of rifle fire. An ailing Graham, suffering severely from lumbago, and able to carry on only because of morphine injections, turned out his troops and signalled to Drury Lowe, who galloped up from Mahsama. Throughout the heat of the day, the troopers, mounted and fanned out, waited for the enemy 'to try conclusions'. For hours the men were exposed to the sun but not to enemy fire, for the distant Egyptian artillery was ineffectual. At three p.m. it was reported the Egyptians were retiring. The weary cavalry went back to camp to eat a meagre evening meal.

Supper was interrupted, for the dawdling Egyptians found their courage at four-thirty, an hour and a half before sunset. A strange time to begin a battle. Making skilful new dispositions to meet the attack, Graham placed his right flank so as to tempt the enemy into an assault where Lowe's cavalry, which was alerted once more, could teach Arabi a painful lesson. When the Egyptians, reinforced by a train with men and artillery (their most powerful arm), pressed forward and seemed ready to take the bait, the veteran Graham sent a young aide-de-camp with specific orders to Lowe: 'Take the cavalry round by our right, under cover of the hill, and attack the left flank of the enemy skirmishers.' Passing to the rear, the impressionable messenger, experiencing his first battle, was infected by some of the rumour and panic spread by less worthy members of the force, a type that is usually to be found behind the battle-area. Graham dispatched one message and Lowe received another, for the excited lieutenant added to Graham's words by saying he 'was only just able to hold his own!'

Wolseley was startled out of his bed by the 'jumpy message' which was relayed by Willis from Tel-el-Mahuta. Willis feared Graham had been defeated and believed the enemy was advancing on Mahsama. He promised to do all he could to hold on, but begged for all available reinforcements. Knowing the imperturbable Graham, with whom he had served in China, and the supreme confidence he had in his men, Wolseley curtly dismissed the request with the comment, 'Willis is a very plucky fellow personally but an alarmist.' The general, nevertheless, decided to dress and ride to Kassassin to look into the matter.

Wolseley's belief in Graham was not misplaced. At seven-fifteen p.m., Graham, assuming the cavalry charge was at hand which would protect his flank, ordered a general advance which compelled the retirement of the enemy. The tired troopers, however, were a little late in getting started and arrived only in time to hasten the retreat. Their attack being delivered in the moonlight, the cavalry used the evening star and the flash of guns as guides. The enemy, surprised by the great dark horses, received them with rifle and shell fire, most of which passed over English heads because of the difficulty of judging distances at night. To get their own guns into action, Baker Russell ordered the 7th Dragoon

Guards to wheel outward so as to allow the four guns of the Royal Horse Artillery to come up. After firing several rounds, the guns in turn made way for the Household Cavalry, led by Baker Russell. Forgetting their fatigue, they responded instantly to his thunderous cry of 'Charge!' With trumpets sounding in their ears and the horses wild with excitement, they came forward in great black waves. The enemy was scattered by swinging blades and heavy horses, many falling on their faces to avoid being slashed. Conspicuous with his white jacket reflecting moonlight was Baker Russell. His horse was shot under him, but 'he laid well about him, killing two or three of the enemy'. According to the official report the cavalry were supposed to have overrun a battery of nine guns, but none could be found the next day. Actually, they never reached the Egyptian batteries, which is understandable, for in the dark it was difficult to distinguish friend from foe. By eight-forty-five Graham ordered a general return to camp.

Wolseley himself, before leaving Ismailia, learned of the brilliant success from the correspondent of the *Daily Telegraph* who called on his way to the telegraph-office. Thanking God, the Chief rode to Graham's camp which he reached at sunrise. He visited his wounded, of which there were eighty, asking how many of the 'Gypies' each had killed. Baker Russell, whom he had made a brigadier a few days before, complained of a sore arm after cutting down so many of the enemy.

Always ready to admit an error in judgment, Wolseley publicly praised the conduct of the Household Cavalry. They proved they could do something more than keep up with the Queen's carriage. With little modesty, he wrote his wife: 'They will probably owe the continuance of their existence to my bringing them here and pushing them well to the front.'[18] His compliments about the Household Cavalry were repeated to the Duke, but Cambridge was furious when he learned that Sir Garnet had made Baker Russell a brigadier. Wolseley let the Duke's words of anger pass without reply, but he told Loo: 'I have quite enough big difficulties here without having to fight little difficulties raised by H.R.H. When it can be said that I have appointed a bad man to an office, it will be time to find fault with my selections.'[19]

The biggest difficulty was still that of transport. Having seized the most practicable advanced post, Wolseley's plan was to hold it and the line of communications until sufficient supplies and men could be accumulated at Kassassin for the final thrust. After the initial chaos of landing, there was the problem of overland transportation. From time immemorial, the Egyptians had used pack animals in the desert. A well-organized mule-train would have maintained a steady flow of supplies moving to the front, yet little concern was shown as to where baggage animals could be procured. Wolseley had relied on his last week in England to make final transport arrangements; but being unfit for work at the time, he left the matter largely to Adye, who regarded such matters as of little consequence. Foolishly, Adye depended on Turkey as his chief source of supply. The Sultan, however, hoping to delay the English, placed an embargo on the exportation of animals until the war was virtually over. Other beasts obtained in Spain and Italy arrived too late.* A few mules were sent from Cyprus in time to be of great value; and the Indian troops, fortunately, brought 2,500 mules of their own. Even then it took time and effort to organize them into an efficient train. 'I have all along said,' Wolseley wrote to his wife, 'that picking up hundreds or thousands of mules did not constitute a transport. The drivers whom we obtain are the *canaille* of Levantine towns, and we really have no authority over them. To buy a canvas and a paint-box is not to have a picture.'[20]

The army had to rely almost entirely upon the canal and railway. Once the obstacles were removed, the steam launches, tow-cutters, and locomotives (arriving at the beginning of September) began to make considerable headway.

The lull in military operations tried the nation's patience. The rapidity of the advance to Kassassin led many to assume that the Egyptian army had been completely routed and the way was open for the final drive to Cairo. The disappointed and ill-informed criticized the 'sloth' and 'torpor', and sarcastically asked whether the army had gone to sleep. Soon there were rumours to the effect that the transport had broken down entirely and that Sir Garnet could not move because of the impossibility of feeding his army. The average civilian, though able to master the strategy, failed to understand how movements in war are rigidly regulated by supply and communications. For every day of fighting there are weeks of preparation and marching. This twelve-day interval of quiet, though the least showy, was, according to Maurice, the most important and 'represented the period of hardest work during the campaign'.

A carping press and an impatient Parliament could not make Sir Garnet move any sooner than he intended. Even Childers, more sensitive to public pressure, failed to stir the general with broad hints about the Government's embarrassment. Wolseley's steadfast refusal to strike a

---

* Mules were ordered from as far away as the United States, though there were reports of Fenian plots 'to blow with dynamite these representations of the corrupting influence of British gold'.

blow until preparations were completed, marked him as a great soldier.

At the end of August, an exotic flavour was added to the army as the Indian contingent, with Sikh lancers, Pathan mountaineers, Baluchi zouaves, and Oudh sepoys, collected around Ismailia. Wolseley was delighted to find his brother, Colonel George Wolseley, among them. At the same time Alison's Highland Brigade, under Hamley, was brought to Ismailia from Alexandria, leaving Wood with his brigade to watch the lines at Kafr Dowar. Wood was greatly disappointed at being left out of the 'big fight', and Hamley regarded it as a slight that half of his force should remain behind. He protested bitterly to his superiors.

No one wanted Wood and his men at Ismailia more than Wolseley. Their absence meant a 'sad weakening' of his force, but he dared not leave Alexandria unprotected. It was one of the many evils, he claimed, 'occasioned by that silly and criminal bombardment of Alexandria, which Lord Northbrook and the Admiralty concocted'.[21]

Arabi was no Nasser. He was neither dynamic nor resourceful. Why Arabi did not make a more determined attempt to harass traffic on the Suez Canal, or destroy the newly-laid pipes conveying fresh water from Ismailia to Port Said, or at least engage in guerrilla tactics along the sensitive supply line to Kassassin, were questions many British officers asked one another. When Arabi did take the initiative, he attacked at the wrong time and at the wrong place – Kassassin, September 9th. This was a result of misinformation supplied to him by Bedouin scouts who had assured him that Graham's force was still very small, and then lied about having cut communications between Kassassin and Ismailia, producing a few cattle that had strayed from the British camp to prove it. Actually there were 8,000 men at Kassassin, with the Guards, a battery, and a regiment of cavalry within reinforcing distance.

At dawn the Egyptians moved out to smash the advance force. They approached in two columns, one from Tel-el-Kebir and the other across the desert from Saliheen on the north. Together, they included nearly eighteen battalions of Arabi's best infantry, thirty guns, and a large body of mounted men.

Under cover of heavy, though relatively harmless artillery fire, the Egyptians came forward with some spirit and drove in the British outposts. However, the firm attitude and determined fire of the British infantry and artillery, far larger than was anticipated, checked the Egyptian advance; and the sight of Drury Lowe's cavalry driving forward, wedge-like, and threatening the inward flanks of the two moving columns cooled their ardour. And when the British took the offensive, they fell back. The repulse became a rout. Foot soldiers took off their boots to run faster and riders pushed the saddles off their camels so as to lighten them in flight. The pursuit continued to just outside the range of the big guns at Tel-el-Kebir.

The British might have taken Tel-el-Kebir that day. But Sir Garnet wanted a crushing victory at this desert fortification, one that would place him in a position to profit from his success and advance directly upon Cairo with his cavalry. A premature blow might give Arabi the chance to defend the capital, or at least burn it, for only a short time before the rebel leader had declared he would destroy the city in the event of his being defeated in the field.

Arriving at Kassassin shortly before noon, Wolseley looked over the situation carefully and then ordered his army back to camp. All about him he heard humorous cuts at the Egyptians and the customs of their country.* There was also some grumbling, even among distinguished officers, who were eager to rush right on into Tel-el-Kebir. A sector of the press took up the complaint and wailed about Sir Garnet's failure to push his advantage. To their way of thinking, he was 'floundering the desert, without plan or objective'. They predicted, almost enthusiastically, his ultimate failure.

While the army was drawing strength from Ismailia daily, Sir Garnet was up before daybreak each day to ride out and have a closer look at Tel-el-Kebir, nine miles away. Often he was accompanied by his brother George. Together they rode over a flat, open plain, absolutely devoid of trees and without marked undulations. To the soldier's eye, this land of colourless sterility offered neither cover nor shelter. Entrenched troops would have an enormous advantage.

With a telescope screwed to his good eye, Wolseley surveyed Tel-el-Kebir, 'the big hill'. He saw the great earthworks on which large bodies of fellahin had laboured for months. The gravelly sand parapets, taller than a guardsman in bearskin head-dress, were faced with a ditch averaging six feet in depth and ten feet in width, and stretched from the Sweetwater Canal into the desert for nearly four miles. At carefully selected intervals, there were well-made redoubts whose salient position gave them a wide command of either flank. Behind these defences, nearly two miles in depth, were the interior works of shelter trenches, rifle-pits, and more artillery crowning points of natural elevation. Arabi's fieldworks, where

* This contempt for foreigners, their customs, and even the very food they ate, was not uncommon among the British. Wolseley liked to tell the story of a British general before Cadiz, who excited the fighting spirit of his men by saying: 'You Englishmen, who are fed upon beef, don't surely mean to be beaten by a d——d lot of Spaniards who live on oranges.'

work was still in progress, were not uniform in strength, and towards the north they dwindled in size. This position, according to spies and prisoners, was held by some 20,000 regulars, supported by 6,000 Bedouin and irregulars, 2,500 cavalry, and 60 guns.

The Oriental was credited with fighting stubbornly behind entrenchments, and Arabi boasted that his men would be invincible behind these lines. But Wolseley was not so foolish as to have his vastly inferior force storm entrenchments up an inclined plain that offered no concealment from heavy guns or high-powered rifles. Yet, to attempt to turn the enemy's position, either on the left or right, would entail a long and tedious march on the hot desert. And what was more significant, he might fail in his object – to come to grips with the Egyptians at such close quarters that they could not shake themselves free except by a general engagement with all their army. Surprise is the essence of war; and when Wolseley learned from his frequent rides forward that Arabi kept a very bad look-out, he resolved to attack without warning precisely at dawn after marching his men under the cover of darkness over the cool, featureless ground.

On the morning of September 12th, all the generals with one staff officer each met Sir Garnet atop the Ninth Hill outside the Kassassin camp. The Chief then led them out a few miles towards the enemy's works. Here they were grouped for some little time watching for the first sign of dawn. Shortly after that moment arrived, mounted sentinels were seen emerging from behind the earthworks. 'Note the time!' said the Chief breaking silence. It was five-forty-five. 'Our attack must be delivered before this hour tomorrow morning,' he continued, 'otherwise those vedettes will detect our presence.'[22]

To the circle of generals about him, Sir Garnet then explained his matured plan for hurling his force of 11,000 bayonets, 2,000 sabres, 61 guns, and 6 machine-guns against the strongest part of the line at daybreak on September 13th. On the left, just north of the canal, he would place Hamley's men, with the Highland Brigade in front and the composite brigade behind. To the right would be Willis's men, with Graham's brigade leading and Prince Arthur and the Guards to the rear. Between the two divisions, Wolseley put Goodenough's artillery with forty-two guns. The artillery, less likely to go astray, would act as a guide between the infantry divisions during the night march and help prevent the possibility of their stumbling or firing upon one another. And should any of the British panic after the attack was delivered, the position of the guns would prevent it from spreading along the entire line. It was a pivot on which either flank might rely in case of reverse. The guns would be in an ideal position to cover a retreat – or exploit a success.

The Indian Brigade under MacPherson would come up on the south side of the canal fully an hour after the main body so as not to disturb the villagers along the cultivated belt who might spread the alarm before the main party was ready to attack. On a level with and supporting Mac-Pherson's men would be the Naval Brigade, moving along the railway upon which they had already placed a truck carrying a 40-pounder. To the rear of the extreme right flank, Wolseley placed the mounted men and two batteries of Horse Artillery which were to circle round the enemy left after daylight so as to threaten the defenders from the rear and pursue them once they had abandoned their entrenchments.

The army was to march in the order it was to fight in. To manoeuvre about before the enemy position was out of the question. However, Wolseley left the exact formation to his division commanders' discretion. Thus, Hamley's men advanced in half-battalions in double company columns at deploying intervals, while Willis's marched in the drill-book formation of half-battalions in colums of companies:

Hamley's 2nd Division           Willis's 1st Division

—  —     —  —          —     —

—  —     —  —          —     —

                                    —     —

                                    —     —

'Well, gentlemen,' the Chief concluded, 'don't talk about it until the orders are issued. I wish you all luck.'[23] The officers saluted, mounted their horses and rode off. There was neither debate nor discussion; Wolseley's words were clear and final. But the commander sensed misgivings, even objections. All knew as well as he that there were elements of uncertainty about a night attack that could not be foreseen or provided for. Soldiers are rarely steady at night ... they can lose their way ... they are prone to panic. The long-faced Adye obviously thought it too bold an experiment. Maurice, the historian, remembered how the cry of an animal encountered at night had roused defenders to danger in the past, such as the celebrated cackling geese who warned the Romans of the approach of the Gauls on their capital. Buller, in his long career as a soldier, could not recall a single campaign where Englishmen did not fire on Englishmen – in the daytime! Drury Lowe was reminded of those terrible panics that turned into a general stampede during the long weird nights in Zululand. Wolseley himself reminisced back to that night in Oudh when a soldier was frightened into loud screams by a snake crawling over his bed. In the madness that followed, a colonel had a terrific encounter with a tree, and another fancied his own leg to be part of a murderous sepoy and shot himself; the normally sedate Sir Hope Grant seized Wolseley's sword and began to brandish it wildly. Wolseley often remarked that while a night march could be the most deadly, it could also be the most difficult of military operations.

Nothing had been done to prepare the British soldier for marching at night since Peninsular days. Yet Wolseley was confident that he had brave, well-disciplined troops, led by reliable officers and directed by an excellent staff, that could bring it off. And like every great captain, Wolseley was capable of conjuring up the blending phases of a proposed battle in his mind's eye, for he possessed a complete appreciation of the ground and understood the habits and reactions of his adversary. Having imagined himself in Arabi's place and carefully weighed every contingency, Wolseley did not hesitate to assume the great responsibility. As Von Moltke advised, 'First ponder, then dare.'

Not until three p.m. were the men told they were to move out that evening to attack the Egyptian stronghold. The camp soon presented an animated scene as gangs of men set to work. Large bodies from each unit gathered round the commissariat stores to collect the hundred rounds of ammunition and two days' rations that were to be carried by each man. As they laboured, there was a general feeling of relief that the period of inactivity and hardship was about to end, and that the time of Arabi's defeat was close at hand. The current camp joke was about the Egyptian officers; each knew *he* would run, but hoped his neighbour would stay and fight. Riding about the camp, dropping words of cheer, was Sir Garnet himself. He admired their spirit. They never looked better or healthier, though the people at home would scarcely recognize them in their rough loose jackets, full of dust and spotted with mud, and their beards beginning to sprout in a most unattractive manner.

To deceive the spies and enemy scouts, the long rows of tents did not come down until dusk. Then they were packed and carried along with other baggage to the railway embankment. All camp fires were left burning and no bugles were sounded as each unit marched off.

The first march was a short one to the area of the Ninth Hill above the

camp. Serried rows of men were told to lie down near the line of telegraph-poles that ran west for 1,000 yards. They had been planted by the
engineers to orient the army in the right direction when the time came to
march on Tel-el-Kebir. Some tried to snatch a little sleep on the bare sand;
others stole a forbidden smoke under their helmets. Some talked quietly.
A few grumbled over the rigid inspection by the officers to see that no
loose cartridges were carried outside their pouches, for it was Sir Garnet's
scheme to rush Arabi's trenches at the point of a bayonet without firing
a shot. It was to be a shock battle such as Wellington fought in Spain.
The more knowing among the privates denounced this 'foolish order' – a
man should have a round handy with which to defend himself. But Wolseley was not going to risk the success of his venture by allowing some
frightened soldier the chance to bang off a shot into the dark at some
imaginary enemy along the line of march.

The Chief did not rest until all the men found, sometimes with difficulty, their allotted resting-place in this world of shadows. Lying down,
Wolseley prayed for success. He admitted to no one but himself that he
was deeply concerned about the outcome of the battle. His reforms were
soon to be tested. Would his confidence in the short-service system, which
he had so vehemently and uncompromisingly advocated, be vindicated?
How his enemies would delight in his failure! Even his friends might
brand him a fool for having attempted something so novel as a night
attack. Wolseley listened to the low hum of voices about him. A staff
officer who was near by, noticed a sad look come over his thoughtful
features. No doubt the Chief wondered how many of these same men
would be alive in a few hours.

Soon all was quiet, and the commander and most of his men slept.

After one o'clock the whispered and electric 'Fall in' was heard. Much
depended upon a good start. After a little confusion, the two divisions
started simultaneously. With a sense of suppressed excitement an army
of ghosts plodded quietly into the Egyptian night. The silence was
occasionally broken by the neighing of a horse, or, as men stumbled, by
muffled ejaculations which were rarely prayerful. All orders were given
in lowered tones and the quiet was strictly enforced. Between the shadowy
lines of the leading brigades and those behind were a series of connecting
files established by Sir Garnet to keep contact and order in the moonless
dark.

The Chief, who had diligently checked the distance beforehand as well
as the precise rate of the march, was assisted by an excellent repeater
watch given him by Lord Airy. By striking the watch, he could learn the

exact time. To Butler, riding beside him, the striking of the ever-longer numbers by this unique instrument 'seemed to draw into tighter twists all the strands of our expectations'.[24]

Piloting the army like a ship at sea was Lieutenant Rawson of the Royal Navy, who steered by the stars, for there was no luminous compass until three years later. Rawson was a native of Canada. And by a strange coincidence, it was on this same night, over a hundred years before, that Wolfe, swathing his army in darkness before Quebec, surprised and defeated the French in the morning. Like Wolfe, Rawson was to die with a bullet in his lung.

There were frequent halts to correct the direction and maintain touch, for despite the vigilance of the officers, especially Sir Garnet and his staff, the formation began to lose shape. A disastrous collision nearly resulted when the rumour of 'enemy horseman in front' caused the centre of the Highland Brigade to hesitate while the wings, failing to hear the whispered warning, began to wheel inward until the dark figures almost faced one another. Unable to distinguish friend from foe, a fatal encounter was in the making. Fortunately, the rifles were not loaded. Alert officers quickly restored order. The rumour was undoubtedly the result of the tendency to exaggerate the sound of the few horses ridden by the commander and his staff, who more than once provoked a nervous challenge from soldiers who believed they might be Bedouin stealing upon them.

The discipline of the men was excellent. But after the final halt of nearly an hour, at three a.m., everyone grew more tense. The night seemed darker and more foreboding than ever. Without warning the deep silence was shattered by 'a peal of wild hilarious laughter' that rang out across the velvet surface of the desert. The offender who jeopardized the safety of the army was seized, bound and chloroformed into quiescence. It turned out to be the paroxysms of a Highlander who had filled his canteen with rum instead of cold tea, which the commander had recommended. No evidence has been found to support the story that Wolseley ordered the hysterical Scot to be bayoneted on the spot.

To Butler, philosopher and poet, it was the mocking sound of an ancient desert and even older stars which had seen greater conquerors – Pharaohs, Moses, Napoleon, and a man leading an ass on which a young woman rode cradling a child in her arms.

Riding some distance ahead of the phantom pageant, until he reached what he believed to be a point only a few hundred yards from the enemy lines, the new conqueror of Egypt dismounted to await developments.

Looking behind him to the east, the commander was jarred by a pale shaft of light – the harbinger of dawn. Striking his watch in disbelief, Wolseley learned it was not quite four-fifty a.m., nearly an hour before sunrise. How could that accursed instrument be so wrong? If sunrise was so close at hand, the attack would surely be too late. While he and his staff struggled to see the hands of their timepieces, the light began to fade. Not until after the campaign did Wolseley discover that the strange light that heralded their attack was the tail of a comet whose nucleus lay below the horizon. Wolseley always reproached himself for not having made a more thorough search for astronomical information before undertaking the campaign.

Battles rarely develop as planned. When the sombre lines closed on Arabi's bulwark of sand, they were far from perfect. With the stars, of which only the North Star and Great Bear were visible all night, moving slightly to the north-west as they set, the British columns, unwittingly, did the same. Because of this error of seven degrees, they approached the earthworks obliquely in the form of an irregular echelon with the left thrown forward. It was actually a stroke of good fortune, for close to the canal, about 500 yards before the line of defence, was an advanced redoubt which Highlanders by-passed to the right. The outlying fieldwork was not seen by reconnaissance patrols, largely because a mirage combined with the angle from which they examined the defences made it appear to be part of the main entrenchment. Had they struck this redoubt, much of the advantage of surprise would have been lost and the British fired upon sooner than anticipated. (According to the rules of the umpires at Aldershot, one quarter of the force would have been declared *hors de combat*.) But the stars in their courses fought against the Egyptians that night. Before that dreadful dawn, they lay peacefully in their trenches, having been lulled to sleep by the nasal sounds of some 400 readers of the Koran, who cared for the army's spiritual needs.

Even the winds, blowing from west to east, were favourable to Wolseley. The dull monotonous tramp of British boots and the crunch of gun-wheels through the sand was wafted back into the desert as the stormers approached. Though none realized it, because of the angle of the march, the brunt of the attack would fall upon the Highlanders. They would strike first and at the highest parapets and deepest ditches near the centre of Arabi's works.

A single shot from the right of the line announced to the sleeping Egyptians the presence of a hostile force. A few more shots followed and a bugle sounded the alarm. Wolseley, somewhat to the right front of the

Highlanders, moved forward to get a closer look in the dim light, hoping the flashes of light before him might provide some guide for future action should it become necessary to improvise. Dismounting, he gave his horse to his brother George to hold and walked ahead. As he peered through his glasses into the darkness, the first Egyptian shell dropped between him and his horse; but, as was so often the case, did not explode – otherwise the commander, with his horse and brother, might have been blown to pieces. An added danger came in the form of inquisitive enemy patrols on white horses. First to detect their approach was Tulloch, who shouted to Butler: 'Good God! Wolseley will be cut off.' Butler spurred his horse forward to warn the Chief as Tulloch brought up the small escort of marines. Fearing the enemy cavalry might change direction and endanger his guns, Wolseley ordered up his own cavalry escort. The Egyptians, who had seen enough, turned back to their lines.

It was a thrilling and anxious moment for Wolseley as he witnessed the Highlanders fade into the fast-dispersing morning mist before them. No longer was there any need for silence. Wolseley heard the sharp click of bayonets in obedience to loud commands, and the shrill blast of bugles. Only the sounds of the pipers were missing, and they were making a vigorous effort to fill the bags which had been deflated as a precaution during the night march. As they approached the sand heaps, there were ringing and sustained cheers. In a steady run the Cameronians, the Gordon Highlanders, and the Black Watch advanced upon the hastily-manned ramparts in two long continuous waves, for during the march the half-battalion double columns had gradually closed in upon one another. They advanced in 'the good old style', thought Wolseley, as he watched the solid ranks, an irresistible breaker crested with the glint of steel. Ahead in the black mound under a lilac sky, he saw a sheet of lambent yellow flame that continued to flash like long streaks of distant lightning. The Egyptian artillery was also in action, sending shells shrieking overhead. But in their frenzied fright, the defenders fired high, their bullets and balls whining wildly on into the desert until they furrowed into a sand-drift beyond. In the narrow strip of 150 yards the stormers crossed, only 200 went down.

The Highlanders tumbled into the deep trench and scrambled for the fiery top, pushing, pulling, cursing, as they slipped in the soft sand and tried to mount each other's shoulders. Bayonet and butt-end tussles followed as the redcoats dropped among white-garbed, swarthy-faced defenders to hack and stab. With desperate courage the surprised Egyptians, most of all the Sudanese, engaged them hand-to-hand. Many gunners, their redoubts entered from the rear, were bayoneted in the back while still working their pieces. And when they fell back, the defenders were unbroken and paused to kneel and fire a parting shot.

The fire from a second line of entrenchments was so severe that the Highlanders hesitated. At one point the Egyptians charged the redcoats, driving them back from the ramparts. There was added confusion when shouts of 'Retire! Retire!' were clearly heard along the ebbing, irregular wave. (It was never learned who said it, but some later believed it to have been uttered by a couple of 'Glasgow Irishmen' with Fenian sentiments.) The treacherous shouts were answered by officers' oaths and counter-commands of, 'No retirement, men! Come on! Come on!' Nevertheless, many redcoats disappeared back into the ditch during the confusion. Hamley rushed forward to where it was hottest with small bodies of reinforcements, which he had retained for such an emergency. Alison, absolutely alone, appeared with a pistol in his only hand to rally the re-coiling men. Mixed groups quickly gathered about his bold figure. The initiative was regained and the advance progressed slowly into the interior retrenchments. By now the bagpipes had recovered their wind and added their encouragement to the attack by playing lustily 'The March of the Cameron Men'.

The pipes of the Irish far to the right sounded in reply. Some fifteen minutes after the Highlanders' assault, at the same moment it reached its climax, Graham's brigade rushed forward. They had not only been a half-mile behind the Highlanders, but had to 'change front-about-quarter left' on the left company of the marines so as to face squarely the wall of flashing flame. They crossed a deeper zone of fire; however, the booming big guns and rattling musketry were generally misdirected. Graham, the fearless giant, with his customary gallantry, led the men over a shallow ditch. Royal Irish, Fusiliers, Royal Marines, York and Lancaster men drove the yielding but again unbroken enemy from successive positions in the now strong dawn.

Goodenough, waiting for more light to advance his guns, trundled them over ditches and parapets, wherever a gap could be found. Their punishing fire was joined by the Horse Artillery who plied the Egyptians with enfilading fire on their desert flank. The cavalry itself, which had gone over a mile astray on the march, galloped up to threaten the enemy's left flank and rear. The Indian contingent, meeting little resistance on the left, swept up along the canal with the Lancers far in front. Boxed in on almost every side, and their line of retreat threatened, Arabi's army was transformed into a mass of fugitives. Small knots of men continued to fight – some gunners with rammers – but most threw down their arms and fled for their lives with cries of anguish and shouts of 'Allah!' Shells bursting overhead added to their panic. Thousands surrendered. The battle was over in thirty-five minutes.

The expression that 'dead men tell no tales' never applied to a battle-field. As Wolseley and his staff rode through the remains of a broken army, they discerned mute but eloquent testimony of what had happened on the field. First came the Highlander dead, huddled in the foremost ditch. Beyond the parapet were men blown to pieces by cannon; others looked as if they had fallen asleep after a long march. The wounded were often encircled by comrades, forgetful for a moment of glory, and acting as if the unfortunate soldier were lying in a peaceful hospital. The commander often stopped to add his comforting words. The number of Egyptians who cluttered the ground became more numerous. Usually they were found on their backs, indicating they had stopped and turned to fire at their pursuers. Wolseley noticed with much satisfaction that the Egyptians had been hit principally in the legs and stomach – his men had fired low and slowly. Seeing a large number of enemy wounded, Wolseley asked that Egyptian surgeons be found and sent up to look after them. As the wounded lay with red blood soaking into the yellow sand, many covered their faces with paper to keep off the flies and the rays of the rising sun.

There was a great thirst among friend and foe. Once the victors had mastered the field, they rushed to the canal to slake their thirst. An incessant cry for water by the wounded was made in several languages. Their suffering was so great, some dragged themselves forward to drink the blood of wounded camels near by. Private soldiers often showed no compassion for their gasping Egyptian foes. One rifleman, encountering dead Egyptians that were slowly roasting in their clothing, drew a pipe from his pocket and lit it from human flames, commenting: 'By —— I never thought I should live to use a dead Egyptian for a light to my pipe!'[25] But most could not restrain their sympathy and gave what help they could. More than one Englishman was shot in the back for his pains.

These poor fellahin, untutored in the art of war and betrayed on every side, found one who stayed to pray over them and write their epitaph. 'Peace be to them,' said Butler, 'lying under these big mounds on the lone desert ... No word should soldier utter against them; let that be left to the money-changers. They died the good death. Dust to dust. They did not desert the desert, and Egypt will not forget them.'[26]

Over 2,000 defenders died that day. Wolseley told Adye on the previous night, 'We shall lose five hundred.' The battle cost him exactly 480 killed and wounded, mostly of the Highland Brigade. There was no accounting the number of Egyptian wounded; the organization of their army had disintegrated. And as Wolseley predicted, once decisively defeated, the fellah soldier would disband and return to his home; his minor wounds would be cared for there, and he would assume the life of a civilian once more.

Riding to the bridge over the canal, a prearranged meeting point for his generals some two miles inside the enemy lines, Wolseley saw the last phase of the battle, or what was by now a rout. The only resistance shown was by an unconquered redoubt near the canal, which was silenced when a British battery came up and exploded its magazine. Everyone was on the run, except for a pathetic old Arab lying on his stomach and firing wildly into the blue air at imaginary foes. On disarming him, he was found to be totally blind. Before Wolseley were Hamley, Alison, and 200 Highlanders, the foremost part of the brigade, rushing into the camp and railway station a short distance north of the bridge. Two train-loads of fugitives made good their escape, but a third was hit by a shell which exploded its ammunition. The train stopped.

The congestion at the stone bridge among fugitives who tried to escape the British cavalry and infantry coming from the north was fearful. Those who could swim jumped into the canal. Once across, they all rushed through a wheat field, which by the time of Wolseley's arrival on the scene had been 'trodden till it looked like a threshing floor'. British artillery left the field strewn with dead men and disembowelled camels and horses.

Those south of the canal fortunate enough to escape bayonet and shell, ran afoul of the Indian cavalry. Rushing along a now open and unrestricted front were rows of 'swarthy bearded faces, fierce with the lust to kill and intoxicated with the easy victory'. They tore about on flying mounts 'tipped in front with fluttering pennons and flashing lance points'.[27] The Biblical expression, 'terrible as an army with banners', was given meaning as the wretched fellahin were spitted on gay lances. If they had stood their ground like disciplined troops, thought Wolseley, they could have emptied most of the saddles before the impaling lances came within striking distance. Instead, they made no attempt to defend themselves, but flung themselves to the sand hoping the horseman would ride over them, or threw up their hands in surrender.

Those who fled before the sabres of British troopers north of the canal were treated in a less sanguinary manner. Many prisoners were taken and, in many instances, Tommy Atkins would give the fleeing fellah a resounding smack on the seat of the trousers with the flat of his sword to speed him on his way.

When Wolseley reached the bridge, the Highlanders paused in their pursuit and gave him a victorious and vociferous cheer. Lady Butler, whose name and canvases were known throughout England, later selected this moment to describe in paint the Chief and his staff. 'After the Battle', charged with emotion and precise in every detail, portrayed the slight and rigid frame of Wolseley, which never relaxed despite the strain of the long march; to the right was Adye with a question framed on his lips regarding the pursuit; behind the Chief was Buller with his horse shying away from a dead fellah; and to the left was her husband, leaning forward to speak with a soldier.*

The conqueror dismounted and stepped over the low parapet on the stone bridge, sat down, and pulled out a cigar. While engaged in a kind of tobacco debauch – six in a row – he smilingly received the reports of his commanders, beginning with the quiet and determined MacPherson; in Wolseley's opinion, 'the best man here'. The Chief calmly issued orders to MacPherson and Drury Lowe for a vigorous pursuit to improve the victory. The former would move at once to Zagazig, the next large centre where Arabi might make a stand; the latter would continue the job of total dispersion of the Egyptians, which was nearing completion.

Lighting another cigar, he wrote a telegraphic dispatch announcing his victory to the people at home. Watching Fitzgeorge, who 'manages the mess admirably', come up to arrange for breakfast, Wolseley thought it might give pleasure to the old Duke to have his eldest son carry home dispatches once the conquest was complete. As it turned out, George Fitzgeorge would be the last bearer of dispatches to receive a pecuniary reward.†

When the commander got up to leave, his horse could not be found. While he rode off on another, his aides made a thorough search for the vanished mount. It was later found in the possession of one of the young officers of a Highland regiment. Much can be said for the boldness and

---

* Though Butler disapproved of this 'unworthy theme' of exulting in triumph over the poor fellah, his wife insisted upon going ahead with the project. Crowds of Highlanders were employed to satisfy her desire for historical accuracy. Sir Garnet, however, posed not on his charger, but on the knee of Lady Wolseley, who tried to keep him from fidgeting. The portrait proved a great favourite and was hung in the Royal Academy. Later, as if to satisfy her departed husband, who hated the sight of it, Lady Butler cut the canvas to pieces.

† Apparently he could use the money, for it cost his father some £150,000 to settle his debts. The Duke never mentioned him in his will.

acquisitiveness of this Scot, whose name was never divulged, for 'the trophy' had an English saddle with the initials G.J.W. stamped plainly upon it.

Looting was proceeding at a furious pace at the large enemy camp a few yards away. By tradition, the belongings of the enemy became the property of the victors. Highlanders, Guards, and Royal Irish, charged through the many rows of abandoned tents. In comic relief to the serious scenes enacted earlier in the day, here a tall Highlander would be garbed in the long flowing robes of a desert sheikh; there a diminutive cockney would be strutting about under an enormous turban, carrying an arsenal of fancy pistols and daggers in a broad, colourful cummerbund. Others rode about on fractious camels and beautiful horses whose owners, in their haste, had taken off on foot. On returning to their respective units, the men were forced to surrender what they had taken. An energetic provost-marshal and his large, stern-faced body of mounted police, acting under Sir Garnet's strict orders, quickly put an end to the pernicious searching.

The behaviour of the soldiers, especially the Household troops, was of an exceptionally high order throughout the campaign. Wolseley could boast that there were only three courts martial in Egypt. (Naturally, not all offenders were caught and punished.) The Duke of Teck, handsome father of the future Queen Mary, who served on Wolseley's personal staff and looked after the foreign military representatives, infuriated his brother-in-law, the Duke of Cambridge, by suggesting that part of his kit was stolen by a soldier servant; if he ever took part in another military campaign 'it would be with German soldiers, who at least were honest'.[28]

Wolseley promised the tip of Arabi's nose to his daughter, but the Napoleon of the fellahin was one of the first to flee the battlefield. He later complained that the British did not even give him time to put his boots on. Unable to escape by train, he and his second-in-command galloped across the desert to Belbeis, where they abandoned their fatigued mounts and ordered a train for Cairo. Arabi, huddled in a coach and weeping, arrived in the capital empty-handed with the bitter news of defeat.

The British were determined not to grant Arabi the three or four days needed to recover his strength, or permit him time to destroy the city, which was his rumoured intention. Crossing the battlefield with tireless energy, the Indian contingent continued on to Zagazig, the 6th Bengal Lancers leading the advance. It was more like a hunt, recalled MacPherson, for the dawn lesson at Tel-el-Kebir deprived the pursuers of any real danger. Fugitives melted into the distance all along the way. Some stopped to surrender, but the British, intent on capturing rolling-stock and breaking communications to Zagazig between various parts of the Egyptian army in the Delta, pretended not to notice them.

Nearing the town at four p.m., the straggling line of Lancers broke into a gallop. Five of the best mounted were first to enter the narrow streets and clatter up to the railway station. Six engines had their steam up and three were already in motion; all were crowded with fugitives. The sweaty troopers dashed daringly into the middle of them and threatened to shoot the drivers. The intimidated drivers either threw up their hands or ran away. The demoralized passengers followed their example. Only one driver had the courage to attempt an escape, but in the excitement ran on to the wrong track and crashed into an incoming train. Thus large numbers of beaten soldiers were prevented from reinforcing the Cairo garrisons or from inciting the populace to riots against the Europeans there.

The Indian cavalry pushed on along the canal to Belbeis where it would join the cavalry division, taking a desert road to the south-west, for the final dash to Cairo. Belbeis, twenty-five miles from Kassassin, was occupied that night after the exchange of a few shots at the railway station, which Arabi had left less than a quarter of an hour before. Here the tired mounted men bivouacked for the night. Because the Horse Artillery, delayed by the narrow bridges over canals and ditches, had not yet arrived, Drury Lowe considered waiting until they caught up. But Stewart and Baker Russell urged him to push on as soon as possible. He hesitatingly agreed.

Thus, long before dawn, they were on their way again, headed for Cairo, thirty-nine miles away. Following the edge of the desert under the blazing sun, they by-passed salaaming peasants with white flags and soldiers who offered to surrender. Much of the heat of the march was ignored because of the intense excitement; no one could say what awaited them in Cairo.

The sun was setting when the advance force reached the suburb of Abbassieh. With magnificent bluff, Stewart went forward with fifty men and demanded the surrender of a garrison of thousands, while the rest of the cavalry remained far behind so as not to reveal the smallness of their force. Arrangements were also made for the capitulation of the Citadel and of Arabi himself. During the night Arabi Pasha, surprised a second time, and Toubla Pasha, in from Kafr Dowar where he commanded, went to Abbassieh to offer their swords to Drury Lowe, who was surrounded by exhausted and famished troopers, many of whom slept bridle in hand.

Arabi's conqueror remained at Tel-el-Kebir after the battle, sleeping in one of the 'smelly' captured tents amidst snoring Guards and Highlanders. Wolseley and his staff left for Zagazig on the afternoon of September 14th, but the single line was in such disorder their arrival was delayed until nine p.m. They spent the night in the railway station and feasted on a tin of meat, a few biscuits, and some claret which the Duke of Connaught providentially brought along; otherwise they would have gone hungry. Buller was at the throttle when they departed for Benha where Wolseley received Stewart's account of the surrender of the capital – how he wished he had a few more men of Stewart's calibre! The submission of the rest of Arabi's army throughout the country was reported in rapid succession.

Cairo. Wolseley saw the morning reflect on the palaces and domes built by long-forgotten sultans. Between soaring minarets, he could distinguish the heavy battlements of the Citadel which was now in British hands. There was a cordial reception at the station. Officials formerly loyal to Arabi were now 'all coffee, cigarette, and obsequious courtesy'.[29] Soon they reached the Abdin Palace, placed at the disposal of the commander-in-chief and his staff by the Khedive. Here in the square of the palace a year before, recalled Wolseley, Arabi with 4,000 bayonets had forced Tewfik to meet his demands.

Passing through the cool corridors into the handsome apartment of satin and gold reserved for him, Wolseley dictated a message to the War Office: 'The war in Egypt is over; send no more men from England.'

Wolseley had indicated to everyone before leaving London the scene of the decisive struggle, Tel-el-Kebir, and had predicted that on September 16th the war would be concluded. He missed by one day.

The news of Tel-el-Kebir, followed by the announcement that Cairo had been taken and the war was over, created a sensation throughout Europe. In England there was great enthusiasm and a deep sense of satisfaction. The Liberal Government, anxious for days as to whether the force was strong enough to accomplish the task before it, was greatly relieved. Gladstone was ecstatic with delight, extending and receiving congratulations. He was most effusive in his praise of Wolseley, whom he promised a peerage. Childers, like Wolseley, had the added satisfaction of knowing that the military reforms had passed the test of efficiency. None was steadier on the march or cooler in the fight than 'Childers' boys', as the critics labelled them. The campaign was an abounding promise for the future.

The Duke told Wolseley he was thoroughly pleased. The night march, the rush before daybreak, the Indian contingent on the flank, the dash to Zagazig, etc. was exactly the thing. He could not have planned it better himself.

Softening towards Wolseley, the Duke wrote to the Queen: 'His great fault is that he is so *very ambitious*, and that he has only a certain number of officers in whom he has any real confidence. If we could, on his return, only modify these two feelings, he would be twice the value he is to his country ... '[30] At Balmoral, on learning of the great victory and that 'darling Arthur was safe and well', Victoria 'felt unbounded joy and gratitude for God's great goodness and mercy'. Two days later, on receiving a letter dated September 3rd, in which Sir Garnet praised the conduct of her Household Cavalry, she could not resist remarking that it was 'the only Long Service Corps in the army'.

Most of Wolseley's critics were either silenced or forced, grudgingly, into an admission as to his ability. Some of his enemies must have felt like the member of the Opposition who, it was said, on learning of Waterloo, rushed into his club and exclaimed: 'There has been a misfortune, Wellington has won a great victory at Waterloo!'

Cairo was an enchanting city to conquerors who had spent weeks in the sterile desert. Sir Garnet lived luxuriously in the most magnificent of palaces 'amidst every variety of stink' with pashas, effendis, prefects, mudirs, bimbashis, beys and other officials streaming in and out. Life from the military standpoint was anything but strenuous, though some like McCalmont wished 'the business had gone on longer'.

Stewart and Butler were given the unsoldierly task of removing the harem women 'of the late Pasha of the blood' from the old palace at Abbassieh, a task which according to the latter involved 'playing a sort of hide-and-seek with them through the palace'.[31]

There were frequent picnics, and Butler arranged for his friends to have 'pemmican at the Pyramids', which Buller pronounced 'nasty'. From atop the Pyramids, Wolseley's imaginative chief signalling officer sent him a Napoleonic message: 'Four thousand years look down on you, the Conqueror of the Pyramids!' To which he received a prompt and unappreciative reply: 'Don't be a fool! Come down.'

The Khedive made a triumphal re-entry on the afternoon of September 25th. Great crowds came to greet and cheer him. How many more might have come out to see him hanged? When he left the capital in mid July,

Arabi found it necessary to protect him from the very people who were now cheering him.

His Highness drove from the railway station in an open carriage. By special request of the Queen, 'darling Arthur' was given the place of honour next to the pale Khedive, while Sir Garnet sat by the side of Sir Edward Malet with his back to the horses. Troops, many in new uniforms, lined the streets to the palace to hold back the multitude as the bands played the 'Khedive's March' and cannon boomed. On reaching Ismailia Palace, the Khedive once more thanked Wolseley for having restored his throne. As McCalmont described it, 'he seemed thoroughly well satisfied at the thrashing we have given his army'.[32] Tewfik then decorated Wolseley with the Sultan's highest award, the Grand Cross of the Osmanieh. A profusion of decorations followed. That night the skies were illuminated with fireworks.

His presence in Egypt no longer required, Wolseley decided to leave for home on October 21st. Because of the general's obvious need for rest, Dr Jackson advised him to go home by sea. Wolseley compromised by going as far as Trieste aboard the fastest ship in the navy. There he was honoured by Austrian military authorities and a special coach was placed at his disposal to take him across the Continent.

Three months before Wolseley, a commoner, had left London, sneaking through his stables in 6 Hill Street to the docks; now on the evening of October 28th, Lord Wolseley of Cairo, and Wolseley in the County of Stafford* (the latter included so as to indicate to his detractors he was descended from a noble line) was welcomed by an enormous crowd at Charing Cross station. Room was found for persons of distinction on the main-line arrival platform, and in turn the Duke of Cambridge, the Prime Minister, the War Secretary, the Duke of Teck, and others stepped forward to offer congratulations. All the while, cheer after cheer rang through the enormous building. In trying to reach the Strand, where even greater crowds were gathered, the party was drawn into an irresistible swirl of humanity.

Lady Wolseley, who met her husband at Dover, noticed Mr Gladstone, who, it was said, had been 'set on his legs' by her husband's victory, being nearly carried off as he 'was sadly pushed and pummelled in the crowd'. 'While he was gasping for breath,' she saw Mrs Childers 'disappear in a

---

* After a great deal of debate, public and private, Wolseley received a barony with a grant of £30,000, instead of an annuity, for he had no son to provide for after his death. The sum represented a compromise. Because of his 'embarrassed finances', Wolseley haggled for £35,000 while Gladstone at first proposed only £25,000. To compensate for this 'shabby treatment', according to Wolseley, he was promoted to the rank of full general.

whirlpool of people double her height'. Lord Granville, the Foreign Secretary, was heard to say, 'This is *your* Tel-el-Kebir.' The burly Duke of Cambridge then 'cleared the way manfully and beautifully' to the carriage, though he was 'jostled unmercifully'. Even then the brougham seemed in danger of being 'crushed like an almond shell by the pressure'.[33]

His stay in London was brief, he having been commanded to Balmoral by Her Majesty. Wolseley dreaded the trip to Scotland. Would he be made to suffer another cutting jibe regarding the short-service system? Of course, he told his wife, 'the poor woman naturally understands nothing of the subject ... having been informed upon military matters by her cousin George and other equally great warriors of his class'.[34] Victoria's letters after Tel-el-Kebir were definitely 'cold'. He and Lady Wolseley carefully pored over every word of correspondence, finding scarcely one approving sentence. Feeling very much misunderstood, he told his wife how he had done all he could 'to mollify the Queen's dislike to me, and to gain her favour'; yet she treated him so badly.[35] Moreover, he had gone out of his way to bestow every courtesy possible on Prince Arthur, whose presence on the battlefield was a constant worry. He even used his correspondence with the Duke to convey indirectly his many compliments concerning Arthur and his military conduct, knowing it would get back to the Queen and the Prince. And how did Prince Arthur reward him? The best His Royal Highness could say to his mother was that Sir Garnet 'is the least fussy General he ever served under'. 'It would be like telling Mrs Langtry,' Lady Wolseley remarked testily, 'that she was *not plain* by way of a compliment.'[36]

Wolseley was wrong. His little side campaign of winning the Queen's affection through her son had succeeded. She was touched by the general's many kind words about Arthur; and the Duke of Connaught was far more impressed with Sir Garnet's brilliance than the latter was aware of. A few days before the General's visit, Victoria wrote, 'If only this *really* great General behaves with tact and good taste when he returns, and does not make injudicious speeches.'[37]

The subsequent interview at Balmoral helped to clear the way for a better understanding. Wolseley began by indulging in fulsome flattery about the Prince, adding, 'I should say more, if I were not speaking to your Majesty.' He tactfully went on to praise the Life Guards and other favourites of the Queen. Then they took turns criticizing Gladstone's Egyptian policy, most of all his failure to hang Arabi because he was 'frightened by so-called "public opinion" and by the Radicals'.* 'How

* After a farcical trial, Arabi was exiled to Ceylon.

different things would have been,' the general concluded, 'had Lord Beaconsfield lived.'[38] The Queen was delighted. Since Victoria's harsh opinions of Sir Garnet were well known at Court, they were astonished when Her Majesty toasted his health at the dinner table and spoke glowingly of his success in Egypt.

On November 18th a Royal Review in honour of the Egyptian expedition was held at the Horse Guards parade-ground, which was reminiscent of the military pageant held by the Prince Regent after Waterloo.

The morning was not propitious. It was ushered in almost unseen, clothed in thin fog. As the day advanced, the fog grew thicker, until by eleven a.m. it was so dark one was reminded more of the ancient plagues of Egypt than the recent victory in that land. Authorities wondered whether the review should be held because of the danger to travellers. As the first gun sounded to announce Her Majesty's approach from Buckingham Palace, the gloomy atmosphere began to clear, and when her carriage approached the saluting point the first gleam of sunshine burst over it. The effect was striking, almost portentous. Then the distant sounds of martial music from different directions were heard as the various regiments converged upon their monarch. None was prouder than Wolseley when the defile of 'boy soldiers' with worn and sunburnt faces displayed 'a strapping stalwartness, a manliness of aspect, and an air of conscious superiority, which belied much of what' had been heard about them.[39]

Wolseley believed the Egyptian campaign, with its precise blending of prudence and daring, was the tidiest little war ever fought by the British army in its long history. So it was.

# THE GORDON RELIEF EXPEDITION

IT was time to relax. After a quick visit to Paris, the conqueror of Egypt returned to spend his spare hours in the cool, green English countryside, which had grown so appealing in the desert. The Duke of Cambridge dreaded another 'spring-cleaning' that would sweep away more of those military traditions which he so cherished, but he found his reform-minded adjutant-general far less aggressive than usual. Wolseley seemed more interested, for the moment, in combating the Channel tunnel project, and, to the Duke's delight, in thwarting the Government's efforts to withdraw virtually all British troops from Egypt. Together, thought the Duke, they might educate the likeable Lord Hartington (later the Duke of Devonshire) on Egyptian affairs; for, as a result of a Cabinet shuffle, Hartington was asked to 'step into the old shoes of Mr Childers' and take over what was regarded by politicians as a difficult and unrewarding post.

Returning to the War Office after a brief visit to Russia, Wolseley heard the disturbing news that the Mahdist rebellion in the Sudan had attained alarming proportions. What had been a small dark cloud up the Nile while he was in Africa, was now rolling northward in great black billows of fanatical hatred that extinguished life and civilization.

It was in the summer of 1881 that Mohammed Ahmed declared with burning eloquence that he was the long-awaited Mahdi, or 'guide'. As the chosen messenger of Allah foretold by the Prophet, it was his mission to regenerate Islam and convert the world to a universal religion with one law, complete equality, and a community of goods. Unbelievers, be they Christian, pagan, or Muslim, would be destroyed in holy war.

The man and the hour were joined. In a profoundly religious land of crude minarets, the oppressed prayed for such a saviour to deliver them from the injustice and venality of Egyptian officials who dispatched brutal and licentious soldiers to collect taxes and suppress the lucrative slave trade. Thousands flocked to his sacred green banner. Called dervishes, or 'poor men', these converts dressed themselves in a dirty white cotton *jibbah* with coloured square checks sewn upon it, and wore a little straw cap on their newly-shaven heads. Vowed to poverty and holy war, few

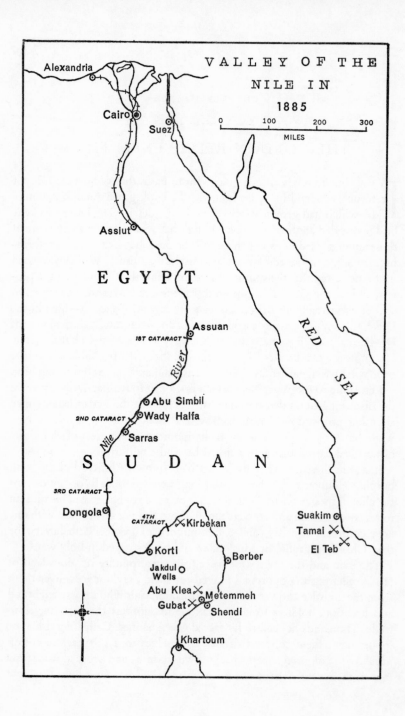

men sought death more. Armed in the beginning with little more than spears and a fanaticism as fierce as that of the followers of the Prophet who conquered half the known world over a thousand years before, the dervishes quickly overran much of the country south of Khartoum, the capital, defeating Turco-Egyptian armies in battle after battle.

Gladstone had been led, very much against his will, into the occupation of Egypt, and certainly he had never bargained for military intervention in the Sudan. It was his declared purpose to get out of Egypt as soon as possible. But like it or not, the British were still in military occupation of a land where the native government was disorganized and incompetent. To pretend that Egypt was an autonomous country under a vague Turkish suzerainty, which preferred to be perversely obstructive, was an absurd political fiction. Though Gladstone refused to admit it, Britain ruled Egypt; though he refused responsibility for the Sudan, Britain was bound to become involved.

Then Gordon, already a national legend, came on the stage. The name of the former and successful governor-general of the Sudan began to circulate privately through officialdom as one that might now be exploited by an anxious Government to arrange for the withdrawal of the garrisons. His name alone, it was said, could do wonders. Wolseley from the beginning felt his employment would be 'most desirable'. Sir Evelyn Baring, the British Agent in Cairo, who had no great liking for Gordon, twice rejected the proposal. As Baring later told Granville, 'a man who habitually consults the Prophet Isaiah when he is in a difficulty is not apt to obey the orders of anyone.'[1]

Charles George Gordon was not an ordinary man. He was half military genius and half religious fanatic. He was best remembered for leading a handful of unwarlike Chinese to miraculous victories over the Taiping rebels, thereby saving China. His escape from injury, despite great personal risks, and his successful efforts in rescuing starving children and outraged women, bred the conviction in his God-intoxicated brain that his was a divine mission. 'Chinese' Gordon subsequently pursued a spectacular career as a Christian Knight challenging the powers of evil in distant lands. Utterly fearless, scrupulously honest, the brilliant eccentric astonished his contemporaries with his saint-like indifference to riches, honours, and women. Chafing under authority, he sought assignments where he was to have a free hand. To the official mind, he was always slightly 'mad'. Baring called him 'half-cracked'.

Wolseley, never a humble man, felt he was 'not worthy to pipe-clay Gordon's belt'. They had remained staunch friends since first cast together on service in the trenches before Sebastopol. After serving together in China, their careers followed divergent paths, but they exchanged letters from time to time, admired one another's successes, and remembered each other nightly in their prayers. Gordon was one of the few acquaintances, said Wolseley, 'who came up to my estimate of the Christian hero. He absolutely ignored self in all he did, and only took in hand what he conceived to be God's work. Life was to him a Pilgrim's Progress between the years of early manhood and the Heaven ... he always longed for.'[2]

Early in January, Wolseley received a message from Gordon, who had been on a pilgrimage to Palestine, telling how he accepted employment under the King of the Belgians in the Congo to suppress slavery. Because of the British Government's disapproval, he would be forced to resign from the army. Would Wolseley be good enough to arrange his pension? Wolseley wired his old friend to come to London to discuss the matter. An appointment was arranged at the War Office on January 15th.

The day after his arrival in England (January 7th), Gordon received an unexpected call from W. T. Stead, enterprising editor of the sedate *Pall Mall Gazette*, while at his sister's home in Southampton. The innovator of the 'interview' in British journalism pressed Gordon for his expert view on conditions in the Sudan. Deceived as to the true nature of affairs, Gordon spoke optimistically of the situation. He opposed evacuation, and like Wolseley, he dwelt on the difficulty of carrying out such an operation.

Making the most of his 'scoop', Stead in large print declared: 'Chinese Gordon for the Soudan!' Why not send the world's greatest leader of irregular forces, he asked editorially, 'to save what can be saved from the wreck in the Soudan?' Other papers took up the cry, appealing to the thoughtful and excitable, the jingoes and humanitarians. The Queen herself hinted to Granville that Gordon might be of assistance.

Wolseley believed more than ever that the situation required the peculiar genius of Gordon, 'God's friend', as he called him. At three p.m. on January 15th, the middle-aged (fifty-one) general, short and spare, came to the War Office to see the adjutant-general. As always, Wolseley was first drawn to his bright blue eyes that 'seemed to court scrutiny, whilst at the same time they searched into your inner soul'.[3] In the long conversation that followed, Wolseley persuaded 'Charlie' to forget about the Congo, a venture which neither he nor the British Government could approve, and told him the Ministry was thinking of asking his assistance in evacuating the Sudan. Gordon expressed his willingness, verbally and in writing, 'to proceed to Suakim and report on military situation of Sudan and return'.

It was more than Gordon's optimism or Wolseley's urging that persuaded the Government to send the eccentric hero to the Sudan. The Gladstone Ministry welcomed an opportunity, without involving the Government financially or militarily, of satisfying public demand and weathering a Parliamentary storm that was brewing over the Sudan. Perhaps Gordon could once more work miracles and settle matters by mere force of his magnetic personality. Granville put pressure on Baring, who now gave his consent, provided Gordon was willing to follow instructions.

Gordon was summoned back to London from Brussels to meet a committee of Cabinet members on January 18th. After breakfasting at Wolseley's home in Hill Street, Gordon was taken by the adjutant-general to the War Office at noon. While Wolseley was in Hartington's office for a last-minute discussion with the Ministers (Hartington, Granville, Northbrook, and Dilke), Gordon warmed himself by the fire and watched the private secretary scribbling before him. With childlike naturalness he asked, 'Do you ever tell a lie?' Before the startled secretary offered a reply, Wolseley came out to usher Gordon in to meet the Ministers. After earnest consultations, Gordon agreed to undertake the Sudan mission. When asked how soon he would be ready to start, Gordon declared his readiness to leave that night on the Indian mail train.

Gordon's instructions, which subsequently created so much controversy, were poorly stated, but clearly implied a future executive capacity in addition to conferring advisory powers. Certainly Baring, under whose direct orders he was placed, did not hesitate to give Gordon authority on his arrival in Cairo to go to Khartoum and carry out the evacuation of the Sudan by withdrawing the garrisons. And before he left Cairo, Granville authorized his being made governor-general of the province. Unfortunately, Gladstone, who was at Hawarden and considered the whole affair of secondary importance, was left with the impression, uncorrected by Hartington's report of the proceedings, that Gordon had been sent merely to report and advise.

As Gordon waited to board a train at Charing Cross station, Wolseley asked him if he had any cash, knowing his friend had a way of losing sight of such trifles. Gordon confessed he had not thought of it. His lordship dashed into a hansom and raced around to various clubs to collect some £200 in small sums from his friends. Not trusting Gordon, Wolseley gave the money to Colonel J. D. H. Stewart of the 11th Hussars who was to accompany him to Africa. Stewart, whom Gordon called his 'wet nurse', later wrote to Wolseley that when they arrived in Egypt, Gordon met his former secretary who was now blind, and generously gave him £100.

Wolseley carried Gordon's solitary kit-bag; Granville took his ticket; and the Duke of Cambridge, who made a surprise visit, held open the carriage door. There was a round of handshakes and a 'God bless you.' The event was faithfully recorded in the morning papers, whose readers were relieved to learn that their hero was on his way to the Sudan to what would surely be another triumph. Queen Victoria, who was somewhat better informed on the matter, recorded in her diary: 'His attempt is a very dangerous one.'

To send a man like Gordon to evacuate the Sudan was a mistake. The Government had chosen a strong man to carry out a weak policy. Gordon, a born fighter who spent his life advancing and obeyed only his conscience, was the last man in the Empire to lead an inglorious retreat. Nor was his the language of retirement. 'Don't be panic-stricken;' ran his first message to Khartoum, 'you are men, not women; I am coming.'

By the end of March, Gordon resolved to defend Khartoum, which he reported could be easily held, and 'smash the Mahdi'. Meanwhile the dervishes of the Eastern Sudan, led by Osman Digna, an ex-slaver whose ambition was kindled by the Mahdi's success, menaced the garrisons of the Red Sea littoral and the port of Suakim itself. The Gladstone Government, concerned more for its own survival than that of the inhabitants of Suakim and its outposts, succumbed to the pressure of an indignant public and their Queen. To pacify at least that corner of the Sudan, a force of British troops under Sir Gerald Graham was sent from Egypt. Wolseley told Hartington that the sooner they dealt with Osman Digna, the better.

Graham defeated Osman Digna's hordes at El Teb (February 9th) and again at Tamai (March 13th). The fighting was bloody and desperate. The fuzzy-wuzzies, with their fanatical disregard for life, won the undying respect of the steady British, who found that neither rapid-firing machine-guns nor Martini-Henrys with expanding dumdum bullets could stop them unless they smashed a skull or pierced the heart. And 'even when the paralyses of death stole over them, in their last convulsions they would try to cut, stab, or even bite … even little boys came brandishing sticks, led recklessly by their parents to the very muzzles of our rifles'.[4] Among those who penetrated the British square was a bounding tribesman who jumped clean over the front rank, only to be impaled on the bayonet of a soldier to the rear. 'How's that, sir?' the amazed soldier asked his superior. 'Well caught!' observed the officer.

After all this trouble and expense, the British Government threw away the fruits of success. Instead of allowing Graham to secure the desert route to Berber to prevent Gordon from being isolated, which the military authorities in the War Office and Egypt favoured, the victorious Graham and the whole of his splendid force were ordered to re-embark by the end of March by a cautious Gladstone Government.

The Suakim expedition was worse than useless. The unsubdued followers of the Mahdi recovered from Graham's blows and soon boasted that the English did not advance because they feared them. Berber, the key to the Sudan, where a small garrison looked in despair for relief, was soon invested and communications to Khartoum were cut. Graham, though a careful commander, was sure he could have sent Herbert Stewart with a couple of squadrons of cavalry to Berber virtually unopposed. He always regretted that he did not dispatch Stewart forward on his own responsibility instead of telegraphing for approval.

Wolseley believed some positive measures must be taken to support Gordon. He suggested to Granville on March 22nd that part of Wood's Egyptian force be sent to Wady Halfa, just below Egypt, for moral support, and six British officers, experts on Sudanese affairs, be sent to Berber to await Gordon's instructions. The matter was referred to Baring, who after consulting military authorities in Cairo, vetoed the proposal. Neither Cairo nor London was anxious to take any steps to improve Gordon's position, though by the end of March Khartoum was surrounded. Gordon could no longer even fight his way out.

Driven by a strong sense of personal responsibility for having placed Gordon in this predicament, Wolseley never relaxed in plumping for a decision. He repeatedly asked to be allowed to take at least a small party to secure Berber as forerunner to a larger expedition, should that become necessary. He even offered to go himself to Suakim, 'not an agreeable summer residence', and take command of the small beleaguered garrison. The mere announcement of such a move, he assured Hartington, 'would make everyone feel that you were thoroughly in earnest'. 'I presume the government,' he told his superior, 'is not prepared to allow General Gordon and his garrison to fall into the hands of the cruel and barbarous enemy now besieging Khartoum ... If you contemplate sending an expedition in the autumn to Gordon's relief, the sooner he is informed the better it will be for him and for our interests.' In the end, he warned, 'the English people will force you to do it whether you like it or not.'[5]

All the while through the months of March and April, Gordon, to keep up the morale of his soldiers, promised the troops that British troops were on their way. Feeling it was the Government's duty to extricate the garrisons, he tried to force the hand of an unwilling Ministry. His proposals were rejected. 'If a boy at Eton,' he wrote during the siege, 'had behaved as the British Government has done, I *think* he would be kicked; and I am *sure* he would deserve it.'

As the Mahdi's coil tightened about the city, a desperate Gordon made final appeals for outside help from other sources. He suggested the Turks be invited to send a force, and if necessary transfer the Sudan to the Sultan. He called for appeals to foreign consuls, the Pope, and British and American millionaires to give financial aid in support of a Turkish expedition. All in vain. In fact, most of his messages were no longer getting through. By the end of April all communications with Cairo were cut. The faint voice was silent.

During the first few months there was no undue alarm, but by May concern for Gordon's safety was widespread. An aroused nation became vocal on behalf of their mute idol. The English people, often mistakenly depicted as a cold, practical race, displayed an almost hysterical sentimentality. There was an enormous protest meeting in Hyde Park. Gladstone was publicly hissed. Churches held special prayers. Royalty added its voice to the public outcry. Funds were raised by public subscriptions to begin a relief expedition. A thousand sportsmen, 'men prepared to go a thousand miles to shoot a lion', were called upon to force their way to Khartoum and rescue Gordon. (Buller, jealous of Gordon's popularity, refused to join, declaring 'the man was not worth the camels'.)

Wolseley, with the popularity of a nation's most successful soldier behind him, renewed his suit to induce the Gladstone Government to send a relief force. But when Lady Salisbury during a chance meeting in the street asked hopefully about the plans and preparations he must obviously be working on, his lordship threw up his hands in a gesture of despair and declared: 'I have nothing to tell you. There are *no* plans and *no* preparations.'[6]

Because of a divided Cabinet, Gladstone managed to avoid any positive action. The supreme body was an ill-assorted political combination of old-time Whigs and ambitious Radicals, of Imperialists and Little Englanders, who had one thing in common: going backwards and forwards in their attitude on Gordon and the Sudan. The words of a popular song written a few years before fittingly described their conduct: 'First she would, and then she wouldn't; and then she said she really couldn't, with a hoop de dooden da.' It was hardly the sort of executive to which England could look for firm, swift decisions. Most inclined to support a relief expedition was the languid, easygoing Hartington, a Whig leader who would have been more at home in the eighteenth century. 'The Duke,' as Stead described him, 'was inertia itself. His don't-care-a-damn frame of mind made him incapable of acting until fully roused ... His strength was to sit still.'

It was this man who could save Gordon if he acted in time. On learning late in June that Berber had fallen a month before, Wolseley redoubled his efforts to rouse the placid Hartington, whom he personally liked and admired. Scarcely a day now passed that he did not importune the War Secretary. 'Remember we cannot command things,' he told Hartington, 'all the gold in England will not affect the rise and fall of the Nile or the duration of the hot and cold seasons in Egypt. Time is a most important element in the question, and indeed it will be an indelible disgrace if we allow the most generous, patriotic, and gallant of our public servants to die of want or fall into the hands of a cruel enemy because we would not hold out our hands to save him.' He concluded with a touching announcement: 'At any rate I don't wish to share the responsibility of leaving Charlie Gordon to his fate, and it is for this reason that I recommend immediate and active preparation for operations that may be forced upon us by and by.'[7]

These words coincided with the first pathetic messages received from Gordon in three months in which he asked the whereabouts of the relief force. The messages provoked a violent outcry in Fleet Street to save him. Hartington, for once, found the courage to take the initiative and force the issue by threatening to resign. Gladstone had to give way. If the leader of the Whig faction left, the Government would fall and the Grand Old Man's precious Franchise Bill would be lost.

On August 5th, the Government obtained a vote of credit (174 to 14) for £300,000 to undertake operations for the relief of Gordon, *should they become necessary*, and to make certain preparations in respect thereof.

The first action Wolseley had to fight was termed 'the battle of the routes'. When the adjutant-general recommended in April that a relieving force move up the Nile valley, his view was challenged by General Sir Frederick Stephenson, the commander of the army of occupation in Egypt. 'Dear old Ben', as he was nicknamed by his admirers, declared that boats would never make it through the cataracts, and he was backed up by naval officers who carefully explored the Nile route. Supported by most of the 'experts' and fellow officers in Egypt, Stephenson advocated the

Suakim–Berber route, which would be shorter – 280 miles as against
1,650 miles from Cairo to Berber – and quicker. With Suakim as a base
the resources of the Empire could be brought closer. The care of the sick
could be better provided for, and even ice would be made available along
this line. 'The balance of testimony and authority,' Gladstone told the
Queen, 'was decidedly against him [Wolseley], and the idea of Suakim
and Berber route ... was entertained in preference.'[8] Even Wolseley himself was silenced for a time when the Government promised a Suakim–
Berber railway, which it was estimated could be built in three months'
time. But when construction was delayed until June and it was learned
that Berber had fallen, Wolseley declared that whatever advantage the
Suakim–Berber route possessed was gone and returned to his original
proposition.

The Nile route, argued Wolseley, had one great advantage – water, the
most serious want in a tropical or desert region. Instead of ice, those on the
Suakim–Berber track, the last hundred miles of which was an almost
waterless desert, would thirst for the foulest liquid. It should be remembered, he further stated, that on the desert the hardy Arab, who eats
vegetables instead of salted provisions, requires from 15 to 20 lb. weight of
water daily. And where the desert traveller would bake under a savage
sun, those in Nile boats would be screened by awnings and fanned by Nile
breezes. Would it be possible, Wolseley asked, to collect sufficient camels
to carry men and provisions in such a thrust across the merciless desert?
For every 1,000 men to move anywhere, 4,000 lb. of foodstuff alone
would be required each day. Two camels, which cost more than one
boat, could carry 700 lb. at most, whereas his Nile boats would carry
three months' provisions for its dozen or so passengers, their camp equipment, ammunition, and all that soldiers require in the field. Nor do boats
have to be fed.

In July a committee of old Red River men, McNeill, Buller, and Butler,
testified as to the absolute feasibility of Wolseley's plan to use the same
small boats up the Nile. According to them, the Nile route would present
less difficulty than the journey to Fort Garry in 1870. Gordon, also, had
favoured the Nile route. By the beginning of August the Cabinet, Radicals
and Whigs alike, leaned towards the Nile approach that seemed to promise
a bloodless regatta up a river, like the Red River expedition, rather than
sponsor another round of violent clashes with Osman Digna in land as
untamed as his followers.

Since Stephenson had little faith in the Nile plan, Hartington thought
that it would be unfair to ask him to assume command. Moreover, rather

than risk failure with a commander who imperfectly understood the Nile plan, he proposed Wolseley to take, temporarily, the chief command in Egypt. Wolseley, who never had the slightest hint from Hartington – whom he saw almost every day – as to what was in the wind, was agreeably surprised.

Hartington did not give Wolseley any indication of what he had in mind because of the possibility of his candidature being rejected. The Radicals, most of all Dilke and Chamberlain (whom Wolseley personally loathed as demagogues), objected to Wolseley heading a large expedition that might result in the reoccupation of the Sudan. The Duke of Cambridge also demurred, complaining lamely that he was being deprived of the services of his adjutant-general. He roused Victoria, who resented the vulgar demand of sending for 'our only General', which she believed was so injurious to the morale of her soldiers. For a brief time there was a heated, triangular exchange of telegrams between the Queen at Balmoral, her royal cousin in Edinburgh, and Hartington at Bolton Abbey. Gladstone, meanwhile, hemmed and hawed. He still hoped, somehow, the expedition might be avoided. To send to the Sudan a determined soldier like Wolseley, eager to save his friend, might commit the Government to war against his will. Hartington, however, once more firmly put his foot down. Gladstone could well ask, what had got into this ordinarily lethargic politician? With the Prime Minister forced to back his War Minister in the selection of Wolseley, the Queen gave way. The decision was popularly approved. Wolseley's ability to calculate with extraordinary accuracy questions of time and distance was well known.

And wherever Wolseley went, the 'gang' was sure to go. First his right hand, Stewart, 'the very best all-round Staff officer'. If necessary Stewart would become his fist and punch his way through to Khartoum. To serve as chief of staff, Buller, the red-faced Mars, stouter than ever and full of good things. Buller was put to work organizing the whole equipment and provisions of the boats. He also generously supplied himself; forty camels would be required to carry his personal effects. Brackenbury, the scholastic soldier, invaluable as an organizer, but not improved in manner or beauty. Wolseley found him 'yellower and certainly much uglier than ever', and still, by far, the most disliked man in the army, from the Duke of Cambridge downwards. The energetic, bustling Wood to command the line of communications of 1,400 miles, with which there was nothing to compare since Napoleon went to Moscow. Wood was already at Wady Halfa preparing the advance base, buying camels, collecting stores and munitions, and arranging for transport up the river.

Though the War Secretary generally supported Wolseley's sections, Cambridge did prevent the transfer of such officers as Baker Russell to the Sudan. Wolseley was nevertheless surprised that he succeeded in getting as many officers as he did. 'The Duke,' he wrote to Lady Wolseley, 'has to be coaxed and flattered and then terrified as one would act if dealing with some naughty little girl or some foolish old woman.'9 For the sake of the army, however, Wolseley wished that Bismarck would make him King of Brunswick.

'The history of the British army,' wrote Childers, 'is certainly one wonderful adventure, and their present advance up the Nile will exceed all previous efforts.'10 It was a feeling shared by every man in the service who wanted to escape the slow poison of soldiering at home. Wolseley was overwhelmed by applications for what promised to be a romantic, swashbuckling enterprise. First in line was the Prince. The Queen, however, not only revived her old objections, but when Gladstone asked that he at least be kept informed regarding important happenings in the Cabinet and the Sudan, she curtly told him that 'secrets should not be divulged to persons who talk too much'.11 Wolseley nevertheless privately agreed to keep him informed as to his movements, and promised to try and find employment for some of his friends. Among the latter was the daredevil Lord Charles Beresford, darling of high society, as much at home on the floor of Parliament as on the quarter-deck of a warship. His daring in taking a gunboat under the very batteries of the Egyptian forts during the bombardment of Alexandria elicited from the admiral the signal 'Well done, *Condor!*' which became a proud slogan throughout the navy. Wolseley soon found 'Charlie' to be frank, clever, exuberant, and always ready to perpetrate the most outrageous practical jokes, which caused the Queen to describe him as 'a trifle cracky'.

Some men risked arrest and possible court martial to join the expedition. Later in Egypt a band-boy was discovered as a stowaway. He defended himself by saying that out of the entire band he was the only one without a medal, and he could not stand it any longer.

The first thing to be done was to arrange for the transportation. Because of his passion to put the Red River campaign on an enormous scale, Wolseley asked Butler, who had just returned from 'across' the Atlantic, to take charge of construction and delivery of the Nile boats, actually man-of-war 'whalers'. They had to be large enough to carry a dozen men with a hundred days' supplies and ammunition in specially designed weather-resistant cases that would fit snugly at the bottom of a boat, and later on a camel's back. Moreover, the whalers must be light enough to be carried on the men's shoulders, but sturdy enough to withstand rapids, whirlpools, and sandstorms; roomy but small of draught; slight and easy to row but lasting. After much experimentation with various models, Butler managed to reconcile the many contradictory requirements in a boat 30 feet long with a beam of 6 feet 6 inches and a draught of 2 feet 6 inches, fitted for twelve oars and a couple of masts.

The Admiralty flatly declared that it would take from two to three months to construct 400 of them. However, it took more than admirals to discourage the impatient Irishman. Orders for the special craft were placed with forty-seven British firms. Working night and day, nearly 100 were ready to leave England's shores in twenty-seven days. Hartington, meanwhile, authorized the construction of an additional 400.

The Nile boats were not received without ridicule. It was predicted that they would be dashed to pieces on rocks, their crews sucked under by whirlpools and devoured by crocodiles. The authorities in Egypt continued to hammer away against the scheme long after the first whaler was launched. Their remonstrances were backed by the 'experts' in England. The London press was strongly opposed to the idea, pronouncing it 'sheer quackery' ... 'a wicked waste of money' ... 'an unfloatable flotilla' ... 'madness'. Tommy Atkins, it was further argued, understood little about sailing and rowing. Wolseley, nevertheless, provided a solution: he would employ Kroomen, who had performed such excellent service in the Ashanti campaign, and voyageurs who had done so much to make his little Red River expedition a success. A steamer was sent to West Africa to collect some 300 of the former. Arriving in Egypt, the strong, happy, obedient Kroomen were even taught a little drill, though they could certainly not be taken into action, for they still boasted of their cowardice as a national trait.

The Canadian authorities were asked to recruit 400 voyageurs, under Canadian officers, though the British Government promised to pay them and accept all expenses. Unfortunately the voyageur class as Wolseley had known them was virtually extinct. The force of 386 men that was hurriedly collected proved to be a microcosm of the Dominion's citizens. There were white men (French-speaking and English-speaking), halfbreeds, and Indians, mainly Iroquois whom Wolseley specifically requested. There were illiterates and men of education. Many were tellers, storekeepers, cowboys, lawyers – anything but voyageurs – who joined for the sheer adventure and good pay of forty dollars per month. Some were to prove worse than useless, capsizing and smashing boats on the rocks before they 'got the hang of it'. Many of the names alone, such as

'Patrick Murphy, Limerick', somehow lacked the flavour of birchbark shooting rapids in the wilderness. The great majority, however, demonstrated their worth many times over. The expedition could actually have used a couple of hundred more, redskins and half-breeds in particular. Strange to say, a close intimacy sprang up between the Indians and the black Arabs of the Sudan, while the latter kept their distance from the chattering Kroomen, whom they called 'English Blacks'.

Working under contract as civilians, the Canadians were placed in a position independent of the officers. There were many instances of insubordination and abusive language to officers. One officer, taking exception to their informal speech, had to teach them better manners with his fists. And since Wolseley had decided to make it another 'soft drink' campaign, it was sometimes found necessary to fix bayonets to prevent voyageurs, who had a strong prediliction for 'fire-water', from raiding medical stores and bartering with the natives.

Knowing that men deprived of liquor crave sweets, Wolseley insisted on substituting tons of jam and marmalade, despite protests at the War Office. It was at least one minor point upon which Wolseley and the Queen could agree when he paid a quick farewell visit to Osborne the day before his departure (August 31st) for Trieste where he would board a man-of-war.

Wolseley hoped to avoid any unpleasant encounters with Royalty, most of all an objecting Cambridge, before his departure. But as soon as Wolseley's appointment was finally confirmed and his plans for a Nile campaign revealed, the Duke raced back from Scotland 'in a devil of a rage, and so hot has been his head and his anger', Wolseley told his friend Lady Neville, 'I am sure he will have a bad attack of the gout.'[12] He did.

Wolseley waited until he was well out to sea on the *Iris* before he sprung his boldest, most revolutionary plan on the Duke. In wavy strokes that suggested the condition of the Mediterranean, he informed his superior at the War Office that he would require a Camel Corps to act as mounted infantry for a possible strike across the desert in the final stages of the campaign. This remarkable commando would be a *corps d'élite* for which he would skim off the cream of all the cavalry, the seven battalions of Guards, and the two battalions of the Rifle Brigade: by taking two officers and forty picked men from each regiment and combining them to form a Heavy and Light Camel regiment and a Guard's Camel regiment, to which was eventually to be attached 100 seasoned marines – a total of sixty-one officers and 1,121 men. A Mounted Infantry Camel regiment, consisting of Sussex and Essex regiments, would join them in Egypt – an additional twenty-five officers and 480 men. To sugar-coat the pill, Wolseley suggested that Colonel Primrose, a friend of Cambridge and Hartington, be offered command of the Guard's Camel regiment, and that a place might be found for the Duke's third son, Major Augustus Fitzgeorge (11th Hussars).

On having recovered his breath, the Duke then denounced the scheme as 'outrageous'. The 'principle is unsound,' he declared, and detrimental to the *esprit de corps* of the regiments. But since Hartington and the Government sanctioned the proposal as a measure that might save Gordon, he did not see 'how it can be refused with propriety'.[13] With commendable speed the Duke brought the detachments together and inspected every man. They landed in Egypt on October 7th. 'A finer shipload of men,' declared one officer, 'never left England.'[14]

The idea of a 'camelry' was vigorously assailed in some quarters. Taking a little of everything, it was said, may be a capital way to make a salad dressing, but it is not the way to make an effective military instrument. The illustrated journals, more in jest than in criticism, offered cartoons of the trooper of the future: one depicted a horse-guardsman on a bicycle; another showed a cavalryman on a zebra and his comrade on a giraffe, which had the advantage of serving also as a portable signal post. The Duke never stopped grumbling about the 'Nile Circus'.

The Duke was nevertheless gratified that his son Augustus would have an opportunity for distinction. Because of his delicate health, however, Cambridge asked that Wolseley find some 'light work' for him. The latter promised to see what he could do, but privately complained how repulsive it would be for him to have to be near the Duke's 'diseased' offspring. 'I think,' he wrote to his wife, 'I had better send this one into the forefront of battle to see if at least one of the lot can stand being shot at. The father could not and the eldest son took precious good care never to expose his useless carcass to danger.'[15]

Arriving in Cairo on September 9th, Wolseley was quartered in the Kasr-el-Noussa Palace where he immediately set to work organizing the expedition, beginning promptly at five-thirty a.m. each day, and working, as always, standing up to a special desk. The work, which he revelled in, was frequently interrupted by ceremonials and reviews, which he believed necessary to popularize the British army in Egypt. Behind the scenes, he used his famous charm to eliminate some of the bitterness between the old garrison and the flood of new officers he was bringing out from England. The latter's arrival, according to one officer stationed in Cairo, caused 'a disjointing of all our noses here'.[16]

M                                    353

There were almost daily conferences with the politicians, namely Northbrook, who accompanied Wolseley to Egypt, and his cousin, Baring. Wolseley keenly resented their efforts to denigrate Gordon. 'They call him mad,' he told his wife, 'because he does not worship the party gods whom Gladstone and Co. have set up.'[17] In defence of his hero, 'Charlie' Gordon, Wolseley could not resist telling Northbrook, 'Whatever may be our opinion as to his policy we must, at least, all feel proud of him as an Englishman at bay, fighting to protect the men, women, and children he was to bring away safely.'[18]

Gladstone insisted that Wolseley's undertaking be strictly limited to one of 'rescue and retire'. The instructions Wolseley received from Granville on September 19th, based upon the Foreign Secretary's consultations with Baring and Northbrook, stated that his objective was to bring away Gordon and Stewart from Khartoum, and whatever Egyptian soldiers and civilians wished to return. Once this had been done, no further offensive operations were to be undertaken, for Egyptian rule in the Sudan should end. Thinking it quite probable that Gordon might refuse to come away, the Khedive was instructed to give Wolseley a secret firman which would allow him to supersede, if necessary, a reluctant Gordon.

Before leaving Cairo, Wolseley predicted to his wife, 'I ought to shake hands with Gordon near Khartoum, about 31st of January next.'[19]

On September 27th, Wolseley boarded a train for Assiut which was described as the most uncomfortable in the world. At Assiut Wolseley and some of his staff boarded the *Ferooz*, one of the Khedive's yachts, and were soon 'serenely breasting the muddy current of the Nile'. All along the river there were scenes of busy preparations. Of greatest interest were the lines of whalers strung out behind motherly steamers. Wolseley, in shirt-sleeves, spent most of his time in his cabin waging his own little war on the flies while trying to read *The Life of Cicero*. This eloquent Roman who 'pandered to the whims of the mob to gain and retain power' reminded him of Gladstone. Could there be anything more absurd, he asked himself, than explaining to a nation the subtle differences between 'surrounded' and 'hemmed in' while Gordon was obviously in great danger? What a pleasure it was to leave all those pusillanimous and vacillating politicians behind.

Pausing at Assuan, Wolseley tried to bring some order to the telegraph service. The Egyptian operators were unaccustomed to working under pressure and often took bribes from correspondents for priority of service. Wolseley now took exclusive possession of the single line south and imposed a tight censorship. Maintaining a line deep in the Sudan would not be an easy task. One poor linesman was seized by Hadendowa tribesmen, tied to a pole and severely burned when the ends of the cut wires were put into his ears so as to make him talk like the singing wires and reveal the white man's plans.

Threading its way through the less formidable First Cataract above Assuan, the royal yacht reached Wady Halfa, the last outpost of civilization beyond which the Roman legions never penetrated. Wady Halfa, when properly rolled off an Arab's tongue, has an impressive sound, but the thousands of Englishmen passing through would pronounce it 'Bloody Half-way'. It was little more than a collection of ill-assorted mud hovels before Wood arrived. Now, as the base of operations, it looked to the newcomer's eye as if 'the goods station of a London terminus, a couple of battalions of infantry, the War Office, and a considerable portion of Woolwich Arsenal had been all thoroughly shaken together, and then cast forth on the desert.'[20]

Tragic news awaited Wolseley in Wady Halfa. On September 10th Gordon had sent Colonel J. D. H. Stewart, together with a few other Europeans, on a steamer down the Nile to run the Mahdi's gauntlet, and inform the outside world of the true and desperate state of Khartoum. Before reaching Dongola and safety, the ship struck a rock. The local sheikh disarmed the party with promises to help them on their journey and then treacherously murdered them. 'If only,' Wolseley exclaimed, 'Stewart had died in battle in place of being murdered like an Irish landlord by a cowardly sulking reptile such as this country and Ireland produce in large numbers! May that murderer fall into my hands.'[21]

Gordon, meanwhile, received the heartening news from Major Kitchener operating out of Dongola, some 250 miles south of Wady Halfa, that a relief expedition for which he had waited so long was under way.

Kitchener was the antenna of the expedition and sole link between Gordon and Wolseley. Daily he risked his life in garnering intelligence and in trying to send and receive messages from the beleaguered city. Rather than submit to torture if caught, the intrepid Kitchener always carried a small bottle of poison concealed on his person. Wolseley, who had by now learned to appreciate the worth of this somewhat headstrong subordinate, heard that his talent for disguise was so exceptional that a soldier once threw a stone at him believing him to be a native who had no business moving about the camp.

Establishing his quarters on board a dabahbeeyeh, or native boat,

Wolseley undertook the organization of transport and supply. Few but the professional soldier could appreciate the logistical labour such work entailed, especially in a land as desolate as the Sudan.

An army, like a serpent, travels on its stomach. Great pyramids of food alone were concentrated at Wady Halfa. The chief ration of meat was represented by 1,608,500 tins of beef from Chicago, called 'bully beef'. There were 1,359,400 lb. of ship's biscuits, 20,800 lb. of pickles, 1,003 pints of champagne (for the sickly), baking powder, lime juice, compressed vegetables, tea, erbswurst, etc. All had to be relayed to a chain of intermediate depots up the Nile from which soldiers could draw rations while keeping intact the supplies freighted in the whalers to the 'fighting base', which was later established at Korti. It would not be until the beginning of November that a sufficient collection of supplies would permit Wolseley's sending forward the main body of his force.

Much of this work had to be entrusted to well-paid native workers, as well as Egyptian soldiers, who refused to be hurried. They required gentleness and persuasion. Religious ceremonies, which involved irritating delays, had to be respected. When one general wired to another to inquire if the Muslims might be allowed to fire a salute at Ramadan, the curt reply was, 'I don't care a Damadam.' The natives, of course, considered the whole proceeding as a foolish waste of money and energy. What a mad people these English must be to send an army to the heart of the Sudan to save one Englishman.

The greatest obstacles were the cataracts. They were to be found wherever ridges of granite crossed the Nile bed. No two were alike, and the most obstructive was the Second Cataract above Wady Halfa, nine miles of grotesquely shaped black rocks tossed by a volcanic convulsion, over which the narrowed river rushed wildly and seethed with whirlpools. The deep gorge called Bab-el-Kebir, the 'Big Gate', between two carved chins of mountain, produced such savage churning torrents that steamers 'forging against it trembled like a whip'.[22] The naval experts pronounced it utterly impassable – all, that is, but Beresford. With the assistance of 4,000 natives who prayed to Allah for aid, and 1,500 British soldiers who used language somewhat the reverse of prayer, the resourceful captain managed to haul the steamers through. Butler's whalers also found a passage. Of the 549 whalers taken through the cataract by November 22nd, 166 navigated the 'Big Gate', the rest were portaged. Only three were smashed. But it was slow work.

Wolseley found time to welcome the voyageurs, some of whom had been with him on the Red River. They were in holiday spirits when their barges put in at Wady Halfa. To amuse themselves some had played cards while others bombarded the natives ashore with biscuits. Their suits of thick grey tweed, black shiny hats, and moccasins gave them a slovenly appearance, but they looked sturdy enough for the boating requirements of the whalers that were turned over to them.

Not far behind were the first detachments of the Heavy Camel regiment. They looked like scarecrows, Wolseley thought, in their out-sized grey serge tunics, loose yellow-ochre breeches, blue goggles and veils he had prescribed for them. He was anxious to see the picture they would make on a camel, most of all the noble 'tin bellies'.

The uninitiated soldier found the camel a curious, unfriendly, almost frightening beast. The miserable animal seemed to suffer from a chronic condition of extreme mental depression. When being fed, saddled, or ridden, the mount would groan and roar complainingly. The brute seemed fiercer than a lion when the novice was treated to the terrifying sight of an open mouth going for the rider with a hideous gurgling sound in its throat. 'He will bite the hand that feeds and tends him,' reported *The Times* correspondent who hoped to make a pet of his camel; 'he knows not gratitude, is bereft of softer passions and looks upon whomsoever approaches him – for whatever purpose – as his bitter enemy'. Ordinarily, however, the camel is a docile beast, one that rarely kicks or bites. Only one soldier was taken into hospital for camel bite.

Wolseley recognized the great risk in trying to train men to handle this novel steed, but he gambled on the British soldier being able to adapt himself once more to the demands of a great empire. Day after day men of the special corps were taught the ways of the camel: how to mount and dismount; how to make him kneel quickly and tie his front legs so that he might provide cover before the onslaught of a charging enemy; how to form hollow squares and other strange manœuvres of all kinds. Few, at first, learned to ride the beast with comfort. They felt insecure perched loosely with their legs crossed in front of them never knowing what the brute was going to do next. 'Very clever camel, mine, sir,' a beginner told an officer. 'Why, he's been playing cup and ball with me for an hour and a half, and he's only missed me twice!'[23]

The camels suffered, too. Many were ruined and killed by improper care. The popular myth that a camel is a hardy, almost indestructible beast that requires little fodder and no water was not easily dispelled. The army, most of all the commissariat, had much to learn about the intelligent management of camels and native drivers, whose numbers were woefully insufficient. The difficulty began with a hurried commander-in-chief who had failed to appreciate the crucial problem of transport and supply where the unfamiliar camel was concerned. Wolseley, moreover, appointed an inexperienced director of transport, Colonel Furse, who collected a company of officers and men no less ignorant than himself. Thousands of beasts were enfeebled by overwork and crippled by improper saddling that produced enormous sores. Worst of all, Wolseley was initially misinformed as to the number of camels needed. Only 8,000, many of whom were old and worn, were procured by officers who knew little of the art of camel buying, where at least 10,000 were required, and 12,000 would not have been excessive.

Feeling his presence was required at Dongola where he could better communicate with Gordon, Wolseley moved forward his scheduled departure from Wady Halfa to October 28th. There was also the problem of dealing personally with the Mudir, the local autocrat whom Sir Herbert Stewart, in command of the forward station, reported as insolent and unco-operative. The Chief, his staff, and an escort of nearly a hundred mounted men took their camels at Sarras, still vibrating from a short, uncomfortable train ride, and proceeded along the Nile. Wolseley personally detested camels. The magnificent female the Khedive lent him proved an unreliable beast, and the disgusting way she gurgled reminded him of Brackenbury.

Not long after departure, the general encountered a cloud of dust coming north which was made by a body of officers. Concluding a brief chat with them, Wolseley tried to put his mount into a trot. Instead, his camel suddenly swerved to join the departing riders and threw him to the ground. Before anyone could assist the Chief, he remounted. The embarrassed Wolseley looked long and hard at Melton Prior, the illustrator-correspondent who was with the group. Realizing that the general feared a forthcoming sketch of his undignified fall, the tactful artist declared, 'I did not see you fall, sir.'[24]

Once more Wolseley was out to establish a local record for speed, to do an eight-day journey in seven. During the day, the party raced along the Nile with frequent short-cuts across the desert. At night, they slept under open skies. It was a desolate region, vast and undefined, with no railways, no roads, no trees, no grass and no water but the winding, shimmering Nile which gave the Sudan life and unity. Some called the scenery picturesque, but to Wolseley it was a forbidding wasteland, like a world destroyed.

Nowhere on earth could the sun be more cruel. During the heat of the day, which has been known to range as high as 140 degrees, even the lizards and flies would huddle under the camel's saddle to escape the sun. The land began to look like hell – with the fires put out. All about the sterile jungle of black rocks glowed like huge coals. Wolseley felt his blood circulate as if it were liquid fire. Soon his brain began to lose touch with reality. The camels with their air of hopeless misery became lost souls in some more evil part of Hades, tormented by impish riders who caused them to moan dolefully. The Nile always restored the senses, soothing parched eyes and cooling baked lips. The muddy water had the taste of thick, rich cream.

The Mudir of Dongola, Mustapha Bey Yawer, was a crafty Circassian, feared and respected throughout his province, and suspected by the British of playing a double game. His professed allegiance seemed more sincere after he defeated the local Mahdist rebels in September and treated the advancing troops to the sickening sight of their severed heads. Wolseley, recognizing his great influence throughout the land, determined to keep the Mudir's loyalty, which might soon be demonstrated by his providing additional camels and food. Kitchener and other British officers warned the general that he was not an easy man to deal with, describing him as vain, calculating, and ill-mannered. Moreover his courage, born of fanatical piety, was extraordinary. When the Mudir went into battle, it was said he demoralized his enemies by throwing sand at them.

The great general's arrival in Dongola began with an affront. As a superior official, Wolseley expected the Mudir to be there to greet him when he stepped ashore from the steamer in which he completed the last few miles of his journey. But only Stewart and lesser Turco-Egyptian officials were on hand for the ceremony. The next day an insulted Wolseley went to the Mudir's residence situated amidst dilapidated mosques and their tottering minarets.

When his lordship entered the courtyard, he was greeted by a mock battle between black Arab warriors staged for his 'entertainment' by the tricky Mudir. As the excitable natives seemed to work themselves up to an uncontrollable frenzy, Wolseley did not know whether to leave or stay. Suddenly with mad yells and screams they rushed at the red-coated visitor. 'I saw the slightest wince on the part of our general,' related one witness, 'as a man raised his spear as though to thrust at him.'[25] Wolseley, nevertheless, passed the Mudir's test.

Over sweets and coffee, an unctuous Mudir shared Wolseley's optimism regarding Gordon's future. The latest news from Khartoum was good. A few hours earlier, Kitchener telegraphed that Gordon had replied to the

Mahdi's offer to surrender by defiantly declaring he would hold the city for years. Wolseley managed the Mudir 'fairly well by flattering him and making him believe he was really a great man',[26] though at times he could be a nuisance. When the devout Circassian was allowed to use the telegraph-line, he insisted on prefacing each message with a chapter from the Koran.

The commander-in-chief kept a punishing schedule: preparing the advance, negotiating with Arab tribesmen in the vicinity, and maintaining control over local authorities. Between five a.m. and noon, he dashed about the city and neighbouring country. All afternoon he was in his office making work for others. Before dinner he exercised the intellect, reading and writing until midnight. Those about him marvelled at the way he kept to such a regimen without the slightest sign of fatigue or irritability.

But Wolseley became vexed when supplies and whalers began to arrive irregularly. Then for five whole days none moved at all. To expedite progress, the general called for his camel and two aides to accompany him on a flying trip back to Wady Halfa. A Scots subaltern calculated that a camel subjected its rider to 1,285 distinct jerks per mile; Wolseley felt every one of them by the time he concluded his fifty camel-bumping miles each day. Not since Gordon had the natives seen anyone travel at such speed. By the time he reached Sarras four days later (November 16th), his camel could barely stand, for like her rider she had little food or water the last day. Wolseley was refreshed that night by a bottle of champagne and the local joke that the poor nuns taken by the Mahdi had married Greek priests – 'Union of the Greek and Latin Churches!'

The chief cause for delay was Buller's dereliction in ordering sufficient coal, which caused all steamers between Assuan and Wady Halfa to stop running. The chief of staff had already remedied the retarding oversight by negotiating a new contract with Thomas Cook and Co. to supply more coal. Such faulty staff work nevertheless cost, according to Wolseley's estimate, at least three weeks' delay.

In Wady Halfa, Wolseley also learned that there was discord among his staff. Dissatisfied with his rank to begin with, Butler chafed under a chief of staff whom he considered incompetent. Wood, meanwhile, was telling everyone that Earle (scheduled to command a brigade) 'is a Sergeant-Major that is quite useless'. And Buller was belittling 'everyone who may possibly enter the lists with him in the military race for distinction'.[27] With bickering, jealousy, and wounded vanities on all sides, the Chief felt that his staff, which should be working as a team, had let him down.

On November 17th, Wolseley received his first direct message from Gordon. He told how he could not read Wolseley's messages because the cipher had been sent away with Colonel J. D. H. Stewart. The food supply was running low and desertion to the enemy was running high as the Mahdi's forces pressed a miserable garrison. 'We can hold out for forty days with ease;' he wrote, 'after that it will be difficult.' Since the message was dated November 4th, it meant his position would become extremely difficult after December 14th. This gave Wolseley less time than he had counted on.

It would be difficult to communicate with Gordon *en clair*, but in an ingeniously disguised message Wolseley conveyed the date, January 7th, for his concentration near Korti. 'For obvious reasons,' he told Gordon, 'I do not give you details how my army is composed, but it is strong enough to wipe Mohammed Ahmed and all his followers off the face of the earth.' At the same time, to please the peace-minded Gladstone Government, Wolseley at least went through the motions of offering terms to the Mahdi who, as he anticipated, ignored them.

On his way back to Dongola, Wolseley composed a stirring message to his men to redouble their efforts on Gordon's behalf. 'It is a difficult thing,' he wrote to his wife, 'for an Englishman to compose an order of this sort. For a Frenchman, and perhaps all other foreigners, the task is easy; he can afford to be heroic and pompous in his expression without being thought ridiculous.'[28]

So as to 'get the last ounce' out of the men with the oars, the general offered a prize of £100 and a place in front on the final march to the battalion which made the fastest run between Sarras and Korti. The Queen sharply censured Wolseley for offering a premium to his men. British soldiers, in her opinion, are always expected to do their utmost! Wolseley was deeply offended.

The appeal to the soldiers' patriotic and sporting instincts began to show results. In addition, the voyageurs were used more efficiently as pilots than as navigators by establishing them permanently in fixed camps near dangerous waters, rather than working them up and down the length of the river.

Whoever called this a 'Nile picnic', declared one of Wolseley's fresh-water sailors, 'I would like to see him with both hands poulticed in a sling.'[29] In the beginning the idea of rowing up the Nile through an almost unknown land appealed strongly to the men's sense of adventure. The future general, Sir Ian Hamilton, related how they felt like 'Boy

Scouts dressed up like Red Indians let loose in a flotilla of canoes'.[30] But the strain of unceasing labour quickly robbed the Nile voyage of much of its glamour.

All hands were turned out at dawn. Following a quick breakfast, they put their blistered hands to the oars to row like galley slaves; or they worked around rapids and sand-banks, which meant back-breaking poling, shoving in water up to their knees, toiling at the end of a rope, or hauling the whaler short distances. The work grew hotter each day as they seemed to catch up with the sun's slow retreat south. On good days, sailing days, they enjoyed gliding on deep, smooth water with the cooling north wind at their back that so frequently swept south to fill the void created by heated air rising from the equatorial regions of Africa. But normally the ever-widening Nile* fought them with treacherous, capsizing currents and hidden rocks that knocked holes in the whalers. Many soldiers never took to the water and lived in fear of drowning. 'You know I know nothing about a boat, or what it ought to do,' wrote one officer in a family letter, 'and I am ashamed to tell you that the whole time I am sweating with terror. And every night when I go to bed I dream of whirlpools and boiling rapids and then I dream I am drowned.' (Less than a score were actually drowned.)

Life was hard in the long line of slow-moving boats. It was hurry, hurry all the way. Tired bodies were infested with lice and often covered with boils, for the slightest scratch might be poisoned by insects, mainly flies. On shore they might be attacked by white ants and other crawling things. Scurvy, cholera, and typhoid often tracked them. They lived where possible off the country or ate unappetizing rations, the more luxurious foods being held in reserve at the bottom of the boat. The little time allowed them after supper was spent mending clothes. The wear and tear of their contest with 'Pharaoh's stream' left many bootless and in rags. Trousers were repaired with biscuit tins. The tartan trews of the Black Watch were patched with old socks. A few preferred to row naked like the Kroomen. But naked or not, they all took a pride in wearing a thoroughly disreputable head-dress, such as a brimless felt hat, a mangy old rabbit skin, a dirty turban or fez. On arriving at Korti, a reporter described them as resembling Falstaff's ragged followers rather than a body of Britain's finest troops. The hard labour, however, had weeded out the unfit and the rest were 'as hard as nails', reported one of Wolseley's aides, 'without an ounce of superfluous flesh upon them, lean, bronzed and muscular, ready and fit to go anywhere and do anything.'[31]

* Because of evaporation and absorption, the Nile is far larger at Berber than at Cairo.

The best time was made by the 1st Battalion of the Royal Irish. Wolseley was 'very gratified' to give the prize to his 'own countrymen', who used the money to buy a silver replica of a Nile whaler. Some attributed the victory to the encouragement of popular, grey-bearded Father Brindle who pulled an oar as well as the best of them. He had the respect of every man in the army from private to general. Wolseley tried several times to have him knighted. Others claimed the Irish won because they had nothing but Nile water to drink.

As Wolseley penned his congratulations to the Royal Irish, he was interrupted by the arrival of Colonel Burnaby. Along with millions of his countrymen, Wolseley was dazzled by the exploits of Burnaby: riding through Russian Central Asia in the middle of winter, ballooning perilously across the Channel, fighting Russians in the Balkans, standing up to fuzzy-wuzzies at El Teb with a shotgun, thereby vindicating, as he asserted, 'the supremacy of the Anglo-Saxon race'. Burnaby was said to be the typical Englishman, a man 'of great strength,* equable temper, simple unostentatious manners', etc. But like Gordon, his erratic undertakings and disregard for authority caused resentment in official circles. The Government was angered by his political attacks on their Sudan policy, which he considered spineless. The Duke was annoyed by his unconventional military deportment. When Burnaby, this 'bad fellow', as Cambridge called him, was refused permission to join the Nile force, his friend Wolseley privately advised him to come to the Sudan on his own where it would be difficult for the War Office to interfere with a commander's requests. Asking for a leave of absence, ostensibly 'to take a trip to the Cape', Burnaby headed straight down the Nile. Wolseley gave him the quickly created job of inspecting staff officer.

'At home it is wine and women,' observed the recently arrived Burnaby, 'but out here, from what I can see, it's men and water.' [32] It was a sentiment heartily seconded by the officers of the camelry, for these men – many of whom were noblemen – were accustomed to the club life, the female companionship, and the military pageants of soldiering in Britain. Few in fact had ever fired a shot in anger. Not that these representatives of the nation's leading families were complaining. They were ready to suffer great hardship and privation – and often did. McCalmont, second in command of the Light Camel regiment, said that their enthusiasm was such they acted as if they 'were going to fight the Battle of Waterloo over again'. [33] At sea, the officers and men of these crack regiments shot to

* On one occasion Burnaby carried two small ponies, one under each arm, from an upstairs exhibit room down to a courtyard.

pieces everything that would float, including an occasional porpoise. On the Nile it was the crocodiles who suffered.

The men on the whalers, or 'Wet Bobs' as they were called, found it difficult to conceal their jealousy as they slaved away like 'poor plebeians' on bully beef and weevil-infested biscuits while 'this band of patricians' rode stately camels and nibbled 'the toothsome jam, cheese and boiled mutton'. It was 'a scurvy trick,' wrote Sir Ian Hamilton, 'and my bleeding gums and loosened teeth taught me once and for all the advantages of belonging to the aristocracy.'[34]

More galling was the news that the camelry would go to the front first and hog all the glory. To overtake the clock, Wolseley had come to the conclusion that his camel commando must be employed in the emergency for which it was created. The danger to Gordon was too great to wait for the whalers to complete the rocky river route on a rapidly falling Nile. A quick relief could be effected by separating Stewart's mobile column of camelry from the river at Korti and sending it the short way across the great Nile bend through 176 miles of desert to Metemmeh. At this point, four steamers sent by Gordon in October would be waiting to load some of the troops. With Beresford and his bluejackets to man the steamers, they would dash the remaining ninety-six miles to a famished Khartoum where, Wolseley believed, the sight of a few redcoats should scare off the besiegers. The river column under Earle, meanwhile, would fight its way along 400 roundabout miles of the mighty Nile to Metemmeh where they could replenish the supplies of the desert column and give support in the relief of Khartoum.

Korti was the fastest growing town in the world as over 9,000 men struggled southward on and along the banks of the Nile to increase its dimensions. When the commander-in-chief arrived by steamer in mid December, he approved Stewart's camp site. It was a refreshing resting-place with its groves of palms shading and fanning the white tents and broad sandy streets framed by well-watered gardens. Singing and laughter could be heard throughout the day in a city animated by warlike preparations and hope. At night, groups of officers and men assembled to hear the band of the Sussex regiment. Music served to renew the strength and restore the spirits of exhausted men who, with split lips and faces 'like raw beef', climbed down from their camels or stepped out of a whaler that had been home for over a month. As a forest of unit flags, together for the first time, rose before the tents, the commander wrote: 'I am gay because I am confident of success. I never was more confident about any operation I had entrusted to me.'[35]  By Christmas most of the desert column had arrived, but the supply of camels was still far from adequate. Thousands of sick animals had to be left behind to die in the desert or at remount depots established on the way. The Mudir's promise to provide additional camels was not kept, and few could be obtained locally.

Wolseley grew fretful. The staff, Buller in particular, who had unfortunately said that Gordon was not worth the camels, had let him down. The doves in the palm tree over Wolseley's tent irritated him with their cooing, which reminded him of that 'old windbag' Gladstone. On hearing that the Prime Minister, the 'real cause of all our difficulties', was ill and could not sleep, he wrote: 'We have been anxiously looking out for Gladstone's death ... I had long ago composed his epitaph, "Here lies W.E.G. a minister of the Crown who for a very long period exercised authority. He found England a first-rate power and died leaving her a weak third-rate power." '[36]

The desert column could wait no longer. To overcome the short supply of camels, a half-post would be built up at the three rocky pools at Gakdul from which the camels might return for their supplies. The preliminary movement began on December 30th. In addition to the camelry, there were the 19th Hussars, engineers, a medical staff corps with bearers, and three mountain screw-guns (the parts screwed together). The entire force with the exception of Kitchener and the native scouts who had left earlier in the day, paraded before the commander-in-chief, moving forty camels abreast. It was an imposing, mile-long spectacle as 2,000 camels, their necks stretching out like ostriches, marched past. The stalwart, bronzed riders kept perfect control over them as they passed Wolseley, and the band played their adopted tune, the old Clan Campbell march, 'The Camels are Coming'. This was the flower of the British army, whose bold, confident manner bespoke centuries of conquest. And they were led, in Wolseley's opinion, by the nation's 'best all-round soldier' – Sir Herbert Stewart.

The parade over, Wolseley rode some distance into the desert where Stewart and the advanced guard saw him standing alone on a little mound. He waved to them and wished them good luck. He stayed to watch the last of the men disappear into that shimmering, remorseless waste about which almost any tale seemed believable. Sceptical natives, who had seen larger parties than this puny force of 1,500 succumb to thirst and the spears of an elusive enemy, prophesied their doom.

The next day, New Year's Eve, while Stewart's men made the hills resound with chorus after chorus of 'Auld Lang Syne', a messenger made his way through the encircling dervishes to deliver a message from

Gordon. The note, postage-stamp size, simply said: 'Khartoum all right. 14. 12. 84. C. G. Gordon.' This hopeful-looking statement was designed to deceive the Mahdi's men should it fall into their hands. A less sanguine verbal message told of the great strength of the enemy and the desperate straits of the garrison, which was consuming the last of the donkeys, dogs, cats, rats, etc., and had grown too weak to bury the dead strewn along the banks of the Nile. 'We want you to come quickly,' said Gordon. But this was qualified by the warning that Wolseley should not leave a hostile Berber behind, which fairly suggested his ability to hold out for a few days more. The messenger further related how the undaunted Gordon, after resting in the afternoon, spent most of the night visiting his outposts to keep the sentries cheered and alert. In the morning he ascended to the roof of the palace to look through his telescope for the first signs of the relief.

Gordon's one hope rested on the swiftness of the desert column, which returned on January 5th with its unloaded camels after depositing the bearded Guards and other detachments to protect the precious wells. An anxious Wolseley rode out six miles to meet his returning desert arm and congratulate Stewart on his successful experiment. The men, who remained in excellent condition, were described by Wolseley as 'the finest lot of men he had ever seen, and could march from one end of Africa to the other'. The camels, however, were another matter; many of these enduring beasts could take no more. Travelling 196 miles in six days, a large number dropped out on the way; others suffered fearfully from large sores, some big enough to put one's fist into. (One soldier did and got a handful of loathsome maggots.) Wolseley wished that 'the visionaries' who wrote so 'flippantly' about the Suakim to Berber route could see the effects of such a desert march.

With only three days' rest, the surviving, overworked camels were sent out again. Stewart, in high spirits, took with him the tardy Beresford, his sailors, and their Gardner machine-gun. Beresford was a source of great amusement, riding a donkey which he named 'Waterford' because the animal had thrown him off his back as many times as that Irish constituency had rejected him as a candidate for Parliament. And as a sailor's remedy for sick camels, he had his boatswain 'caulk the seams' by stuffing oakum and tar into their backs.

It had been Wolseley's intention to accompany Stewart to Metemmeh where Earle, who was already moving up the Nile to take Berber, would join him on the final drive to Khartoum. But Hartington insisted the commander-in-chief should remain at Korti where he could conveniently receive reports from both columns and at the same time remain in constant telegraphic communication with the Government, whose concern was perhaps demonstrated by the 17,000 words relayed on the line in a single night.

Enduring all the risks without actually being part of the advancing column was the worst possible torment for Wolseley. Unlike a battle against a European foe, Stewart's defeat, Wolseley knew, could mean the cruel annihilation of all his men, such as occurred at Isandhlwana. 'This is the first time in my life that I have been chained to the rear in a campaign,' he told Buller, 'and I hope it may be the last. To lead a storming party a day would be child's play to the anxieties of this position.'[37] Wolseley confessed that his nerves were not as good as they used to be. As a responsible commander, he decided to give up smoking, then tea, and soon contemplated doing without claret at his supper of thin soup and bread. When someone asked about the large supply of cigarettes he kept in his tent, Wolseley told him they were for Gordon, a heavy smoker, to whom they would be presented when Stewart opened the way to Khartoum.

Stewart, a humane Englishman, said regretfully: 'I don't like unnecessary slaughter, but I'm afraid we shall have to kill five hundred or so of the poor devils before we can establish ourselves in Metemmeh.'[38] The Mahdi had his own thoughts on the subject of killing. Forewarned of Stewart's intentions by his half-dash to Gakdul, he gathered over 10,000 of his finest warriors to intercept and massacre the British.

The dervishes, however, first waited for the desert to take its toll. On leaving the refreshing wells of Gakdul, the British plodded between two fires, the blazing sky and the heated sands. The endurance of man and beast was tried to the utmost. 'Camels breaking down in all directions,' wrote a Hussar in his diary, 'and the native drivers are falling down and shrieking for water.'[39] Some foolishly gulped their ration of yellow, stinking water early in the day. One soldier offered another a sovereign for a drink, another his watch and chain.

A march of forty-three miles over a waterless tract brought the army before the wells of Abu Klea. Here the men, many with tongues thickening and lips turning black, learned the disheartening news from their protective screen of Hussars that the enemy held the vital wells in force, obviously determined that the British should never reach water. With the tantalizing thought of an abundance of water almost within reach, the desert column bivouacked and tried to rest on the eve of what Winston Churchill described as 'the most savage and bloody action ever fought in the Sudan by British troops.'[40]

Their night roughly broken by incessant sniping and the beating of tom-toms, the men breakfasted and formed up into a square. The camels, save for those carrying ammunition and water, were left behind in a garrisoned zariba of brushwood and boxes. Marching slowly to preserve formation over broken ground, the little band continued down a dark, narrow valley, at the end of which stood the wells protected by hundreds of enemy flags. The moving fortress paused repeatedly to answer the fire from the hills and close up the sluggish camels. Within 500 yards of the now animated banners, Stewart halted once more to restore the dragging rear and care for the wounded. Without warning, 5,000 cleverly concealed Arabs rose from a near-by ravine. They ran forward in perfect order, their disposition resembling a trident with mounted men forming the three points and a sheikh at each tip. 'It looked like a Hyde Park meeting coming towards us,' wrote one soldier.[41] But their murderous intent soon became apparent. Like so many demons in human form, the fuzzy-wuzzies pranced and leaped towards the smoke of the square with a kind of thirst for death. The shouts in their deliriums of hate were like the roar of the sea. Some threw pages of the Koran into the air with passages underlined in blood.

At first, thinking that these 'poor beggars' would never close the ground between them and the massed fire, Englishmen pitied them. But skirmishers fleeing to the square masked the fire of their comrades. One fat sergeant never got back. Even after the tremendous blast of rifle fire commenced, it seemed to have no slowing effect upon the charging dervishes. Their attack veered off the left front of the square, a bristling wall of bayonets spitting fire, and fell with full force on the left rear face made vulnerable by a gap in the line. Riding out of the gap, wading into them single-handed, was the heroic figure of Colonel Burnaby, unmistakable in his Royal Horse Guards uniform of blue. Unhorsed and with blood gushing from his jugular vein, he continued to fight with 'the wild strokes of a proud man dying hard'.

Savage scenes were enacted as British soldiers grappled with brawny Arabs who poured through the gap wielding two-edged swords and six-foot spears. The Gardner gun, from which wonders were expected, was pushed into the gap where after the first few rounds it jammed. The sailors were bowled over in the rush, including Beresford, who was one of the few to jump up again. Many defenders in the gap had to rely on 'sheer pluck and muscle' when their rifles jammed. Those who trusted the steel of their bayonets discovered to their horror that they bent like blades of tin. On entering a dervish body, they stuck fast like a cork-screw. Added to the mechanical failures were human ones. Some soldiers facing about and firing into the square at charging Arabs, shot several of their own men in their excitement. And when what appeared to be a box of cartridges was hastily ripped open, hundreds of gold sovereigns rolled on to the ground. For a few seconds the battle was forgotten by the greedy men near by who scrambled wildly until every last piece disappeared. No less amazing was the sight of one fine old sheikh, his horse never swerving to left or right, bounding into the middle of the square where he planted his banner and began reading a scroll from the Koran until shot down. 'If any man deserved a place in the Muslim paradise,' declared a British officer, 'he did.'[42]

The camels, a source of weakness on the march, now became a pillar of strength. Acting as a living breastwork, indifferent to spears and bullets that thudded into their hides, they broke the momentum of the charge. For a moment the dervishes 'did not know what to do; some crept under the camels, and were shot on the other side'.[43] The framework of Englishmen, some fighting nearly back to back, rallied and closed the gap. All the dervishes inside died. Slowly, sullenly, the outside assailants, their fiery violence expended, drew back. Grapeshot discouraged them each time they turned as if to attack again. A few of the 'dead' Arabs in and about the square who had been shamming, or momentarily stunned, suddenly came to life and engaged single Britons in some fascinating Homeric duels. One soldier exclaimed he now understood how the Romans could enjoy gladiatorial contests.

With three hearty cheers, British style, the square reformed some thirty yards away from the carnage. On the knoll behind them lay seventy-four dead Englishmen spattered with dust and blood. Burnaby's body was covered with a Union Jack. Beresford and a fellow officer agreed over a cigarette that 'it was hard to have to die without knowing who had won the Derby.'[44] As the wax-faced, stiffening carcasses were buried and the wounded cared for, a staff officer counted over 1,100 dervishes, many of whom still wore fiendish expressions on their faces and little cases tied to their arms containing Muslim prayers which the Mahdi promised would turn infidel bullets to water.

Water was now more important than bullets. What little spare water remained was given to the groaning wounded. Men fainted and others suffered great agony from a tongue that filled their mouths. The Hussars soon reported the wells unoccupied, and an army slaked its great thirst with muddy water that would have been declared unfit under ordinary conditions. It was a drink they remembered all their lives. The zariba was transferred to the wells and not until very late the next day did the weary force, reduced by nearly a quarter of its strength and nearly 180 miles from reinforcements, resume its march towards the Nile and towards an enemy of undetermined strength. 'Tomorrow I intend taking Metemmeh,' vowed Stewart to an aide, 'and if Gordon's steamers are there I will the day after [January 20th] send them to Khartoum with Wilson.'

The British soldiers were defeated that night by dense scrub and untrustworthy guides who led them in circles. Hundreds of camels went astray. Whenever the men halted, they dropped like logs and were asleep almost before they hit the ground. Luckily the enemy did not choose to attack in the dark. The sun finally came to the aid of the desert column and showed them the way. Atop a gravelly ridge they were treated to the sight of the distant blue Nile and smoke which they believed was made by Gordon's steamers. A few miles to the north they also saw dervishes swarming out of Metemmeh bent on keeping them from reaching the river. The Englishmen realized they would have to fight again as they did at Abu Klea if they were to survive.

Before marching on, Stewart ordered breakfast and rest behind a flimsy square of boxes and saddles. A somewhat chastened enemy, meanwhile, seemed to prefer Remingtons to spears. Firing accurately from good cover, their bullets caused considerable loss. Stewart received a wound, obviously mortal, just above the groin. Five minutes later, in a steady hand, the dying leader wrote goodbye letters to his wife and mother. 'I know,' he told the latter, 'you are proud of my being hit like this.'[45] Since Burnaby, whom Wolseley had designated as second in command, was dead, Sir Charles Wilson took over. Having consulted Stewart, Wilson left the wounded and baggage in a zariba and prepared to fight his way to the Nile.

'If ever a little British army looked like walking to certain death,' observed Beresford, 'it was that thin square of infantry.'[46] Probably not a man would have survived if the dervishes had not left their concealed positions to charge. The British, with no skirmishers before them this time, commenced firing as coolly as they would at Aldershot on a field day. The front ranks of the enemy peeled off and disappeared into the tall grass. In one instant dervishes were coming forward wildly; the next, they were engaged in a no less wild movement to the rear, sweeping the spectators from the villages before them. The enemy wounded were bayoneted to prevent their slashing and firing at the passing square. A completely spent army with half-dead camels reached the Nile just as the young moon shone on the water. The wounded were lifted in their litters to see the glorious water for which they had fought. Not long thereafter contact was made with Gordon's waiting steamers.

Communications to Korti were irregular and infrequent. 'Consumed with anxiety', Wolseley was tempted to take one of his aides and gallop across the desert to learn the fate of the desert column. On January 17th, the day of Abu Klea, Wolseley was at Twelve Mile Hill, a water-post outside Korti, enjoying the comforting sensation of being that much closer to Stewart and his gallant men. Four days later a bashi-bazouk messenger brought news of the victory. The commander was saddened by the heavy loss. Poor Burnaby! At least persons in high places would no longer hound him, thought Wolseley. It was gratifying to learn that no dervish who got into the square lived to boast of having slain an Englishman, and above all, that Stewart, thank God, was still unharmed.

But not until his men reached Khartoum would the general be able to relax. Wolseley's hair, like Gordon's, suddenly grew whiter. Every afternoon he rode to the commanding knoll south of the camp to scan the horizon with his telescope for the first sign of any news. Every day he wrote of his concern for Stewart, as if he had a premonition of harm befalling him. 'I am nervous about Stewart,' he told his wife, 'for his loss – even being wounded – would really, at this moment, be a national calamity.'[47]

Before dawn on the morning of January 28th, while Wolseley was reading his morning passage from the Bible, an exhausted messenger told him of the Battle of Gubat, or as the natives called it 'the Battle of the Square Which Reached the River', and of Stewart's grievous wound. Wolseley knew instinctively that he would not survive. It was like losing a brother. Writing a consoling letter to Lady Stewart, Wolseley declared, 'if I were a woman, I would sooner be his widow than the wife of half the men I know.'[48] It bothered him a little, however, to remember that Stewart, like Colley, did not believe in a revealed religion. Surely, Wolseley thought, our Maker would not punish unbelievers in the way clergymen and priests would have us believe. He hoped there would be some kind of United Service Club in the hereafter where old soldiers might meet.

A flood of congratulatory messages put Wolseley in better spirits. The Queen was 'rather gushing'. Hartington, who added his felicitations, was annoyed that her message did not go through the War Office, as it properly should. All these telegrams – from Cambridge, the Lord Mayor, the Khedive – were posted for the men to read. Von Moltke, Germany's greatest soldier, expressed it best when he spoke of the desert column as 'a band, not of soldiers but of heroes'.* Wolseley waited in vain for word from Gladstone.

The Royal Irish, meanwhile, volunteered to foot it across the desert to reinforce Wilson's little force. At their head was Buller who was to take over the command. The more Wolseley thought of Wilson being in charge, the more he worried about Gordon's safety. He wrote home, 'Sir C. Wilson, very useful for political work, is no soldier; this is his first dose of fighting, and it has entirely hurt his nerves.'[49] If only he had commissioned Beresford, 'that splendid fighting man', to succeed, or been allowed to employ the quick acting, decisive Baker Russell. Such men would drive the point of the sword home.

Wilson, more accustomed to desk-work than leading men in the field, was running the army as no army should ever be run – by committee. A handful of senior officers were called in for regular consultation. Colonel Boscawen, the second ranking officer, whom Wolseley described as 'having neither nerve, determination or experience', was given executive command when there was fighting to be done. 'Wilson is rather an old woman who doesn't know anything about drill and funks the responsibility,' complained one soldier; 'everyone gives their opinion and advice in the freest manner, from the junior subaltern upwards, and the man who gets Wilson's or Boscawen's ear last, his advice is followed.'[50] Beresford, afflicted with a painful carbuncle so that he could scarcely walk, angrily complained that he could not get Wilson to make up his mind about anything. 'I felt a great change had come over the spirit of the men,' wrote another officer, 'the confidence which was everywhere apparent under Sir Herbert Stewart had vanished.'[51]

Concerned for the safety of his sadly diminished force, the cautious Wilson lost three valuable days in a vain attempt to take the dervish position on the Nile and in making reconnaissances up and down the river. It was not until the morning of January 24th that Wilson seemed to remember the object of the expedition. Hope ran high when he took two of the steamers, actually converted gunboats, and a small detachment of the Royal Sussex, who would wear red tunics at the end of the journey to frighten off the dervishes before Khartoum.

Gordon was right when he wrote that a handful of redcoats was all that was required. Father Ohrwalder, a prisoner in the Mahdi's camp because he refused to renounce his faith, relates how news of the defeat at

* The future Kaiser Wilhelm II, however, expressed his Anglophobia by writing, 'May the Mahdi chuck them all into the Nile.'

Abu Klea put the discouraged Mahdi in mind to raise the siege and retire to Kordofan. The Prophet began to have revelations that called for retreat. All of his council of caliphs and emirs, save one, favoured a withdrawal. The sight of a score of men in scarlet would have sent the Mahdi on a *hegira*. Wilson's delay restored confidence and gave support to the arguments of the solitary councillor, Mohammed el Kerim, who wisely held that nothing was to be lost by an assault: if it failed there was still time to retire; if it succeeded the English would not dare to come any farther. On the night of January 25th it announced that the Mahdi opportunely had a second vision that the city would be delivered into his hands on the following morning.

Exploiting the gap in the ramparts caused by a falling Nile, 40,000 dervishes streamed in and overwhelmed the feeble defenders. The fighting was over in minutes, but the looting, massacre and rape continued. Nor did the women who cut their hair and put on men's clothes escape. Only after 4,000 were dead did the Mahdi call a halt.

Gordon had been first to die. His head was cut off and taken to the Mahdi, where it was identified and hung on a tree to be speared, cursed and spat upon by his followers. This was the fate of the man Butler called 'the bravest, the purest and the most truthful Englishman of his time'.

Two days later Wilson's steamers arrived to be greeted by shells and the jeering shouts of Mahdists lining the banks which announced the death of Gordon. Turning downstream, the steamers were wrecked near an island. Wilson was close to suffering Gordon's fate when Beresford came to the rescue in a steamer caulked with rags and rotten from age. He saved the party and successfully fought his way back. Behind them, at the bottom of the Nile, lay twenty redcoats.

Beaten by forty-eight hours. For the first time in a long and brilliant career, Wolseley tasted the bitterness of failure. He always spoke of February 4th, the day he received the news, as the saddest day of his life; it left him 'utterly knocked out'. His first thoughts were for Gordon. Though his death was not confirmed, he prayed that his friend had died quickly.

If only Stewart had lived, Wolseley said over and over again, the steamers would have started immediately for Khartoum. 'I hate to see Sir C. Wilson,' he wrote home, 'because I cannot help remembering that he *might* have been at Khartoum easily the day before it was betrayed.'[52] Military opinion was almost unanimous in its condemnation of Wilson. But Wilson, soldier in uniform only, did the best he could in a situation that would have been trying to the most seasoned leader. He lost two days where weeks were lost owing to the lack of coal on the lower Nile and the faulty preparations for the camel transport, for which the staff and, therefore, the commander-in-chief himself was responsible. All this, of course, pales into insignificance when compared to the long months Gladstone allowed to pass before he was forced to act on Gordon's behalf. It was he who made it a race against the clock where an oversight, a mishap, an error in judgment could upset the most careful calculations and lead to failure.

Since Abu Klea, Wolseley had experienced many shocks and surprises, but none equalled the news that the timid Government, with uncommon rapidity, decided to avenge Gordon and 'smash the Mahdi at Khartoum'. They left it to a stunned Wolseley to decide when to attack and offered whatever reinforcements were required, cost what it might. A fresh expedition was to be sent to Suakim and a railway constructed to Berber as quickly as possible. Graham was selected to command once more.

This sudden reversal in policy was dictated by public wrath. The dramatic death of Gordon, more shocking than any ordinary defeat, evoked powerful emotions. A day of national mourning was observed. The Queen, made ill by the news, expressed the feelings of her subjects when she sent an accusing telegram to Gladstone, Hartington, and Granville. At no stage in his political career was Gladstone more unpopular.* An unrepentant Gladstone, who never had a word of praise for Gordon, nevertheless cowered before a vote of censure. To satisfy the general cry for vengeance, heard even in his own party, he and his colleagues in the Ministry outjingoed the jingos with fearful sounds and violent threats.

Talleyrand warned that public opinion provided a useful check but a dangerous guide for governments. At first Wolseley glowed with anticipation for the chance to regain his professional pride by destroying the Mahdi's army. 'If I can only kill him,' he told his daughter Frances, 'it will be a very happy finale to our expedition up the Nile.'[53] But his common sense began to prevail. The army was not formed with a view to besieging Khartoum. This could not be done until autumn, which meant paying the heavy penalty of sizzling for six months under the Sudan sun. Wolseley privately told his friends that he feared the new campaign would be the biggest, most costly war since Waterloo.

Wolseley ordered Berber to be taken 'by hook or by crook'. This was to be the jumping-off place for a large-scale, cool weather campaign. The

---

* It was believed by many, Wolseley among them, that on the night Gladstone learned of Gordon's death, he remained callously indifferent and took a lady friend to the theatre.

city would be hit by the river column from the north and the flying desert column from the south. Buller, though spoiling for a fight, soon reported the desert column could no longer 'fly' – or sit for that matter. Behind him was an army of 50,000 howling fanatics, flushed with success, with orders to surround and destroy him. His transport was in a deplorable condition, and the men's boots were worn through. Buller had to issue the sickening order to retire quickly rather than risk having his retreat cut off. Eating as much as they could hold, Buller's men threw the rest of the stores into the Nile and marched back to Korti. Enemy snipers pelted them all the way. The camels were so badly shot up that in order to keep in the water when they drank, Beresford kept plugging them with oakum. As they died, the men ate their humps as a change from the monotonous fare of bully beef. When the rear-guard, composed of the Royal Irish, straggled, Buller threatened he would not jeopardize the safety of his column by waiting for anyone. Father Brindle frequently went back with a borrowed pony to haul them in, threatening to excommunicate those who continued to lag behind.

Why the Mahdi didn't attack this way-worn, disheartened remnant of an army remains a mystery. Only once did the Arabs skirmish as if to attack; it was the one time Buller's stern face brightened. Receiving the men on their return to Korti, Wolseley told them: 'It was not your fault that Gordon has perished and Khartoum has fallen.'

The river column fared better. But an abnormally low Nile and problems of supply slowed its progress. The discovery that nearly a third of the biscuits were unfit because of faulty soldering of the tins was most discouraging. That same day a force of 2,000 dervishes decided to contest their advance. The Battle of Kirbekan (February 10th) was of an old-fashioned kind. The South Staffordshire Regiment changed to red and the Black Watch to kilts. Bayonets flashed and pipers struck up. While the Arabs were held in a light frontal attack, a decisive flanking one was delivered. The British loss would have been slight had not Earle stuck his head into a hut still held by dervishes. Brackenbury took over and conducted the retirement to Korti ordered a few days later.

The ragged army, united once more, proceeded to summer quarters in the province of Dongola, where many sat around with the forlorn look of tenants at an Irish eviction. All the romance of the expedition was gone. The voyageurs, though Wolseley wanted them to stay on, unanimously voted to go home. (It was reported they were in a drunken state all the way across the Atlantic.) The Kroomen, some of whom mutinied, were forced to stay.

To steady the loyal native population of Dongola, Wolseley solemnly pledged to defend them. England, he said, would never desert her friends. She was determined to smash the Mahdi if it took a hundred years. When some sons of the desert visited one of the stations commanded by General Dormer and spoke of the miraculous powers of the Mahdi, Dormer took out the glass eye that replaced the one lost in the Crimea, tossed it into the air, caught it, and restored it to its place asking if he could do that? The visitors ran off in panic.

To manage affairs in Dongola more effectually, Wolseley proposed that he be made governor-general. The Queen came to his support and suggested to Lady Wolseley that her husband should 'even THREATEN to resign if he does not receive strong support and liberty of action'.[54] But Gladstone felt the general was as unfitted for the position as a Turkish Pasha. Gladstone, in fact, was opposed to there being any governor-general of the Sudan.

To put the commander-in-chief in closer touch with Suakim, Hartington asked him to move up to Cairo. Wolseley objected to taking leave from his soldiers in the torrid Sudan. It had the odd look of letting them 'stew in their own juice'. The Government, Wolseley complained, seemed to want to put him in a bad light. Nor would they, to his annoyance, publish his reasons for the retreat to Dongola. Actually Wolseley, suffering from eye-strain, diarrhoea, and overwork, needed the relaxation afforded by an Egyptian palace and the presence of his wife and daughter who came out from England.

On March 30th, 1885, while a joint Anglo-Russian commission was settling the disputed areas of the Afghan frontier, Russian troops attacked the village of Pendjeh. Pendjeh, which no one had ever heard of before or has remembered since, was suddenly described as the gateway to India! The Afghans were unperturbed, but Gladstone spoke of 'unprovoked aggression' on the part of the Russians. Vigorously thumping the imperial drum, the Prime Minister demanded a vote of credit for £11,000,000 and alerted the reserves. Deserters were told all would be forgiven if they returned to serve their Queen and country. The nation was convulsed by a war crisis. And since every soldier was needed for a war against Russia, all offensive operations in the Sudan must cease.

Gladstone later spoke of the crisis as heaven-made. The stress of the hour permitted him to pull quietly out of the Sudan imbroglio, while the large sum of money allowed him to defray the expenses of the Nile expedition. His own party was reunited: Radicals were pleased by the revocation of his pledge to avenge Gordon; the Whigs were no less gratified by his unexpected stand against Russia, for it could no longer be said that the Government was indifferent to the preservation of the Empire. Of course, once the Pendjeh affair served his purpose, Gladstone suggested arbitration to the somewhat bewildered Russians. It was a masterly display of adroit political tactics. 'I don't so much object,' once grumbled a member of Parliament, 'to the Grand Old Man always producing the ace of trumps from up his sleeve, but I do object to his saying that the Almighty put it there.'

Wolseley vigorously protested against a policy of 'butcher and bolt' in the Sudan. The news, however, did not come as a surprise. Wolseley was sure from the very beginning there would be no conflict with Russia. Warlike words out of the mouth of a man who had vehemently assailed any belligerent stand growing out of a question of prestige and honour did not ring true. Wolseley argued that the power of the dervishes would be increased and that one day it would be necessary to meet and crush it. At least hold on to Dongola, he pleaded. But his counter-proposals were given scant consideration. When complete evacuation was ordered on May 11th, Wolseley seriously considered resigning from the service.

Gladstone had made him look ridiculous. 'I made promises to the Sudan people on the faith of Mr Gladstone's announcement in Parliament,' he wrote to a friend, 'that have "*blackened my face*" in this land of Egypt and that make me long to sneak out of it.'[55] Thousands of loyal natives who had put their trust in a British pledge were abandoned to the merciless fury of rapacious dervishes. War, disease, and famine wrought by the Mahdist movement were to account for the lives of 6,000,000 persons.

Entrusting the retrograde movement to Buller, who made it a brilliant triumph of organization, Wolseley decided to investigate the situation at Suakim where the army was to be broken up and the railway stopped once more. While he was away, Lady Wolseley privately wrote to the Queen asking leave for her husband, which was granted. Back in Egypt, Wolseley lingered in Cairo only long enough to make a few last-minute arrangements for defence and to purchase a white donkey requested by the Queen. After finding just the right one, the general learned to his chagrin that Her Majesty wanted a *male* donkey, not a female. 'But surely,' he commented to his wife, 'the Queen has plenty of male donkeys in her service already.'[56]

Before Wolseley's departure, the Gladstone Government tried to apply salve to the general's wounded pride by bestowing upon him a vacant ribbon of St Patrick; but they gave him infinitely more pleasure by abdicating from power on June 10th. Wolseley's hatred for that 'old heartless brute', Gladstone, never died. He always reversed the initials G.O.M. (Grand Old Man) to M.O.G. (Murderer of Gordon). A statuette of Gladstone on his mantel, much to the surprise of Wolseley's visitors, was always turned to face the wall because he couldn't stand the face of the 'old crocodile' looking at him. Not unlike many a good Conservative of his time, the Wolseley dog was taught to growl on the word 'Gladstone!' Wolseley's favourite story was about a boy from Eton arguing with a boy from Harrow about the relative merits of their respective schools. 'Well, anyhow,' declared the Etonian proudly, 'Wellington was at Eton.' To which the youth from Harrow replied, 'Well, anyhow, we never had a beast like old Gladstone.'

Years later, when Wolseley received a card of admission to attend Gladstone's funeral at Westminster Abbey, he wrote on the back of it: '28.5.98. Could not go to the funeral of a man who had all through life preferred office to the honour and good of England.'[57]

For a brief time Wolseley nourished the hope that the Salisbury Government might halt the retreat from the Sudan. But the new government soon made it emphatically clear that they had no desire to alter their predecessor's policy. Salisbury, however, saw to it that Wolseley and his men were publicly thanked. And feeling the expedition failed through no fault of its commander, the Prime Minister made him a viscount, and by special request of the Queen the title was to descend to his daughter.

The Mahdi died on June 20th, some say of smallpox, others of debauchery. His successor, Caliph Abdullah, tried, as Wolseley predicted, to invade Egypt. The dervish leader was discouraged, however, from any further offensive movements by his defeat in the Battle of Ginnis at the end of the year. It was not until a decade later that Kitchener, with superior weapons and the advantage of Wolseley's earlier experiences, had the good fortune and glory to settle the 'dishonourable affair'. Having destroyed the Caliph's army at Omdurman, Kitchener took the Mahdi's bones from a hallowed monument, burned them to ashes, and tossed them into the Nile. 'Gordon has been avenged,' wrote Wolseley.

# CHAPTER SIXTEEN

# EPILOGUE

AFTER his failure to rescue Gordon, Wolseley predicted to a friend, 'the sun of my luck set when Stewart was wounded'.[1] He believed that he had passed the meridian of his career. Had he succeeded, the feat would have been pronounced brilliant as he was proclaimed around the globe. Now there were only the malicious voices of detraction as his enemies exulted in his personal failure. Smarting from his first and only reverse, wearied by his exertions, depressed by the death of Stewart, friend and foe alike expected the returning Wolseley to be somewhat subdued. Instead, Wolseley came back full of fight, eager to advance the cause of reform and correct the defects uncovered while campaigning in the Sudan.

With wrathful indignation, Wolseley raised a terrific row over jamming rifles and soft swords and bayonets. They cost the lives of so many good men fighting dervishes. He told of one pursued soldier who dragged the body of a bayoneted Arab for some distance before he could disengage – and then his rifle jammed. 'I will hang these rogues as high as Haman,' he vowed angrily, 'even if I have to appeal to the last court – public opinion.'[2] The press caught the fever and the 'sword scandal' provided bitter remarks in Parliament. It was difficult to fix the blame, but in the end an investigating committee was formed and the Government obediently complied with the recommendation that the testing of armaments should be turned over to the military rather than remain in the hands of the munitions makers.

Wolseley renewed his attack on the seniority system. In a suppressed dispatch, which in some mysterious manner found its way into a leading journal, the adjutant-general complained that during the Egyptian campaigns of 1882–5 he was compelled to leave his best battalions in the rear while inferior ones were sent to the front, because he could not expose the officers and men to the gross incompetence of their commanders. He contended it was criminal to place the lives of gallant soldiers in the hands of officers 'who were deplorably ignorant of the elements of their profession', and attained high rank only because of the seniority system.

Then an article signed 'Centurion', which was believed to have been written by Wolseley himself, appeared in the *National Review* which was no more gentle in its criticism. Finally, Wolseley, very Irish in his impetuosity, began to use strong language on the subject of seniority in after-dinner speeches.

The Duke of Cambridge naturally resented this public appeal. Several times he reprimanded his subordinate for ignoring 'legitimate channels of communication to the commander-in-chief'. But regulations governing the writings and speeches of officers were not clear, and Wolseley refused to surrender this advantage so long as shortcomings of the military were not remedied.*

The fiery and volatile Wolseley, knowing he was too powerful to be either ignored or silenced, never stopped fighting those monumental obstructions, tradition and officialdom, to give England a real army: one 'ready to go anywhere and do anything', as he put it. He paid the penalty of being ahead of his time. Distrusted and disliked by the old school, he was regarded more than ever as the army's worst enemy.

The Duke continued to fight the pertinacious adjutant-general every step of the way. With bitter animosity, the old gentleman declared, 'Every change has been made at the right time, and the right time is when you cannot help it.' The commander-in-chief took pride in acting as a drag on the wheels of progress. And there were moments when it was all Wolseley could do to prevent backward measures. At such times, he told Lady Wolseley, 'I could have murdered him with pleasure.'[3] An angry Wolseley would write letters to 'that foolish Cambridge' that were insultingly critical of his attitude, put them into his desk, and the next day 'rub out anything I may in cooler moments think too strong'.[4] An exasperated Wolseley would frequently express to his wife the wish that 'H.R.H. would go abroad or to the devil for a little and let me either have command of the army or leisure to enjoy life with you.'[5]

Despite the Duke and his allies, Wolseley, with the assistance of Wood, Buller, and other reformers, succeeded in keeping the army abreast of rapidly changing times. Machine-guns, magazine rifles, rapid-firing cannon with high-explosive shells, and other up-to-date arms were introduced. An unorthodox mounted infantry (which the Duke favoured) was raised and trained under the supervision of Baker Russell. The Intelligence department was greatly expanded with Brackenbury placed at its head. An effective scheme for mobilization was adopted. The supply

* He also got himself into trouble in America at this time by attacking the military reputation of 'Mr U. S. Grant'.

and transport of the army was reshaped. Wolseley was truly the father of the modern British army.

Many of the improvements he had hoped to introduce were still unborn when Wolseley turned his office over to Buller in 1890, but the battle for reform was nearly won. Wolseley was comforted by the knowledge that at least the foundation had been laid. A tired, less militant Wolseley left the War Office to assume command of the forces in Ireland. He accepted his being 'shelved' with little objection. Even his appearance changed. Trimming his fierce, waxed moustache short, like that of the ordinary British soldier, gave him a kindlier appearance. Wolseley could have had the command in India, which he so desperately wanted a decade before, but he now preferred a less strenuous, more peaceful assignment away from controversy. Let Roberts stay in India, he advised. In the back of his mind, Wolseley had the notion that should the Duke, who was already over seventy, retire, he would be in a far better position to succeed him. Before leaving London, Wolseley found himself, almost against his will, liking and disliking Cambridge by turns, just as the Duke did him. Somehow, once the cares of office were put aside, a curious grudging affection came to the surface.

In Ireland Wolseley found a more active outdoor life. None too soon, for he felt the 'poisonous atmosphere at the War Office' was destroying him physically. He and Lady Wolseley enjoyed collecting bric-à-brac and furnishings for their handsome Dublin residence, which was depressingly named the Royal Hospital. They entertained lavishly, far beyond the table allowance of £100 a year.

Yet, it was in many ways a lonely life. No one could ever replace Colley and Stewart, his dearest comrades. Only when Maurice or Butler came for a visit did Wolseley enjoy the intimate companionship afforded by old friends. Much of their lively, even brilliant, conversation revolved around their current writings. Most of Wolseley's spare hours were spent labouring over his biography of Marlborough. It was his principal contribution to literature, though his two-volume work never got far beyond his hero's early life. He also produced a novel under an assumed name which has been happily forgotten.

After his five-year stint, Wolseley was ready to leave this 'rainy and squally island' – the cemetery of a reforming soldier's power. The disloyalty of so many of his countrymen pained him; the squalor of back streets depressed him; the provincial society bored him; the climate began to affect his health, and especially that of Lady Wolseley. Wolseley, now a field-marshal (1894), also thirsted for something more stimulating than the 'mild orgy of red wine and red roses' to be found at the banquets of various literary societies. Believing that he would succeed the Duke as head of the army, he now impatiently counted the days until the ageing veteran retired.

In the spring of 1895, Rosebery's Liberal Government, determined to modify the office of commander-in-chief and cut the ties that bound the service directly to the Sovereign, persuaded the Queen, who cherished the hope that her soldier son, Prince Arthur, would soon secure the post, to ask her kinsman to resign. The Duke was not in a compliant mood. Feeling he was being 'summarily *turned* out', Cambridge briefly fought an embarrassingly childish but futile rear-guard action. The decision was kept from the public until June 1st when Mr Campbell-Bannerman, the War Secretary, made a fulsome speech in the House plastering the venerable Cambridge with panegyrics and telling how His Royal Highness 'makes way in order that certain changes may be introduced'.

It was universally assumed that Wolseley, the most accomplished and deserving soldier, would be announced as successor. But the Liberal Government, offended by Wolseley's outspoken opposition to Home Rule for Ireland, entertained some new notions on the subject. Making a party rather than a public decision, Rosebery decided to recommend Buller for the office.

Wolseley, meanwhile, optimistic in his ignorance, was blissfully yachting in the North Sea. While in London in April, he learned that the Duke was being pushed out of office and confidently anticipated the call, never doubting that the Liberals, who had exploited his name and talents for years, would offer him the post. Moreover, Campbell-Bannerman, though a 'Little Englander', had been a personal friend and collaborator on army reforms since they worked together under Cardwell.

While still at sea, a flood of messages relayed from the north of Scotland and Norway repeated the open secret that the War Secretary was preparing to appoint the pupil not the teacher. They urged him to hurry back to defend his interests. To Wolseley it was a 'sudden knockdown blow ... delivered to me *below the belt*.'[6] Rushing back to his wife at Homburg before going on to London, he told her he 'felt the shame of being thrown aside as if I were worn and useless'. He blamed two men for the indignity and injustice caused by his supersession. First Buller, a 'false friend' who owed him everything, for deliberately undermining his influence. Second the Duke, whom he 'always despised as a poor nerveless "ends" of cowardly flesh', for pressing the former's candidacy out of 'venomous hatred and spiteful vengeance'.[7] (It was no secret that the

Duke preferred the reserved Buller, who did an excellent job as adjutant-general, but he was hardly in a position to dictate his successor.)

Before his arrival in London, the 'Wolseley luck' once more asserted itself. At the very same sitting after Cambridge's retirement was announced, an unlooked-for vote of censure was carried against the Secretary of War over the short supply of cordite. The next day the Liberal Government resigned. With the Conservatives in power under Salisbury, the field seemed wide open in the matter of succession. Rumours were thick about the chances of Wolseley, Roberts, and Buller. Even the aggrieved Duke somewhat foolishly resurrected faint hopes, though Salisbury refused to consider reversing the several measures adopted by the retiring War Secretary relating to the War Office.

There was little Wolseley could do in London before returning to Ireland. His hands were tied. It was out of the question that he boldly ask Salisbury for the post; he would never put himself 'on a level with the advertising Roberts'. He could only look to his friends to 'pull strings' as a dramatic struggle of backstairs intrigue developed. Furthermore, with the question still undecided, Wolseley felt he could not look his old comrades in the face. 'Had I run away or brought about some great military disaster,' he confided to one of his old 'gang', 'I could not have been treated worse than the late government proposed to treat me.'[8]

Wolseley soon heard on 'the best authority' that Roberts and all his friends were 'moving heaven and earth to get Lansdowne [the new War Secretary], who of course knew him well in India, to make him boss at the War Office.'[9] And he feared that Buller might still be the favourite since the army was evenly divided between himself and Roberts. 'The two Field-Marshals are too clever and too outspoken,' observed a friend on the inside, 'the Cabinet would prefer a plodder [Buller] to a genius.'[10]

The Queen, as was to be expected, had very definite ideas on the subject. She began to hope that her son, the Duke of Connaught, might now qualify for the office. Victoria told Salisbury that Roberts was 'absolutely impossible because of ignorance of military affairs outside India … She recognized Lord Wolseley's claims but demurred strongly to his great imprudence and his fondness for a clique.'[11] The Queen suggested that Wolseley might be more advantageously employed as Britain's representative to Germany where her grandson, Kaiser Wilhelm II, desired a military ambassador. The Kaiser, she reported, 'jumped' at the opportunity of getting a soldier like Wolseley.

On being told that the Duke of Connaught was in the running, a strangely generous Wolseley let it be known he was prepared to step aside and accept the Berlin assignment. 'I had years ago,' he told Sir John Ardagh, 'had it conveyed to the Queen that I would never stand in his way.'[12] Salisbury and Lansdowne, meanwhile, concluded that while there was some question as to which was the best man available, none had better credentials for the office than Wolsleley.

'Thank God for all his mercies!' declared Wolseley on receipt of their decision early in August. 'I feel as a man condemned to death must feel when suddenly reprieved,' he wrote to Lady Wolseley who was still on a holiday in Germany.[13]

The Queen, always a poor loser, telegraphed Lansdowne: 'I sanction Wolseley's appointment but I do not think it a good one.'[14] The same day she advised the War Secretary to 'impress upon Lord Wolseley the absolute necessity of not having anything to do with the Press'.[15]

The other contestants took their defeat gracefully. Roberts seemed happy with his new Irish command. Buller, though disappointed, stayed on as adjutant-general to serve and support Wolseley loyally. How far he had intrigued on his own behalf is not clear, but his part in the affair was not altogether creditable. It was reprehensible that he made no effort to acquaint an old friend such as Wolseley with what was afoot. Wolseley was nevertheless willing to forgive and forget. However, when the Wolseleys added a horse to their stable which proved to have a somewhat unreliable, if not treacherous disposition, they named it 'Sir Redvers'.

By the time the Duke made his undignified exit in November, Wolseley found it in his heart to forgive him for all the slights and injuries inflicted over the years. Imagining how he would feel when forced to retire from the military stage five years hence, Wolseley felt genuinely sorry for the 'royal retrograde'. Cambridge responded to Wolseley's expressions of sympathy by assuring him 'that if and when we have differed, it has been on public grounds only, and not from any personal reasons.'[16] Wolseley invited him to drop in during office hours, at any time. And when the Duke did, the new commander-in-chief would make a show of asking the advice of an old man who had had thirty-nine years' experience on the job.

The prize lost some of its glitter when Lansdowne hastened to inform the new commander-in-chief that the powers of the office would be considerably narrowed more or less along the lines indicated by his predecessor, Campbell-Bannerman, who had in turn been guided by the findings of the Hartington Commission. The Hartington Commission originally recommended (1890) that when the Duke stepped down a chief-of-staff system should be instituted; it was held that excessive centralization of power weakened the sense of responsibility among other military department heads, thus reducing their efficiency. At the time, Wolseley and royalty closed ranks to prevent a 'catastrophe'. Wolseley, more concerned with the extension of civilian power in the army than the preservation of royal patronage, called it a step backward. (Wolseley thought he detected the hand of the ambitious 'Brack', one of the commissioners, behind this scheme, for he was obviously the best man fitted to be chief of staff under a war secretary.) Campbell-Bannerman in the end rejected the recommendation, but agreed to reduce substantially the power of the commander-in-chief, while that of the civilian Secretary of War would be increased. It remained to the Conservatives, no less intent on increasing civilian control, to carry out a half-hearted compromise by creating a five-headed monstrosity with the commander-in-chief supervising the other four major department heads (adjutant-general, etc.) in a general way, while all four were directly responsible to the War Secretary, who could consult them without reference to the commander-in-chief. Wolseley was thus given overall responsibility without any real control. The incoming commander-in-chief soon realized that the dignity of his position had been considerably lowered and complained he was 'the fifth wheel on the coach'. This false position was especially galling to an officer who had looked forward for years to attaining the highest position of military authority, only to find it had been emasculated.

It became increasingly difficult for a man with Wolseley's temperament to adjust to this subordinate role. He could never fully accept the fact that Lansdowne was his absolute and impregnable master. How could an ignorant civilian, Wolseley asked, be allowed to dictate to a soldier on professional matters? It would be as if he, a military man, were to lay down the law on scientific matters to Louis Pasteur.

It was an unequal struggle. Lansdowne not only had the political authority, but he was an exceptionally clever man, who played the role of omnipotent War Secretary to the hilt. He dealt firmly with Wolseley's efforts to provide the army with a single military head whom the nation could look to as professionally responsible for its efficiency. To Lansdowne's advantage, the time had passed when 'our only General's' calculated indiscretions on public occasions could muster powerful popular sentiment on his behalf. Wolseley's star was fading. Roberts and Kitchener, capturing headlines with their soldiering abroad, were the new public idols. Moreover, Wolseley's health was bad. It began with a severe attack of influenza which nearly killed him shortly after taking office. Indigestion and what he called 'Indian fever' tormented him more than ever. Soon his memory became faulty. Most of all, Wolseley grew sick of his anomalous position with Lansdowne pressing unduly his civilian authority on one side, and 'insubordinate department heads' ignoring him on the other. He complained: 'I am badgered and hampered by a pack of Secretaries of State, Surveyor Generals, etc., etc., etc. who thwart and oppose me until I am nearly mad'.[17] For all practical purposes, Lansdowne was the commander-in-chief and Wolseley was reduced to being 'the vice-chairman of a debating society'.

Into this atmosphere of confusion at the War Office the South African crisis intruded. At each stage of the crisis from 1896 on, Wolseley tried to impress upon the Government that war with these sturdy farmers would be an extremely difficult undertaking. He called for a substantial increase of forces on the spot. 'A display of power,' he advised, 'would be the surest way to secure the peace.' Wolseley wrote to his friends: 'Let us not lead others into temptation should be a daily prayer on the lips of every British Cabinet Minister. It is wicked to pretend to be weak when we are strong.'

As the danger of war mounted, Wolseley insisted on the purchase of horses and transport, the mobilization of an army corps in England, and the creation of a fresh corps to be on hand to reinforce the first. Wolseley warned 'that if war comes we shall be obliged to send the largest force that has ever left our shores to take part in it, and the distance being great, it will be in all respects the most serious business we have ever had on hand.'[18] Butler, whom Wolseley had helped to place in South Africa as High Commissioner and general in command, supported this view, claiming it would take an army of 200,000 to hold South Africa. Because of his views, the critical, embarrassingly pro-Boer Irishman was replaced.

Aside from a small increase to the strength of the army, Lansdowne and his Government obstinately scorned the commander-in-chief's insistent recommendations. The politicians objected to the cost and feared they might be accused of aggressive measures while attempting to settle the dispute by peaceful negotiations. This failure to make adequate preparations was to cost Britain dearly.

When war began, Wolseley had the great personal satisfaction of witnessing reservists present themselves with alacrity. Once more the Cardwell system had proved itself. Throughout the war, as the difficulties Wolseley predicted materialized, he successfully laboured to reinforce the poorly prepared advance-guard 7,000 miles away until a force of 267,000, with its full complement of artillery and cavalry, landed in South Africa. Rarely has a better army embarked from England's shores.

But disaster struck first. Unit after unit marched off to defeat and surrender. South Africa again became the graveyard of soldiers' reputations. None was buried deeper than that of Sir Redvers, who would have preferred to serve as chief of staff with Wolseley as commander-in-chief in the field. The Buller of the Boer War was not the Buller of old. He was an absolute failure. Ten years of strenuous labour at the War Office left him sluggish in mind and body. But no one sheds a tear over a general who is destroyed by overwork and lack of exercise. Wolseley was 'thoroughly disappointed in him for he has not shown any of the characteristics I had attributed to him; no military genius, no firmness, not even the obstinacy which I thought he possessed when I discovered him. He seems dazed and dumbfounded.'[19]

Not all of the muddle was on the battlefield. The major military departments at the War Office, working under great strain, remained unco-ordinated. The prevailing attitude was 'you fight your war, I'll fight mine.' Wolseley was no less guilty than the rest. It was later claimed that the commander-in-chief never passed the reports of the Intelligence department to the Office of the Secretary of State. Wood, then serving as adjutant-general, told how Lansdowne minuted papers directly to him, but always received them back through the office of the commander-in-chief because Wolseley insisted upon it. When the Government decided to send Roberts to supersede Buller, with Kitchener as chief of staff, they didn't bother to consult the commander-in-chief.

Why didn't they send Wolseley? He had South African experience and knew the army better than any man living. Roberts, at 66, was no younger than he. The Government spoke unconvincingly of how they could not spare him from the War Office, and they suggested that his health was too delicate. Wolseley angrily insisted he was in excellent shape. However, he could no longer conceal his true physical condition. He was as cheerful as ever but, as one visitor noticed, he seemed 'to have lost some of the abnormal mental activity which he had displayed in the past, and he had the air of a somewhat tired man.' And by now his memory had noticeably decayed. He could not remember the immediate past. Wolseley would meet an old comrade and declare: 'I'm delighted to see you, no one told me you were coming!' A short time later he would see the same individual and repeat his welcome: 'Oh! how nice to see you – nobody told me you were coming!'[20] It got so bad that there were times when he didn't even recognize his own secretary. On occasions he would write a brilliant report, go home, and the next day deny he was the author. 'It was rather a faulty memory than a mental failure,' one of the

War Office officials observed, 'and things went on pretty well in spite of it.'[21]

Waging war against 'simple Christian farmers' left England with few friends in the community of nations. Fearing an attack by some great hostile power, Wolseley demanded that troops be raised and measures be adopted essential to home defence. When the Government refused to act, Wolseley threatened to resign. The Cabinet hesitated for two days and then gave way. It was a small victory, but the only one he could boast of.

Wolseley viewed his success with mixed feelings. If they had accepted his resignation, he would at least have been released from the cares of office. 'I have lost all interest in my work,' he confided to his wife; and he was heartily sick of working with an insulting, domineering 'little whippersnapper of a War Office clerk whom chance of birth has made into a Secretary of State'. Lansdowne was so unlike himself, he told Lady Wolseley, having 'a small mind and feminine disposition'.[22]

As the century came to a close (November 1900), the greatest soldier England produced since Wellington was retired. The Government recalled the popular Roberts to take his place. Wolseley saw little justification for the lavish reception that attended Roberts's homecoming. The Queen bestowed upon him an earldom and the blue ribbon of the garter. Parliament voted him a sum of £100,000 for his great national service. Everyone, including Roberts, acted as if the war was over, though it dragged on for another year and a half.

The retiring commander-in-chief hoped that Roberts, whom he faithfully and energetically supported in all his requests for men and supplies, would put his enormous popularity to some practical good by completing the army system he had done so much to establish. But Wolseley feared that 'cute, little, jobbing showman' was so much of 'a snob as regards Dukes and Earls, that he will give way to society and preserve'.[23] A friend at the War Office later confirmed his fears by declaring 'Bobs, Jobs, Snobs & Co.' had taken over.

There were no expressions of thanks for Wolseley's half-century of service. Instead of crediting him with foresight during the South African crisis, it was broadly hinted that he was responsible for the major calamities because he had under-estimated Boer strength and the force that would be required to subdue them.

' "Jaw" is king,' declared Wolseley. The prevaricating politicians who flatter the crowd, he observed, were masters in England. And the greatest liar of them all, the fountainhead of calumny, was Lansdowne, 'half

Frenchman* and whole cad!' Wolseley resolved to defend his honour in the House of Lords and do a vital service to his nation by exposing the defects in the administration of the army.

On 'army night', March 4th, 1901, the galleries were so crowded one would imagine the Church or rents were in jeopardy. Members of the House of Commons packed into their seats, thoughtfully located at the far end of the Chamber so that only part of the proceedings might be heard. Privy Councillors swarmed to the steps of the throne. It was widely rumoured that the Olympian calm of the House of Lords was to be exploded 'as someone was thrown to the lions'. They watched in profound silence as a little old man, stiffly erect but broken by his long struggle to give England a better army, rose and read a dignified speech which had obviously been prepared with great care. They strained to hear for the delivery was feeble. But the point was clear: had he been given the authority, the war would have followed a more satisfactory course. Wolseley temperately refrained from attacking any person, condemning instead the administrative system in the War Office for the lamentable set-backs. He pleaded for an improved status for the commander-in-chief who was in a better position to be acquainted with the needs of the army than a civilian selected by the Prime Minister from among his political supporters, one who was not only ignorant of army affairs, but served interests which were not military. These faults, Wolseley warned, must be corrected to preserve the efficiency of the army and the highest interests of the Empire.

Provoked by this exposé, Lansdowne sprang to his feet. Exhibiting anger publicly for the first and only time in his political career, Lansdowne lashed out in a vicious personal attack on his former associate. With a pitying contempt which so often characterizes the disdainful, urbane politician, he ridiculed the competence of the witness. He asserted that commander-in-chief's duties were actually of great importance, and that if his lordship had paid greater attention to them, the Government might have profited from the employment of auxiliary forces throughout the Empire which were neglected during his term in office. Never changing the falsely pleasant, almost sneering smile on his face, Lansdowne wounded Wolseley with the unsupported remark that he should have admonished them, that Ladysmith† was a bad position,

---

* It was generally supposed that his grandfather was an illegitimate child of Talleyrand.

† When Wolseley spoke of a defensive force being placed in 'the position of Ladysmith' he meant Biggarsberg, twenty miles to the north. Knowing Natal as intimately as he did, Wolseley considered Ladysmith, which was enclosed by commanding hills, to be the last place in the area to bottle up a garrison.

and that more than one army corps would be required to defeat the Boers.

In the debate that followed, Hartington and Salisbury tried to remove the sting from their colleague's ungenerous allusions which insinuated that the former commander-in-chief had wilfully and consistently neglected his duties. Nothing could, however, efface the bitterly offensive public attack on the reputation of a renowned soldier whose successful campaigns had won for him the thanks of this same Parliament many times. Far worse, the allegations were delivered at a time and in a way that would prevent verification or refutation.

Eleven days later Wolseley returned to an animated House of Lords which Lord Rosebery now described as 'a cockpit'. Pleading in a voice breaking with emotion, he asked the Government to produce all papers relating to the allegations made by Lansdowne and to the statements he had made in rebuttal. Wolseley admitted he did not *fully* anticipate the course of events during the war; however, he was certainly aware of the risks and persistently recommended measures long before they were adopted. Lansdowne in his rejoinder went so far as to confess that for political reasons the military advice of the ex-commander-in-chief was at times ignored, but he and his Government resisted the demand for papers on the technical grounds that they were too confidential to divulge. Surely, thought Wolseley, this man must be descended from the notorious Talleyrand who believed that man was given a tongue to conceal the truth.

Wolseley's motion was supported by only thirty-eight peers. A red-faced Roberts voted with the majority. Wolseley wrote to his wife: 'I am disgusted to death with the treatment I received from that poor little contemptible creature Lansdowne and the clique that supported him. If I were ten years younger I should move heaven and earth to have it out with him, but now it is too late.'[24] Never again would he enter the House of Lords. He would wait for history to vindicate him.

This last passage of arms was a sad end to a brilliant career. Wolseley retired into silence and obscurity. The Government allowed him to abandon all the ceremonial obligations associated with his many honorary offices. Occasionally he was recognized by a small crowd of boys or 'idle people', as he called them, but he always wished they 'would keep their attention for Lord Roberts or Sir Evelyn Wood, who like them'. Soon his name was hardly ever mentioned in the press. 'I do think it odd,' remarked Sir Ian Hamilton, a Roberts man, 'that so original a mind had passed away, leaving so little remembrance behind it.'[25] Wolseley's name was quickly forgotten because he refused to 'soldier to the gallery', and he was too impersonal, too English, ever to allow the people around him to see his human side. Wolseley was admired, but he was too detached to win the affection of the ordinary run of soldier or officer. When in civilian clothes, people rarely recognized the unassuming Wolseley. They would often remark: 'Does not that man remind you of somebody?'[26]

The last twelve years were dull years. What little pleasure Wolseley could squeeze out of life was derived from reading, writing, and visits to places of historic interest. Serving a recluse, Wolseley's valet complained he was losing caste in the service of 'so very quiet a nobleman, who does not even go to the races!'[27] At the insistence of friends, he wrote an incomplete, wordy autobiography up to the Ashanti War, but the story of his varied experience was poorly organized owing to a patchy memory. On a visit to his old Chief, the sentimental Butler had the painful experience of no longer being recognized.

Wolseley died on March 26th, 1913, at his winter residence in Mentone, France, the result of complications arising from a slight chill. He always dreaded 'dying in bed, like an old woman'; he would have preferred meeting death in the open air with his face towards England's enemies, like the thousands of his countrymen who in a few months would salt the earth of foreign fields with their bones. He did much to prepare them for that struggle. When a German general later called the army of 1914, the Old Contemptibles, 'that perfect thing apart', he was speaking of an army Wolseley helped to create.

Britain was without her proverbial luck when the Boer War and World War I failed to coincide with Wolseley's career. Next to Wolseley, even Kitchener was a poor organizer. 'The tragedy of Wolseley's life,' commented one of the Wolseley 'ring', 'was that he never encountered a foe worthy of him.' The master of the small war remained an 'inheritor of unfulfilled renown'.

The War Office officials decided to give Wolseley's memory the highest tribute with all possible pomp and every mark of honour. On March 31st, 1913, his body was borne through a heavy, depressing fog to St Paul's. Behind the flag-draped coffin and the poignant figure of a riderless charger were representative units from all branches of the service. The South Staffordshires, his first regiment, recalled dim memories of a slim subaltern leading a suicidal charge against a Burmese stronghold. There were units to remind one of Sebastopol, Lucknow, and Peking. Present were the Rifles he took through the forests of North America and the jungles of West Africa. The shrill, wailing notes of the Highlanders rang out as they did long ago before Sekukuni's stronghold and at Tel-el-Kebir. And there were the Royal Irish who paddled the long Nile in the race to Korti. At the end of the march came the Household Cavalry, the men who had ridden with Wolseley against Arabi Bey.

The coffin was laid to rest near to Wellington, where all his life Wolseley had wished to be.

# NOTES

---

## CHAPTER I – THE SUBALTERNS' WAR

1. Garnet W. to Wellington, Sept. 23rd, 1850, P.R.O., W.O. 31/1001.
2. Garnet W. to Raglan, Jan. 9th, 1851, ibid.
3. Frances Ann W. to Wellington, Sept. 22nd, 1851, ibid.
4. Garnet W. to Richard W., April 11th, 1863, Wolseley Papers, Hove.


## CHAPTER II – BLUNDERS AND HEROICS

1. Garnet Wolseley, *The Story of a Soldier's Life*, Constable & Co. (London, 1903), 1, 85.
2. Garnet W. to Buller, Sept. 15th, 1886, Buller Papers, P.R.O., W.O. 132/2.
3. Garnet W. to Frances W., Oct. 6th, 1890, Hove.
4. Sir William Francis Butler, *Akim-Foo, The History of a Failure*, S. Low, Marston, Low & Searle (London, 1875), 40.
5. Garnet Wolseley, 'The Old Trenches Before Sebastopol Revisited', *The Royal United Service Magazine*, XXXVIII (Nov. 1894), 116.
6. Ibid.
7. Garnet W. to Dowager Lady W., July 20th, 1855, Hove.
8. Lady Harriet Wantage, *Memoir of Lord Wantage*, Smith, Elder & Co. (London, 1907), 74–5.
9. Garnet W. to Dowager Lady W., June 13th, 1855, Hove.
10. Wolseley, *Life*, I, 148.
11. Ibid., 159
12. Garnet W. to Louisa W., Aug. 18th, 1894, Wolseley Papers, Royal United Service Institution Library (R.U.S.I.).


## CHAPTER III – THE DEVIL'S WIND

1. Wolseley, *Life*, I, 229.
2. Garnet W. to Richard W., Aug. 14th, 1857, Hove.
3. Ibid., Sept. 28th, 1857.
4. Wolseley, *Life*, I, 272.
5. Garnet W. to Richard W., April 29th, 1859, Hove.
6. Ibid., Nov. 28th, 1857, Hove.
7. Wolseley, *Life*, I, 309.
8. Garnet W. to Richard W., Nov. 28th, 1857, Hove.
9. Sir James Hope Grant, *Incidents in the Sepoy Mutiny*, Blackwood & Sons (Edinburgh, 1873), ed. Henry Knollys, 193.
10. Sir Charles Alexander, *Recollections of Thirty-nine Years in the Army*, S. Sonnenschein & Co. (London, 1898), 130–1.
11. William Gordon-Alexander, *Recollections of a Highland Subaltern*, E. Arnold (London, 1898), 260.

12. James Pope-Hennessy, *Monckton Milnes*, Farrar, Strauss & Cudahy (New York, 1955), II, 99.
13. Garnet W. to Richard W., March 18th, 1859, Hove.
14. Ibid., April 7th, 1858, Hove.
15. Sydney Henry Jones-Parry, *An Old Soldier's Memories*, Hurst & Blackett (London, 1897), 239.
16. Garnet W. to Richard W., April 29th, 1859, Hove.

## CHAPTER IV – THE SHOPKEEPER'S VENGEANCE

1. Garnet W. to Matilda W., Oct. 23rd, 1859, Hove.
2. William Russell, *My Diary in India in the Year 1858-59*, Longmans, Green & Co. (London, 1960), II, 340-1.
3. Garnet W. to Dowager Lady W., Oct. 15th, 1859, Hove.
4. Garnet W. to Caroline W., July 26th, 1859, Hove.
5. Garnet W. to Dowager Lady W., March 18th, 1855, Hove.
6. Garnet W. to Richard W., March 23rd, 1859, Hove.
7. Ibid.
8. Ibid., Aug. 7th, 1859.
9. Jones-Parry, *Memories*, 25-4.
10. Ibid.
11. Garnet W. to Caroline W., Jan. 14th, 1860, Hove.
12. D. F. Rennie, *The British Arms in North China and Japan*, J. Murray (London, 1864), 184.
13. Garnet W. to Matilda W., May 6th, 1860, Hove.
14. Stanley Lane Poole, *The Life of Sir Harry Parkes*, Macmillan & Co. (New York, 1894), I, 275.
15. Robert Swinhoe, *Narrative of the North China Campaign of 1860*, Smith, Elder & Co. (London, 1861), 275.
16. Wolseley, *Life*, II, 25.
17. Sir James Hope Grant, *Incidents in the China War*, Blackwood & Sons (Edinburgh, 1875), ed. Henry Knollys, 65.
18. Arthur Fisher, *Personal Narrative of Three Years' Service in China* (London, 1863), 391-2.
19. Count Maurice d'Hérisson, *Journal d'un Interprète en Chine* (Paris, 1866), 173-4.
20. Swinhoe, *China Campaign*, 92.
21. Lane Poole, *Parkes*, 373-4.
22. Garnet W. to Frances Ann W., Aug. 27th, 1860, Hove.
23. Garnet Wolseley, *Narrative of the War with China in 1860*, Longmans, Green, Longman & Robe (London, 1862), 130.
24. Ibid., 138.
25. Ibid., 136.
26. Rennie, *British Arms*, 126-7.
27. Wolseley to Frances Ann W., Aug. 27th, 1860, Hove.
28. G. Allgood, *China War, 1860*, Longmans, Green & Co. (London, 1861), 49.
29. Sir Richard Harrison, *Recollections of a Life in the British Army*, Smith, Elder & Co. (London, 1908), 87.
30. Garnet W. to Caroline W., Sept. 22nd, 1860, Hove.
31. Wolseley, *Life*, II, 68-9.
32. Swinhoe, *China Campaign*, 261.
33. Ibid., 300.
34. Wolseley, *War with China*, 227.
35. 'Journal of an officer of the 67th Regiment during the North China Campaign of 1860', *The Royal United Service Magazine* (Feb. 1874), XVIII, 65.

36. Garnet W. to Matilda W., Oct. 23rd, 1860, Hove.
37. Ibid.
38. Grant, *China War*, 209–10.
39. Garnet W. to Richard W., Jan. 20th, 1861, Hove.
40. Ibid.
41. Wolseley, *Life*, II, 90.


CHAPTER V – THE BURNING EDGE OF WAR

1. Garnet W. to Richard W., May 8th, 1863, Hove.
2. Ibid., Sept. 14th, 1862.
3. John Black Atkins, *The Life of Sir William Howard Russell*, J. Murray (London, 1911), II, 39.
4. Wolseley, *Life*, II, 132.
5. Ibid., 133.
6. Garnet W. to Col. McCabe, Aug. 13th, 1899, Maurice Papers.
7. Garnet Wolseley, 'A month's visit to the Confederate headquarters', *Blackwood's Magazine* (Jan. 1863), XCIII, 20.
8. Wolseley, *Life*, II, 141.
9. Wolseley, *Blackwood's*, 29.
10. Garnet W. to Richard W., Nov. 4th, 1864, Hove.
11. Garnet W. to Matilda W., Nov. 1863, Hove.
12. Garnet W. to Richard W., March 23rd, 1859, Hove.
13. Ibid., June 3rd, 1865.
14. Ibid., Dec. 7th, 1865.
15. Wolseley, *Life*, II, 160.
16. G. T. Denison, *The Canadian Magazine* (Oct. 1895), V, 496.
17. Garnet W. to Richard W., Sept. 9th, 1866, Hove.
18. Ibid., Aug. 8th, 1866.
19. Gustave Paul Clusaret, 'My Connection with Fenianism', *Litell's Living Age*, CXIV (1872), 357.
20. Garnet W. to Richard W., March 17th, 1857, Hove.
21. Ibid., July 13th, 1863.
22. Garnet W. to Frances Ann W., no date, Hove.


CHAPTER VI – REDCOATS ON THE RED RIVER

1. Sir Joseph Pope, *Correspondence of Sir John MacDonald*, Doubleday (New York, 1921), 124.
2. Garnet W. to Richard W., April 6th, 1870. Hove.
3. Wolseley, *Life*, II, 171.
4. Garnet Wolseley, 'Expedition to the Red River', *Blackwood's Magazine*, CIX (Jan. 1871), 62.
5. Garnet W. to Richard W., Oct. 29th, 1862, Hove.
6. George Lightfoot Huyshe, 'The Red River Expedition', *The Royal United Service Magazine* (1872), XV, 78.
7. 'Proclamations to the Loyal Inhabitants of Manitoba', June 30th, 1870, P.R.O., W.O., 107/9, No. 2.
8. Joseph F. Tennant, *Rough Times, 1870–1920* (Winnipeg, 1920), 40.
9. Wolseley, *Blackwood's*, 72.
10. Garnet W. to Richard W., June 3rd, 1870, Hove.

# NOTES

11. Wolseley, *Blackwood's*, 170.
12. George Lightfoot Huyshe, *The Red River Expedition*, Macmillan & Co. (London, 1871), 190.
13. Wolseley, *Blackwood's*, 176.
14. Lewis Butler, *Sir Redvers Buller*, Smith, Elder & Co. (London, 1909), 25-6.
15. Huyshe, *Red River*, 222.


## CHAPTER VII – FROM INKSHED TO BLOODSHED

1. Sir Edmund William Gosse, *Aspects and Impressions*, Scribner's Sons (New York, 1922), 283.
2. Sir George Arthur, *A Septuagenarian's Scrap Book*, T. Butterworth Ltd (London, 1932), 117.
3. Winwood Reade, *The Story of the Ashantee Campaign*, Smith, Elder & Co. (London, 1874), 363.
4. Sir Robert Biddulph, *Lord Cardwell at the War Office*, J. Murray (London 1904), 221.
5. Wolseley, *Life*, II, 268.
6. Ibid. 266-7.
7. Sir Henry Morton Stanley, *Coomassie and Magdala*, Harper & Brothers (New York, 1874), 7.


## CHAPTER VIII – FIRE LOW, FIRE SLOW

1. Wolseley, *Life*, II, 279.
2. George Alfred Henty, *The March to Coomassie*, Tinsley (London, 1874), 157.
3. Reade, *Ashantee Campaign*, 216.
4. Garnet W. to Cambridge, Nov. 21st, 1873, Royal Archives, Windsor.
5. Reade, *Ashantee Campaign*, 395-6.
6. Melton Prior, *Campaigns of a War Correspondent*, E. Arnold (London, 1912), 14.
7. Garnet W. to Richard W., Nov. 3rd, 1873, Hove.
8. Reade, *Ashantee Campaign*, 395-6.
9. *Vanity Fair* (1874), XI, 203.
10. Garnet W. to Glover, Jan. 17th, 1874, Glover Papers, Royal Commonwealth Society Library.
11. Sir Henry Brackenbury, *The Ashanti War*, Blackwood & Sons (Edinburgh, 1874), I, 413.
12. Reade, *Ashantee Campaign*, 241-2.
13. Ibid.
14. Stanley, *Coomassie*, 213.
15. Brackenbury, *Ashanti War*, II, 84.
16. Reade, *Ashantee Campaign*, 297.
17. Prior, *War Correspondent*, 18.
18. Wolseley, *Life*, II, 342.
19. Stanley, *Coomassie*, 201.
20. Ibid.
21. Ibid.
22. Ibid., 354.
23. Brackenbury, *Ashanti War*, II, 343.
24. Sir Edmund Fremantle, *The Navy as I have known it*, Cassell & Co. (London, 1904), 247-8.

## CHAPTER IX – CHAMPAGNE AND SHERRY DIPLOMACY

1.  George Earle Buckle, ed., *The Letters of Queen Victoria* (extract from the Queen's Journal, March 22nd, 1874), second series, J. Murray (London, 1926–32), II, 331.
2.  Garnet W. to Frances Ann W., March 23rd, 1874, Hove.
3.  William Monypenny and George Earle Buckle, *The Life of Benjamin Disraeli, Earl of Beaconsfield*, Macmillan Co. (New York, 1920), II, 645.
4.  Garnet W. to Frances Ann W., March 23rd, 1874, Hove.
5.  Sir Francis William Butler, *The Life of Sir George Pomeroy-Colley*, J. Murray (London, 1899), 121.
6.  Carnarvon to Garnet W., April 30th, 1875, Carnarvon Papers, P.R.O., 30/6, No. 38.
7.  Ibid., Feb. 16th, 1875.
8.  Wolseley, *Life*, II, 317.
9.  Sir John Robinson, *A Lifetime in South Africa*, Smith, Elder & Co. (London, 1900), 37.
10. Alan F. Hattersley, *Portrait of a Colony: The Story of Natal*, University Press (Cambridge, 1938), 94–6.
11. Garnet W. to Richard W., June 2nd, 1875, Hove.
12. Garnet W. to Louisa W., April 8th, 1875, R.U.S.I.
13. Broome to Carnarvon, April 26th, 1875, Carnarvon Papers, P.R.O., 30/6, No. 38.
14. Garnet W. to Louisa W., April 8th, 1875, R.U.S.I.
15. Butler, *Colley*, 122.
16. Sir William Francis Butler, *An Autobiography*, Scribner's Sons (New York, 1913), 173.
17. Butler, *Colley*, 121-2.
18. Hattersley, *Portrait*, 120.
19. Garnet W. to Louisa W., April 25th, 1875, R.U.S.I.
20. Alan F. Hattersley, *Pietermaritzburg Panorama*, University Press (Cambridge, 1938), 68.
21. C. W. de Kiewiet, *The Imperial Factor in South Africa*, University Press (Cambridge, 1937), 44.
22. Butler, *Autobiography*, 175.
23. Garnet W. to Carnarvon, May 29th, 1875, Carnarvon Papers, P.R.O., 30/6, No. 18.
24. Garnet W. to Louisa W., May 13th, 1875, R.U.S.I.
25. Ibid.
26. Ibid., May 18th, 1875.
27. Hattersley, *Portrait*, 121.
28. Robinson, *Lifetime*, 38–9.
29. Ibid., 39.
30. Ibid.
31. Garnet W. to Richard W., June 2nd, 1875, Hove.
32. Garnet W. to Carnarvon, June 2nd, 1875, Carnarvon Papers, P.R.O., 30/6, No. 18.
33. Garnet W. to Richard W., June 2nd, 1875, Hove.
34. Carnarvon to Garnet W., July 14th, 1875, Carnarvon Papers, 30/6, No. 18.
35. Garnet W. to Carnarvon, May 7th, 1875, ibid.
36. Garnet W. to Carnarvon, May 29th, 1875, Carnarvon Papers, P.R.O., 30/6, No. 18.
37. Ibid.
38. Garnet W. to Louisa W., June 16th, 1875, R.U.S.I.
39. Ibid., June 22nd, 1875.
40. Ibid.
41. Ibid., Aug. 27th, 1875.
42. Ibid.
43. Ibid.
44. Ibid.
45. Ibid.
46. Butler, *Autobiography*, 189.

## CHAPTER X – A MODERN OTHELLO

1. Garnet W. to Richard W., Feb. 18th, 1878, Hove.
2. Butler, *Autobiography*, 190.
3. Sir John Adye, *Soldiers and Others I have known*, Jenkins Ltd (London, 1925), 26–7.
4. Archibald Forbes, *Souvenirs of Some Continents*, Macmillan & Co. (London, 1885), 161.
5. Garnet W. to Louisa W., July 18th, 1878, R.U.S.I.
6. Garnet W. to Salisbury, Aug. 5th, 1878, Register of Letters on Cyprus Correspondence 1878–9, Add. Mss. 41324, British Museum.
7. Garnet W. to Louisa W., Aug. 5th, 1878, R.U.S.I.
8. Ibid.
9. *Army and Navy Gazette* (June 5th, 1888), XIII, 380–1.
10. Lady Anne A. Brassey, *Sunshine and Storm in the East*, Holt & Co. (New York, 1880), 270.
11. Garnet W. to Salisbury, Aug. 4th, 1878, Cyprus Register, British Museum.
12. Garnet W. to Cambridge, Oct. 9th, 1878, R.A.
13. Archibald Forbes, 'Fiasco in Cyprus', *Nineteenth Century* (Oct. 1878), IV, 617.
14. Sir Hugh McCalmont, *The Memoirs of General Sir Hugh McCalmont*, ed. and completed by Sir C. E. Callwell, Hutchinson & Co. (London, 1924), 150.
15. Garnet W. to Louisa W., Aug. 5th, 1878, R.U.S.I.
16. Edward Vizetelly, *From Cyprus to Zanzibar*, C. A. Pearson Ltd (London, 1901), 16–17.
17. Forbes, *Nineteenth Century*, 620.
18. Sir Samuel Baker, *Cyprus as I saw it in 1879*, Macmillan & Co. (London, 1879), 441.
19. Garnet W. to Salisbury, Oct. 25th, 1878, Cyprus Register, British Museum.
20. Charles Rathbone Low, *A Memoir of Lieutenant-General Sir Garnet J. Wolseley*, Bentley & Son (London, 1878), 280.
21. Garnet W. to Greaves, Jan. 14th, 1879, Cyprus Register, British Museum.
22. McCalmont, *Memoirs*, 149.
23. Ibid., 149–50.
24. *The Times*, Aug. 7th, 1878, 10.
25. Garnet W. to Salisbury, Aug. 20th, 1878, Cyprus Register, British Museum.
26. Low, *Wolseley*, 356.
27. Garnet W. to Salisbury, April 8th, 1878, ibid.
28. Garnet W. to Mr Bourke, April 8th, 1878, ibid.
29. Garnet W. to Warren, May 1st, 1878, ibid.
30. Mrs Andrew Scott-Stevenson, *Our Home in Cyprus*, Chapman & Hall (London, 1880), 24.
31. McCalmont, *Memoirs*, 151–2.
32. Viscountess Frances Wolseley, 'Life and Letters of Lady Wolseley', unpublished manuscript, Hove, I, 18.
33. Scott-Stevenson, *Cyprus*, 67.
34. Butler, *Autobiography*, 197.
35. Garnet W. to Cambridge, Feb. 26th, 1879, R.A.
36. Garnet W. to Salisbury, Feb. 18th, 1879, Cyprus Register, British Museum.
37. McCalmont, *Memoirs*, 152.

## CHAPTER XI – CATCHING CETEWAYO

1. Sir George Richards Greaves, *Memoirs of General Sir George Greaves*, J. Murray (London 1924), 140.
2. Monypenny and Buckle, *Disraeli*, VI, 431.
3. Ibid., 435–6.
4. Ibid., 433–4.

5. Garnet W. to Richard W., June 4th, 1879, Hove.
6. W. H. Clements, *The Glamour and Tragedy of the Zulu War*, J. Lane (London, 1936), 109.
7. Hon. Gerald French, *Lord Chelmsford and the Zulu War*, J. Lane (London, 1939), 272.
8. Ibid., 242.
9. Garnet W. to Richard W., June 4th, 1879, Hove.
10. Butler, *Colley*, 234.
11. Garnet W. to Louisa W., July 4th, 1879, R.U.S.I.
12. 'Editorial Notes', *The Royal United Service Magazine* (July 1880), XXIV, 367–8.
13. 'With the Irregulars in the Zulu War', *The Royal United Service Magazine* (March 1880), XXIV, 380.
14. Archibald Forbes, *Barracks, Bivouacs, and Battles*, Macmillan & Co. (London, 1910), 317.
15. Alexander Wilmot, *History of the Zulu War*, Richardson & Best (London, 1880), 197–8.
16. Garnet W. to Cambridge, Aug. 8th, 1879, R.A.
17. Greaves, *Memoirs*, 253.
18. Monypenny and Buckle, *Disraeli*, VI, 459.
19. Garnet W. to Louisa W., July 10th, 1879, R.U.S.I.
20. Ibid., Aug. 26th, 1879.
21. Garnet W. to Cambridge, July 11th, 1879, R.A.
22. Garnet W. to Buller, July 13th, 1879, Buller Papers, P.R.O., W.O./132.
23. Garnet W. to Louisa W., Aug. 13th, 1879, R.U.S.I.

## CHAPTER XII – TAMING THE TRANSVAAL

1. Garnet W. to Louisa W., Sept. 15th, 1879, R.U.S.I.
2. De Kiewiet, *Imperial Factor*, 249.
3. Garnet W., to Louisa W., Sept. 29th, 1879, R.U.S.I.
4. Ibid., Sept. 11th, 1879.
5. Ibid., Dec. 23rd, 1879.
6. Ibid., Oct. 15th, 1879.
7. McCalmont, *Memoirs*, 166.
8. Garnet W. to Cambridge, Nov. 24th, 1879, R.A.
9. McCalmont, *Memoirs*, 169.
10. William MacDonald, *Romance of the Golden Rand*, Cassell & Co. (London, 1933), 167–8, 176.
11. Ibid., 176.
12. Lord Francis Wallace Grenfell, *Memoirs of a Field-Marshal*, Hodder & Stoughton Ltd (London, 1925), 193.
13. Sir Henry Brackenbury, 'The Transvaal Twenty Years Ago', *Blackwood's Magazine* (Nov. 1889), CLXVI, 743.
14. Low, *Wolseley*, 385.
15. MacDonald, *Rand*, 178.
16. Ibid., 180–1.
17. Garnet W. to Louisa W., Dec. 2nd, 1879, R.U.S.I.
18. Monypenny and Buckle, *Disraeli*, VI, 473.
19. Brackenbury, *Blackwood's*, 749.
20. Ibid.
21. Garnet W. to Louisa W., Nov. 10th, 1879, R.U.S.I.
22. Harrison, *Recollections*, 230.
23. Garnet W. to Louisa W., Feb. 15th, 1880, R.U.S.I.
24. Ibid., July 16th, 1895.
25. T. F. Carter, *A Narrative of the Boer War; its Causes and Results*, 3rd ed., J. Macqueen (London, 1883), 89–90.

26. McCalmont, *Memoirs*, 178.
27. Garnet W. to Richard W., April 21st, 1880, Hove.
28. Garnet W. to Louisa W., April 18th, 1880, R.U.S.I.
29. Ibid., Feb. 15th, 1880.
30. Garnet W. to Richard W., April 21st, 1880, Hove.

## CHAPTER XIII – OUR ONLY GENERAL

1. Garnet W. to Louisa W., March 20th, 1880, R.U.S.I.
2. Ibid., April 18th, 1880.
3. Lord Napier of Magdala, *Letters of Field-Marshal Lord Napier of Magdala*, ed. H. D. Napier (London, 1936), 30–1.
4. Forbes, *Souvenirs*, 171–2.
5. Maurice to Wolseley, no date, Maurice Papers.
6. Wolseley, *Life*, II, 234.
7. Garnet Wolseley, 'Long and Short Service', *Nineteenth Century* (1881), XX, 559.
8. Charles Williams, *The Life of Lieut.-Gen. Sir H. E. Wood*, Sampson (London, 1892), 206.
9. Garnet W. to W. H. Smith, Dec. 27th, 1885, Hambleden Papers, National Register of Manuscripts, series §1, packet L.
10. Sir Ian Hamilton, *Listening for the Drums*, Faber & Faber Ltd (London, 1944), 150.
11. Sir Philip Lee, *King Edward VII; A Biography*, Macmillan & Co. (New York, 1925–7), I, 558.
12. Ibid.
13. Arthur Ponsonby Ponsonby, *Henry Ponsonby, Queen Victoria's Secretary; His Life from His Letters*, Macmillan & Co. (London, 1942), 93.
14. Ibid.
15. Cambridge to Victoria, Nov. 10th, 1881, R.A.
16. Ibid., Nov. 6th, 1881.
17. Garnet W. to Louisa W., July 31st, 1880, R.U.S.I.
18. Extracts from the Queen's Journal, Nov. 28th, 1881, Buckle, *Letters*, second series, III, 249.

## CHAPTER XIV – THE COUNTERMARCH OF MOSES

1. Cambridge to Victoria, July 20th, 1882, Buckle, *Letters*, second series, III, 311.
2. Garnet W. to Louisa W., Sept. 4th, 1882, R.U.S.I.
3. Frances Wolseley, 'Lady Wolseley', I, 80.
4. Garnet W. to Louisa W., Aug. 17th, 1882, R.U.S.I.
5. Ibid.
6. William Charles Francis Molyneux, *Campaigning in South Africa and Egypt*, Macmillan & Co. (London, 1896), 230–1.
7. A. E. P. B. Weigall, *A History of Events in Egypt, 1798–1914*, Blackwood & Sons (Edinburgh, 1915), II, 158.
8. Garnet W. to Cambridge, Aug. 28th, 1882, R.A.
9. Butler, *Autobiography*, 223.
10. Garnet Wolseley, 'The Military Question of Today', *The Royal United Service Magazine* (April 1893), XXV, 754.
11. Butler, *Autobiography*, 237.
12. Sir John Frederick Maurice, *The Military History of the Campaign of 1882 in Egypt*, H.M. Stationery Office (London, 1888), 50.

13. Butler, *Autobiography*, 225.
14. Ibid.
15. Ibid., 227.
16. Sir John Frederick Maurice, 'Critics and Campaigns', *Fortnightly* (July 1888) V, 120–1.
17. C. Royle, *The Egyptian Campaign, 1882 to 1885*, Hurst & Blackett Ltd (London, 1900), 158.
18. Garnet W. to Louisa W., Aug. 31st, 1882, R.U.S.I.
19. Ibid.
20. Ibid., Sept. 10th, 1882.
21. Ibid.
22. McCalmont, *Memoirs*, 218–19.
23. Ibid., 219.
24. Butler, *Autobiography*, 231.
25. Arthur V. Palmer, 'A Battle Described from the Ranks', *Nineteenth Century* (March 1890), CLVII, 404.
26. Butler, *Autobiography*, 237.
27. C. F. Winter, 'A Canadian's Recollections of Tel-el-Kebir', *Canadian Magazine* (May 1912), XXXIX, 59.
28. James Pope-Hennessy, *Queen Mary, 1867–1953*, Allen & Unwin Ltd (London, 1959), 101.
29. Butler, *Autobiography*, 239.
30. Cambridge to Queen, Oct. 12th, 1882, Buckle, *Letters*, second series, III, 347.
31. Butler, *Autobiography*, 239.
32. McCalmont, *Memoirs*, 223.
33. Louisa W. to Mrs Goschen, Oct. 30th, 1882, R.U.S.I.
34. Garnet W. to Louisa W., Sept. 28th, 1882, R.U.S.I.
35. Ibid.
36. Louisa W. to Garnet W., Oct. 19th, 1882, R.U.S.I.
37. Victoria to Granville, Oct. 11th, 1882, Buckle, *Letters*, second series, III, 346.
38. Extracts from the Queen's Journal, Oct. 30th, 1882, ibid., 354–6.

## CHAPTER XV – THE GORDON RELIEF EXPEDITION

1. Lord Evelyn Baring Cromer, *Modern Egypt*, Macmillan Co. (New York, 1908), I, 448.
2. Wolseley, *Life*, I, 147.
3. Ibid., 148.
4. Frederic Villiers, *Days of Glory*, George Doran Co. (New York, 1920), 68.
5. Garnet W. to Hartington, April 13th, 1884, Wolseley Papers, W.O. Library.
6. Lady Gwendolen Cecil, *The Life of Robert, Marquess of Salisbury*, Hodder & Stoughton, Ltd (London, 1921), III, 103.
7. Garnet W. to Hartington, July 24th, 1884, Wolseley Papers, W.O. Library.
8. Gladstone to Victoria, Feb. 5th, 1885, Buckle, *Letters*, second series, III, 559.
9. Garnet W. to Louisa W., Dec. 20th, 1884, R.U.S.I.
10. E. Spencer Childers, *The Life and Letters of the Rt. Hon. Hugh C. E. Childers, 1827–1896*, J. Murray (London, 1901), II, 30.
11. Sir George Compton Archibald Arthur, *Concerning Queen Victoria and Her Son*, Robert Hale (London, 1943), 175.
12. Lady D. Nevill, *The Life and Letters of Lady D. Nevill*, Methuen (London, 1919), 123.
13. Edgar Sheppard, ed., *George, Duke of Cambridge: A Memoir of His Private Life Based on the Journal and Correspondence of His Royal Highness*, Longmans, Green & Co. (London, 1906), II, 135.
14. Lord Edward Gleichen, *With the Camel Corps up the Nile*, Chapman & Hall (London, 1888), 4.

NOTES

15. Garnet W. to Louisa W., Sept. 27th, 1884, R.U.S.I.
16. Ardagh to a friend, Nov. 7th, 1884, Ardagh Papers, P.R.O., 30/40, §2.
17. Garnet W. to Louisa W., Oct. 1st, 1884, R.U.S.I.
18. Ibid.
19. Ibid., Sept. 13th, 1884.
20. Sir William Francis Butler, *The Campaign of the Cataracts*, Sampson, Low, Marston, Searle & Rivington (London, 1887), 214.
21. Sir George Compton Archibald Arthur, *General Sir John Maxwell*, J. Murray (London, 1932), 6.
22. Lord Charles William De la Poer Beresford, *Memoirs*, Methuen & Co. (London, 1914), I, 228.
23. Adye, *Soldiers*, 115.
24. Prior, *War Correspondent*, 204.
25. Ibid., 206-7.
26. Garnet W. to Cambridge, April 4th, 1885, R.A.
27. Garnet W. to Louisa W., Nov. 25th, 1885, R.U.S.I.
28. Ibid., Nov. 30th, 1884.
29. Charles Perry Stacey, *The Nile Voyageurs, 1884–1885*, Publications of the Champlain Society (Toronto, 1959), 71.
30. Hamilton, *Drums*, 175.
31. Adye, *Soldiers*, 127.
32. Thomas Wright, *The Life of Colonel Fred Burnaby*, Everett & Co. (London, 1908), 272.
33. McCalmont, *Memoirs*, 230.
34. Hamilton, *Drums*, 176.
35. Garnet W. to Louisa W., Dec. 18th, 1885, R.U.S.I.
36. Ibid., Dec. 8th, 1885.
37. Garnet W. to Buller, Feb. 16th, 1885, Buller Papers, P.R.O., W.O. 132/2.
38. Gleichen, *Camel Corps*, 71.
39. Sir Percival Scrope Marling, *Rifleman and Hussar*, J. Murray (London, 1931), 130.
40. Sir Winston S. Churchill, *The River War*, Longmans, Green & Co. (London, 1902), 63.
41. Lord Douglas Dundonald, *My Army Life*, E. Arnold (London, 1926), 38.
42. Sir Charles Wilson, *From Korti to Khartoum*, Blackwood & Sons (London, 1886), 29.
43. Dundonald, *Army Life*, 38-9.
44. Beresford, *Memoirs*, II, 271.
45. Osborn and Johnson Wilkinson, *The Memoirs of the Gemini Generals*, A. D. Innes & Co. (London, 1897), 424.
46. Beresford, *Memoirs*, II, 276.
47. Garnet W. to Louisa W., Jan. 22nd, 1885, R.U.S.I.
48. Wilkinson, *Gemini Generals*, 423-4.
49. Garnet W. to Louisa W., Jan. 27th, 1885, R.U.S.I.
50. Marling, *Hussar*, 136.
51. Dundonald, *Army Life*, 52.
52. Garnet W. to Louisa W., Feb. 22nd, 1885, R.U.S.I.
53. Viscountess Frances Wolseley, 'Lady Wolseley', I, 134.
54. Victoria to Louisa W., March 3rd, 1885, Buckle, *Letters*, second series, III, 619.
55. Nevill, *Nevill*, 125.
56. Garnet W. to Louisa W., May 14th, 1885, R.U.S.I.
57. Viscountess Frances Wolseley, 'Lady Wolseley', I, 421.

## CHAPTER XVI – EPILOGUE

1. *The Royal United Service Magazine*, LVII (April 1913), 446.

2.  Garnet W. to Lady W., Feb. 22nd, 1885, R.U.S.I.
3.  Ibid., Jan 2nd, 1887.
4.  Ibid., Nov. 29th, 1890.
5.  Ibid., April 4th, 1887.
6.  *The Royal United Service Magazine*, LVII (April 1913), 446.
7.  Garnet W. to Louisa W., July 22nd, 1895, R.U.S.I.
8.  Garnet W. to Ardagh, Aug. 24th, 1895, Ardagh Papers, P.R.O., 30/40, §1.
9.  Garnet W. to Louisa W., July 3rd, 1895, R.U.S.I.
10. Swaine to Garnet W., July 26th, 1895, R.U.S.I.
11. Lord Thomas Newton, *Lord Lansdowne*, Macmillan & Co. (London, 1929), 131.
12. Garnet W. to Ardagh, Aug. 10th, 1895, Ardagh Papers, P.R.O., 30/40, §2.
13. Garnet W. to Louisa W., Aug. 9th, 1895, R.U.S.I.
14. Newton, *Lansdowne*, 134.
15. Victoria to Lansdowne, Aug. 17th, 1895, Buckle, *Letters*, third series, II, 553.
16. Willoughby Verner, *The Military Life of H.R.H. George, Duke of Cambridge*, J. Murray (London, 1905), II, 401.
17. Nevill, *Nevill*, 131.
18. Garnet W. to Victoria, Sept. 12th, 1900, Buckle, *Letters*, third series, III, 398-9.
19. Garnet W. to Louisa W., Feb. 17th, 1900, R.U.S.I.
20. Gosse, *Impressions*, 289.
21. Sir Neville Lyttleton, *Eighty Years' Soldiering*, Hodder & Stoughton Ltd (London, 1927), 169-70.
22. Garnet W. to Louisa W., Aug. 1st, 1900, R.U.S.I.
23. Ibid., Oct. 2nd, 1900.
24. Ibid., March 22nd, 1901.
25. Hamilton, *Drums*, 183.
26. Gosse, *Impressions*, 275-6.
27. Ibid., 278.

# INDEX